A LIBERAL CHRONICLE

SOURCES FOR MODERN BRITISH HISTORY

General Editors: Kathleen Burk, John Ramsden, John Turner

REAL OLD TORY POLITICS: The Political Diaries of Robert Sanders, Lord Bayford, 1910–1935
Edited by John Ramsden, 1984

THE DESTRUCTION OF LORD ROSEBERY: From the Diary of Sir Edward Walter Hamilton, 1894–1895
Edited by David Brooks. 1987

THE CRISIS OF BRITISH UNIONISM: The Domestic Political Papers of the Second Earl of Selborne, 1885–1922
Edited by George Boyce. 1987

LABOUR AND THE WARTIME COALITION: From the Diary of James Chuter Ede, 1941–1945
Edited by Kevin Jefferys. 1987

THE MODERNISATION OF CONSERVATIVE POLITICS: The Diaries and Letters of William Bridgeman, 1904–1935
Edited by Philip Williamson. 1988

THE CRISIS OF BRITISH POWER: The Imperial and Naval Papers of the Second Earl of Selborne, 1895–1910
Edited by George Boyce. 1990

PATRICK GORDON WALKER: Political Diaries, 1932–1971
Edited by Robert Pearce. 1991

PARLIAMENT AND POLITICS IN THE AGE OF BALDWIN AND MACDONALD: The Headlam Diaries, 1923–1935
Edited by Stuart Ball

A LIBERAL CHRONICLE

Journals and Papers of

J. A. Pease,
1st Lord Gainford

1908–1910

Edited by

Cameron Hazlehurst
and
Christine Woodland

British Library Cataloguing in Publication Data

CIP information for this book is available from the British Library

ISBN 1 872273 00 9

PUBLISHED BY THE HISTORIANS' PRESS
9 Daisy Road, London E18 1EA
Printed in England by Anthony Rowe Ltd

Contents

Preface and Acknowledgements

In 1965 a 24 year old Australian doctoral student embarked on a still unfinished quest for the surviving private papers of the members of the Asquith government. Among the first fruits of the search was the discovery of a large collection of correspondence, diaries, press-clippings, official memoranda, memoirs, photographs, and ephemera relating to the life of J.A. Pease, 1st Baron Gainford.

Fifteen volumes of diaries were found. The first covered three months in Cambridge in 1880; others dealt with visits to Ireland (1887), South Africa (1897), Ecuador and the Panama Canal (1921–2), and parliamentary events (1892–3, 1895–6, 1897–1900, 1900–08, 1905). But the most important three volumes began with the accession of Asquith to the premiership in 1908 and continued to the formation of a coalition government in May 1915.

In *A Liberal Chronicle*, Christine Woodland and I print the text of the diary from March 1908 to May 1915. Our edition of the text, interspersed with other relevant documents, notes, and commentaries, will appear in two parts. This first volume covers the years 1908, 1909, and 1910 and reproduces all but the last two entries in the manuscript journal that is now MS Gainford 38 in the Library of Nuffield College, Oxford.

The Gainford Papers were deposited at Nuffield College by Jack Pease's grandson who became the 3rd Lord Gainford in 1971. They have been available to scholars for a quarter of a century and have been widely quoted in books, theses, and articles. Dr M.W. Kirby's monograph, *Men of Business and Politics*, The Rise and Fall of the Quaker Pease Dynasty of North-East England, 1700–1943 (George Allen & Unwin, 1984), made excellent use of the collection at Nuffield College as well as other family papers.

Christine Woodland and I had hoped to produce our edition of the diaries in the late 1970s. But unforeseen personal and professional responsibilities intervened. Our conception of the work also changed. The rather austere editorial framework originally envisaged has evolved into a more elaborate edifice.

We have attempted to identify and provide basic biographical information for every person mentioned in the text. On the assumption that few readers will have the breadth of expertise to put more than a small proportion of Pease's entries into context, we have added explanatory footnotes and commentaries on most of the subjects to which he refers. In compiling this supplementary material we have been aided by a very large number of people – descendants of men and women about whom Pease wrote, librarians, archivists, fellow scholars, officers of professional associations, clubs, and societies, and others with special knowledge which they volunteered in response to our letters and published appeals for help.

We are particularly indebted for sustained assistance and guidance over many years to Christine Kennedy and Eleanor Vallis (Nuffield College Library), Jane Langton and Lady de Bellaigue (Royal Archives), and Dennis Porter, Helen Langley, and Colin Harris (Bodleian Library).

In addition, for advice on particular points and assistance we are grateful to: Douglas Agnew, the Hon. Charles Allsopp (Chairman, Christie's), Carole Angier, Eric Bellamy (The National Motor Museum), Dr Richard Bingle (India Office Records, British Library), Katharine Bligh (House of Lords Record Office), Lord Blyth, Eleanor Brock, Dr Michael Brock, Dr David Cuthbert, Dr Roy Douglas, the late 4th Lord Derwent, Baroness Elliot of Harwood, Alistair Elliot (The Library, University of Newcastle upon Tyne), J.G. Ellis, Professor David Fahey, Dr Charles K. Fairbanks, Geoffrey Ford (University of Bristol Library), Janet Friedlander (National Union of Teachers), Dr José F. Harris, R.J. Hill (Lord Chamberlain's Office), Martin Gilbert, Edwin Green (Archives, Midland Group), Dr Rob Irving, Dr Patricia Kelvin, Dr A.G. Kenwood, the Marquess of Lansdowne, Dr Keith Laybourn, Emeritus Professor Alan McBriar, Emeritus Professor Oliver MacDonagh, I. F. Maciver (National Library of Scotland), Professor Shula Marks, Professor A.J.A. Morris, Professor Bruce K. Murray, Lord Norton, Dr John Padley (University of Sheffield), Dr Martin Petter, Lord Polwarth, Profesor Martin Pugh, Dr A.W. Purdue, Sir David Reynolds Bt, Dr R. Robson, Will Schofield, Richard J. Shoobridge, Dr Roderick Suddaby (Imperial War Museum), Dr Anne Summers (British Library), M.D. Tuckfield (Automobile Association), Kenneth Vaus, Roderick Walker (Lincoln's Inn Library), Patricia J. Williams (St Deiniol's Library), H.P. Willmott, A. Wilson (Stranraer Branch Library), Sarah Wimbush (National Portrait Gallery).

For granting or facilitating access to private papers and for permission to quote from documents we are grateful to Her Majesty the Queen, and to the late 5th Marquess of Aberdeen and Temair, P. Audley-Miller, Lord Bonham-Carter, the late Lady Burke, the late Randolph S. Churchill, Lady Hermione Cobbold, Lord Craigmyle, the late 28th Earl of Crawford, Dr Pauline Dower, Sir Hugh Elliott Bt, Lord Esher, the late Judy Gendel, Lord Glenconner, the late J. Gulland Osborne, the late Viscount Harcourt, the late Miss Anne Holt, Dame Christian Howard, the late Mrs A.D. Ingrams, the late Mrs K. Idwal Jones, the late Mildred Kirkcaldy, George Lane Fox, the late John Lehmann, Lady Lyell, Sir Hector Monro, Elizabeth Orton, J. Gurney Pease, Lord Ponsonby, the Hon. Sir Steven Runciman, the late 2nd Viscount Samuel, the late J.H. MacCallum Scott, Mrs B. Simon, the late Lord Southborough, the late Dr A. Stokes, Hallam Tennyson, Martin Vogel Jr, Rev. Francis W. Vye S.J.

Successive research and secretarial assistants have contributed greatly to the preparation and amplification of the text: Angela Joly, Mayling Stubbs, Sue Lloyd, Susan Enever, and Christine Alabaster in Oxford; Jan Brazier, Dr Marion

Stell, Carol Flanagan, Jeannette Horrocks, Pauline Barratt, Jean Dillon, Beverly Gallina, Jan Hicks, Pearl Moyseyenko, Brenda Unwin, Janice Aldridge, Helen Macnab, Lois Simms, Marie Penhaligon, Christine Waring, and Diane Crosse in Canberra.

For alerting us to errors, obscurities, and infelicities remaining in the penultimate draft we are grateful to Professor Kenneth O. Morgan, Professor John Turner, and Professor F.B. Smith.

The presentation of the work for publication, including keyboarding, layout, indexing, and final editorial queries has been the responsibility of Anthea Bundock. Her skills, resourcefulness, and perseverance have been a critical factor in bringing the project to fruition.

To Lord Gainford we are deeply indebted for entrusting us with the task of editing his grandfather's diaries. And, above all, for being more patient and supportive than we had a right to expect when the enterprise was so long delayed.

Early work on the project was greatly aided by the Twenty-Seven Foundation, Nuffield College, and The Queen's College, Oxford. The British Council provided a timely air-fare. Queensland University of Technology has supported the closing stages of editing and preparing the text.

Finally we must acknowledge the crucial assistance of the Institute of Advanced Studies at the Australian National University which funded the greater part of the research on which this book is based. Without the continuing commitment of resources which the ANU made possible a work on this scale could not have been contemplated.

Cameron Hazlehurst
Brisbane, August 1993

*   *   *

The text which appears here is a complete transcription of the original except for a few unintelligible passages. Pease's punctuation is slapdash. We have, therefore, inserted or deleted commas, apostrophes and dashes where not to do so might lead to confusion. Unnecessary stops at the end of abbreviated words have been removed. The spelling and capitalisation of the text are also erratic. We have retained enough of Pease's variations to convey the flavour of the original but have occasionally corrected what would otherwise look odd. We have printed his persistent spelling of 'negociations' and capitalisations which seem from the context to convey some intended emphasis. Presumed slips of the pen and misspellings have been silently corrected; attention is drawn to the corrections where they seem to signify a noteworthy unfamiliarity with a person, place, or institution. (Spelling Edwin Montagu with a final 'e' was a common error; spelling Count Metternich with a 'k' was not. Pease could not have been expected to know that Ivy Pretious spelt her name with a 't'.)

The diary is obviously not always written on the day to which it refers. Where we have established that it is mis-dated we have explained why a different date is more likely. Where passages clearly have been added to an entry after the original was written this is noted.

We follow conventional practice in enclosing doubtful readings and conjectural dates in square brackets with a question mark. Pease's style is often so cryptic that it would be visually disturbing to insert obviously missing words in parentheses or to make frequent resort to 'sic'. However, peculiarities or omissions in interpolated letters by other writers are recognised and rectified conventionally.

Every individual mentioned in the text has a biographical note. Most biographies are grouped together at the back of the book. The exceptions include (a) several people who are mentioned only once and whose relevant details are included in a commentary or footnote, (b) those who are mentioned by title rather than name (e.g. the Lord Mayor of London) and who are identified on the page where they first appear, (c) those about whose identity we are uncertain – probable, possible, or conceivable identifications being given in a footnote or commentary; and (d) the two whose identity totally eludes us.

Editorial commentaries are italicised. Readers who prefer to read the text alone can therefore readily skip the italicised interpolations. In some cases, however, even expert readers will find something new in the commentaries. Although the period covered by this book is short it touches upon a large number of issues and long-forgotten incidents. The editors have been reminded frequently of the limits of their own knowledge. As the footnotes and acknowledgments testify we have drawn on a wide range of unpublished as well as published sources in clarifying and developing some of Pease's more allusive remarks and observations.

The introduction that follows provides background on Pease's life up to March 1908. The second volume of *A Liberal Chronicle* will have an introduction briefly outlining the author's political achievements and standing by 1911 and a postscript on his career after 1915.

Introduction

As Liberal Prime Minister from 1908 to 1915, H.H. Asquith had five Chief Whips: George Whiteley, J.A. Pease, the Master of Elibank (Alick Murray), Percy Illingworth, and John Gulland. Of all these men entrusted with parliamentary management and political organisation in the country 'Jack' Pease is the only one known to have kept a substantial diary.

Pease had started a diary several times and there are surviving fragments dealing with a term in Cambridge in 1880, overseas travels, parliamentary events in the later 1890's, and the formation of the Campbell-Bannerman ministry. But it was not until April 1908 when he was 47 that he managed to establish a regular diary-keeping habit. The new discipline was prompted by his move closer to the centre of affairs as he waited in the wings to succeed George Whiteley. For the next seven years Pease kept a faithful record of the significant political events with which he was concerned. The journals on which this edition is based cover Pease's years as Chancellor of the Duchy of Lancaster and President of the Board of Education as well as his nineteen months as Patronage Secretary to the Treasury, the office conventionally held by the government Chief Whip.

Some other colleagues in the Asquith government kept political journals – John Burns, Lord Carrington, Charles Hobhouse, and 'Loulou' Harcourt are the best-known (though Harcourt's twentieth-century diaries seem to have disappeared). But none was closer to the Prime Minister than Pease whose diary is a uniquely authoritative source of information on the workings of Westminster and Downing Street in one of the most turbulent periods of twentieth century political history. Although he was restored to the ministry, but not the Cabinet, as Postmaster-General in 1916, Pease rarely returned to diary-keeping after he became a casualty of the formation of the coalition government of May 1915.

The diary entries vary from a few words to several pages, generally written on or very close to the date to which they refer. They are frequent during parliamentary sessions; and, from the time Pease joined the Cabinet early in 1910, they include information about almost every Cabinet meeting he attended as well as others he heard about from colleagues. The political sensitivity of much that he wrote moved him to use locked volumes until February 1915.

Pease wrote what was essentially an aide-mémoire. There are abundant signs of haste and tiredness. The spelling and punctuation are erratic. There is no evidence of stylistic pretension. And, although there are occasional passages which betray pride in achievement, the diary's preoccupation is with others, especially the Prime Minister. It is primarily a record of things heard, seen, and done in Parliament and 10 Downing Street. Family matters rarely intrude; and a separate sporting diary celebrates Pease's prowess with the gun. If Pease was introspective, his journal does not betray his thoughts. If his private life had passions or peccadilloes, he evidently felt no need to leave clues. Guileless as his writing is, its revelations of self are small and infrequent. When he embarked late in life on an autobiography – a project that was never completed – he had slender resources from which to reconstruct what he had himself felt, believed, and tried to do.

In a government of many talents and much ambition, Pease had few illusions about his own prospects. He was grateful to be given a vantage point close to the centre of power. If his standing was always too modest to satisfy his wife, the daughter of a military hero, it nevertheless enabled him to make notable contributions to maintaining the Liberal majority and the momentum of reform. When he lost his seat in the general election of January 1910 he might well have retired from politics and attempted to resurrect family fortunes severely diminished by a financial collapse in 1902. But Asquith, who rated him a good second class man, offered him a place in the Cabinet and told him to find himself a seat. Walter Runciman, whom he was eventually to succeed as President of the Board of Education, thought this elevation a scandal.[1] Edwin Montagu, David Lloyd George, and Winston Churchill all expressed reservations about Pease's talents and judgment in particular contexts. But, for all his colleagues' condescension about his capability, Pease alone of Asquith's Chief Whips attained Cabinet rank. It could be argued that his promotion was more a matter of good fortune than ability. Certainly, it must be granted that Illingworth's performance from 1912 onwards was unblemished by the political or personal failings which barred the ascent of Whiteley, Alick Murray, and Gulland. The 'straight, competent, fearless' Illingworth, as Lloyd George eulogised him, enjoyed the full confidence of the Prime Minister but was denied the possibility of higher office by his premature death in 1915. Whiteley and Murray were clearly responsible for their own fates. And Gulland, who was undeniably a casualty of war politics, never seemed to have the measure of the Chief Whip's job let alone qualities fitting him for the Cabinet.[2]

Joseph Albert 'Jack' Pease was one of eleven members of his Quaker family to sit in the House of Commons in the nineteenth century. Although he was the only Pease who can properly be considered a career politician, his emergence in

---

1   Runciman to Hilda Runciman, 15 Feb. 1910, Viscountess Runciman MSS.
2   For Lloyd George's tribute to Illingworth see *War Memoirs of David Lloyd George*, 6 vols, Ivor Nicholson & Watson, 1933–36, Vol. II, 1933, p. 746. In *Memories and Reflections 1852–1927* (2 vols, Cassell, 1928, Vol. 1, pp. 190–92) Asquith's praise for 'one of the straightest man I have ever known, and one of the most lovable' is subtly juxtaposed to a pointedly qualified portrait of the Master of Elibank. Pease is not mentioned in Asquith's two volumes.

local government as Mayor of Darlington at the age of 29, then as MP for Tyneside three years later, testified to a powerful dynastic imperative.[3] Pease's older brother, father, grandfather, and great uncle were among the ten other members of the clan who had preceded him to Westminster. Five years after he entered Parliament, a friendly journalist wrote that the Peases 'must surely form the largest family party in the House. Such a contingent would be well worth securing for any cause or ism if families voted *en bloc;* it is well-known, however, that they carefully eschew anything like uniformity of opinion and action.'[4]

According to the historian of the Victorian Quakers, Joseph Pease, the first Quaker to sit in the House of Commons, had 'an inconspicuous career in the House'.[5] A different adjective might justifiably have been used for someone who had the reputation of being 'the best-dressed man in the House of Commons, where, in his deep claret or mulberry suit, his knee breeches, silk stockings and buckled shoes, he always looked as if he had come from a levée.'[6] Moreover, Joseph Pease was conspicuous in other senses. He was a potent industrialist, a founder of the town of Middlesborough, an ardent anti-slavery advocate, and – to the chagrin of many Friends – a protectionist and an opponent of limiting children's hours of work.

Jack Pease's father, Joseph Whitwell Pease, sat as MP for South Durham for 20 years from 1865 and then for Barnard Castle until his death in 1903. His first duty was the management of the family's extensive coal, iron, woollen, railway, engineering, and banking interests. A patriarchal businessman and great philanthropist, Sir Joseph Pease Bt, as he became, was President of the Peace Society and of the Society for the Suppression of the Opium Trade. Active in the campaign to repeal the Contagious Diseases Acts, he moved the abolition of the death penalty in 1886 and presented the first disarmament proposals of the Society of Friends to Parliament in 1889. As Chairman of the North Eastern Railway he was a pioneer of industrial conciliation and arbitration. On more general political issues, he was cautious about franchise reform and a late convert to the secret ballot. He was a consistent opponent of female suffrage ('Boadicea and Joan of Arc might have been geniuses, but both had come to an untimely end.') He was also deeply troubled about Irish Home Rule and tried to dissuade

---

3   On the Pease family background see M.W. Kirby, *Men of Business and Politics*: The Rise and Fall of the Quaker Pease Dynasty of North-East England, 1700 1943, George Allen & Unwin, 1984; Maurice W. Kirby, 'The failure of a Quaker business dynasty: The Peases of Darlington, 1830–1902', David J. Jeremy (ed.), *Business and Religion in Britain*, Gower Publishing, Aldershot, 1988, pp. 142–63.

4   *The Echo,* 1 Aug. 1897, in Elizabeth Isichei, *Victorian Quakers,* Clarendon Press, Oxford, 1970, p. 205.

5   Isichei, *Victorian Quakers,* p. 196.

6   Sir Timothy Eden, *Durham,* 2 vols, Robert Hall, 1952, Vol. I, p. 247.

Gladstone from pressing his Home Rule Bill in May 1886 when it seemed certain to splinter the Pease family as well as the Liberal Party.

Joseph Pease had turned down a minor office under Gladstone. When first offered a baronetcy he had declined. No Quaker had previously accepted such a title. Three Quakers were sounded out in 1882 and this time, according to Sir Edward Hamilton, Pease 'accepted with avidity'. Twelve years later he showed no such avidity for a proffered peerage. But his standing as a respected parliamentary veteran was recognised when in 1899 he was asked by the Chief Whip to propose the election of Sir Henry Campbell-Bannerman at a party meeting convened to confirm the emergence of a new Liberal leader in the House of Commons.[7]

Unhappily, none of Sir Joseph's achievements or honours was to have a greater impact on the public mind or his younger son's political prospects than his monumentally disastrous conduct of the family's financial affairs. As Dr Kirby has meticulously recounted in his study of the Peases' business history, Sir Joseph ruined himself and his children. He had his integrity as the trustee of his niece's estate judicially impugned, and barely escaped the final humiliation of bankruptcy in 1902. But for the timely support of Christopher Furness and a consortium of friends, family, and associates, Jack Pease's career – in politics as well as in business – would have been extinguished before he held office.

Sir Joseph Pease died a broken man less than a year after the collapse. His elder son Alfred, with a drastically reduced fortune and a sick wife, was forced to accept government employment in South Africa. Jack Pease alone clung to the

---

7   In addition to Kirby's accounts, and press cuttings in the Gainford MSS, these paragraphs draw on Anon., *Fortunes Made In Business*, 2 vols, Sampson Low, Marston, Searle & Rivington, 1884, Vol. I, pp. 363–79; Mrs Stuart Menzies, *Modern Men of Mark*, Herbert Jenkins, 1921, pp. 217–52; R.J. Irving, *The North Eastern Railway Company 1870–1914*: an economic history, Leicester University Press, Leicester, 1976, pp. 29, 46–7, 56–65, 107, 137; Victor G. Plarr, *Men and Women of the Time*: A Dictionary of Contemporaries, Geo. Routledge & Sons, 14th edn 1895, p. 660; Nancy E. Johnson, ed., *The Diary of Gathorne Hardy, later Lord Cranbrook*, 1886–92: Political Selections, Clarendon Press, Oxford, 1981, pp. 269, 796; Paul McHugh, *Prostitution and Victorian Social Reform*, Croom Helm, 1980, pp. 174, 246; Virginia Berridge and Griffith Edwards, *Opium and the People*: Opiate Use in Nineteenth-Century England, Yale University Press, New Haven, 1987, pp. 176–92; H.L. Malchow, *Gentlemen Capitalists*: The Social and Political World of the Victorian Businessman, Macmillan, 1991, *passim*; Robert Byrd, *Quaker Ways in Foreign Policy*, University of Toronto Press, Toronto, 1960, pp. 139–40; A.B. Cooke and John Vincent, *The Governing Passion*: Cabinet Government and Party Politics in Britain 1885–6, Harvester Press, Brighton, 1974, p. 435; Sir J.W. Pease to W.E. Gladstone, 14 and 20 May 1886, W.E. Gladstone MSS, Add. MS 44497, ff. 223, 246; Sir Edward Hamilton's diary, 30 April 1882, Dudley W.R. Bahlman, ed., *The Diary of Sir Edward Walter Hamilton 1880–5*, Clarendon Press, Oxford, 1972, p. 261; T.E. Ellis to Sir J.W. Pease, 2 Feb. 1899, Gainford MSS, 5.

House of Commons. Elected for the Tyneside division in 1892 he had put a first foot on the ladder of preferment as parliamentary private secretary to John Morley, Chief Secretary for Ireland in the Gladstone and Rosebery ministries. 'He talks the party platitudes glibly and with intelligence. But he does not utter a single idea of his own'. Thus Joseph Cowen's renegade Liberal daily the *Newcastle Daily Chronicle* (29 June 1892) had described Pease in an election supplement whose partisan candour was not far off the mark.[8] It was true that at Cambridge – where his contemporaries included Wentworth Beaumont and Harry Paulton – Jack had cut a bigger figure at cricket, tennis, riding, polo, hunting, and athletics, even drama, than in the examination hall. Earlier, when crammed by Mandell Creighton, he may have been exposed to 'the political significance of all historical events' but was singularly uninspired by his year under the Embleton vicarage regime.[9] Creighton was to argue in his inaugural lecture as Dixie Professor of Ecclesiastical History in 1885 that all study should 'develop the power of observation rather than supply opinions'.[10] By then, armed with a modest pass degree and deeply immersed in the affairs of Pease and Partners Ltd 'Collieries, Ironstone Mines, Limestone Quarries, Fire Clay Works', Jack was freely sharing both observations and opinions with his father:

> I am not very sure that the inequality of the capabilities of miners as compared to farmers in looking after themselves is sufficient reason for having freedom of contract in the Employers Liability Act as opposed to the stringent clause in Agricultural Holdings Act, as supported by the Liberal party. I personally would like to see freedom of contract in both, it's just as much an insult to a farmer to say you can't look after your own interest as to say the same to the miner. Do you think you are consistent?
>
> (14 June 1883, Gainford MSS, 2/2)

---

8 On the politics of the *Newcastle Daily Chronicle* and the Pease family's involvement in the northeastern press see Maurice Milne, *The Newspapers of Northumberland and Durham*: A Study of their progress during the 'Golden Age' of the Provincial Press, Frank Graham, Newcastle upon Tyne, [?1971], pp. 90-1, 144-7, 154-6, 203-4; Alan J. Lee, *The Origins of the Popular Press in England 1855–1914*, Croom Helm, 1976/1980, pp. 97, 135–6, 174–5, 214.

9 Tom Gibson Carmichael, later a Liberal MP, came up to St John's in 1878, the same year Pease started at Trinity. Carmichael switched from science to history after two years and was sent to Creighton for urgent instruction. Carmichael's widow records that Creighton 'carefully adjusted his teaching to the needs of the embryo statesmen' in his care. (*Lord Carmichael of Skirling*: A Memoir prepared by His Wife, Hodder & Stoughton, [?1930], p. 81).

10 Peter R.H. Slee, *Learning and a liberal education*: The study of modern history in the universities of Oxford, Cambridge and Manchester 1800–1914, Manchester University Press, Manchester, 1986, p. 77.

I can't see what ultimate gain we can have by slaughtering thousands of the Soudanese, at a considerable loss to ourselves, in both men and money. Gladstone no doubt will in the House prove the course he has taken was the correct one, but he can by words prove anything.

(20 February 1885, Gainford MSS, 2/5)

I certainly can't go with the G.O.M. in his Home Rule Scheme – the bad lot are merely going to be allowed to dictate to us at the expense of the law abiding landowners.

(12 April 1886, Gainford MSS, 3)

Before his adoption meeting for Tyneside on 8 April 1891 the young candidate had learned to mute his dissent from the Grand Old Man, and had blended Liberal verities, local prejudices, permissible preferences, and a sprinkling of idiosyncrasies into a creed that would serve him well over the next fifteen years. As a loyal Gladstonian he now put Home Rule 'in a very prominent position' and was predictably in favour of reduced army and navy expenditure, religious liberty, local option and Sunday closing, and freeing necessaries of life from taxation.

On labour matters he favoured a Ministry of Labour, courts to deal with employer/employee contracts and wrongful dismissal, and a tribunal of conciliation to avoid lock-outs and strikes. Shipowners, he contended, should be led to take an interest in the lives of seamen by extending the jurisdiction of coroners' inquests to deaths at sea and by making it impossible to insure ships and freight to their full value. Children should not be allowed to work in factories or mines until they were twelve (ten was still the permitted age). Sunday labour should be lessened but he did not support an Eight Hours Bill. Secondary and continued education should be brought within the reach of all, and technical and manual instruction should be available throughout the country. He wanted allotments for working men and, when questioned at the Co-operative Hall, Wallsend, prudently admitted sympathy for productive cooperation and profit sharing.

Radical constituents were warmed by Pease's support for taxation of ground rents and unearned increment, and for the abolition of primogeniture and entail, the hereditary principle in the House of Lords, hereditary pensions and 'keeping up palaces for the use of Her Majesty's distant relations'. On electoral reform he was for one man one vote, equal electoral districts, residential qualifications (three to six months), payment of returning officers' fees from the rates, and payment of MPs. When the country was 'ripe for manhood suffrage', he told a questioner, 'he would not be far behind but he did not think it a practical question at present.' Like his father he was opposed in principle to women's suffrage.[11]

---

[11]   *Newcastle Daily Leader,* 9 April 1901.

His subsequent election address was trimmed of unnecessary disclosures and reinforced with obeisance to Welsh and Scottish disestablishment. It also highlighted his abhorrence of the 'unjustifiable and demoralising' opium traffic and signalled his interest in the abolition of hanging and flogging in prisons ('revision of the Criminal Code and modification of the death penalty'). Three years later, the political agenda was headed by the need for 'effective limitation' of the power of the House of Lords. Favouring increased economy in public expenditure, and a thorough investigation of the incidence of rating and taxation, Pease agreed that the 'problem' of old age pensions would be 'best solved by the application of those principles of self-help, which have produced such satisfactory results in connection with the work of our Trade Unions and Friendly Societies'.

With a well-known name, a safe seat, and adequate talent, an affable young Liberal businessman with good connections was unlikely to remain a back-bencher. Pease could be said to belong to the class of 'hereditary Liberals' like the Buxtons and Trevelyans identified by Leonard Woolf.[12] His Quaker credentials, his reputation as a sportsman, and his judicious pursuit of causes like anti-slavery which were no threat to party unity, augmented his potential. He avoided any obtrusive entanglement in the ambitions and strategies that split the Liberals after the fall of the Rosebery government. When Campbell-Bannerman became Liberal leader in the Commons, with Herbert Gladstone as his Chief Whip, Pease's appointment to the Whips' Office was one of the least surprising of the consequential moves.

Palmerston was reputed to have defined a good whip as 'a man who can say like a gentleman what no gentleman would say'.[13] Pease was too genial and courteous ever to say what no gentleman would say. But to Herbert Gladstone he was a candid friend and indefatigable lieutenant, warning his Chief of rumblings that he was spending too much time interviewing candidates and seeing deputations while neglecting the House of Commons. A junior whip's duties involved long hours ensuring an effective Liberal presence in the House, monitoring the movements of MPs, seeking explanations and administering rebukes to those who transgressed with ill-judged votes or unapproved absences. There was a constant round of entertainment to be provided and endured. Here Pease's wife Ethel ('Elsie'), only daughter of the Liberal Unionist MP Maj.-Gen. Sir Henry Havelock-Allan Bt VC, was a formidable ally. Ambitious for her husband, with a finely honed instinct for social distinctions, she promoted his career with a zeal barely contained by discretion. Unabashed by the knowledge that her father-in-law had been pressed incessantly by his son to economise, she

---

[12] Foreword, Charles Philips Trevelyan, *Letters from North America and the Pacific 1898*, Chatto & Windus, 1969, p. xii.

[13] Sir Mountstuart E. Grant Duff's diary, 4 May 1896, Sir Mountstuart E. Grant Duff, *Notes from a Diary 1896, to January 23, 1901,* 2 vols, E.P. Dutton, New York, 1905, Vol. I, p. 55.

bemoaned to him the inadequacy of their sixteen bedrooms and six sitting rooms at Snow Hall on the Tees near Darlington: 'we must have a house to live in not a middle class villa.'[14]

Unobtrusive as a whip should be, Pease could not avoid declaring himself in some key divisions over the Boer War. Though he cast several votes against the Salisbury government, he denied that he was a pro-Boer and claimed in the general election of 1900 to have 'consistently supported Ministers in all the steps they have thought it necessary to take to bring the war to a steady and successful end'. A key episode in this balancing act was reported to his father on 23 October 1899: 'I voted for the £10,000,000 on Friday, but I never gave a vote more willingly than the one on Thursday in support of Stanhope's amendment as a protest against J.C.'s diplomacy.'[15]

Though never in the vanguard of social reform, Pease could conscientiously put his name to electoral appeals for 'social legislation for the benefit of the people'. He introduced a Cottage Homes Bill to provide in every parish for houses where parish councils could place poor old people of good character. Ostensibly a welfare measure, the bill was in reality a device for circumventing the pauper voting disqualification. If parish councils rather than boards of guardians were responsible for the houses, the inmates could not be paupers. The bill got a second reading and was buried by the government in a select committee.

Pease's seasoning as a political campaigner was advanced by the loss of his seat in 1900 and his transfer to a sparsely populated Essex constituency. Reflecting on his misfortune in Tyneside he told his father:

> One is rather apt to resent the knock-out blow and it is difficult to come up smiling, but after all, the solid respectable steady workman nearly everywhere went for me – the stupid, the sullen, the soaker, the sunken, and the society elector went for my opponent. He had been bribing for some time, and influenced a section, – but it was the increased plural vote and misrepresentation which I had to face, and in the face of khaki fever I could not overcome.
>
> Good wages also told against me, and the Liberal registration secretary is no organiser, and we had only half a canvass.
>
> I shall soon forget the annoyance of having been defeated and political life has no great charm, though I presume it is one's duty to try and serve others, but if I'm not wanted I can find plenty to do elsewhere.[16]

---

14   Ethel Pease to Sir Joseph Pease, 10 Jan. 1900, Gainford MSS, 5.
15   Two years later Philip Stanhope was outraged by Pease's openly expressed preference for the imperialist Herbert Samuel to succeed Alfred Pease as Liberal candidate for Cleveland. Conventionally, whips were publicly neutral between candidates. Stanhope's reiterated complaints and Pease's explanations are in the Gladstone MSS, Add. MS 46022, ff. 121-3; 46060, ff. 39-53.
16   J.A. Pease to Sir Joseph Pease, 12 Oct. 1900, Gainford MSS, 5. For elaborations of the reasons for his defeat see Pease's letters to Campbell-Bannerman, undated,

Eight months later Pease was confiding to the electors of Saffron Walden that he had been turned out of the north east not only by 2600 out-voters but by Roman Catholics told by their priests to vote Tory or be in peril of their souls. A by-election following the sudden death of Armine Wodehouse had launched him into a new style of candidature. Denying rumours that he was a teetotaller bent on depriving working men of their beer, and that his firm had just sacked 200 men, he commended himself to the farmers and rural workers of Essex on the ground of his identification with agricultural and other interests.[17] Barely plausible as this appeal was, he managed to increase the Liberal majority. *The Morning Post* assured its readers on 3 June 1901 that:

> Mr Pease is a Radical Imperialist, and his return will do nothing to assist the class of members of whom Mr Labouchere and Mr John Morley are the leaders. He said himself that Home Rule was not one of the questions at issue.

In Essex, agricultural rating, tithe rating, and the sugar tax were arousing more interest than the South African War. Alfred Pease, who was to find himself increasingly out of sympathy with his younger brother's political flexibility, was:

> ... not very enthusiastic about Jack's politics – he is now posing as favourable to the Agricultural Rates Act and only objecting to it because it did not give Essex a fair share – he opposed the bill tooth and nail before – he told the Newcastle people that his Coal Tax necessitated Pease & Partners sacking 200 men – he now resents the quotation from him as a lie! and what I do not like at all is his wobbly attitude on the war – it is not respectable to run any risk of being called a pro-Boer and it might not pay.[18]

At Westminster Pease's 'imperialist' credentials were to be searchingly scrutinised. When a 'war to the knife and fork' broke out among the Liberal leaders he was one of 40 MPs who declined an invitation to dine in tribute to H.H. Asquith on 19 July 1901 while assuring him that he retained their 'full confidence' in his work on behalf of the Liberal Party.[19] But 'for the sake of humanity' he felt obliged to vote for Lloyd George's motion on women and children in South African camps. He let it be known that he deplored some of Lloyd George's utterances and the method by which the subject had been initiated. Privately he counselled his father 'knowing how strongly you feel

---

(Campbell-Bannerman MSS, Add. MS 41235, f. 256) and Herbert Gladstone, 21 Oct. 1900 (Gladstone MSS, Add. MS 46022, f. 112).

[17] *East Anglian Daily Times,* 13 and 21 May 1901, Gainford MSS, 58, ff. 14–15.
[18] A.E. Pease's diary, 28 May 1901, Pease MSS.
[19] C.P. Allen and others to Asquith, 28 June 1901, Asquith MSS, vol. 10, ff. 5-6.

about the war (as I do) ... to conceal these views when you speak' at a forthcoming party meeting:

> I think tolerance and tact are essential *now* in the interest of unity, progress, peace, justice and economy. When the war is over, things should work alright if we can avoid irritating the Asquith and Grey section at this moment.[20]

Stigmatised for his brief association with Lloyd George in the division lobby, Pease insisted that he was 'decidedly no pro-Boer'. By the winter of 1901 he had wobbled so far in the other direction that he was rejoicing in a speech to his constituents at the supposedly imminent return to active political life of Lord Rosebery. 'He believed that under his leadership the principles of which they were proud would come to the front and with ... Rosebery as their helmsman the ship of State ... would sail into smooth waters before long'.[21]

If Rosebery was a disappointment to Pease and others who despaired of their leaders' jealousies, it was family financial disaster and his father's death which had the most sobering impact. To compound his embarrassment, Arthur Henderson (Sir Joseph Pease's election agent for eight years) was returned for Sir Joseph's Barnard Castle seat not as a loyal Lib–Lab but as the triumphantly independent LRC candidate.[22] Though well-disposed towards Henderson, Pease had no choice but to endorse the Liberal candidate H.G. Beaumont who insisted on fighting against the wishes of the party leadership. When asked by Beaumont for his support, he had pointed out to Herbert Gladstone on 29 June 1903:

> the difficulty of an official Liberal opposing a Labour candidate at the very time when the Liberals were endeavouring to come to an arrangement with Labour reps. throughout the country and how much I was indebted to Henderson's assistance in the Saffron Walden division.[23]

After a timely absence in Mexico and North America, Pease was re-elected to the board of Pease and Partners in 1904, dependent as never before on his emoluments as a director. As the Tory government stumbled to its inglorious end, the temporarily subdued junior whip re-emerged as a political strategist.

---

[20] J.A. Pease to Sir Joseph Pease, 7 July 1901, Gainford MSS, 6.

[21] *Saffron Walden Weekly News,* 5 July 1901, 29 Nov. 1901; *Essex and Halstead Times,* 7 Dec. 1901, Gainford MSS, 58, ff. 23–4.

[22] A.W. Purdue, 'Arthur Henderson and Liberal, Liberal–Labour and Labour Politics in the North-East of England, 1892–1903', *Northern History*, vol. XI, 1976 for 1975, pp. 195–217; F.M. Leventhal, *Arthur Henderson*, Manchester University Press, Manchester, 1989, pp. 8–18; R.I. McKibbin, 'Arthur Henderson as Labour Leader', *International Review of Social History*, vol. XXIII, Pt 1, 1978, pp. 83–5; Chris Wrigley, *Arthur Henderson*, GPC Books, Cardiff, 1990, pp. 25–31.

[23] Purdue, 'Arthur Henderson', p. 210.

Liberals and Labour had the same objects he told an interviewer for the *Northern Weekly Echo* (23 June 1905): 'Many social reforms which the working classes want could be promoted by administrative measures almost as much as by legislative.'

When Campbell-Bannerman formed his administration it was clear that Pease's rehabilitation was not yet complete. There had been press speculation that he would be appointed Patronage Secretary. As Liberal front benchers went backwards and forwards from the new premier's home in Belgrave Square, Pease was in Darlington unaware until the mail arrived on December 10 that he had been summoned on December 8 to see Campbell-Bannerman on the 9th. He arrived in London on an overnight train in time to read about the new Cabinet in the morning papers. The ensuing interviews on December 11 are best described in contemporary notes by Pease headed 'My Official Life' (Gainford MSS, 37).

I was taken into drawing room where Campbell Bannerman promptly joined me. Genial and pleasant as ever, trembling with characteristic nervousness he told me he wanted to know what my position was, and whether I would take an under secretaryship or a junior Lord of the Treasury. I told him I was dependent upon a salary from P & P – explained to him the character of this family business, how it had been created, the extent to which settlements were invested therein, and pointed out that if I vacated my directorship I practically would burn my boats behind me, and after a term in office had expired, I might find myself without either occupation or emolument. I assured him of my desire to serve with and under such a cabinet as he had formed. He then asked me if I was a good linguist, I admitted I had no claims in that direction, he said, well about the only undersecretaryship still vacant was that of Foreign Affairs, and Sir Edward Grey must have a good linguist behind him.

He said he had offered to Elgin, the Foreign Secretaryship, but he knew not a word of any foreign language! He then discoursed for some minutes on the absence of any difference which existed as far as politics were concerned, and drew a vivid picture of Asquith marching up and down his room downstairs, asserting there was a unanimity of political view by every person in the government. Campbell Bannerman said if 'there were any points of difference they were ones of method in detail which could easily be met.' And there was nothing now to prevent smooth working, and the king was very pleased with his 'very efficient set of ministers'. He said he would like me to serve as a junior lord, and thought it was ridiculous that I should give up such a Directorship as P & P – but others should be vacated. In order to be satisfied on the point he would like me to see Herbert Gladstone and Bob Reid (Home Secretary and Lord Chancellor) and ascertain their opinions on the point, and come back and tell him.

I found Herbert Gladstone at 2 Cowley Street. After congratulating him I told him the point upon wh. I had come to see him. He said, his view was that with a continuing office as an under secretary, he thought no directorship which involved work even in the autumn could be held, but he saw no objection to the retention of such a directorship for a junior lord, whose work when Parl was not sitting could be done by a post bag.

We then told me he had been anxious to go to the Admiralty, but had to give way to pressure from Campbell Bannerman. He told me that my claims for Head whip had been prejudiced by my financial trouble, and such an appointment would have opened the door to unpleasant criticisms.

Apart from his brief flirtation with the idea of Rosebery as the saviour of the Liberal Party, Pease had been loyal to Campbell-Bannerman in opposition.[24] Though he might have wished for a better place it was no disgrace to be a junior whip when room could not be found in the Cabinet for Herbert Samuel, Winston Churchill, Walter Runciman, or Reginald McKenna. The man chosen to be Chief Whip was the wealthy cotton manufacturer and former Conservative George Whiteley. Herbert Gladstone 'seemed much surprised when I pointed out how unpalatable Whiteley would be to the other side,' Pease noted:

As a convert he is naturally disliked, apart from his lacking in other qualities. His business capacity is assured and he expects much from him. I thought it a thankless post, full of responsibilities and any breakdown of machine would be attributable to him.

Mindful of repeated Liberal attacks in recent years on the persistence of minister-directors in Tory Cabinets, Sir Robert Reid had misgivings about the propriety of a minister taking the emoluments, salary, or fees of a director. Reid's doubts were brushed aside by Campbell-Bannerman.[25] So Pease went to face the electors of Saffron Walden as a Junior Lord of the Treasury. In the midst of the Liberal landslide in 1906, Pease had a hard fight. The former Chief

---

[24]   After Rosebery's Chesterfield speech, Pease suggested to Herbert Gladstone on 13 Jan. 1902 that divisive influences could be thwarted if Campbell-Bannerman would 'endorse the patriotic note, the critical attack on the Government & the constructive policy laid down by Lord R.' (Gladstone MSS, Add. MS 46022, f. 115).

[25]   Campbell-Bannerman announced that 'all public directorships held by members of the present Government have been given up by Ministers on their acceptance of office'. Honorary directorships, directorships of philanthropic undertakings, and directorships in private companies were permitted. Private companies were not statutorily defined until 1907 and the definition was wider than was envisaged in Campbell-Bannerman's policy. The guideline was redefined so as to cover family affairs and interests not primarily engaged in trading. The Prime Minister was to exercise discretion in interpreting the guidelines. (PREM 1/342; PD, Commons, vol. 350, 152, cols. 1937–8, 31 July 1939). By early 1908 Lords Elgin, Aberdeen, and Portsmouth, E. Robertson, J.E. Ellis, and H.E. Kearley, as well as Pease all still held directorships. H.H. Asquith imposed more stringent conditions, making exceptions only for Aberdeen, Pease, and his own brother-in-law H.J. Tennant. (Barry McGill, 'Conflict of Interest: English Experience 1782-1914', *Western Political Quarterly*, vol. XII, no. 3, Sept. 1959, p. 819).

Whip's provision of £500 was especially welcome. 'The Tory pressure on agricultural labourers at this time of year is more effective than in the summer when harvest has not been got in', he told Herbert Gladstone, 'and I had difficulty getting supporters up to the poll.'[26]

For the next two years Pease was to have the far harder task of educating and disciplining a fractious backbench host in which the survivors of the opposition years were outnumbered by 181 neophytes. He was not happy in the Whips' Office. Charged by Whiteley with responsibility for compiling a sessional record of the voting record of Liberal MPs he offended several who believed they had been traduced by inaccurate listing of alleged hostile votes or unpaired absences. One particularly aggrieved old member advised him to drop his 'inquisitional' return 'as an ungentlemanly and possibly libellous proceeding and which I feel sure is not countenanced by the Prime Minister'.[27]

Meanwhile Whiteley himself was provoking even stronger antagonisms. R.C. Lehmann's experience was not unique. Although recently appointed Chairman of the Liberal Publication Department, Lehmann had joined Jack Seely and 56 others in voting for a reduction in the army by 10,000. This unsuccessful attempt to persuade the government to pledge retrenchment for the following year led to an invitation to come to the Chief Whip's room. There Lehmann found himself being berated 'as if I had been a schoolboy and he a headmaster'. During a heated quarrel Lehmann warned Whiteley that if he continued to hector and bully errant backbenchers he would 'make a ghastly failure of his whipship, and that he hadn't been a Liberal long enough to warrant him in taking this line.'[28] Similar sentiments were recorded by Walter Runciman's wife Hilda after lunching with the editor of *The Westminster Gazette* and his wife:

> Mrs S said some severe things about George Whiteley, about whose appointment I hear many severe things said, chiefly based on the fact that he pokes in the ribs without discrimination and is too much impressed with power of money in party organization.[29]

---

[26] J.A. Pease to Herbert Gladstone, 27 Jan. 1906, Gladstone MSS, Add. MS 46022, f. 150.

[27] A.C. Morton to J.A. Pease, 13 Feb. 1907; and complaints from T.C. Taylor and J.D. Rees, Gainford MSS, 85.

[28] R.C. Lehmann's diary, 19 March 1906, Lehmann MSS.

[29] Hilda Runciman's diary, 17 [March] 1906, Viscountess Runciman MSS. In Whiteley's defence it should be said that he himself had been an exceptionally generous donor to party funds, giving £20,000 in 1906. (T.O. Lloyd, 'The whip as paymaster: Herbert Gladstone and party organization', *English Historical Review*, Vol. LXXXIX, No. CCCLIII, Oct. 1974, p. 806).

Some of Whiteley's difficulties were no doubt the result of inexperienced members chafing over unfamiliar but customary modes of parliamentary management. 'One has to deal with a great mob of new members, most of them absolutely ignorant of the ways of Parliament', Pease's colleague Herbert Lewis lamented.[30] Hilaire Belloc, for example, was angered by the Chair's 'inability' to see him because his name was not on the Whip's list of MPs wishing to speak.[31] But the Chief Whip's limitations were increasingly a cause for concern at 10 Downing Street. The Prime Minister's principal private secretary Arthur Ponsonby, noticed with distaste how Whiteley 'enjoyed the money squeezing part' of the 'degrading occupation' of compiling the honours list.[32] Vaughan Nash, Ponsonby's colleague in Campbell-Bannerman's office was comprehensive in his denigration: 'he seems to me quite devoid of any mind or political quality'.[33]

Whiteley knew of Pease's eagerness for employment elsewhere. When a vacancy was expected in the Under Secretaryship at the Local Government Board he broke the news that the Prime Minister proposed to nominate someone (T.J. Macnamara) rightly regarded as 'a great authority on local rating'. In any case 'if a man takes a minor advance as his reward, it almost seems as if he had an idea that his value was inconsiderable.'[34] Pease did not intend to let an inordinate sense of his own worth stand in the way of even a modest advance. 'I want you to know,' he wrote to Campbell-Bannerman on 4 January 1907, 'that if there is at any time when you are making ministerial changes, any post you could offer me which might be regarded as promotion, a change would not be unwelcome'.[35]

While he had, as he reminded the premier, 'little chance of showing administrative ability', Pease had already earned himself a rebuke from *The Daily News* on 6 October 1906 for not doing as whips were supposed to do: 'hold their tongues, and leave the expression of delicate points of policy to men who have the responsible direction of it'. Incensed by Labour's behaviour in the Cockermouth by-election, he had told a meeting in Peebles that, if similar

30 J.H. Lewis's diary, 24 April 1907, Lewis MSS.
31 *The Manchester Guardian*, 24 and 25 Jan. 1907. Belloc had pledged to divide the House over Chinese labour in the debate on the Colonial Office vote. He alleged that Alfred Emmott in the Chair offered to 'see' him if he agreed not to divide. It was small comfort to be publicly instructed by *The Manchester Guardian*'s London correspondent that the House could have been divided merely by shouting 'aye' or 'nay' at the appropriate time. Belloc had his revenge in *Mr Clutterbuck's Election*, Eveleigh Nash, 1908, *A Change in the Cabinet*, Methuen, 1909, and with Cecil Chesterton in *The Party System*, Stephen Swift, 1911.
32 Ponsonby's diary, 3 July and 5 June 1907, Ponsonby MSS (Shulbrede).
33 Nash to Arthur Ponsonby, 28 Jan. 1907, Ponsonby MSS.
34 G. Whiteley to J.A. Pease, 15 Jan. 1907, Gainford MSS, 88.
35 Copy, Gainford MSS, 85.

methods and tactics were repeated, the Liberal Party would give 'that section of the Labour Representation Committee little quarter'.[36] Pease's strategy for dealing with Labour was to yield gracefully in the country what could not be held, and to portray the parliamentary socialists as a vexatious and uninfluential fringe group. It was not Keir Hardie, but men like John Wilson, Richard Bell, Enoch Edwards, Thomas Burt, and Charles Fenwick who, he contended, most effectively represented labour interests from within the government ranks.[37] Unlike his brother Alfred whose lack of sympathy with 'socialistic' legislation was soon to be followed by his withdrawal from the Liberal ranks, Jack Pease's difficulties with the 'New Liberalism' were practical and tactical, not philosophical.[38]

As Campbell-Bannerman's health declined, Pease's hopes for preferment shifted to his most likely successor, the Chancellor of the Exchequer. Fortuitously learning that the Local Government Board had made no progress in the preparation of an English valuation bill he seized the chance to demonstrate to Asquith his alertness on politically sensitive issues. Liberals in the House and the country were expecting action on land values and a hastily produced bill might be a fiasco.[39] The absence of Campbell-Bannerman abroad in December 1907 gave Pease the excuse he needed for writing to Asquith '(in my private capacity!)', on another matter that also 'may be worthy of cabinet consideration'. Arthur Henderson (the LRC Whip) had called for tea at Pease's Darlington house, Headlam Hall, a few nights earlier on his way to a meeting in his constituency. Henderson told Pease that his party were 'going to fight many industrial seats at the next election'. If the Liberals wanted to 'prevent a lot of

---

36 The speech was widely reported: see for example *The Daily Chronicle*, 6 Oct. 1906. On Oct. 9, Campbell-Bannerman concurred with Lord Ripon that 'our Whips have been too frisky and too noisy: they have mistaken their proper function'. (Ripon MSS, Add. MS 43518, f. 121).

37 Praise for the 'Labour representatives in the House of Commons who are loyal to Sir Henry Campbell-Bannerman' was a notable feature of Pease's speech to the Northern Liberal Federation at Stockton-on-Tees on 14 December 1907 (*Essex and Halstead Times*, 2 Dec. 1907, Gainford MSS, 58, f. 143).

38 Among Quakers, Seebohm Rowntree's analysis and advocacy of remedies for unemployment and poverty had been influential. A Friends Social Union carried forward a program of study, debate, and publication from 1903. A Socialist Quaker Society was active and respected. (W.H. Marwick, *Quaker Social Thought*, Woodbrooke Occasional Papers 2, Friends Home Service Committee for Woodbrooke College, 1969, p. 15). For Alfred Pease's objections to the domestic policy of the Liberal government see his letters to Herbert Samuel, his successor in the Cleveland constituency, 4 and 19 Aug., 2 and 5 Sept. 1908, Samuel MSS, A155 III, ff. 135, 137, 147 149.

39 Asquith had been contemplating the taxation of land values since early in 1906 (Sir Edward Hamilton's diary, 1 March 1906, Hamilton MSS, Add. MS 48683, in John Brown, 'Scottish and English land legislation 1905–11', *The Scottish Historical Review*, Vol. XLVII, 1, no. 143, April 1968, p. 76).

Tories getting in representing a minority' they should introduce the second ballot. Pease saw merit in this (though he seemed not be be clear about the difference between a single transferable vote and other preferential systems). There are, he concluded, 'several obvious objections to the 2nd ballot'.[40]

Much as Pease might aspire to a Cabinet post, his best prospect of promotion was to step into Whiteley's shoes. The Chief Whip's health had suffered and, as his principal deputy, Pease had borne a greater burden in the closing months of 1907. In December 1905 Pease had been isolated in Darlington at a critical time and had taken no initiative on his own behalf. With the seriousness of the Prime Minister's ill-health an open secret by early 1908, he was determined not to make the same mistake twice. Self-assertion might not yield the most coveted prize. But at least his claims would not go by default.

---

[40]   J.A. Pease to H.H. Asquith, 15 Dec. 1907, draft, Gainford MSS, 85.

Chapter 1

The Asquith Succession

Sir Henry Campbell-Bannerman resigned as Prime Minister on 3 April 1908. Three days later H.H. Asquith left for Biarritz where King Edward VII awaited him. Among the large correspondence that arrived during the new premier's absence was a letter from Jack Pease:

Private & Confidential   April 8. 1908
Headlam Hall
Gainford

My dear Asquith,

As one of your greatest admirers may I tell you, how delighted I am that you are now Prime Minister, & how heartily I wish you health & strength to occupy for many years the highest position a man can attain.

If, as I assume, some changes are pending, may I ask you not to overlook my record. I *hate* writing about myself, but it is only my due that you should know when C.B. induced me to strengthen his whips' staff, in 1897, he told me that such a sacrifice made by me whilst we were in opposition, might probably be a step to a more responsible post hereafter.

In 1905 when he had nearly formed his government he sent for me, & told me he had been misinformed about my readiness to accept office, but that he could still offer me the under-secretaryship for Foreign Affairs. I said I should be glad to accept the position, but I asked if Edward Grey remained in the Commons, would it not be expected that his subordinate should be a peer. C.B. at once admitted the force of this, & then asked me if I would become a junior Lord & work under Whiteley. He urged that with a staff ignorant of whips' duties, my experience would be of value, & as he appeared to think that in this way I could best serve the party I agreed to do so.

I do feel, that *my eleven years* work as a whip does entitle me to some recognition by promotion & may I add that not only would the responsibilities of an administrative department be more congenial to my tastes, but also I think better adapted to my capabilities.

A telegram here: Headlam Gainford would bring me up in about six hours at any time to talk things over with you, if you would like to see me.

Forgive me for writing to you when you have so much to attend to, and believe me with heartfelt congratulations.

Ever yours,
Joseph A. Pease

P.S.   Montagu said you would like to know the attitude of the party to the Eight

Hours Bill (for Mines) – I enclose you a memorandum on the subject for perusal at your leisure.[1]

(Asquith MSS, vol. 11, ff. 51–2)

JAP (as Pease will usually be described in the following commentaries and notes) had actually been appointed a whip in 1897 by Sir William Harcourt. His memory had also enhanced Campbell-Bannerman's studiously guarded reference to the Under-Secretaryship at the Foreign Office. According to JAP's own contemporary note of an interview on 11 December 1905, the Prime Minister had said 'well about the only under-secretaryship still vacant was that of Foreign Affairs, & Sir Edward Grey must have a good linguist behind him.' (Gainford MSS, 37). JAP had already admitted that he 'had no claims in that direction', notwithstanding the fact that his French was probably better than that of Grey who was supposed to be 'trying to learn' French months before he took office at the end of 1905. Certainly JAP did not speak it with a Northumbrian accent as Grey reputedly did. (Lord Balcarres' Diary, 21 September 1905, John Vincent, ed., The Crawford Papers: *The journals of David Lindsay twenty-seventh Earl of Crawford and tenth Earl of Balcarres 1871–1940 during the years 1892 to 1940, Manchester University Press, Manchester, 1984, p. 86; Runciman to W.M. Crook, 22 August 1919, Crook MSS; Edgar Vincent, Viscount D'Abernon,* An Ambassador of Peace, Pages from the diary of Viscount D'Abernon ..., *3 vols, Hodder and Stoughton, 1929–30, vol. i, p. 66). The Under-Secretaryship was offered to Lord Burghclere (1846–1921) who, as Herbert Coulston Gardner, had been Liberal MP Essex (Saffron Walden) 1885–95 and President of the Board of Agriculture 1892–5. Burghclere so 'clearly showed that he considered it a degradation that I took it as a virtual declining' Campbell-Bannerman told Lord Ripon on December 13. (Ripon MSS, Add. MS 43518, f.63). The post was then offered to Lord Edmond Fitzmaurice who had held it in the Gladstone government from 1882 to 1885. 'Grey agreed to E.F. cordially faute de Burghclere: now he prefers B' who said he had been misunderstood. (Charles Hobhouse's diary, 19 Dec. 1905, Edward David, ed.,* Inside Asquith's Cabinet: From the Diaries of Charles Hobhouse, John Murray,

---

1 The Coal Mines (Eight Hours) Bill proposed to limit the miners' working day to eight hours. Despite the coal owners' arguments that it would reduce coal output by 10% and lead to increases in the cost of coal of up to 9d. per ton, it received the royal assent on December 21. It did not, in the end, include in the limited hours the time miners spent reaching the coal face or the reverse journey. JAP's memo has not been traced. But his own argument – that the bill met the needs of the midlands and south Wales coalfields but would 'unduly prejudice commercial interests, and dislocate a trade which is now economically carried on and is giving good employment under conditions and hours which give general satisfaction' in Durham and Northumberland – is succinctly put in a letter to Herbert Gladstone, 15 April 1908. (Gladstone MSS, Add. MS 46022, f. 159).

1977, p. 54). Fitzmaurice, who was virtually bilingual in English and French, accepted and was created Baron Fitzmaurice.

Asquith replied to JAP two days after he returned from Biarritz:

Private   20 Cavendish Square W.[2]
12 April 1908.

My dear Jack,
 I found your letter on my return from Biarritz. I knew that you had a preference for some administrative office over your present post, and in the changes which are being made I should have been glad to give effect to your wish. But the situation is rather changed by Whiteley's private intimation to me that health &c will oblige him very shortly to give up the post of Chief Whip. There is no one in the party who possesses the same qualifications as yourself to succeed him, & I need not say that the office is one of the most responsible & important in the Government. That is my reason for doing nothing for you at present.

Yours very sincerely,
H.H. Asquith

Tuesday 14 April[3] ... I called upon Asquith at Grosvenor Square[4] – he was dressed in blue flannel jacket & at once welcomed me. He told me he had asked Whiteley to stay on as Chief Whip until the adjournment at the end of July, that he would ask the King to make him a peer. Asquith spoke highly of the efficient way he had managed the business of the House, and urged him to stay on, although Whiteley himself, owing to insomnia was anxious to be relieved earlier of his work.
 When I sympathised with the P.M. in the difficulties of altering C.B.'s ministry, he said on the whole those I have shelved have been very nice. I did

---

2   20 Cavendish Square was the Asquith's London house from 1894 to 1920. On Asquith's appointment as Chancellor, Margot Asquith said that 11 Downing Street was too small for their family. It was therefore occupied by Herbert Gladstone. (Roy Jenkins, *Asquith*, Collins, 1964, p. 161). When the Asquiths moved into No. 10 they leased 20 Cavendish Square first to Sir Bache and Lady (Maud) Cunard, and then to George Cornwallis-West.

3   JAP misdated this entry April 7. His first few diary entries were written several weeks after the events to which they refer. We have omitted the opening paragraph which paraphrases and misdates JAP's letter of April 8, and muddles other dates.

4   'Grosvenor Square' was probably a slip of the pen for 'Cavendish Square'. None of Grosvenor Square's residents in 1908 was likely to have been Asquith's host. Asquith's father-in-law, Sir Charles Tennant Bt, had lived at 40 Grosvenor Square till his death in 1906, bequeathing it to his son Edward who moved to Queen Anne's Gate in December 1906. The lease of 40 Grosvenor Square was sold to Sir Daniel Cooper in 1908. (Sir Edward Tennant's diary, 23 Nov. 1906, Glenconner MSS; Irwin Dasent, *A History of Grosvenor Square*, Macmillan, 1935, p. 222).

not mind about Portsmouth that was easy, but Elgin and Tweedmouth were very unpleasant interviews for me, but Tweedmouth took it well, also from Lough I got a nice letter when I made him a P.C. but I had difficulty getting it out of the King.

Tweedmouth's fate had been sealed a month earlier when The Times *military correspondent, Colonel Charles à Court Repington, leaked the extraordinary but true story that the First Lord of the Admiralty had replied to a private letter from the Kaiser, and had revealed Britain's naval estimates to the German Emperor before they were presented to Parliament.   (W. Michael Ryan,* Lieutenant-Colonel Charles à Court Repington: A Study in the Interaction of Personality, the Press, and Power, *(Ph.D. thesis, University of Cincinnati, 1976, pp. 201–14). Tweedmouth may have taken his interview 'well' but he wrote to Asquith on April 11, refusing the Lord Presidency of the Council, as a 'consolation prize', and adding 'You don't trust me – why not give me a watch dog, say Runciman or Winston with a seat in the Cabinet.' (Asquith MSS, vol. 11, ff. 87–8). Asquith persuaded him to reconsider and he finally agreed to become Lord President. (Asquith to Edward VII, n.d. and 12 April 1908, Asquith MSS, vol. 19, ff. 255–6, 261). Elgin's feelings were expressed uninhibitedly in a letter to his colleague in misfortune Tweedmouth: '... I feel that even a housemaid gets a better warning' (20 April 1908, Tweedmouth MSS). Asquith had offended Elgin by the casual offer of a marquessate which Elgin declined.   The King had approved the marquessate for Elgin, and was delighted 'that supreme ass Portsmouth is shunted altogether'. (Edward VII to the Prince of Wales, 8 April 1908,* RA *AA25.35).*

He then asked me my criticism on his new appointments, I said from a whip's point of view, Fowler was no use in the Cabinet, he had no following in the House.[5]   That McKinnon Wood, was a force among the London Liberal Members, & to have him inside the Ministry would strengthen the Govmt. Masterman was a most unpractical politician, he was an idealist who let loose below the gangway could do & had done mischief, but I was glad his tongue was tied & that he might see the difficulties of putting into practice his theories at the Local Govmt Board. Asquith said there was no other place for him, but he would like to have seen McKinnon Wood at the L.G.B. As for Seely, I said he had

---

5   An 'artfully laid' trap had failed to dislodge the aged Fowler: 'Morley, by arrangement, suggested ... that the time had come for both of them to tender their resignations, knowing of course that his would not be accepted.' (Sir Almeric FitzRoy's diary, 31 May 1910, Sir Almeric FitzRoy, *Memoirs*, 2 vols, Hutchinson [?1923], vol. I, p. 411). Proposals in 1902 and 1907 to translate Fowler from the Commons to the Lords had been shelved because of gossip about his son. (Lord Knollys to Campbell-Bannerman, 28 Oct. 1907, Campbell-Bannerman MSS, Add. MS 52513, ff. 98, 102).

worked loyally with us, deserved his position through his work in the country & for the ability he had displayed, & as long as he was outside the ministry he had an influence which was capable of weakening the Govmt in case of any disagreement. Asquith then asked me about organisation. I admitted I was not fully acquainted with Parliament Street[6], but my general impression was not favourable. I thought information was collected but not used. He told me Arthur Acland certainly had some criticisms to make on the Nat. Lib. Fedtn & I had better get from him his views, & think the whole matter over before I took up the position of Chief Whip. We then discussed Whiteley's characteristics & his methods, the way in which money had been collected from those given honours was obviously most distasteful, but the chest was fuller than it had been since the days of Pitt, & the sooner the securities [and] consols were taken out of Whiteley's name & put into Trustees the better. 1/2 a million nearly in hand.[7] I pointed out the inconvenience of having to step into a position at end of July – that this meant Parliament St would remain unreformed until the autumn session. Asquith said he would see whether the change could be effected on the 26th June when honours would be conferred.

As all my friends thought I had deserved better at C.B.'s & Asquith's hands after 10 years of whip's work, I asked him if I could – as an apparent recognition to keep their tongues quiet – be given a P.C. Asquith said I think it would come better when you get your position in July.

House of C. reassembled on 27 April. Whiteley asked me to see Asquith, with a view to his being liberated on June 26 – & told me how hard it was to keep things quiet, & at the same time to get his constituency prepared for an election.

On Wed. May 6 dined with Arthur Acland. He went at some length into the incidents connected with the formation of C.B.'s Govmt in Dec. 1905. How he had spent 4 or 5 hours one evening, with Haldane & Grey persuading them to enter. After 2 hours Grey & Haldane left him, & he then heard they had decided not to go in, he sat with them until 1.0 the same night & finally Grey said he would join. In the morning Herbert Gladstone called upon him offered him a safe seat told him C.B. would send for him, that he waited 3 days in London, & how neither C.B. or Gladstone had ever explained their conduct, in not sending for

---

6   The National Liberal Federation, the Liberal Central Association (of which the Chief Whip was *ex officio* chairman), the Liberal Publication Department, the Home Counties Liberal Federation, and the London Liberal Federation were located in adjoining offices in Parliament Street. The National Reform Union also had a London office nearby.

7   Whiteley handed over £519,000 '(actual and collectable, all good money) ... less under £5000 overdrawn at the Bank' and £400,000 in Consols. (Whiteley to Asquith, 29 May 1908, Asquith MSS, vol. ll, ff. 139–40).

him, or giving any reason for their change of mind. He subsequently thought he could serve the Party, as president of the Nat. Lib. Fedtn & for 2 years had been brought into contact with its so called work.[8] Hudson was a personal friend, but he said Hudson was lazy, the organisation was independent of the Government, it passed resolutions at its routine meetings, & votes of condolence & congratulations when deaths occurred or honours were given. I admitted my impression was no work was done to arouse latent Liberalism or stimulate organisation in the constituencies, & Hudson now gave me the impression he was suffering from swelled head, & that it was a great mistake to have conferred a knighthood on him after the election. Acland said I had exactly struck the nail on the head, but he advised me not to take any action to arouse annoyance but just to go my own way & ignore the Nat. Lib. Fedtn, but to treat them with deference. The agents he said, in the country always played into each others' hands & never admitted inefficiency. I explained to him my ideas of a whip's duty to be at the House & look after the machine & its work there, but to devolve the organisation into districts, all of which should centralise their information at Parliament Street. I alluded to the hopelessness of trying to do the work from head quarters which ought to be done locally, & as an instance alluded to the meeting held at 42 Parlmt St. the day before, even with Lloyd George McKenna Winston Churchill present, the shortcomings were admitted but the remedies not found. Churchill had, that very day, told me how glad he was that I was to follow Whiteley, & that he had not known before that day (that through Whiteley's indiscreet references to his executive of his early retirement) that he was to be relieved, & that I could rely on him (W. Churchill) to back me for all he was worth. W. Churchill & I talked over Freddie Guest, as a man who would take up organisation in the midlands & work it. Two days later I explained to Churchill that if F.G. made a

---

8   See T. Boyle, 'The Formation of Campbell-Bannerman's Government in December 1905: a Memorandum by J.A. Spender', *Bulletin of the Institute of Historical Research*, vol. XLV, Nov. 1972, pp. 283–302. Reporting a conversation with Edmund Gosse in 1915 about the formation of C.B.'s government, Elizabeth Haldane wrote that her brother and Grey called on Acland but were 'not influenced by his advice.' (Elizabeth Haldane's diary, 21 Sept. 1915, Elizabeth Haldane MSS). Nevertheless, Acland was obviously treated badly. Believing he had been asked to consider taking a peerage and leading the government in the Lords – not, as JAP recorded, to come into the Commons – he was then completely ignored. An unpublished note by Lord Rosebery, 17 June 1906, based on a conversation with Spender, shows that Spender had suggested putting Acland in the Lords when Campbell-Bannerman refused to make Haldane Lord Chancellor. In 'the hurly burly the strengthening of the H of Lds drops out of sight, & so does Acland'. According to Rosebery, Spender and Acland had together drawn up an account of the formation of the government – presumably the 'Memorandum by J.A. Spender' printed by Boyle. Rosebery's note is in the Beaverbrook MSS, Harriet Irving Library, University of New Brunswick. For contemporary versions by Acland see his undated letter to Lord Tweedmouth (Tweedmouth MSS) and letter to Lord Ripon, 15 Dec. 1905, Ripon MSS, Add. MS 43638, ff. 98–101.

scheme work, I would then promote him to hony organising secretary & give him a status among the agents in visiting the constituencies, but that his Colonel (Cecil Bingham) & Tweedmouth (his uncle) had warned me he might not be reliable.   W.C. said his tact energy & perseverance helping him had been remarkable, & the way he organised the fight at Dundee & stimulated work for the cause of his return left nothing wanting.[9]

Whiteley's debilitating insomnia had not responded to a prolonged rest cure in 1907.   With Campbell-Bannerman's retirement seemingly imminent, Elsie Pease had written disconsolately to JAP on 27 January 1908:

… I suppose Asquith will shift Whiteley as soon as he can & I don't see any one to be Whip but you – & should so much rather you had anything else. I am so bored with the party & the endless civility to 'terrors' which it entails, & the ceaseless toil, unless it should lead to something better but I know this is selfish & you must take anything that is offered you & be thankful for it.

(Gainford MSS, 86)

Elsie's irritation with the Chief Whip surfaced again a little later:

Make Whiteley do his own work. Why should he take the pay & put so much on you – of course it brings you more prominently into contact with ministers but I don't hope for much from the brutes as with you as No 2 the whipping goes alright & it looks bad to climb down & shift up Chief Whip – acknowledging W is a failure – & it means throwing over Herbert Gladstone …

(undated letter, [? March 1908], Gainford MSS, 86)

The news that the Chief Whip had advised his constituency association of his impending resignation appeared in the press on May 19. The Daily Mail, The Daily Telegraph, and The Times tipped JAP as Whiteley's successor. The Daily News (May 20) thought that he would be popular with Unionist, Irish, and Labour MPs as well as Liberals. The Manchester Despatch (May 19) suggested that a more popular choice would be the Master of Elibank 'for his courtly manners and his perfect tact are united to a shrewd business head and a thorough understanding of the party organisation'. Other possibilities were J.H. Whitley, an unpaid Junior Lord of the Treasury, who was thought not to want the job, and the Lancashire barrister MP Sir Joseph Leese.

---

9   Churchill, defeated in Manchester in the by-election caused by his elevation to the Cabinet, was standing for the Dundee seat vacated by the newly ennobled Edmond Robertson, Lord Lochee.   He was returned comfortably on May 9.   Guest, Churchill's assistant private secretary, became the first chairman of the Western Counties Liberal Federation.

Only The Daily News *lobby correspondent seems to have discovered Pease's unwillingness to take the post. In the few hours before it became clear that JAP had accepted, the* News *man reported that Asquith would look outside the Whips' office. Ivor Guest, R.C. Lehmann, and Sir Edwin Cornwall (previously whip of the Progressive Party in the London County Council) were mentioned. But by the afternoon of May 20* The Westminster Gazette *lent its authority to reports that JAP was the chosen man, and predicted that he would be 'successful in a post of singular difficulty and complexity'. Several newspapers used the opportunity to dilate on the office of Chief Whip: 'a name invented when members of Parliament were sportsmen as well as legislators ... A good Whip must be omnipresent and omniscient – the first to enter the House and the last to leave it – as Sir A. Acland-Hood was in the days of the Unionist Government.'* (The Daily Mail, *19 May 1908). 'He is the general manager of the concern. He has to deal with many men of many moods, each one of whom looks to him for help and guidance, some of whom are at times wayward and others occasionally wilful.'* (The Northern Echo, *20 May 1908).*

Friday 22 May Lord Tweedmouth telephoned me he wanted to see me, & he called at 8 Hertford St[10] – the object of the visit was to give me advice on whip's work, but none was volunteered, but I forced him to give me his views, on my staff, Elibank's work, the causes of his success 1893–5. Always be in the Lobby, & every day see the P.M. in the morning before the day's work begins were the most practical pieces of advice.[11]

He then proceeded in a disjointed way to allude to his grievance, his views on Admiralty work, the necessity of getting rid of Fisher who had been 1st Lord too long. He proceeded to tell me he had been living with Mrs Sands[12], & intended to marry her, & hoped Elsie & I would receive her, & that he knew such a step was for his happiness, his method of life would be known if he did not. I was much perturbed. I merely told him that I only wanted him to be happy, but I saw

---

10   The Peases' London house.
11   Tweedmouth's sister, Lady Aberdeen, ascribed his success to a brilliant series of parties at Brook House, to the Liberal Social Council founded by Lady Tweedmouth (who died of cancer in 1904), and to a very full social calendar seasonally punctuated by fishing, shooting, and hunting. (*Edward Marjoribanks Lord Tweedmouth KT 1849–1909 Notes and Recollections*, Constable, 1909, p. 23).
12   Possibly Maud Sands, 'the other woman' in the Hartopp divorce of 1902, a former actress described by Sir Edward Clarke, counsel for Lady Hartopp, as 'a very beautiful woman who was living apart from her husband, and who was known to be accessible to gentlemen who were prepared to pay somewhat heavily for her favours'. (Gerald Isaacs, 2nd Marquess of Reading, *Rufus Isaacs, 1st Marquess of Reading* ..., Hutchinson, 2 vols, 1942/45, vol. 1, pp. 96, 98–100). In March 1908 it was rumoured that Tweedmouth was going to marry the widow of the 2nd Baron Inverclyde. (JAP to EP, 9 Mar. 1908, Gainford MSS, 520).

he was not in possession of his powers of judgment, & felt inclined to go to Asquith. But he told me he had just seen Asquith, & that Lady Margt Orr Ewing & Lady Ridley his nieces[13] both approved of his intention.

Monday 25th called on Asquith in his room at House of C found him much upset, Tweedmouth was a 'raving lunatic'. It appears he dined with Lady Hindlip[14] on the Friday evening, after he saw me, & his behaviour excited comment. Lady Ridley had spoken to Asquith & Asquith wired for Dudley Marjoribanks from Liverpool, Lady Aberdeen from Ireland & Sinclair from Scotland. He was placed under care at his house in Seymour Street. I talked over business matters relating to work in House, & Whiteley's retirement on June 2d so that election in Pudsey should take place on 20th before honours list on 26th, as we agreed that for Whiteley to go to the Peers during an election would be disastrous, & would be used by the Labour candidate as an argument why he should be supported, rather than a party which whilst making peers, said they objected to them.[15]

Asquith seemed surprised that the King knew about Tweedmouth's condition, when they met Fallières French President[16] at Victoria Station the King said 'How terrible about Tweedmouth we will speak about it tonight' (i.e. at the State Banquet when they would again meet).

I had some talk with Loulou Harcourt about my prospective duties & work, & also about Tweedmouth's methods of life, to which was attributed his mental condition.

---

13 Lady Margaret Orr-Ewing's mother, Anne, Duchess of Roxburghe, was the fourth daughter of the 7th Duke of Marlborough. Tweedmouth had married the Duke's third daughter, Lady Fanny (d. 1904). The Duke's eldest daughter, Lady Cornelia, had married the 1st Lord Wimborne; their daughter, the Hon. Rosamond ('Rose') (1877–1947) a gifted sculptor and musician (DBE 1918) had married the 2nd Viscount Ridley, whose mother was Tweedmouth's sister. Thus Lady Ridley was Tweedmouth's niece twice over.

14 Probably Georgina ('Minnie') (d. 1939), widow of the wealthy brewer 2nd Baron Hindlip, whose cook was 'wonderful'. (G. Cornwallis-West, *Edwardian Hey-Days* or A Little about a Lot of Things, Putnam, 1930, p. 128). But possibly Agatha (1879–1962), wife of the 3rd Baron, a noted traveller and big game hunter with her husband who was Unionist junior whip in the Lords 1907–14. No Hindlip papers for this period have survived.

15 Pudsey, in the West Riding of Yorkshire, had been Whiteley's constituency since 1900. The results of the by-election, which took place on June 20, were: J.J. Oddy (Un.) 5444; F. Ogden (Lib.) 5331; J.W. Benson (Soc.) 1291. Benson was an unofficial Labour candidate. The 1906 contest had been a straight fight between Liberal and Unionist candidates.

16 (Clement) Armand Fallières (1841–1931), President of France 1906–13, made a state visit to London 25–28 May 1908, including an inspection of the Franco–British Exhibition at Shepherd's Bush.

The deterioration of Tweedmouth's mental condition may have been hastened by the deeply embarrassing revelation in March 1908 of his 'private' correspondence with the Kaiser on naval policy. But his 'incapacity and ignorance' were already a subject of Whitehall gossip. (C. Spring-Rice to Lord Cranley, undated, Stephen Gwynn, ed., The Letters and Friendships of Sir Cecil Spring Rice, *2 vols, Constable, 1929, vol. 1, p. 113). He had reluctantly accepted Asquith's offer of the Lord Presidency, resenting his removal from the Admiralty ostensibly to make way for a First Lord in the House of Commons. On May 18, he delighted the Opposition by describing Haldane's army scheme as a gamble. In a tribute to Campbell-Bannerman the same day he remarked on the late Prime Minister's fidelity to his wife in language so unflattering to the late Lady Campbell-Bannerman that the passage was suppressed by Hansard and the newspapers. (Balcarres' diary, 30 May 1908, Vincent, ed.,* The Crawford Papers, *p. 109). The next day, answering questions relating to McKenna's administration of the Admiralty 'he prefaced his speech by an exordium, almost incoherent with temper ... declared he had no official knowledge of the matter, and indulged in some acrimonious jocularities at the expense of the Privy Council and its functions, as concentrated in the hands of the Lord President, who, he announced, "has nothing to do."' (Almeric FitzRoy's diary, 23 May 1908, FitzRoy,* Memoirs, *vol. I, p. 352).*

On May 20 Tweedmouth sent the King a bizarre invitation to participate in a variety entertainment with Tweedmouth's fifteen unmarried nieces 'very bright but very proper'. (Sir Philip Magnus, King Edward the Seventh, *John Murray, 1964, pp. 375–6). Asquith informed the King that Tweedmouth was 'unhinged' (undated letter, tentatively dated 21 May 1908 by the Royal Archives, RA R29/15), and later recalled for Venetia Stanley:*

His was a tragic case, for he was one of the sanest & most high-spirited of mankind. I shall never forget my bewilderment when, in the course of a longish tête-à-tête in the Cabinet room, it gradually dawned upon me that he was off his head. Rosie Ridley & I spent a whole Saturday afternoon in search of a mad doctor who would certify him to be insane, and at last dragged old [Sir Thomas] Barlow from a death bed to do what was necessary.[17]

The Times *(28 May 1908) announced that Tweedmouth was suffering from insomnia and a complete rest had been ordered. He died in September 1909.*

---

17 Asquith to Venetia Stanley, 31 Oct. 1914, Venetia Montagu MSS, Michael and Eleanor Brock, eds, *H.H. Asquith Letters to Venetia Stanley*, Oxford University Press, 1985 (1st edn 1982), p. 300. Tweedmouth's youthful high spirits had led to the near starvation of a small boy at Harrow who was locked up without food to do some Greek lines for him. Later he was obliged to flee from Oxford to Paris to escape arrest for leading a group which burnt and destroyed books and papers in Christ Church library. ([Julian Osgood Field], *Uncensored Recollections*, Eveleigh Nash & Grayson, 1924, pp. 231–3).

26 May 1908 House up at 9.30 – got business through in the way I wanted, &
went to the Court Ball.

Had 10 minutes chat with Lord Rosebery. I told him that I wanted a working
arrangement with the Liberal League. He said I want it to be dissolved, now
Asquith is Prime Minister, there is no longer any reason for it, but I have been
overruled, but he suggested I should see Allard. Lord R. described his sensation
in his uniform, as that felt by a tortoise, with a head out shell above, & cold &
flabby underneath.

*The Liberal League was one of the organisations which inevitably would be of
concern to a new Chief Whip. Formed in February 1902, incorporating the
Liberal Imperial League, it had Lord Rosebery as president, and a formidable
quartet of vice-presidents: Asquith, Grey, Fowler, and Haldane. Its secretary,
William Allard, was one of the most respected organisers in the Liberal party.
JAP himself, in spite of his sympathy with Asquith and admiration for Rosebery,
does not seem to have been a member of the League. At Glasgow on 10 March
1902, Rosebery had said that if the League were not founded on political truth
and justice it did not deserve to prevail. Campbell-Bannerman easily out-
manoeuvred Rosebery and his principal lieutenants in 1905. When Haldane
warned Whiteley early in 1907 that the League 'would "flutter the dovecotes"
(or some such expression) if not properly regarded in respect of patronage',
Campbell-Bannerman extinguished the threat by instructing the Chief Whip to
tell Haldane that 'any claim to separate recognition of the Liberal League would
mean a reconstitution of the Government'. (Note by Lord Rendel, 31 March
1907, [F.E. Hamer, ed.],* The Personal Papers of Lord Rendel, *Ernest Benn,
1931, pp. 170-1). With Asquith's assumption of the premiership, and other
League leaders entrenched in the Cabinet, it was not clear what purpose the
League served. After flirting with the idea of merging with the Unionist free
traders Rosebery now wanted to give Asquith as much support as possible. But
other League figures, apprehensive about the influence of Lloyd George and
Churchill on Liberal policy, would not allow the League to die. (Alan Sykes,*
Tariff Reform in British Politics 1903–1913, *Clarendon Press, Oxford, 1979,
pp. 168–82).*

27 May 1908 A writer for 'The World' newspaper interviewed me with a view
to writing a sketch of my career.[18]

May 28 Had a talk with Asquith about honours, procedure, and work to be put
down for the following week. He said he had his honour list very full.

---

18 The interview was published 1 July 1908 as part of a series entitled 'Celebrities at
    Home'. As well as a brief biography of JAP and his wife, the article included a
    detailed description of his London home. (Gainford MSS, 58, ff. 170–1).

Dined with Charles Henry of H. of C. sat by Mrs Levy Lever who suggested she had ambitions (baronetcy obviously wanted). The American military attaché's wife[19] on the other side. I was called to the House as supply down for the day was through. We got all report stages on paper but Irish talked on last report vote for 1½ hours, and we got through after 11.0 the money resolution for Irish University Bill, much to annoyance of obstructionists, who thought they had defeated the chance, by allowing supply to run through without debate.[20]

29 May   Played Wilkins Treasury official at Golf at Mitcham & won by 5 & 3. Dined Jeffersons,[21] sat by Mrs/?Lady Cunard.[22]   Went on to Partingtons to evening party. Mrs Asquith talked of her health. Went on to Mrs Arthur James's Ball in Grafton St, & talked to Arnold Morley about Tweedmouth, he had recently had a chat with him, but could not understand him properly.

Oswald and Clara Partington gave a reception 'to meet the Prime Minister' (The Times, 30 May 1908) to which JAP took his wife and daughter before going to the ball held by King Edward's friend Venetia James. The following day he escaped to Littlestone where both Herbert Gladstone and Thomas Lough had houses conveniently near the golf club. Lough, who had invited JAP on May 21 (Gainford MSS, 86) 'to get out of the fuss and gossip for the weekend', had other matters on his mind.

[May] 30 & 31   I stayed at Littlestone, found Lough much opposed to Govmt's action in regard to sugar convention. I agree with his view – as a Free Trade govmt we have little excuse in remaining in convention for further 5 years but his motive for criticisms seems hostility owing to his having been cleared out of ministry.

---

19   Mrs Sydney A. Cloman.

20   The Irish Universities Act, establishing the Queen's University, Belfast, and the National University of Ireland as non-denominational institutions, was opposed by a handful of Ulster Unionists. The National University – a federation of colleges at Cork, Dublin, and Galway (with the theological college at Maynooth affiliated) – was obviously intended to be 'Roman Catholic in spirit and atmosphere'. (Austen Chamberlain to Mary Chamberlain, 1 April 1908, Sir Austen Chamberlain, *Politics From Inside:* An Epistolary Chronicle 1906–1914, Cassell, 1936, p. 103; Leon Ó Broin, *The Chief Secretary:* Augustine Birrell in Ireland, Chatto and Windus, 1969, pp. 21–5).

21   Possibly the H.W. Jeffersons of 12 Berkeley Square.

22   Probably Lady Cunard (1872–1948), wife of the 3rd Bt, but possibly her sister-in-law, Mrs Gordon Cunard. American born Maud Burke, known in later years as 'Emerald', married Sir Bache Edward Cunard in 1895. Edith Howard married Gordon Cunard in 1889; he succeeded his brother as 4th Bt, 1925.

The Government had renewed the 1901 Sugar Convention Act. The original convention, between Britain, Austria–Hungary, Belgium, France, Germany, Italy, the Netherlands, Spain, and Sweden, had stated that the signatories would suppress direct or indirect bounties for the production or export of sugar and impose duty on any imported sugar which had benefited from such bounties. Britain agreed not to pay any bounty on sugar produced in her colonies and to allow no preferential treatment to colonial sugar. The convention had been modified to allow 'bounty-fed' sugar from Russia to be imported into the convention states without attracting duty. This modification was bitterly attacked by many Liberal MPs, led by Lough, as a betrayal of Free Trade. The Cabinet had resolved on May 6 to use an expected Budget surplus to reduce the sugar duty. On May 25, Lloyd George had confided to Austen Chamberlain 'I wanted to keep the sugar duty on and use it for pensions!' Chamberlain later learned that the reduction of the sugar duty was 'on the dictation of the Whips' to arrest the adverse electoral tide. (Austen Chamberlain to Mary Chamberlain, 26 May 1908 and 27 Feb. 1909, Chamberlain, Politics From Inside, pp. 109, 153–4).

June 1   Asquith gave me 20 mins. in his room at House after Questions – had several small matters about procedure to discuss. I told him the position of the Labour Party, how broken up they were in faction. That the Liberal Labour men had decided to stay on our side of House although their unions had passed a resolution to induce them to work with the L.R.C. who sat opposite us. I asked Asquith to take all opportunities to notice them rather than the L.R.C.

June 2   Saw Masterman married King Hy VII Chapel at the Abbey.[23]   After talking over with H.H.A. opportunity sought for by Radicals to censure L. Loreburn for not making Lib. J.P.s, decided to give facilities.

Loreburn annoyed many Liberals by refusing to take political affiliation into account when appointing new JP's. His predecessor, Lord Halsbury, had appointed only Conservatives to the Bench and thus created a great political imbalance. In defence of his appointments Loreburn pointed out that customarily he accepted the advice of the Lords Lieutenant and that nearly all of these were Conservative. Of the 7,000 magistrates appointed between January 1906 and November 1909, there were 3,197 known Liberals. The attacks on Loreburn had been particularly bitter in 1906 7. The problem was resolved in 1910 when a royal commission recommended the formation of advisory committees. Loreburn's successors, Haldane and Sankey, followed his policy of

---

[23]   He married Lucy Lyttelton (1884–1977), daughter of General the Hon. Sir Neville Lyttelton, C-in-C, Ireland 1908–11.

appointing the best candidate regardless of party. (R.F.V. Heuston, Lives of the Lord Chancellors 1885–1940, *Clarendon Press, Oxford, 1964, pp. 153–7).*

June 3   Saw Asquith from 1 to 1.15 about business for following week and off to McKenna's wedding at St Margts.[24] This day the following came to me about honours which they pressed me to give them.   Duckworth (Kt.1) Rees (Kt or Indian order) Layland Barratt (Bt. 10) Barnard (Kt) Tomkinson (P.C.0) Philipps J. (Peer. 30).

Asquith said if A.H.D. Acland would not take Peerage, Philipps might perhaps get it but list full. He told me I would get a P.C. on King's birthday, but not now as I had hardly been promoted & it would look as if I was in too great a hurry. Government turned awkward corner thro' my having put down for this day motion for holiday adjournment, & the anti sugar convention group could not get direct issue, & a Division. This opportunity for discussion convention the only one I could give them.

June 4   Asquith saw King in regard to Honours list. I asked him if there was any chance of Strathcona being made an Earl, as if so I thought I could get some help for the party from him. He admitted he had forgotten to speak of this, but it was not too late.

I saw Whiteley and discussed who I might tap of his list – he thought of Roberts (Herbert) & Barker (John) – but much lamented nothing could be got out of Kearley who Asquith had promised.

---

[24]   He married Pamela Jekyll (1889–1943), younger daughter of Sir Herbert and Lady Jekyll, the latter being one of Asquith's oldest friends. Harold Baker told Cynthia Asquith on 5 June 1915 that 'Jack Pease had been expelled by McKenna from his house in the country where he was staying because he was seen holding Pamela's hand.   Apparently McKenna is a monster of jealousy as well as of most other things.' (Lady Cynthia Asquith, *Diaries 1915–1918*, Hutchinson, 1968, p. 38). Writing to Pamela McKenna on 16 November 1909 Admiral Fisher referred to 'your friend Mr Pease' (Arthur J. Marder, ed., *Fear God and Dread Nought*: The Correspondence of Admiral of the Fleet Lord Fisher of Kilverstone, 3 vols, Jonathan Cape, 1952–9, vol. II, Years of Power 1904–1914, p. 279). By 1912 the friendship had deepened. JAP kept some letters from that year in a special box. The partly destroyed label reads '...Private letters from Mrs McKenna wh... in love w...' JAP's daughter, Miriam commented 'I should explain that Pamela McKenna had "soul-friendships" ... She was always a friend of Mother's and mine. Moreover if any lady made advances to Father Mother gave him hell promptly and the lady disappeared from the scene! Pamela was so devoted to her husband Reggie that she could not live after he died.' (Gainford MSS, 89). Reginald McKenna died on 6 September 1943. His wife died after falling from a moving train on 1 November 1943; the inquest recorded an open verdict. (See P. McKenna to M. Bondfield, 27 Sept. 1943, Bondfield MSS, 2/25).

H. Lewis grumbled to Elibank about his position, not being 2d whip to me, & asked for support for administrative office. Asquith promised him he would try & give him a vacancy if it occurred but Lewis feared he might be overlooked. After House was up, I told Asquith the negotiations I had had today with Paulton in regard to Allard & the Dissolution of the Liberal League. My idea is to place Allard at Free Trade Union – get rid of Carter & Miss Pretious, to Eastern Counties & Women's Free Trade Union & have a real live Free Trade organisation. Gave Asquith my scheme for organisation to look over.

The Times *had announced on June 2 that the Master of Elibank was to be second whip. The rest of the team was Herbert Lewis, Captain Cecil Norton, J.H. Whitley, Sir Edward Strachey, and John Fuller. Lewis had responsibility for monitoring the movements of English and Welsh MPs and recording pairs. Relieved of some of his former House of Commons duties, JAP was to give greater attention to broader questions of party organisation.*

It was to be nearly two years before the Liberal League could be wound up. It was in disarray over the 1909 Budget but was briefly important again to Haldane and Grey in March and April 1910 when a Cabinet split seemed likely over the House of Lords. Meanwhile, William Allard's cause was pressed by Edwin Montagu who believed – mistakenly as JAP's diary establishes – that 'the best organiser in the Liberal Party' had been boycotted by JAP and Jesse Herbert, the treasurer of the Liberal Central Association (Montagu to V. Asquith, Feb. 1909, S.D. Waley, Edwin Montagu: A Memoir and an Account of his Visits to India, *Asia Publishing House, 1964, p. 32). Herbert had no love for the League, especially J.M. Paulton, who had alleged serious inefficiency in the Liberal party organisation in 1903. But he had not proscribed Allard who was given a senior organisational post at Liberal headquarters the following year. (Sykes,* Tariff Reform in British Politics, *pp. 68, 186).*

*The Free Trade Union (and the Women's Free Trade Union) had been formed in July 1903 with the aim of safeguarding 'the free import of Food and Raw Material ... [and maintaining] the general principle that taxation should be imposed for revenue purposes only.' (*The Liberal Year Book for 1909, *Liberal Publication Department, 1909, p. 15). It produced leaflets, posters, and other publicity material. Although distinct from the Liberal Party machine it was linked through Sir Robert Hudson who was secretary of the Liberal Central Association and the National Liberal Federation, treasurer of the Liberal Publication Department, and a member of the Free Trade Union's executive and organising committees. In decline after 1906, during the January 1910 election the Free Trade Union had 50 offices open throughout England employing over one thousand speakers. (Neal Blewett,* The Peers, The Parties and the People: The General Elections of 1910, *Macmillan, 1972, pp. 332–5). On 15 May 1909, Montagu complained to the Prime Minister that the impending marriage and departure of Miss Pretious, the secretary of the Free Trade Union, meant that*

'the odious and useless Carter is to be left to dominate the whole body.'
(Montagu MSS). Ivy Pretious had proved to be congenial as an anti-suffragist
and a talented organiser with responsibility for 70 constituencies including all of
London. 'I cannot think what I shall do at the W.F.T.U. without her!' Molly
Harcourt had lamented. (M. Harcourt to L. Harcourt, 27 April 1909, Harcourt
MSS, uncat.; Bertrand Russell to I. Pretious, 14 Sept. and 15 Oct. 1908,
Tennyson MSS). Wallace Carter, who had been Whiteley's private secretary
before being berthed at the FTU in January 1908, was not dislodged until made
a better offer in 1911 to run the Home Rule Council.

JAP's 'scheme for organisation' was a plan to decentralise the Liberal party
machine which was reported in the press on 4 July 1908. Because the party now
had more seats to defend, and more of its men had to spend eight months of the
year in Westminster, JAP wanted to divide the organisation into nine district
federations each with a paid organising secretary. London, the Home Counties,
Wales and Monmouthshire, and the Eastern Counties were already federated.
The Northern Counties and Yorkshire were partly federated but the Midlands,
West of England, and Lancashire and Cheshire remained to be brought together.
Asquith, having observed the vitality of the federated Scottish Liberal
organisation during the previous winter, was thought to favour the extension of a
*more cooperative approach to political campaigning. (*The Daily News, *4 July*
1908). With the Chief Whip or his representative on each executive committee,
quarterly reports to the Chief Whip by the organising secretary, annual financial
statements and statistical information to the Chief Whip, and supplementary
funding arranged with the Chief Whip, JAP could expect to be better informed, if
not more powerful, than his predecessors who were reliant on the National
Liberal Federation and the Liberal Central Association's contact with individual
associations.

Gave him particulars as to possible vacancies Taunton, Tamworth and Honiton.

Sir Edward Boyle KC, Conservative MP for Taunton, was in ill-health and his
retirement was expected. The by-election took place 23 February 1909; Boyle's
grandson, the Hon. William Peel (Con.) was successful. In 1906 Arthur
Ponsonby had represented the Liberals but he was now MP for Stirling Burghs
and the Liberals did not contest the election. The Conservative MP for
Tamworth, Sir P.A. Muntz Bt, died 21 December 1908 and presumably was in ill-
health when JAP was considering the situation. F.A. Newdigate-Newdegate
[sic] was returned unopposed. Honiton was the seat of Sir J.H. Kennaway. He
did not in fact retire until 1910 but as he was Father of the House and aged 70 in
1908 JAP may be excused for thinking his retirement imminent.

Chapter 2

Taking the Reins

5 June 1908   At 11.20 found Asquith with Margot and Violet trying a motor in Downing Street[1] – after the examination of so important an asset in relation to a Prime Minister's movements, retired into the Cabinet room, where H.H.A. does all his work.

Discussed with him steps to be taken in regard to 8 Hours Bill, & whether government should introduce the measure with 8 Hours to include or exclude drawing. I advocated the course of least resistance, but admitted it was not a strong course but in my judgement necessary owing to past declarations of ministers & the pledges of many supporters, viz– to bring in a bill to include hours of drawing miners, but to say this inclusion was not vital, but having regard to the economic conditions, the govmt recommended this course as a step to 8 Hours but that if 8 Hours hard & fast could not be carried, the responsibility of the Bill not passing must rest with those who were not prepared to accept 8 Hours containing a provision to exclude winding from the time limitation.

'Drawing' meant winding or winching miners from the surface to the pit floor and vice versa. The government had originally proposed including this time in the eight hours daily the miners would be allowed to work. As a concession, winding-time was not to be included in the eight hours for the first five years of the bill's operation; finally the Lords' amendment excluding winding-time altogether was accepted.

I suggested the Cabinet must decide before Monday the 15th, whether the old aged Pensions Bill should be treated as a money bill, & no eleven o'clock rule should operate (a resolution necessary to secure this) or whether the Committee & other stages should be regulated by a guillotine motion. We could not send such a bill upstairs, as the work before committees would now last until July 15.

---

1   Asquith had owned two cars for several years, a Darracq and a Siddeley. (*The Car*, No. 315, 3 June 1908). His new acquisition was the 14–16 hp Darracq; introduced late in 1907, it had a top speed of 40 mph, did 26 mpg, and cost £375. Leicester Harmsworth, Liberal MP for Caithnesshire and brother of Lord Northcliffe, was a major shareholder in the highly successful firm that marketed Darracqs in Britain. (Reginald Pound and Geoffrey Harmsworth, *Northcliffe*, Cassell, 1959, p. 293). Asquith did not drive.   His chauffeur Herbert Harwood had two speeding convictions, the most recent on March 16 for driving his 'very busy' master at a greater speed than 10 mph in St James's Park. (*The Times*, 17 Mar. 1908).

Asquith said it was essential we should pass the bill before the Budget & give the Lords something to do.

On the first four days of a sitting week no contentious business was considered after 11.00 pm unless a special resolution was passed to permit it. Government business had precedence at every sitting except Tuesday and Wednesday evenings after 8.15 pm until Easter and Whitsun respectively. Use of the guillotine was increasingly favoured rather than reduction of the limited time available for private members' business. The Liberal Year Book 1909 *(p. 102) forecast that 'the lessons of experience will result at no distant date in the further perfection of a system which no ministry is now likely to abandon.' Treating the old age pensions legislation as a money bill would have avoided the need for the guillotine as the 11.00 o'clock rule did not apply to money bills.*

I spoke about O'Hagan's disappointment at not being given Admiralty work with Tweedmouth absent, & he asked me to write Crewe thereon & to say he would be glad if he O'Hagan could be entrusted with some government department to reply for in H. of Lords.

Asquith said Buxton was very pleased with Granard's work at the P. Office & that Ripon his co-religionist had nothing to do with Granard being also given Admiralty work.

He (H.H.A.) told me the King had not demurred to the honours list, except for grumble there had been too many Knights. Crewe had sent in several names & he thought his list must be cut down.

He said Whiteley had been skating on too thin ice, in selling honours & asked me to pursue different course. I said I had no intention of associating money & titles, but was anxious to interest those I could in helping my scheme for devolving work on Local Federations which I should have to subsidize if constituencies were to be effectively organised.

I saw Herbert Roberts congratulated him on prospective baronetcy & he said he recognised the necessities of party & asked me to suggest what help I would like. I said £5000, he offered £4000 with further £1000 if I needed it.

A whip's duties included minimising breaches of discipline by members of the parliamentary party. JAP was disposed to deal with isolated cases with a light hand. But there were occasional flagrant and concerted demonstrations that could not be condoned. On June 4, twelve Liberal, 22 Nationalist, and 25 Labour MPs voted against a visit proposed by the King to the Tsar at Reval. One of them was Arthur Ponsonby, formerly private secretary to Campbell-Bannerman for whose Stirling Burghs seat he had been elected less than a fortnight earlier. Ponsonby's papers contain Pease's rebuke and the reply.

Private   June 5, 1908
                                           12 Downing Street, SW

My dear Ponsonby,

May I say with how much pain I see your name in the list of those who voted against the King's visit to Russia.

Quite apart from the loyalty expected from you to the party you have been returned to support, I would have thought the statement made by Sir Edward Grey would have had some weight. Obviously he is in a much better position to judge the situation, & he intimated that the very objects which we all desire & which you intended doubtless to promote by your vote would be only frustrated by any abandonment of the King's visit.

On an occasion like yesterday, it is no excuse to say 'Oh the Government were safe enough, & I wished to express by my vote my horror at the things done by the Russian Government'.

The question I submit you ought to ask yourself is, can I justify the course I have taken if the Government is defeated. Remember the enormous issues at stake, quite apart from the merits of the one vote put from the chair.

As an old member with strong Quaker views of my own, may I say as a friend that influence can be exercised much more effectively by loyalty and quiet pressure behind the scenes than by hostile votes given. Especially when given without any intimation in advance to the whips of your intention.

Surely at least we may expect such an intimation in future, so that ministers may be advised of the views of those they are supposed to lead.

Yours sincerely
Joseph A. Pease

I would like to have a chat with you – but as Whitsuntide is upon us, please excuse my perhaps too plainly writing what I feel.

Ponsonby was unchastened:

Shulbrede Priory
Lynchmere
Haslemere
5.vi.08

My dear Pease,

Thank you for your letter. I could not have let you know before-hand how I was going to vote because I did not make up my mind completely till the end of the Debate. In fact I went in with strong views on the subject but quite ready to be talked over by Grey. I do not think the objections were answered. I consider a visit from our King is the greatest compliment we can pay to another nation and I think to advise such a visit at such a moment was ill timed and unwise (& detracts from the value of these royal visits which have been so successful hitherto). I cannot believe Grey himself was anxious for it and should suspect that Charlie Hardinge & Benckendorff were at the bottom of it and in the judgment of neither of these two have I the smallest confidence. Then it seems to me unfair that the matter should be brought before the House a day or two before the King actually starts so that any protest that is made which must have the appearance of a desire to reverse the decision has all its force taken from it [? chiefly] from the fact that it comes too late. I gave my vote as I did because I don't think the K ought ever to have been advised to go to Russia because I think Czar as an autocrat must be held personally responsible for what has taken place in Russia (just as the Sultan is &

you remember the outcry in England at the visit of the Kaiser to Turkey in 98 just after the massacres) & because I think the opportunity for discussing the visit was given at a moment when all protest was too late.

Grey really did not defend the visit but got out of it by mixing it up with the Convention of which I was entirely in favour. The one was a diplomatic & political move which made for peace the other a special compliment for which there was no real need at the moment.

I cannot take the view that a vote of this kind is a vote for the defeat of the Govt although I quite understand that this is the view you are obliged to take. Any real prospect of the Govt being in danger wd at once outweigh the considerations produced by the particular question under discussion – nor do I hold that blind acquiescence in everything the Govt does, is asked of one.

But I can assure you I do not intend to be troublesome in this respect and I shall probably get my conscience completely under control before long.

Yours

Honour was satisfied. 'I am only anxious we Whips may know so far as possible the views of supporters before Divisions are taken, so as to be able to advise Ministers of their intentions. I know,' JAP concluded tamely, 'it is not always possible.' (JAP to Ponsonby, 9 June 1908, Ponsonby MSS).

June 6 Asked John Barker if he would accept Knighthood, he said NO, he was volunteered to do what was right by party, but wanted a baronetcy & went into reasons, & past creations.

John Barker, the Kensington draper, had twice unsuccessfully contested Maidstone, winning it at the third attempt in 1900 only to be unseated on petition. Although his business interests were in London and Paris, and his home was in Bishop's Stortford, he heeded the party's call and fought the marginal seat of Penryn and Falmouth in 1906. At 68, with a majority of 97, and a record of service in local government and agricultural societies, Barker could reasonably aspire to a baronetcy. As the owner of the largest polo pony stud in the country, he could also afford one.

June 7 I wrote to Asquith & told him how John Barker felt. Got a letter from Warwick asking for honour for Norton,[2] for hospital help during war. I sent it on to Haldane.

---

2 Possibly Arthur Trehern Norton (1841–1912); surgeon St Mary's Hospital, London; surgeon lieut. col. and commandant London Volunteer Medical Staff Corps; member, War Office Committees for the development of the Volunteer Medical service; CB 1897. But conceivably Charles Leigh Adderley, 2nd Lord Norton (1846–1926), a large landowner in Warwickshire who disposed of most of his property in 1911 because of the growing burden of taxation. He had been an assistant Local Government Board inspector and private secretary to his father as

June 9   At Downing Street – arranged for work for 10th.

June 10   Arrived at House of Commons from Darlington to find House up at 6.30. Votes agreed to with 2 Divisions. The possible adjournment of the House anticipated on 11th over action interfering with Indian Press.

A Newspapers Act had been passed by the Indian Legislative Council the preceding Monday, June 8. Sir Henry Cotton, Lib. MP Nottingham (East), who had served in Bengal in various capacities before becoming an MP, feared that the new act empowered the government to send a magistrate to close any newspaper office and confiscate its plant without any judicial hearing being held. In 1882 Lord Ripon had repealed the Vernacular Press Acts and had attempted to let the Indian Press have the same freedom as the British. But by 1908 sections of the Indian press were inciting their readers to violence and the experiment was seen to have failed. Lord Ripon himself had assented to Morley's suggested modifications to the Indian government's proposals, particularly because judicial safeguards had been incorporated. But the government was unable to reply to criticism because it had not yet received a copy of the Act. Restrictions were finally reimposed in 1910.

Whitley gives Acland Hood wind of movement, after Speaker [Lowther] had stopped Liberals putting it down. Speaker thus indirectly given away. Whitley told me situation, & how anxious Asquith was to avoid the adjournment, as he had a dinner of 20 Liberals at his House. Mentally I condemned Whitley's conduct I could not have done it, though doubtless a useful end was served, as Sassoon got the tip & I woke up on

June 11   to see blocking motion in Sassoon's name appearing in the Notice Paper. Called on Asquith at 1.15. Discussed how to deal with old aged pension Bill. Asquith & I agreed that guillotine was quickest and best method, rather than suspension of 11'clock rule.

The decision to closure the committee stage of the Old Age Pensions Bill by compartments (following the second reading debate on June 16 and 17) was taken before the precise terms of the Opposition's amendments were known. Asquith was unmoved by Balfour's objection that the propriety of any particular 'gag' resolution could not be determined before the amendments were seen.

President of the Board of Trade. No Norton received any recognition in 1908 or 1909.

I asked Asquith about honours; he showed me the list – put his pen through several. He asked me whether Philipps incident trying seduce a girl barred him from Peerage, I said NO.[3] He talked about J.B. Robinson (S. African fame) youthful indiscretion, scandal states he was obliged to marry his wife under pain of being shot for having seduced her. We agreed he did the honourable thing![4]
We discussed the rival advantages in including John Barker or Layland Barratt among baronets this time (26th).

Asquith told me Trevelyan (George Otto) & Acland (Arthur) had declined peerages. I pressed for Borthwick baronet, Fleming knight and R.J. Price to be included in this list.

Thursday afternoon (June 11) Asquith asked me into his room & strode up & down as is his wont in discussing matters, said I want you to see whether we should postpone the consolidated fund bill & some supply until the autumn, & find time for some progress with the licensing bill before end of July. I told him

---

3 J.W. Philipps, millionaire shipowner and Liberal MP for Pembrokeshire, had married the orphaned heiress Leonora Gerstenberg (d. 1915) in 1888. There is no hint of the alleged attempt at seduction in P.N. Davies, 'Business Success and the Role of Chance: the Extraordinary Philipps Brothers', *Business History,* vol. XXIII, no. 2, July 1981, pp. 208–32, or in Edwin Green and Michael Moss, *A Business of National Importance*: The Royal Mail Shipping Group, 1902–1937, Methuen, 1982.

4 Botha had recommended an honour for Robinson because of his advocacy of a large measure of self-government to the South African colonies. A baronetcy was announced on 27 July 1908 but Robinson was furious that he had not received it in 1907. He had given Lewis Harcourt £10,000 in 1905 for Liberal Party funds. Harcourt diverted it to the Home Counties Liberal Federation, the Free Trade Union, and the Liberal Radical Union. Robinson was then induced by Herbert Gladstone to provide another £10,000 for the next general election. Sir Francis Hopwood of the Colonial Office told Churchill on 15 November 1907 that Robinson claimed he had spent enormous sums 'to a great extent at the bidding of the Government, and that he understood from the Prime Minister, and also I gather from you, that it would be alright.' (Randolph S. Churchill, *Winston S. Churchill,* Vol. II, Companion Part 2, Heinemann, 1969, p. 699). T.O. Lloyd in 'The whip as paymaster: Herbert Gladstone and party organization', *English Historical Review,* vol. LXXXIX, no. CCCLIII, Oct. 1974, p. 810, says that Robinson 'made no claim based on a bargain about party funds.' But there was a perceptible sub-text in the reference to 'enormous sums' spent at the government's bidding. (Cf H.W. MacCready, 'Chief Whip and Party Funds: The Work of Herbert Gladstone in the Edwardian Liberal Party, 1899 to 1906', *Canadian Journal of History,* vol. 6, no. 3, Dec. 1971, p. 290). Robinson married Elizabeth Ferguson of Kimberley in 1877 and she bore him four sons and five daughters who survived infancy. The story that he 'had been flogged for the seduction of Elizabeth Rebecca Ferguson in the main street' was widely publicised three years later when Robinson pursued the author of a libellous book through the courts. (Geoffrey Wheatcroft, *The Randlords,* Simon & Schuster, New York, 1987, pp. 60, 237).

I thought we could find time for both before the end of July, & then leave the House with only the budget & there would be no object in criticising it, as such delay would mean no fewer government bills but only less holiday. He said he thought Education, 8 Hours might have to be dropped or carried over with the Port of London Bill to another Session, so also the Housing Bill.

Following unsuccessful attempts in 1907 and earlier in 1908, the new Education Bill made fresh concessions to Anglicans and Roman Catholics over religious instruction. The bill proposed that public primary schools should be established in all school areas where a demand for them was made. These schools would be paid for from the rates. They would provide an education similar to that provided at the existing board schools. There would be no religious tests for teachers. This would eliminate the single-school areas, where the only school was a 'non-provided' school. 'Non-provided' schools, that is private, religious, or charitable schools, would be allowed to 'contract out' of multiple school areas; and, if they met standards of efficiency established by the Board of Education, would receive parliamentary grants but not rate aid. Unable to secure Anglican support, the government withdrew the bill at the committee stage early in December. (Benjamin Sacks, The Religious Issue in the State Schools of England & Wales 1902–1914: *A Nation's Quest for Human Dignity, University of New Mexico Press, Albuquerque, 1961, pp. 62–8).*

The Port of London Bill had been introduced by Lloyd George on April 2. It embodied many of the recommendations of the royal commission chaired by Lord Revelstoke. It provided for the establishment of the Port of London Authority (PLA), which would take over the powers of such bodies as the Thames Conservancy and the Watermen's Company. The PLA was empowered to improve facilities in the docks, which were paid for by levies on goods and shipping using the port. The bill was given the royal assent on December 21.

The Housing and Town Planning Bill, designed to fight slum housing and the uncontrolled growth of towns, empowered local authorities to build houses without first obtaining County Council permission. It gave powers for the compulsory purchase of land; permitted large loans to rural areas; made obligatory the establishment of County Medical Officers' inspection of housing; and authorised the drawing-up of town planning schemes. Introduced by John Burns in March 1908, its complexity and the powers conferred on the Local Government Board annoyed the Tories who blocked its progress. Reintroduced in 1909, it eventually passed into law at the end of the year after the second reading was deferred nineteen times. (Enid Gauldie, Cruel Habitations: A History of Working-Class Housing 1780–1918, *George Allen & Unwin, 1974, pp. 304–5; Kenneth D. Brown,* John Burns, *Royal Historical Society, 1977, pp. 139–41, 144–5, 149–51; Charles W. Pipkin,* The Idea of Social Justice: A Study of Legislation and Administration and the Labour Movement in England and France between 1900 and 1926, *Macmillan, New York, 1927, pp. 150–3).*

We must aim to get:
Old Aged Pensions, Irish University, Children, Prevention of Crime, Licensing & Finance & Consolidation Bill.

The government 'got' all these bills except Licensing, the major item of parliamentary business in 1908. Introduced by an unenthusiastic Asquith on February 27, it proposed the reduction of the number of licenses to sell alcohol by 32,000 – one third of those then in existence. This reduction was to be achieved by 1922, when the number of licences allowed was to be in accordance with a fixed ratio to the population. Local veto – prohibition referendums in local government areas – was also to prevail from 1922. Those losing their licences were to be compensated (less generously than under Balfour's 1904 legislation) by a levy on the remaining licence-holders. The bill also included changes in the hours licensed for the sale of drink. Attacked by the Conservatives as an assault on property, the bill was defeated in the Lords on November 27. (David M. Fahey, 'The Politics of Drink: Pressure Groups and the British Liberal Party, 1883–1908', Social Science, vol. 54, no. 2, Spring 1979, pp. 82–3).

Under the Children Act, parents were made more responsible for their children's actions; imprisonment for those under fourteen was prohibited and limited for those between fourteen and sixteen; juvenile courts were established; and reformatory and industrial schools were brought under a regime of certification and inspection. (George K. Behlmer, Child Abuse and Moral Reform in England 1870–1908, Stanford University Press, Palo Alto, 1982, pp. 220–1; David Dewar, The Children Act, 1908: and other Acts affecting children in the United Kingdom, William Green & Sons, Edinburgh, 1910). The Prevention of Crime Act provided for young offenders to be sent to Borstal schools for up to three years or to be allowed out of prison on licence, and for less stringent conditions for long-term prisoners.

I placed to credit of my a/c £30,000 at London & Westminster Bank. The clerk said this is the biggest cash payment ever received in Bank notes he had had experience of, Holden's son[5] gave it me night before, I trusted it in a govmt dispatch box – as I never knew them tampered with.

The Prince of Wales dined at the House tonight – Speaker, & Chairman of Committees (Emmott) present, Lord Advocate, Lord Valentia, Sir Weetman Dickinson-Pearson, Sir Arthur Bigge, Godfrey Faussett, Derek Keppel, Seely, Churchill, self, Birrell, it went off pleasantly.

---

5   Probably Ernest Illingworth Holden (1867–1937); 2nd Baron Holden 1912. His father was Sir Angus Holden, 2nd Bt (1833–1912); woollen manufacturer in Bradford and France; Mayor, Bradford 1878–80, 1886; Lib. MP Bradford (East) 1885–6, E. Riding of Yorkshire (Buckrose) 1892–1900; 2nd Bt 1897; Baron Holden 4 July 1908. The peerage was announced on June 25.

June 12   Saw Lord Blyth – who asked to pay 2 sums of £2,500 to us ¹/₂ yearly in place of annual sums of £5000 in June, I agreed.[6]   June 12 – Asquith gave garden Party to Liberal Party & L.R.C. Liberal members & their wives – a great success fine afternoon.

The success of the Prime Minister's garden party owed something to the presence of the controversial dancer Maud Allan.   'There is no getting away from the fact that ours is a Nonconformist Party, with Nonconformist susceptibilities and Nonconformist prejudices', Edwin Montagu warned, but 'it is equally characteristic of our Party that so many Members who object to meeting the lady were able apparently to recognise her'. (Montagu to Asquith, n.d. [?19 June 1908], copy, Montagu MSS, Box 3, AS1/7/13).

Monday June 15   Came up from Nuneham[7] where I had been spending Sunday with Loulou Harcourt (present in party Lord & Lady Craven, Mr & Mrs Lawrence – he deputy chairman of L. & N.W.R. Co. – Launcelot Smith,[8] Mark Sturgis, Mr & Mrs Stanley – she née Fellowes – Mr & Mrs E. Stonor & daughter,[9] Elsie & M[iriam] B[lanche] P[ease]).

---

6   Sir James Blyth, a philanthropist, 'all blather and a mere self puffer' but who did little to help his local member (JAP) in the 1906 election, had been ennobled in 1907. (JAP to H. Gladstone, 27 Jan. 1906, Gladstone MSS, Add. MS 46022 f. 150). The 3rd Lord Blyth advised us that he had no papers concerning his grandfather.

7   Nuneham Park, the Harcourt family seat, built 1760–1833; the original village, including a medieval church and churchyard, was moved to make room for the park. Lewis Harcourt added a terraced Italian garden completed in 1913.

8   Probably Lancelot ('Launcie') Grey Hugh Smith (1870–1941), a friend of the Harcourts; stockbroker; principal delegate, British Mission to Sweden 1915: 'precise, cheerful, business-like, and not very much more'. (Asquith to Venetia Stanley, 21 March 1915, Michael and Eleanor Brock, eds, *H.H. Asquith Letters to Venetia Stanley*, p. 494; on terminating a love affair with Jean Rhys in 1912 he paid her an allowance until she married. (Carole Angier, *Jean Rhys*, André Deutsch, 1990, p. 676). But possibly Launcelot Eustace Smith (1868–1948); chairman and managing director, Smith's Dock Co., North Shields; his father, T.E. Smith, was MP for Tynemouth and North Shields 1868–85.

9   Probably the Hon. Edward ('Eddy') Alexander Stonor (1867–1940); Clerk, House of Lords; Principal Clerk and Taxing Master of Private Bills, House of Lords. He was a member of the Camoys family, leading Oxfordshire Roman Catholics, and a friend of the Harcourts and Cravens. In 1894 Lewis Harcourt had tried to arrange Stonor's promotion to a Treasury Clerkship, but the Civil Service Commissioners insisted that his qualifications were insufficient (Harcourt's diary, 20, 21 and 27 Mar. 1894, Harcourt MSS). He married in 1899 Christine Alexandra (d. 1958), daughter of Richard Ralli. Their only child was Francis Edward Stonor (1900–1976). There were, however, a son and a daughter from her first marriage to Ambrose Ralli.

Showed Harcourt a letter I sent Asquith as to my views on 8 Hours Bill in case they could do without me at the cabinet which Asquith had asked me to attend at 12.0.[10] Harcourt agreed we should limit the bill to underground work.

I showed him my scheme for federating counties to promote & reform organisation in the constituencies. He approved.

Harcourt, who had sat for Rossendale since 1904, was sent on July 3 a 'Suggested Scheme of Re-Organisation' for the constituencies in Lancashire and Cheshire. The proposed new Liberal Federation was to consist of a council, elected annually, composed of 'the sitting members accepting the Liberal whip, the recognised Liberal candidates, and two representatives from The Liberal Association in each constituency, totalling about 200 Members.'

Only one point in the scheme provoked Harcourt to insert an amendment. 'Individual subscriptions and donations must be raised wherever possible', Pease suggested, to augment the minimum constituency association subscription of two guineas a year. Mindful of previous bickering over fund-raising, Harcourt added 'but without prejudice to the interests of existing Liberal organizations whether national or local.' (Harcourt MSS, 440, f. 106). The establishment and financing of the Lancashire and Cheshire Liberal Federation are explored in P.F. Clarke, Lancashire and the New Liberalism, *Cambridge University Press, Cambridge, 1971, pp. 206, 215–16.*

At 11.30 met Mond, Henry, Spender, Donald (Daily Chronicle), Elibank & Maclean & we discussed purchasing W. Gazette. – & what terms we could press Newnes to accept. £40,000 in shares suggested.[11] Called in by Asquith to No. 10. I placed before him scheme of work for time up to July 31.

Gave him my reorganisation scheme to criticise.

He asked me some questions about guillotine motion for Wednesday, & I explained what we had arranged with Lloyd George on Friday.[12]

---

[10] This letter does not appear to have survived in either man's papers; Asquith did not mention it in his Cabinet letter to the King.

[11] For JAP's role in orchestrating the purchase of *The Westminster Gazette*, the daily evening paper founded by George Newnes in 1893 to promote the Liberal cause, see Stephen Koss, *The Rise and Fall of The Political Press in Britain*, Vol. Two: The Twentieth Century, The University of North Carolina Press, Chapel Hill, 1984, pp. 101–2. Having been given three weeks to make an offer, and fearful that Lord Northcliffe was 'lying in wait to buy serious journals at fancy prices', the Liberal whips had convened 'a meeting of capitalists'. (J.A. Spender to L. Harcourt, 3 June 1908, Harcourt MSS, dep. 440, f. 89).

[12] Lloyd George proposed to guillotine discussion of the Old Age Pensions Bill by allotting five days to the Committee Stage, one day to the Report Stage, and one day to the Third Reading. The motion was passed 311–99.

Tuesday June 16   Talked over with Asquith, the possibility of Kearley's resignation of Board of Trade Under Secretaryship, & his aspiration to the Lords. He Kearley had told G. Whiteley he did not want a baronetcy & was tired of his work, & wanted freedom & leisure. Asquith asked me, if that was all. I said I suspect therefore he does not like to serve under Winston Churchill & that W.C. does not consult him enough, & that I thought he Asquith had better send for Kearley. Asquith said I hope there will be no more of that sort of thing I repeated Whiteley's demand for money, & that I must insist on getting it. He was amused at Whiteley's opinion to me that Kearley was not the sort of man for a Peerage, 'Pot calling Kettle black' & two birds of a feather couldn't damn each others' plumage without exciting amusement.[13]

I spoke about Fitzmaurice being made a Knight as the London Co. Co. engineer for Rotherhithe tunnel, & alluded to precedent of Sir Alex Brunel.[14]

I told Asquith about Wynford Philipps's seat, & he generally approved of my scheme of reorganisation.

Wynford Philipps had informed his Pembrokeshire constituents in April 1908 that he would not be standing at the next election because of the strain on his health. Philipps denied rumours that he wanted the seat to go to Winston Churchill who had been defeated at Manchester North-West on April 24. Walter Roch, a local solicitor, was chosen as Philipps' successor. His Conservative opponent, J. Lort Williams, had arrived in the constituency only a few days before the 1906 election, and had polled very badly. Now, however, he was well known and expected to offer a strong fight. As Philipps was about to be ennobled as Baron St Davids, a by-election was called for July 16. According to The Times, *by no means an impartial source, the Conservative campaign was much better run. Certainly, on polling day they had many more cars than the Liberals. Nevertheless Roch was elected.*

---

13   Kearley got his peerage two years later, having been made a PC in 1908. JAP explained to the Master of Elibank on 18 November 1910 that Whiteley had suggested to Kearley that 'generosity might be further acknowledged by a peerage. I think Kearley rather resented the suggestion, but he told me that if he later on took a peerage he would like to voluntarily help the Party by £25,000 or so, but he wasn't going to buy it. I merely thanked him and there the matter was left.' It was therefore up to Elibank to see if the new Lord Devonport 'would like to respond in the direction indicated by him, at the interview I first had with him'. (Murray of Elibank MSS, 8802 ff. 146–7; G.R. Searle, *Corruption in British Politics 1895–1930*, Clarendon Press, Oxford, 1987, pp. 148–9).

14   JAP presumably meant Sir Marc Isambard Brunel (1769–1849); civil engineer and inventor; he designed the Thames Tunnel between Rotherhithe and Wapping, which was built 1825–1842, and the equipment needed to build it; Kt 1841 for his work on the tunnel; FRS 1842; father of Isambard Kingdom Brunel.

Wednesday June 17   Asquith away at Cambridge all Wed. 17 June Degree being conferred on him.[15]   Lloyd George conducted guillotine motion through House – with tact, present with him on bench most of sitting.

I saw Kearley & made arrangements with him to help us by £25 – & others five fives as wanted (assuming he left govmt.).

June 18   Asquith sent for me at 1.0 –

I told him the London Co. Co. Chairman[16] had been to see me about Fitzmaurice's honour – Asquith decided to defer it.   I told Asquith about negociations for purchase of Westminster and told him I was sanguine to carry it through.   We discussed business, & he put 8 hours on Monday – Old Aged Pensions Ctee for next two days.

I told Asquith the situation which had arisen between Labour men & the LRC group, & how in self-defence of their own seats they were to have their freedom curtailed, by declining to oppose a socialist or other candidate recommended by the L.R.C. Executive, and that 8 M.P.s intended to kick out.

On June 16, the Lib–Lab trade union group (JAP's 'Labour men') in the House of Commons had voted on the terms of an agreement with the Labour Party one of whose clauses bound the members of both groups to 'in no way oppose either members of the Labour party or the trade union group, or candidates endorsed by the Parliamentary Committee of the Trades Union Congress and by the executive of the Labour party'.   The Times reported on June 17 that this decision had been carried by 16 votes to 8.   The following day two of the trade union MPs, Henry Vivian and Fred Maddison, wrote to the secretary of the group Charles Fenwick objecting that 'we should be prevented from defending the best friend of Labour on the Liberal side, even if he were a workman, when attacked by a middle-class Socialist endorsed by the executive of the Labour and Socialist party'.   (The Times, 19 June 1908).   Vivian and Maddison may have spoken for the eight whom JAP thought 'intended to kick out'.   (According to the Labour Leader on June 19 there were only seven dissentients).   But the Miners' Federation decision to join the Labour Party, announced on June 5, had fatally undermined the trade union group which by the end of 1908 had dwindled to 'an almost negligible rump'.   (H.A. Clegg, Alan Fox, and A.F. Thompson, A History of British Trade Unions Since 1889, vol. I 1889-1910, Clarendon Press, Oxford, 1964, pp. 391-2; Roy Gregory, The Miners and British Politics 1906-1914, Oxford University Press, 1968, pp. 28–52).

---

[15]   The Prime Minister received a DCL. 'As a politician', the Public Orator said, he 'had been conspicuous for his fidelity to his friends'. (*The Times*, 18 June 1908).

[16]   Henry Percy Harris (1856–1941); member, LCC 1892–1910 (chairman 1907–8); barrister 1881; leader, Moderate Party 1904–6; Con. MP Paddington (South) 1910–22; KBE 1917.

June 19 Asquith at Birmingham – told me on the 20th he was very pleased with his reception and whole tone of the proceedings of the National Liberal Federation.

Nearly 2000 delegates, the largest number in the Federation's history, attended the annual meeting on June 18 and 19. Resolutions were passed in favour of taxation of land values and remission of tea and sugar duties; and the Liberal programme of educational and licensing reform was endorsed. Asquith's speech at the Hippodrome was a wide-ranging review of the government's record.

June 20 Garden Party at Windsor – Asquith asked Elsie where I was, she told him at Sandwich recruiting, he said nothing but I know he wished he had been there too!

The royal garden party was notable, not for JAP's absence, but for that of four MPs who had not been invited. Arthur Ponsonby, Keir Hardie, and Victor Grayson were singled out because of their vote on June 4 against the King's planned visit to the Tsar. A fourth MP was excluded because of his sullied financial reputation. (Sir Sidney Lee, King Edward VII, *A Biography, 2 vols, Macmillan, 1925/27, vol. II, p. 588). There is no record of the fourth man's name in the Royal Archives, but he was identified in the contemporary press as Harry Marks, proprietor of* The Financial News, *Conservative MP for Kent, Isle of Thanet 1904–10. Marks had been described as a 'dishonest rogue and a scoundrel' by Mr Justice Bigham during the London and Globe Finance Corporation bankruptcy proceedings in 1902. He had been elected at a by-election in 1904 which split the local Conservative association. A breakaway Tory group ran an independent candidate against him in 1906. (F.W.S. Craig,* British Parliamentary Election Results 1885–1918, *Macmillan, 1974, p. 305; Dilwyn Porter, 'Journalist, Financier, "Dishonest Rogue", "Scoundrel": the Life and Times of Harry Hananel Marks, M.P', Moirae, 8, 1984, pp. 65–88).*

In spite of a long record of dubious financial dealings Marks had escaped prosecution. However, when his butler was sentenced in April 1908 to six months' imprisonment for stealing silver worth £47 the Liberal Thanet Times *renewed its attacks on a local member who remained 'free to pursue his peculiar policy of plunder'. (Dilwyn Porter, '"A Trusted Guide of the Investing Public": Harry Marks and the* Financial News *1884–1916', R.P.T. Davenport-Hines, ed.,* Speculators and Patriots: *Essays in Business Biography, Frank Cass, 1986, p. 11).*

Marks's Liberal opponent in 1904 and 1906, Joseph King, had now been nominated for Somerset North. JAP's 'recruiting' mission to Sandwich – a Cinque port in the Isle of Thanet constituency – could therefore have been in pursuit of a Liberal candidate for the safest Conservative seat in Kent. Asquith may have preferred to be anywhere but Windsor. He had no particular fondness for Sandwich; as he told Venetia Stanley on 20 January 1913, it was 'not a pretty place – tho' less gaunt than Littlestone – with very fine air and splendid golf, & a half-dozen millionaires' villas'. (Venetia Montagu MSS).

June 22   Looked in at 1.0 – talked over the suspension of the 11 o'clock rule – we agreed it was a tall order to rush the 8 hours bill, and he said he would give another 1/2 day if appealed to.

He offered to come to Wimborne House on July 7th to give a send off to our New Midland Federation scheme.

June 23   Sent for at 1. o'clock – told him of my interview with Sir Walter Foster, and how sore he still felt at the non-recognition of his services. He said what does he want. I told him a Suez Canal directorship – a most unsuitable man – a Director of Lunacy is more the thing in the gift of the Chancellor. He thinks his constituency would be influenced to liberalism by a favour to their member. Such ideas are purely freaks of the imagination.[17]

I asked him to influence Marnham to stand again for Chertsey. He said he would if I pointed him out some time.[18]

We talked over the incident of the night before, in which the miners jeopardized the 8 hours bill by voting against an adjournment. Their childishness he condemned. I told him I had pointed out their folly, but they were afraid their constituents would not understand a postponement.[19]

I asked him if the King had made any trouble about honours. Oh! Yes a good deal about Whiteley's, but that was some time ago.[20] He said the King didn't like Robinson's peerage, as he has been influenced by Cassel and other anti-Robinson group financiers, but he could not find out anything against his domestic bliss. He was forced at the point of a pistol to marry his wife before the

---

[17]   Foster, MP for Derbyshire (Ilkeston) since 1887, Chairman of the National Liberal Federation 1886–90, and a junior minister 1892–5, had been made a Privy Councillor in 1906. He appears to have received no recognition of his services in 1908, but see 27 January 1910 for the circumstances of his elevation to the peerage.

[18]   F.J. Marnham, a retired stockbroker unexpectedly elected in the 1906 landslide, had a majority of 95; in April 1909 he informed the Chertsey Liberals that the strain of parliamentary life was too great and he intended to stand down. F.G. Newbolt was chosen as Lib.–Lab. candidate but was defeated by Donald Macmaster, KC, a Canadian; the Conservative majority was 4,613. In December 1910 the Liberals did not put forward a candidate.

[19]   The miners' MPs complained that the bill was far too important to go through in one night. Asquith promised to grant them a day or half-a-day in a fortnight.

[20]   Writing from Windsor Castle on June 15, Lord Esher told Harcourt 'The list of honours, I hear, is so long that the P.M. has been asked to cut it down! This applies to "knights and baronets".' (Harcourt MSS, uncat.).

first child was born but there had been 10 others and the marriage had been a success. He told me he would be late at the House and to answer for any points of business raised.

June 24   Cabinet meeting did not see Asquith until he came into the House. He then told me Whiteley had seemed excited about there being no schedule discussion, under the Guillotine resolution, and the alteration of the bill by allowing a sliding scale for old aged pensions, so as to avoid a hard line at an income of 10/- ought to be discussed. I told Asquith I could arrange ½ a day by recommitting the Bill.

In the evening the govmt were disinclined to give way to the sense of the House, and were pressing their proposal to diminish the pro rata contribution to old couples living together. I told Asquith I thought we should be beaten and that Ll. George must give way. Ll. George gave way with great dexterity and told the party he must ask them not to press other amendments as he had no more money to meet further demands. An awkward corner was got round thanks to Asquith's readiness and confidence to accept my advice.

The 'awkward corner' was all of Asquith's making, the pensions policy and legislation having been developed under his direction. In 1911, Lloyd George recalled having 'added up the cost of the amendments which he had had to consider and that they came to £62,000,000 – the Government's income being then about £200,000,000.' By removing the provision that married pensioners living together would receive less than single pensioners Lloyd George was elated that he had captured the party for £334,000, and 'rallied all the party with that concession to resist further pecuniary demands'. (Sir Henry N. Bunbury, ed., Lloyd George's Ambulance Wagon: *Being the Memoirs of William J. Braithwaite 1911-1912, Methuen, 1957, p. 71; E.P. Hennock,* British Social Reform and German Precedents: *The Case of Social Insurance 1880–1914, Clarendon Press, Oxford, 1987, p. 148; Lloyd George to William George, 25 June 1908, William George,* My Brother and I, *Eyre & Spottiswoode, 1958, p. 221). In 1912 Percy Alden estimated that the addition of over 163,000 aged paupers would raise the cost to £13,000,000 a year. (*Democratic England, *Macmillan, New York, 1912, p. 161).*

June 25   Asquith sent for me at 12.0. He said he thought we were well out of the difficulty of the night before. I told him the only alternative would have been for Ll. George to promise to meet the case on report without pledging himself to go the whole hog.

We discussed Hudson's attitude to my scheme and I told Asquith I thought he was loyal and ready to work with and not against us.[21] I was anxious to find a strong man to look after organisation, but Freddy Guest was regarded with suspicion and though Winston's friend, he was not acceptable in many quarters. Asquith asked me to keep my eyes open.

I told him of Furness's scheme to acquire the W. Gazette and the wishes of others not to join him but run together on an equal footing, making themselves liable for £5000 down and later further £5000 and I thought I could find ten willing to go in, but it was a pity to lose this money if Furness would do it all.

Asquith asked me to raise £1500 to enable Schreiner to be engaged to defend Dinuzulu. Winston had written an unwise letter, and committed us before he left office, but we could not take the defence up as a government without creating difficulties.

Dinuzulu (Dinizulu) (c. 1869–1913), a son of the Zulu paramount Chief Cetewayo, returned from exile to Natal in 1897 as a local chief and induna with a salary of £500 p.a. There had been disturbances in 1906 in which, the Natal government asserted, Dinuzulu had been involved. Martial law and press censorship were proclaimed and some 3000 Africans killed. At the Colonial Office it was felt that the Natal government had over-reacted and in private there was strong disapproval of the Natal government's entire administration of native affairs. From the beginning of the rising Churchill had advocated imperial intervention to protect the Africans; this policy was rejected for fear of protests from all the self-governing colonies. In December 1907 Dinuzulu was persuaded, on the promise of a fair trial, to surrender himself peaceably to an inquiry into his alleged complicity in the disturbances. An English KC, E.G. Jellicoe, was retained to augment the Natal defence team but resigned after three weeks, protesting in a letter to the Colonial Office about the procedures being followed in the preliminary examination. Jellicoe's letter was published in The Daily News, *10 February 1908. The Governor of Natal was told by Lord Elgin, the Colonial Secretary, that 'H.M.G. are directly responsible for the procedure adopted in the trial. The obligation is therefore one of honour.' Dinuzulu did not have the funds to obtain the best counsel (the former Cape Colony Prime Minister, W.P. Schreiner). Rather than further antagonise the Natal government by paying directly for Dinuzulu's defence, the British ensured that 'private benevolence' provided most of the money. In April 1909 the British government accepted Dinuzulu's sentence of four years imprisonment, £100 fine, and the*

---

21   Hudson was loyal but he and JAP seem to have had little to do with each other. In 1903 Hudson had admitted to a *Punch* journalist having 'achieved a great reputation for shrewdness and wisdom just by keeping my mouth shut'. The reputation was enhanced by his biographer, J.A. Spender, who forgot that Pease had been Chief Whip. ('T' [Joseph Peter Thorp], *Friends and Adventures*, Jonathan Cape, 1931, p. 69; J.A. Spender, *Sir Robert Hudson*, Cassell, London, 1930, pp. 121, 203).

forfeiture of his position and salary of induna; *but Crewe, the then Colonial Secretary, insisted that some provision be made for his maintenance. (Ronald Hyam,* Elgin and Churchill at the Colonial Office 1905–1908, *Macmillan, 1968, pp. 239–62; Shula Marks,* Reluctant Rebellion: The 1906–8 Disturbances in Natal, *Clarendon Press, Oxford, 1970, pp. 249–93; Shula Marks to CH, 10 Jan. 1991). The 'unwise' letter to which Asquith refers is possibly that in Churchill, Winston S. Churchill,* Vol. II, Companion Part 2, *pp. 752–3. But Elgin had also indicated privately to the Governor of Natal that he was prepared to broach the subject of payment of counsel with HMG. (Elgin to Sir Matthew Nathan, 14 Feb. 1908, Nathan MSS, Rhodes House MS 371/115).*

June 29   Asquith sent for me at 12.50. He asked me, Have you anything to tell me. I replied Yes. On Thursday only one cabinet minister was present to support the salary of the Secy. to Scotland, & a whipup & a few voting against Sinclair's salary, would have meant defeat.[22] On the previous Friday no cabinet ministers were present and unless I was better supported I could not induce the rank and file to attend.

I told him Alec Hood had agreed to my scheme of work for the following week and that we had a lot of pressure for subjects in supply & only 7 more days to offer!

Organisation was discussed and I suggested Master of Elibank as likely to make a good man to work up the country & appoint candidates. He was anxious for such a post, and would take it if he got £1200–£1500 a year with or without a seat in the House.[23]

I alluded to the scandal of vast sums being obtained by the King, or the Master of the Household Sir Chas Frederick or by [?firms] who were behind the scenes for the sale of royal warrants to traders. Asquith agreed it was best for the Master of Elibank to lay papers from Hill of Belfast, Ross & son Aerated water-makers, and Newton's application for £2,000 before Lord Knollys.

Neither the records of the Master of the Household's Department and the Lord Chamberlain's Office nor the papers in the Royal Archives illuminate this alleged 'scandal'. A royal warrant would have had unique marketing appeal for W.A. Ross & Sons, Aerated Water Manufacturers since 1879, well-known for

---

22   The debate had not been simply on the salary of the Secretary for Scotland but on his entire office. It was proposed that £11,600 be granted to the office for its expenses and salaries. The debate was not concluded in the time allotted.

23   Herbert Gladstone had planned but not implemented a new position of Vice-President of the Liberal Central Association to assist the Chief Whip with organisation outside Parliament. The Elibank appointment was not pursued; but Jesse Herbert, the LCA Treasurer, was given greater responsibility for candidates. (Lloyd, 'The whip as paymaster', pp. 812–13).

Ross's 'Royal Belfast' ginger ale, telegraphic address 'Rossroyal Belfast'. (Webster's Red Book of Commerce or Who's Who in Business 1907, *p. 620).* *'Hill of Belfast' probably was not a firm but may have been Lord Arthur Hill PC (1846–1931), 2nd son of 4th Marquess of Downshire, who had been a Unionist MP for West Down and Comptroller of the Household in the 1880s and 1890s and sat again in the Commons for six months 1907–08. Hill's daughter was married to the eldest son of Sir George Brooke Bt, chairman of George F. Brooke & Son, Dublin wine merchants, and a possible source of trade gossip. 'On one occasion my Company was offered the bestowal of the Royal Warrant by a firm of wine merchants in London for a payment of £800.' (Angus Watson,* An Autobiography, *Ivor Nicholson & Watson, 1937, p. 187). Among competing brands, Ross had to contend with the Idris Royal Mineral Waters ('Special Appointment to His Majesty the King'), produced by T.H.W. Idris, Liberal MP for Flint Boroughs 1906–10. Other competitors with royal warrants were Jewsbury & Brown, A.J. Caley & Son, Frazer & Green, H.D. Rawlings & Co (ginger beer in 'The Crown Jar'), and Schweppes. Whatever suspicions there may have been about Sir Charles Frederick they were evidently not shared by successive sovereigns who made him KCVO (1908), GCVO (1910), and KCB (1911). Sir Douglas Dawson, Comptroller of the Lord Chamberlain's Department, also appears to have had an unblemished career (GCVO 1911, KCB 1924). The Master of Elibank was Comptroller of the Lord Steward's Department. There appears to have been no Newton in royal employ at this time. Though the sense of the entry does not suggest it, a conceivable Newton was Sir Alfred Newton Bt, formerly Lord Mayor of London, and chairman of Harrod's, a store which had not yet been given a royal warrant.*

June 30 I had only a short interview with Asquith – on business which I suggested he should place before the Cabinet on the morrow.

The question of recommittal. The number of days to be allotted for the licensing bill guillotine. At 4.0 attended deputation of London Members. Asquith heard Dickinson advocating special claims for attention to London questions – Equalisation of Rates. Asquith asked how a practical scheme could be proposed with local autonomy, if there was no unification of authorities, & asked for suggestions. He alluded to Port of London Bill as a measure peculiarly beneficial to London but recognized some progress should be made with London questions – Licensing, Housing, Old Aged Pensions, London shared with others and specially benefitted that area. [His words were: 'We do hope next session to make substantial progress. I ask for the relative priority of all the subjects of legislation you wish to attain. I ask also, not a bill, but the heads of practical suggestions so [as] to attain the equalisation. Whilst retaining local autonomy. The govmt. are anxious as soon as possible to meet the wishes of London Members'. N.B. A clever reply – it pleased the M.P.s – & placed on them an impossible task which their advocacy of equalisation compelled them to accept.']²⁴

The large area encompassed by the London County Council differed widely in the value and type of properties and the needs of its inhabitants. Attempts to remedy this disparity (equalisation of rates) had been made as early as 1867 when a Metropolitan Common Poor Fund was established. In 1894 a rate of 6d. in the pound was levied on all boroughs but spent according to population. The problem was eased by providing some services at county level, for example, the police and poor law, and later by block grants from the central government. (Sir Gwilym Gibbon and Reginald W. Bell, History of the London County Council 1889–1939, *Macmillan, 1939, pp. 94, 179, 193). London rating reform was contingent on the recommendations of the royal commission on the poor laws and a projected broader readjustment of national and local finance. But the failure of the government to proceed with a valuation bill was causing concern in Liberal ranks.*

Wrote Asquith late at night that care must be taken as to recommittal of Old Aged Pensions Bill as Tories meant to debate it and extend scope of recommittal.

I also alluded to having raised for Lehmann £700 for defence of Dinuzulu, & with his salary and other friends enough secured.²⁵

July 1 After cabinet – told Asquith I proposed to fight Ramsay MacDonald at Leicester. He approved, with Maddison and Sir Edward Wood. I wrote Wood accordingly.

In the two-member Leicester constituency the local Liberals under Alderman Wood had strongly supported Ramsay MacDonald for one of the seats in the 1906 general election. On the resignation of the other member, the Lib–Lab Henry Broadhurst, Franklin Thomasson had been elected for the Liberals in March 1906 without Labour opposition. Thomasson's newspaper The Tribune *having collapsed early in 1908 leaving him with losses of hundreds of thousands of pounds, he did not plan to stay in Parliament. Meanwhile, although control of the Leicester Liberal association had passed to a group determined to resist the advance of socialism, JAP's scheme came to nothing. Fred Maddison (whose election expenses had been paid by successive Liberal Chief Whips since 1897)*

---

24 The bracketed passage was added in the margin by JAP after the entry had been completed.

25 R.C. Lehmann MP, a barrister and former editor of *The Daily News*, was organising the Dinuzulu defence fund. The Natal government, having wrongfully suspended Dinuzulu's salary on his arrest, was prevailed upon to give the £500 owing to him to his defence counsel. (Marks, *Reluctant Rebellion*, p. 273).

chose to stay and fight at Burnley where H.M. Hyndman had split his vote in
1906. In January 1910 Hyndman again split the vote and Maddison lost. Sir
Edward Wood did not stand; and MacDonald was not opposed in January or
December 1910. Eliot Crawshay-Williams, the Liberal candidate in January
1910, conducted his campaign in Leicester with 'the knowledge that behind the
scenes there was the general understanding that Liberal and Labour were
working in amity, if not actually in co-operation'. MacDonald had publicly
deprecated the attempt of the SDP to take root in his locality and he
acknowledged Liberal support after the first 1910 election. (Eliot Crawshay-
Williams, Simple Story: An Accidental Autobiography, *John Long, 1935, p. 95;*
see also David Cox, The Rise of the Labour Party in Leicester, *M.A. thesis,*
University of Leicester, 1959, pp. 61–3; Chris Cook, 'Labour and the Downfall
of the Liberal Party, 1906–14', Alan Sked and Chris Cook, eds, Crisis and
Controversy: *Essays in Honour of A.J.P. Taylor, Macmillan, 1976, pp. 51–3;*
George L. Bernstein, 'Liberalism and the Progressive Alliance in the
Constituencies 1900–1914: Three Case Studies', The Historical Journal, *vol. 26,*
no. 3, 1983, pp. 629–37; David Marquand, Ramsay MacDonald, *Jonathan Cape,*
1977, p. 93).

He [Asquith] told me if we could not get an agreement about recommitting
Old Aged Pensions Bill we would take small bills on Monday evening.

Asquith announced business for the next week in the House as follows:

BUSINESS OF THE HOUSE

Mr BALFOUR (City of London), asking for information as to next week's
business, inquired especially whether then, or in some subsequent week an
opportunity would be given for discussion on the Army Estimates for the Special
Reserve, a matter of very great importance, on which the House of Commons had
really had no opportunity of raising questions on the policy of the Government.
Referring to the Prime Minister's earlier statement as to the recommittal of the
Old-Age Pensions Bill, he intimated that he was unconscious of any bargain or
arrangement on this matter, and he imagined that the House would take its own
course as to the manner in which it would use its time.

Mr ASQUITH, in repeating the arrangements for Monday, agreed that there was
no question of a bargain, but he must plainly state that if there was any disposition
shown to extend the scope of the discussion on the recommittal of the Old-Age
Pensions Bill he would have to reconsider whether he should propose the motion at
all. On Tuesday he would take the report stage of the Old-Age Pension Bill, and,
in order to leave an interval between report and third reading, take the latter on
Thursday instead of Supply, which would be taken on Wednesday, the Navy
Estimates being put down. Vote 5 would be taken first, then Vote 14, and
afterwards, if time permitted, Votes 13 and 15, the remainder of the sitting being
devoted to the Scottish Estimates – the Fishery Board and the Local Government
Board Votes. On Friday would be taken the motion customary at that time of the
Session relating to the sitting of the House after 11 o'clock, and afterwards unless

an arrangement was arrived at in the interval with regard to the report stage of the Irish Universities Bill, a procedure resolution relating to that measure. He would consider the suggestion as to Army Supply, although four days had already been given to it.

Mr BALFOUR pointed out that they were broken days.

Mr ASQUITH promised to look into the question.

Mr J.F. HOPE (Sheffield, Central) asked if it was intended that there should be no longer interval between the recommittal of the Old-Age Pension Bill and the report than the time between the close of Monday's sitting and the sitting of Tuesday.

Mr ASQUITH – Yes, Sir, that is the case.

I dined with Speaker a private dinner. Saw Asquith at Jack Tennant's house Bruton Street[26] after the House was up at 11.0.

I told him of the situation the Labour party were going to create over Keir Hardie not having been invited to the Windsor Garden Party. That Bobby Spencer (Lord Althorp) had told him the reasons for admission or omission of names on the King's list could not be given, and when pressed he said he had nothing to add.

Keir Hardie, Arthur Ponsonby, and Victor Grayson had been excluded from the royal garden party given for Members of Parliament on June 20 because of their part in criticising the King's proposed visit to the Tsar at Reval. In the absence of an explanation from the palace, all Labour MPs were now asking to be omitted from royal invitation lists. Hardie had been persuaded by Ponsonby to see the King's action as 'an insult to my constituents and an attempt by the sovereign to influence votes of members by social pressure'. Labour members were soon mollified by the lifting of the ban on Hardie and Grayson. But the King was slower to forgive the Liberal Ponsonby, whose father had served Queen Victoria and whose brother was the sovereign's assistant private secretary. Ponsonby explained that he was attacking the government's advice to the King and not the King himself. But, as Sir C.P. Ilbert, Clerk of the House of Commons, noted 'The K. looks at all these things from a personal point of view.' (Ilbert's diary, 6 July 1908, Ilbert MSS, H.C. Lib. MS 72). Ponsonby eventually apologised and was invited to a State Ball at Buckingham Palace. (Raymond A. Jones, Arthur Ponsonby: The Politics of Life, *Christopher Helm, 1989, pp. 56–7).*

3 July I wrote the following letter to John Fuller, Vice Chamberlain, which best describes the situation:

---

[26] Tennant lived at 33 Bruton Street.

8 Hertford Street   July 3, 1908
Mayfair

My dear John,

Please tell Bobby, that the P.M. thinks that he should take no further notice of letters from Keir Hardie on the subject of invitations issued by His Majesty. Bobby has already said, he has 'nothing to add' to his previous letter, and he should now adhere to that position and add nothing. The less said the better.

Ramsay MacDonald may be sincere and not so slippery as some think he is, but members of the group can't all be trusted and further difficulties might arise if any attempt is made to restrain the L.R.C. members from dragging His Majesty's name into the gutter press, and utterances of the L.R.C. members.

Any such attempt would probably prove abortive whilst if it is not made, no reason will have been given for not sending invitations to any of the four MPs and if they, Keir Hardie and his friends, seek to puff themselves and gain notoriety their action may recoil on them. Their public references to His Majesty may be deplored but the risk must be run. Silence is the course Asquith advises.

Yours ever
Joseph A. Pease

Monday July 6   Told Asquith we had been in a minority on Irish Estimates – he said well you know where I was. I said yes, but the House is demoralized when ministers' attendances are so poor.[27]

I told him if Lord Spencer resigned his Lord Lieutenancy, he would want Bobby (Lord Althorp) to succeed him, but that the Northampton people would prefer Lord Northampton. He said well Spencer need not then resign.[28]

I discussed the business of the house and time for supply and the Irish Univ. guillotine.

I then told him what I wanted him to say at Wimborne House on the Tuesday, and what course I suggested. He fell in with the idea.

July 7   Talked matters over, and Asquith told me to talk things at Cabinet next day.

Mr and Mrs Ivor Guest gave a luncheon on July 7 for Liberals interested in party reorganisation. JAP chaired the meeting which followed and outlined his scheme for the Midlands federation. Asquith expressed his approval; a motion, to set up a committee to ascertain local Liberal associations' views, proposed by

---

27   Asquith was in the Commons on the previous Thursday afternoon to answer questions. No division was taken on the estimates for Irish education. We have been unable to obtain further information about Asquith's whereabouts.

28   Viscount Althorp, his half-brother, succeeded the ailing Spencer as Lord Lieutenant of Northants on 14 October 1908. (Peter Gordon, ed., *The Red Earl:* The Papers of the Fifth Earl Spencer 1835–1910, 2 vols, Northamptonshire Record Society, Northampton, 1986, vol. II 1885–1910, p. 361).

Lord Beauchamp and seconded by Sir Charles McLaren, was carried unanimously. (The Times, 8 July 1908). Edwin Montagu warned the Prime Minister: 'Pease's reorganisation scheme – so attractive in the abstract – should not be spoiled by persons. I hope it will not be "Wimborne – Housed". Pease has rather rushed things and Hemmerde is not a very popular person! Do you remember Randolph Churchill's attempt to capture the Conservative organisation. The son is very like the father!' (Montagu to Asquith, 14 July 1908, copy, Montagu MSS, Box 3, AS1/7/14).

Wednesday July 8   Attended Cabinet. Asquith asked me to state my proposals in regard to business to the recess. I said I saw my way to bring matters to a conclusion on August 1. There were 2 schemes: 1 guillotining the Irish University Bill the other having the Irish to talk for 3 days on it, but no all night sitting. We discussed the two – agreed to adopt the latter and bring on Finance Bill on July 14 and 15.

I told the cabinet Birrell must drop the sites clause for Ecclesiastical buildings to enable nonconformists to support the Bill.

An amendment to the Irish Universities Bill would have allowed the erection of chapels within the precincts of the new universities, providing this was done by private benefactions. It was first struck out in Grand Committee, reinstated in the Lords, and finally removed when the bill returned to the Commons. JAP's strategy involved outmanoeuvring the Tories as well as placating the nonconformists. As Lord Midleton lamented to Lord Selborne on 9 September 1908: '... we put back into Irish Universities Bill the right of R.C.'s to have a chapel in their college, wh the N.C.'s had forced Asquith to take out. This would have been a real argument with those who accuse us of onesidedness & bigotry. Commons sent it back & we surrendered without a murmur.' (Selborne MSS, 3/73).

We fixed up supply days – slotting the 5 days as best we could – Runciman Grey and Churchill all asked to have their votes not taken![29]

I got leave to massacre 4 small bills. I told the Cabinet they must meet on Oct 13 to get work through and to the Lords by Christmas. Asquith said NO we meet on the 19th. I said NO you don't. Crewe proved I was right and ministers had to give way, as House of Lords could not be rushed. We discussed number of days to be allotted to Licensing Bill – and Asquith arranged a committee of Samuel, Thring, he and I should draw up scheme. I got leave to star Sir F. Banbury's Bird Bill – after Suspension of 11 o'clock rule passed.[30]

---

[29]   We have found no explanation for these requests.

[30]   In June 1908 Sir Edward Grey's friend W.H. Hudson published *The Land's End: a naturalist's impressions in West Cornwall* in which he drew attention to the practice of killing birds which migrated to Cornwall for the winter by luring them on to small

July 9   Saw Asquith about business, at House arranged to have all in order for him the following morning. He quickly grasped all the points — the quality and quantity of bills we were to get through.

July 10   Saw him again in his room 11.50 and explained situation and gave him lists of bills. Precedents for motion to suspend.

On the evening of July 11 the Eighty Club – 'a number of gentlemen who are willing to give assistance by speaking at Clubs, Debating Societies, Liberal Associations, Public Meetings, and also by delivering lectures on political subjects' – held a dinner in JAP's honour at the Waldorf Hotel. Responding to a toast by Lord Loreburn, JAP expressed his concern as Chief Whip at the unreliability of the Unionist free traders who 'did not at the present time vote with them so largely as it was hoped at one time they would'. He went on to praise the 'great assistance' given to the Liberals by 'the trade unionist section of the Labour members' whose 'influence behind the scenes had been much greater than their record in the public eye'. By contrast the help of 'the other section of the Labour party' had only been 'spasmodic':

> The Government had never been able to rely upon them, although he believed that many of them owed their return to Liberal votes. (Cheers). He criticized their action on the Committee stage of the Old-Age Pensions Bill, remarking that in 31 divisions that section had recorded 267 individual votes against the Government and 517 votes for the Bill ... He believed that the electors would realize that it was the Liberal party, helped by the trade union section, who ought to receive credit for the Bill, and not those who might seek to obtain a cheap popularity by claiming that they were in favour of more extreme measures. (Cheers).

JAP was proclaiming that pressure in the division lobby would be less effective than 'the friendly remonstrance behind the scenes, the quiet influence on Ministers in their rooms, or through the Whips'. (The Times, 13 July 1908).

July 13   Sent message I had nothing to raise before the House met.

July 14   Same message but would see him in the House. We had a meeting in his room at 4.0.

---

fishhooks. Sir Frederick Banbury introduced his Wild Birds' Protection bill to prevent this on June 17; it received the royal assent August 1.

Chapter 3

Whip in Hand

15 July 1908   At 11.30 elected formally by the Treasury Board to the Patronage Secretaryship.   Present the Prime Minister Lloyd George Capt Norton H. Whitley, & C.H. Hobhouse (financial Secy) & Sir George Murray.   The P.M. moved my appointment there being no other nomination I was called to the Table.

A cabinet was then held at No. 10. I sent in at Asquith's request a copy of my scheme.

He asked me into his room after questions – & told me the cabinet had struck out the clause in Licensing guillotine resolution giving to the Chairman or Speaker power to postpone the consideration of any amendments if he thinks that having regard to their relative importance & the opportunity for discussion other amendments should have precedence, & might proceed to other amendments or clauses without putting to the House the postponed ones.

He assented to a proposition I made viz I undertook to sweeten the guillotine by speaking to the Press men as to the proposal regarding allocation of time on report to be determined after committee stage.

He told me Lloyd George thought the House not the Ch. should determine these matters. In putting closure the House decided for itself – but the Chairman should be gingered up.

July 22   Saw Asquith after cabinet, he told me what the cabinet had decided re Welsh bill he admitted it could only be for shop window purposes.

Following the Liberal victory in the Pembrokeshire by-election on July 16 Asquith had been 'quite choky'. Lloyd George told him 'with uplifted forefinger' that the Welsh 'deserve Disestablishment. The Welsh members have been very good – they have not worried you at all.' Asquith agreed: 'but how can we do it?' 'I want you to give me 5 days next Session' said Lloyd George who told JAP's colleague in the whips' office, Herbert Lewis, that the reply to be given by the Prime Minister to a Welsh deputation on July 23 would be 'all right' (Lewis's diary, 17 July 1908, Lewis MSS 1943, 10/231). In his Cabinet letter to the King Asquith said he would reply to the Welsh deputation next day that proposals for dealing with the disestablishment of the Welsh Church would be submitted to Parliament but that this would not commit the government in the next session. (RA 29/41). A disestablishment bill was introduced in April 1909 but withdrawn two months later. (Kenneth O. Morgan, Wales in British Politics 1868–1922, *University of Wales Press, Cardiff, 1963, pp. 238–40).*

July 23 Interviews during the past week with Asquith have been brief & short – a word on the bench about progress, times for sittings & asking advice on small matters. He remains the same, always decided and approachable, & withall ready to listen to anything that is said before giving a decision.

Today a meeting of the Free Churches representatives from Wales, called on him in his room to urge Welsh disestablishment & disendowment for Wales. The Rev Evan Jones, Thomas & others spoke for different churches.[1]

Asquith said 'it is our hope and it is our intention to submit next session proposals to Parliament which may be satisfactory. We may be defeated in our intention as we don't know what events may be before us but if we are it will be through no default of ours'. This satisfied them as the deputation realised the difficulties. He had a garden party at No. 10.

The Prime Minister's day ended with a dinner in his honour with parliamentary colleagues who had attended Balliol College.

Lord Knollys telephoned me to ask whether the King should patronise today Mining Exhibition to which Montgomery had pressed his presence.[2] I said it would be popular – but I thought Montgomery had interests to serve, but was a decent man but needed no great attention, nor did he possess much weight.

July 27 Asquith late at House – had a few words on Bench at 4.0 & again at 11.0. He asked me my autumn plans. I told him home for 6 weeks, a shooting visit or two later at Gleneagles & Keir, & Hutton Castle. He said do come for a few days if you can to Slains Castle, Port Erroll – excellent golf at Cruden Bay.[3]

---

1 Sir Alfred Thomas introduced the delegation of Welsh MPs and religious leaders to the Prime Minister and Chancellor of Exchequer. Published reports are consistent with JAP's paraphrase of Asquith's qualified assurance.

2 The Liberal MP H.G. Montgomery had organised the first Colliery Exhibition in 1903, of which the world's Mining Exhibition at Olympia, 11–31 July 1908, was a further development. The King did not attend.

3 In his hunting diary JAP recorded that he spent 12 August 1908 at Grantley with Sir Christopher Furness and family. They shot 307 grouse. JAP then went on to Allenheads and Raby More for shooting (Gainford MSS, [75]). From August 25 to 29 he was at Glen with Eddie Tennant and a large family party of Tennants and Asquiths. (Glen Visitors' Book, Glenconner MSS). Gleneagles was a Perthshire house owned by the Earl of Camperdown. Keir, in south Perthshire, was the family seat of the Stirlings, close friends of Lord Rosebery, and the home of the soldier, scholar, and poet, Archibald Stirling, later Con. MP West Perthshire 1917–1918. Hutton Castle belonged to Lord Tweedmouth. It was leased by Jack Tennant who bought it in 1915 for £23,000. (EP to JAP, 17 Sept. 1915, Gainford MSS, 93). JAP

I said I only want to trouble you in the recess about honours. He said I want to confer 2. 'a P.C. on you and Samuel. Don't you think he deserves it for his work.' I heartily assented. 'Other honours must be limited – a few baronetcies'. We sat up until 4.0 getting bills through.

July 28 I asked him at 7.30 about his meeting at Leeds & suggested Oct 9. He agreed, & then asked me to luncheon to meet Sir Arthur Godley Bryce & Mrs Bryce (Ambassador USA) Sir George Murray, Lady Sassoon, & the Spenders. Asquith gave me letters to read from Hobhouse re method adopted by LRC labour men in having all their requests put through them from labour organisations in constituencies – an organised system to cut out Liberal MPs from securing Kudos from their supporters.

Also a letter from Arthur Acland who had a long grievance about Westminster Gazette & not being on the Board.

Spender talked freely about position after lunch & Mrs Spender spoke vehemently against McLaren, but he said he did not coincide with her view. This in my ear only.

Attended a meeting at 4.0 in Asquith's room to hear view of Protestant deputation protesting against illegalities of clergy in Ch of England. Asquith's reply very sympathetic. He said: The remedy is to give Home Rule to the Church of England – opinion in the not distant future will secure more & more converts to this view. This not question today. The Church derives her vitality from the fact that formularies & ceremonies have been such that men of various definite views find satisfaction in the formularies & ceremonies. Elasticity & power of development in the Church is a sign of the Times. Odds 50 to 1 in favour of white surplice being found in churches now in place of black surplice of my boyhood.

2 Arguments

   (1) The right of laymen to have rubrics performed in accordance with law of land – often law flouted – as long as Church is established by laws formularies sanctioned by Kings Parliaments the laws should prevail.

   (2) All advantages of a state Church accepted by the Church clergy, but repudiate others which are equally sanctioned by State connection.

Only Promise Given

Glad to have suggestions as to remedy. Hands full, & pledges to redeem that I should give a respectful consideration to points raised.

In the mid-nineteenth century it was still normal for Anglican clergy to wear only a cassock for their religious duties. The introduction of the white surplice had caused riots and disturbances in many parishes, where the surplice was seen

---

shot there frequently. Slains Castle, owned by the Earl of Erroll, was rented by the Asquiths for the summer.

as an affront to the Protestant Reformation. Similar problems, such as chanting and the use of incense, divided the church throughout the century. A royal commission established to consider ecclesiastical discipline reported in July 1906 in favour of liturgical reforms that would tend to 'greater elasticity' (PP, 1906, Cd 3040, XXXIII, 1–90). The eucharistic vestments were worn in over 150 churches in the London diocese. Following Cosmo Lang's move from Stepney to York early in 1909 white chasubles and copes were seen more frequently in the northern province. Lang advocat ed legalising the 'six points' for which the ritualists contended but subjecting them to episcopal regulation. E.A. Knox, Bishop of Manchester, led the opposition to Anglo-Catholic changes, with the support of about a quarter of the episcopal bench. Private members' bills were introduced in 1906, 1907, and 1908. The deputation of MPs, introduced by Sir George Kekewich, urged Asquith to act immediately to prevent 'ecclesiastical disorders'. The prolonged controversy culminated in the parliamentary debates over a proposed new, optional, prayer book in December 1927. (G.I.T. Machin, Politics and the Churches in Great Britain 1869–1921, *Clarendon Press, Oxford, 1987, pp. 293–4).*

July 30–31 Asquith conciliatory to Opposition. I suggested he should give them credit for help in passing small bills & he did so – & got credit for a clever move & one which may oil the wheels in future with Opposition whips. Had a stormy time on 30th of electric powers Bill. Churchill intended getting all 3, so I suggested alteration of standing orders. Opposition attacked innovation. Asquith withdrew whereupon Churchill wrote a strong letter to Asquith as follows:

> 'My Dear Prime Minister … It is in your power I presume to override (Emmott's ruling) & to secure their second reading in the first week of the new sitting of the House. … I feel bound to submit these considerations to you, & to point out that the procedure which has been abandoned was not proposed by me but by the Chief Whip, & that he gave me his assurance that he would consult you before placing any motion on the paper.'

I told Asquith it was alright & the bills would come on in October. As the Division approached, Burns went to Asquith & said we would be defeated. Lloyd George asked me to have it talked out. Whitley & Norton showed white feather. I told Asquith we ought to get 50 majority but 20 was my lowest estimate. We got bill by 48 – fear that a Trust would kill municipalization & local interests.

Three Electricity Supply Bills proposed for the London area entailed the rationalisation and expansion of existing electricity undertakings. Churchill pointed out that London's electricity should be the cheapest in the nation, although it was in fact double the price of Newcastle's. The Tyneside NESCO network was the largest in Europe. An attempt to launch a similar operation in

London had been thwarted. The defeat of the Progressives on the London County Council in 1907 had also doomed legislation aimed at expanding the LCC's role. The bills, which eventually were passed in December 1908, were opposed by the London boroughs which did not wish to lose any of their autonomy and by those with an interest in the existing generators. Emmott's diary does not mention the incident. (On the technological and political complexities of London electricity supply, see Leslie Hannah, Electricity before Nationalisation: A Study of the Development of the Electricity Supply Industry in Britain to 1948, *Macmillan, 1979, Chs 1 and 2).*

Aug. 1   Had a final word with P.M. about bills to be taken in autumn – India Loans Bill &c.[4] – & he shook me warmly by the hand & said 'I am grateful for all you've done'. I told him how delighted I was to work under him & thanked him for his kindness & the great help he had been to me. He asked me to Scotland Slains Castle Sept 25–29.[5]

Between general elections one of the Chief Whip's most important tasks was ensuring the selection of suitable parliamentary candidates. JAP's correspondence with Noel Buxton over possible vacancies in Norfolk illustrates some typical difficulties. Buxton, believing that the 68 year old sitting member for Norfolk North, Sir W.B. Gurdon, was likely to retire before the next election, was anxious for the nomination in this safe Liberal seat. On July 13 JAP had seen 'no reason to apprehend Gurdon's retirement' and wanted Buxton to 'tackle Mid Norfolk' (Noel-Buxton MSS, Duke University), where Lord Kimberley's 24 year old heir, Lord Wodehouse, had managed the rare feat in 1906 of reducing a Liberal majority of 574 to 27. But Buxton was not impressed with his chances in Mid Norfolk. He had fought Ipswich unsuccessfully in 1900. He won Whitby at a by-election in June 1905 only to be turned out by 17 votes in 1906. Now he wanted the safety of the large Liberal majorities which Gurdon had enjoyed since 1899. JAP wrote to him from Darlington on 6 August 1908.

---

[4]   The East India Loans Act authorised the Government of India to raise up to £20 million in Britain secured on Indian revenues for railway and irrigation construction and £5 million for other general purposes.

[5]   'There are no grouse and hardly any trout:' Raymond Asquith complained when staying at Slains in 1903, 'but it is only 2 miles from a 2nd rate golf course'. There were big stables, a collection of pictures of William IV, but no bathrooms. 'It is large, dark, cold, damp and empty – full of the noise of waves and seagulls, bleak but not wild, and uncomfortable without being in the least romantic ...' (R. Asquith to Frances Horner, 12 Aug. 1903, John Jolliffe, *Raymond Asquith*: Life and Letters, Collins, 1980, p. 107).

Private
My Dear Noel,

I want to see you very much inside the House, but I am afraid waiting for what people call "certainties" is a policy which courts disaster.

Seats can only be won and kept by hard work, and if ever there was a Tory seat of course Whitby was it, it has only once been won. If ever there has been a Liberal seat it is Mid Norfolk, which has only once been lost.

No one regards the present occupant even at the last election as a serious politician, & he is retiring, & when I offered it to you subject of course to local Liberals accepting my suggestion I was offering you the best Liberal seat which I am likely to have at my disposal for you. I have now asked someone else if he can be induced to come out & work to take it, & he has not finally decided.

In my judgement there are nowadays no certainties anywhere except Wimbledon & The City for the Tories, & possibly St. George's, Hanover Square & Westminster.

Work & the right men can in my judgement win every other seat for Liberalism, & Free Trade, as against Toryism & Protection. We have nothing to fear among intelligent Electors for such causes as we represent. It is not always easy to get the right men to stand, nor to induce them to work in the right way.

I have lots of applicants for seats who themselves consider they have claims for safe seats, far superior to yours, I tell them exactly what I tell you. "Safe seats don't exist" & that it is only by settling down to work in a constituency that headway can be made. My interest is not to compare claims but to get the *best candidates* out. In the seats now held by Liberals, the choice has practically been made for all those in which we know Liberal sitting members are retiring – & I honestly can't hold out much prospect of a better chance than Mid Norfolk. But if you think you have a better chance in winning a Tory seat where a Liberal isn't yet out, or think you know of a Liberal seat for which you can get the reversion let me know which it is, & I'll do my utmost to help you, if no one else is in the field.

Yours sincerely,
Joseph A. Pease
(Noel-Buxton MSS, Duke University)

Buxton declined a further offer of Mid Norfolk on August 11. 'I shan't forget you, but I can't promise *anything better', JAP wrote. On December 15 JAP was able to offer South Huntingdonshire where the retiring Samuel Whitbread had a majority of 469 in an electorate of 5272. But Buxton was not persuaded. (Noel-Buxton MSS, Duke University). His information about North Norfolk was accurate; Gurdon stood down at the January 1910 election and died four months later. With a house in the constituency and the support of the Farm Labourers Union, Buxton prevailed in a fiercely contested pre-selection battle with a headquarters nominee 'of less radical hue'. (Mosa Anderson,* Noel Buxton: A Life, *George Allen & Unwin, 1952, pp. 42–3).*

Whichever seat Buxton contested in Norfolk he was certain to face only a Conservative opponent. Elsewhere Liberals were increasingly confronted with Labour candidates splitting the 'Progressive' vote. The Conservative win at Pudsey was followed by another in Haggerston on August 1. In a letter to the editor of The Nation *published on August 15, Arthur Ponsonby questioned the electoral policy being pursued by the new Chief Whip.*

Sir, I am glad to see that *The Nation* has used the result of the Haggerston election to call attention once more to the too frequent occurrence of a divided battle which ends in the return of the Tory.

Let us hope that, by a careful testing of the various methods for meeting this danger which are offered by proportional representation, second ballot, and alternative vote, the Government will include in their Electoral Reform Bill some scheme for dealing with this unsatisfactory state of affairs by legislation.

But in the meanwhile cannot something be done, and in view of the fact that a Reform Bill will probably meet with rough handling from the House of Lords, ought not something to be done to unite the army of progress against the heavily subsidised forces of Protection and Toryism?

It is important to remember that there is no distinct line of cleavage among the Progressives. The Left Wing of the Liberal Party shades off through Labor into Socialism, and what is required, to my mind, is a change of policy at headquarters, not only directed towards the better organisation of Liberalism in the country, but more especially with a view to abandoning the attitude of suspicion and hostility towards the Independent Labor Party which has characterised the *régime* since the General Election, for one of conciliation, compromise, and even encouragement.

This latter was the policy adopted by the Chief Whip before the General Election. Not ostentatious alliance, for that is not possible, but the judicious selection of seats that might be left to Labor, reciprocal concessions, the determined avoidance of three-cornered fights, the careful choice of an advanced Liberal candidate where Labor was strongly represented in the constituency but had no candidate; in short, a diplomatic policy of deliberate co-operation whenever possible. It required undoubtedly judgment and skill to deal with delicate situations and confer with dissentient local associations. But the Chief Whip of the time realised that, not by accentuating the differences in constructive policy, but by unity and agreement in attack, the best results from the constituencies could be obtained. The consequence was that, without hindrance or internal discord, the voice of progress was able to find expression to the fullest extent throughout the country at the election.

I will not enter into the question as to who has been to blame for the growth of antagonism between the two sections that has arisen since January, 1906. It is sufficient to know that it exists, and that the Tories have to some extent succeeded in fanning the flames by alarming moderate Liberals with their highly-colored and ridiculously over-drawn pictures of the dangers of Socialism.

There is talk in the Liberal ranks at times of fighting Socialism as a method of dealing with this difficulty. Nothing, in my opinion, would be so fatal. Socialism is not our enemy. The few Socialists in the House of Commons vote nine times out of ten with the Government, and when they do not it is only because they are eager to quicken the pace, and on these occasions many Radicals join with them. Our enemy still remains, and will remain for years to come, a deeply-rooted prejudiced, retrograde Toryism, which has at its disposal vast wealth and powerful influence with which to win over the still unthinking and indifferent portions of the electorate. To fight Socialism, which cannot be detached from Independent Labor, which, in its turn, cannot be detached from Trade Union Labor and Radicalism, will produce a rift widening in time to a chasm right through the party of progress. It is true that this chasm may in time form itself from the natural tendency of political forces, but it would be a fatal mistake to engineer such a split, a mistake which our real enemy would greatly rejoice in, as it would inevitably result in their supremacy again, perhaps for another generation.

Yours, &c.

Arthur Ponsonby

JAP responded privately, attempting to explain that the growth of antagonism was not of his making:

Private & confidential

Headlam Hall,
Darlington
August 25 1908

My dear Ponsonby,

Some one has kindly sent me the Dumfermline Journal for August 22nd in it I see a letter of yours dated August 8th which appeared first in The Nation of August 15th – I am interested in your views, and I candidly want your help. You have been behind the scenes and know what difficulties are. You say:–

'What is wanted; is a change of policy at headquarters, not only directed towards the better organisation of Liberalism in the country but more especially with a view to abandoning the attitude of suspicion and hostility towards the Independent Labour Party'.

You admit ostentatious alliance is not possible, but the judicious selection of seats that might be left to Labour reciprocal concessions, – & a diplomatic policy of cooperation whenever possible.

I am anxious for this & have done my best to promote it, and therefore I can't advocate 'a change of policy.'

Let me tell you, as an illustration, of one instance of how I have tried to cooperate. Henderson, the leader of the LRC group, I supported on his platform before the election, I proposed him on one of his nomination papers. Last year he holds a meeting close to my House does not ask me any longer to come on to his platform but I ask him to my House, & entertain him. We have a long friendly talk, he tells me the LRC & ILP groups will not directly or indirectly cooperate that they intend to run candidates in as many constituencies as they can. That groups of irreconcilables exist in every constituency and McDonald tells me their leaders can't control them, & they insist on fighting us at nearly every election, the question of money for expenses is the only restraining influence. Henderson tells me that nothing but a second ballot will prevent Tories in many constituencies from getting in, whom he at any rate regards as his enemies, in the same way as you & I do.

I agree with you, any proposal to obtain majority representation will secure rough treatment from the Lords but none the less I am anxious that such a measure should pass the Commons before the General Election.

Henderson now makes my task no easier. He is reported in The Clarion 26/6/08 to have said at a Labour & Progressive Association meeting in his constituency in June that he 'was prepared to make his next appeal to the constituency on that one issue' of socialism.

I ask for some reciprocal concessions but not before, but after I offer them. Good progressive radicals (like say Joseph Walton) who have never given a Tory vote, are now to be opposed by an ILP man – Hobhouse in Bristol, and other 35 sound Liberals are to be opposed. Our man will in every case poll more than the ILP candidate. Am I to stand quietly by and try to withdraw our progressive candidate to give the minority group a chance and allow the break up of Liberal organisations?

I insist so far as I can on Associations being placed upon the broadest democratic basis; I put forward for labour constituencies labour candidates whenever they can be found & approved.

As you are a practical man I want your friendly advice. You are not satisfied with the position neither am I. Is the fault mine? What more can I do?

Yours very sincerely

Joseph A. Pease

(Ponsonby MSS)

Ponsonby's practical advice – to 'induce' Labour to negotiate by 'putting up a Liberal to oust some of their best men' – did not commend itself to JAP. 'I don't like any use being made of the power we possess to threaten opposition if it can be avoided' he told Ponsonby on August 30. (Ponsonby MSS; Martin Petter, 'The Progressive Alliance', History, vol. LVIII, Feb. 1973, pp. 49–50). The problem for the Liberals was compounded by the rivalry within the Labour movement of the Independent Labour Party and the Social Democratic Federation. Within a week the death of the Liberal MP in the two member constituency of Newcastle-upon-Tyne brought out a group of socialist 'irreconcilables'. The Liberals nominated Edward Shortt to succeed Thomas Cairns. The Labour Party National Executive persuaded the Labour candidate J.J. Stephenson to withdraw. But the Social Democratic Federation, with the support of some ILP branches, nominated their own candidate E.P. Hartley. The SDF candidate antagonised the ILP and the local suffragists by refusing to pledge himself to oppose any future franchise reform restricted to manhood suffrage. (Sandra Stanley Holton, Feminism and Democracy: Women's Suffrage and Reform Politics in Britain 1900–1918, Cambridge University Press, 1986, p. 67; Christine Collette, For Labour and for Women: The Women's Labour League, 1906–1918, Manchester University Press, 1989, p. 75). At the by-election on September 24 the seat fell to the Conservative, G. Renwick, though his vote was less than that of the Liberal and Socialist votes combined. The voting was further confused by the presence of at least 2000 Irish voters who supposedly had been influenced to vote against the Liberals because of the banning of the carrying of the Host in the Eucharistic Congress Procession in London earlier in the month. (Marquand, Ramsay MacDonald, pp. 109–11; The

Annual Register. A Review of Public Events at Home and Abroad for the Year 1908, *Longmans, Green, 1909, p. 197; A.W. Purdue, 'The Liberal and Labour Parties in North-East Politics 1900–14: The Struggle for Supremacy'*, International Review of Social History, *vol. XXVI, 1981, no. 1, pp. 15–16; Asquith to Shortt, 19 Sept. 1908, Shortt MSS).*

During August I received two letters from Asquith – first asking my opinion as to when he should give Poynder a peerage he had promised him. I told him not to commit himself to November & to tell Poynder he would see him after his return. On August 25 he wrote

(Slains Castle)

My dear Jack. Many thanks for your letter. I have written accordingly to Jack Poynder. We shall be delighted to see you & Mrs Pease & your daughter here on September 25th. Winston arrived this morning & the McKennas have been here in their yacht for the last two days. Yours ever H.H.A.

Asquith gave a more expansive account of events in Aberdeenshire to a new friend Dorothy Beresford on August 29:

... The great excitement of the present week was the arrival in our little bay of the 'Enchantress' – the magnificent Admiralty yacht, with the First Lord and Mr McKenna on board. She lay here for three days ... We had the officers to lunch & dinner, & dined with them on the yacht, & took a short cruise, finishing up as a climax with a great & rather grim family golf match – the McKennas, husband and wife, against Violet & me. I am glad to say that we triumphed over them, but Pamela, who has only begun to play since she married three months ago, showed considerable proficiency & indomitable courage.

Since they left we have had Winston Churchill here for a couple of days. Unfortunately he could not bring his beautiful fiancée.[6] He was in excellent form, climbing over dangerous rocks like an antelope, and perorating on every imaginable subject at all hours of the day & night.

(Kidd MSS)

I wrote to him [Asquith] about Newcastle election September 16; on September 22 1908 he wrote again from Slains.

Dear Jack.

Many thanks for your letter. The situation in Newcastle appears to be as confused as possible.

I am extremely sorry to have to write that I am afraid we must give up the pleasure of seeing you & Mrs Pease & your daughter here on Friday.

My girl Violet had a nasty fall on the rocks here just as it was getting dark here on Saturday evening. She was quite alone, except for her dog, & we searched for her unavailingly for the best part of four hours. At last she was found lying unconscious at the top of a grass slope, up which she had managed to crawl. The

---

6   Churchill and his 'beautiful fiancée', the twice previously affianced Clementine Hozier, were married on 12 September 1908, after a 32 day engagement.

result is that she is suffering from a nervous shock & has to be kept in bed & in absolute quiet. So far [no] other untoward symptom has developed but as you will understand we have to keep the house as quiet and empty as possible.

I was due at Balmoral yesterday but did not go. If the Dr gives a favourable account I shall go there today for a couple of nights.

Yours ever H.H.A.

October 3 Travelled from Forfar to Earlston to attend Prime Minister's meeting. He spoke for about 50 minutes to a packed audience in a tent, a hard headed listening audience. We afterwards motored to Hutton Castle 25 miles. The P.M. was quiet, & all the talking was done by Mrs Tennant & me driving to Hutton. Party only Asquiths, Tennants & I. After dinner, we played Bridge for 2$^{1/2}$ hours, it is extraordinary that Asquith takes such an unconcealed interest in the game, after playing a successful hand his face beams with childish delight. When the reverse occurs his mobile lips are twisted & pulled almost in contortions. Conversation at dinner turned on golf, successes by individuals at various recreations, & merits contrasted.

The party at Lord Tweedmouth's Hutton Castle had heard Asquith speak to a meeting of over 4000 people organised by the Scottish Liberal Association. In a marquee 220 feet long and 60 feet wide, the audience was necessarily attentive. Interrupting suffragettes were readily ejected as all women were required to sit together near exits. The premier's main theme was the government's land policy, particularly for Scotland. He argued that the policy was a simple extension of the 1885 Crofters Act which had helped stem rural depopulation and urban congestion by encouraging crofters to stay on their land. Greater security encouraged them to build better houses and use better agricultural methods. The Scottish land bill extended this policy to small holders. Asquith claimed that fears for landlords' rights and existing interests could not be justified after a reading of the government's proposals, but that if there was any glaring omission, the bill was open to amendment. Despite his support for the content of the bill, Asquith failed to say when it would be reintroduced into the Commons after its recent defeat in the Lords. This presumably deliberate obscurity was noted by Balfour in a speech a few days later. (See John Brown, 'Scottish and English land legislation 1905–11', The Scottish Historical Review, vol. XLVII, I, no. 143, April 1968, pp. 72–85).

Sunday October 4 A very hot still sunny morning I took my Dispatch box under a large Beech tree to deal with my correspondence.

About 11.00 Asquith came to me, took a chair & for 2 hours and a half talked confidentially to me.

He first dwelt upon the recent cabinet crisis, of which up to the present nothing is known. Gladstone's apathy in connection with The Eucharist procession in London in September he severely condemned, he described how no notice was taken either by Henry head of the Police, or by the Home Office. Henry is a RC & asserts he had been advised of the intention to process early in August, arranged the course, but had no knowledge of the Eucharist being a feature outside the Cathedral, & therefore took no counsel from the Home Office. When Asquith's attention was drawn to the intention only 6 days before the procession he at once wired in confidence to Lord Ripon to secure the voluntary abandonment of the Eucharist procession. The telegram was sent on to The Archbishop, & Asquith called it a gross breach of confidence. He wrote strong letters to Gladstone & Ripon and they both resigned. Gladstone on the plea that his Department had been in error for which he was censured, & Ripon on the ground that R Catholicism had received a blow in the face of Protestantism, by the Govmt forcing the withdrawal of the Eucharist from the procession.

Asquith went into great detail, in regard to the incident, & explained how he had induced his colleagues not [to] be precipitate. Any such public action would exaggerate the importance of the incident. It was deplorably mismanaged, but he had himself no other course to take, if the law was to be respected (though he admitted it had on other smaller matters of the same kind often been winked at) & peace preserved. As it was he said, there was great danger, & regrettable incident was only just avoided. The Archbishop's last steps in to the Cathedral he said had been described to him, as similar to the effort of a Derby winner to get past the post.

Though he was critical of Gladstone's handling of the affair, Asquith had assured the Home Secretary on September 23 'how anxious I am to retain a colleague and friend whose services I value so much. It is clear that you have been very badly served by Henry ...' Having seen Sir Edward Henry's explanation, Asquith concluded on September 29 that 'it reduces his error of judgement to one of relatively small dimensions'. (Gladstone MSS, Add. MS 45989, ff. 191, 196). But Gladstone, and his permanent under-secretary Sir Edward Troup, had performed very poorly. (Jill Pellew, The Home Office 1848– 1914: from Clerks to Bureaucrats, *Fairleigh Dickinson University Press, Rutherford, 1982, pp. 83–6). Asquith asked Gladstone to consider going to the Lords as Lord President in place of Tweedmouth, but this rather half-hearted proposal was not pressed. The idea had been put to Asquith by the King who also suggested replacing Gladstone with Harcourt. (Esher's diary, 26 Sept. 1908, Esher MSS, 2/11). Eventually, Fowler, now Viscount Wolverhampton, was transferred from the Duchy of Lancaster to the Lord Presidency, a move which disappointed the King who had been pleased with his work at the Duchy. (Haldane to Asquith, 30 Sep. 1908, Asquith MSS, vol. 11, ff. 194–5). Ripon resigned on September 14. Age and ill-health, not policy differences, were mentioned when the resignation was announced on October 9. Despite this incident, illegal Roman Catholic processions continued and in 1909 one such procession led to rioting and disorder. The police were instructed to use their*

powers of prevention where they feared serious obstruction, inconvenience, or
breach of the peace. (Asquith's Cabinet letter to the King, 23 June 1909, Cab.
41/32/22).

We then talked, walking round the garden about the alterations in the
Government necessitated by Tweedmouth's resignation (which Lady Aberdeen
had induced him to voluntarily send, in a perfectly sane letter). Asquith dwelt
upon the weakness of the speaking ministerial strength in House of Lords and
asked me about Burghclere, Robertson E (Lord Lochee). Morley & Fowler were
now too old & declined, & everything was left to Crewe & Lord Chancellor.

After thinking over Liberal Peers, I said I saw no one who would carry much
weight. Sandhurst & Northampton, I suggested for consideration. Asquith said
the King always seemed favourable to Northampton being given some post &
had advocated him. He The King was very much annoyed at the Eucharist
procession, & said whilst personally he liked Herbert Gladstone he regarded him
as wholly incompetent for his office, & had urged the acceptance of his
resignation the previous week at Balmoral. I undertook to find out about
Lochee's health, he had written to say he was quite equal to work again &
Asquith seemed to favour him, as an able man.[7] Haldane wrote from Balmoral
(Oct 3) to say that the King preferred Burghclere. Crewe condemned
Northampton he was politically lazy & he had not helped him in the Lords. We
then went through various matters connected with business for the autumn
session & time table – methods for securing alteration of Procedure, re
resolutions & time now wasted before money bills could be introduced. The
party's attitude to Home Rule, he argued whilst we favoured the principle we
could not foresee the platform upon which the next election would be fought. I
showed him a letter from Maddison on the opposition of labour to the socialism
now being preached, urging the govmt to go steady.[8]

We then had a long talk on Lloyd George's relations with Mrs Charles Henry
I assured him I thought the scandal was founded on platonic relationship due to
pushing American Jewess's desire to get on socially. Asquith said his visit to
Berlin, as a Peace promoter, & to secure reduction of Navy was mistimed. The
Emperor only laughed at Ll. George's motoring tour, & he became ridiculous

---

[7] Edmond Robertson's ill-heath may have cost him Cabinet rank in April when he
     aspired to the Duchy of Lancaster but was consoled with a peerage. (Lady
     Southwark, *Social & Political Reminiscences*, Williams & Norgate, 1913, pp. 219–
     21). The account of his removal from the ministry in Cameron Hazlehurst, 'Asquith
     as Prime Minister, 1908–1916', *English Historical Review*, vol. LXXXV, no.
     CCCXXXVI, July 1970, p. 504, gives too much weight to Arthur Lee's critical
     assessment of his competence.

[8] Maddison's letter has not survived in either JAP's or Asquith's papers.

going round with the Henrys & Harold Spender.[9] He & Edward Grey had concocted a really strong telegram stopping him from making an ass of himself, which they sent to him on his arrival at Berlin through the Embassy.

Lloyd George's ostensible aim on his motoring tour of Germany had been to study the German systems of old age pensions and sickness insurance but while there he had also put out feelers to discuss the possibility of arms limitations. Asquith's description of these events to JAP is less than fair: there is evidence that he and Grey had encouraged Lloyd George, only asking him to stop his attempts after an interview between the German Emperor and Hardinge at Cronberg in which the former displayed great intransigence and passion on the question. Certainly the language of the telegram sent to Berlin cannot be described as 'strong'. (Michael G. Fry, Lloyd George and Foreign Policy, *vol. one,* The Education of a Statesman: 1890-1916, *McGill–Queen's University Press, Montreal, 1977, pp. 97–103). Asquith himself told Grey on August 24: 'I cannot say that I think any real harm has resulted from these indiscretions, and in my letters to L.G. I have, without assuming a scolding tone, made your view and mine pretty plain.' (FO 800/100/136–7).*

We then had a chat on Lloyd George's limitations – his laziness which was such a trouble to Sir George Murray.[10] I alluded to his constant interviews with Churchill but I thought there was really no intrigue but Winston in many ways was a child. Asquith agreed and said Loulou Harcourt was not in the group, & he would like to have given him promotion to the Home Office. He saw no

---

9   'Not since Sancho Panza went abroad with the Don has there been anything quite to equal' Spender's performance, A.G. Gardiner told Charles Masterman on September 14. (Masterman MSS, A 3/5/6). In a letter to Julia Henry, who had returned early to England, Lloyd George recounted on 23 August 1908 that Spender had been so bemused by the attention of the press that he had left behind two-thirds of the luggage when the party travelled to Hamburg. (Lady Henry MSS). Elsie Pease found the Henrys obnoxious, especially the 'pushing American Jewess' (not 'heiress' as transcribed by Bruce K. Murray, *The People's Budget 1909/10: Lloyd George and Liberal Politics*, Clarendon Press, Oxford, 1980, p. 111, and from what is described as the diary of 'a Junior Whip' by Bentley Brinkerhoff Gilbert, *David Lloyd George, a political life*: The Architect of Change 1863–1912, Ohio State University Press, Columbus, 1987, p. 352). 'These people are a pestilence to me ... so I can barely be civil to them ... I will not go out with 2nd rate people when I have a girl out' Elsie told JAP on 7 March 1908. (Gainford MSS, 86).

10   Lloyd George's 'laziness' was a popular theme of his departmental and ministerial subordinates. 'He refuses to read any office files or papers, but likes people to come and talk', Charles Hobhouse recorded in his diary on 5 August 1908. In late June Asquith had instructed Hobhouse, the Financial Secretary, to 'come and see him weekly on the financial position' (David, ed., *Inside Asquith's Cabinet*, p. 73).

difficulty in making a precedent for Crewe to remain at the Colonial Office and to be President vice Tweedmouth. The King wanted Fowler to remain at the Duchy, but if he had saved money there for the King, it was no reason to prevent his promotion to Privy Seal.[11]

[*October 5*] On the following morning October 5, came a letter from Lord Ripon, in which he asked there should be no delay in the acceptance of his resignation & he would do it on the ground of health & age, & inability to attend to duties, he at the same time thought awkward questions might arise after Parliament met, & he might not be able to agree with the attitude his colleagues might take place [sic]. Asquith said he had no longer any compunction in accepting the resignation, as Ripon's grounds were now those he could accept as sufficient. The concluding portion of Lord Ripon's letter was couched in most friendly terms & alluded to his satisfaction of Asquith's government associated with the passage of work based on progressive principles govmt. For upwards of an hour we then discussed those upon whom honours should be conferred at the November distribution. The following were the names he selected out of a list I advocated, taken out of my application for honours Book. I said nothing about myself, but he said I was to be a PC.

Privy Councillors
   Sir Charles McLaren. Herbert Samuel & J.A. Pease. Irish PC – Lord Pirrie (who would be elected unanimously for Dublin Lord Mayoralty if he would stand). The King had already hesitated but had agreed to this.[12]

Baronets
   John Barker MP. C.E. Shaw MP. O. Williams MP. E. Hatch

---

[11]   Eventually Fowler, by then Viscount Wolverhampton, replaced Tweedmouth as Lord President; he in his turn was replaced by Lord Fitzmaurice. Crewe remained at the Colonial Office but also took over the Privy Seal from Ripon.

[12]   Lord Pirrie, the Belfast (not Dublin) shipping magnate, had been ennobled in 1906 over King Edward's objections. He had been an Irish PC since 1897. His appointment as a Knight of St Patrick was announced in *The Times* on October 9. As none of the other members of the order would attend a public investiture with him he was privately invested by the Lord Lieutenant. (Lee, *King Edward VII*, vol. II, pp. 451–2).

Knights. Duckworth MP. Dalziel MP. Luke White MP. Fordham H.G. E.D. Walker Scott J.W. ?Mackie[13] [indecipherable name][14] (if he would accept I might find out) ?Martin Dr Carlaw. Arts &c – Beerbohm Tree[15], Bodington (Leeds) T. Hardy[16]. Frampton (sculptor) J.J. Thomson. There were a few others left over for consideration & Asquith said the civil servants' list would also have to be considered.

Mrs Asquith then joined us, & soon let out the differences between her views & Asquith's on some of his colleagues. She dwelt upon Lloyd George's failure as probable at the Exchequer, the slimness of Tommy Shaw who she did not trust. I spoke up for him. We discussed Ure too & his great ability. Asquith said I would much sooner have the Lord Advocate to discuss Scotch Small Holdings with than the Scottish Secretary. He is a really able man though he doesn't look it & brains always appeals to the Prime Minister. Before dinner we had another chat for an hour, over various peers, who he should appoint as Lord Lieutenant for East Riding. Lord Nunburnholme was the only resident Liberal except Lord Derwent who was mad. Francis Johnson Asquith suggested but I said he was a Tory though a nice fellow.[17]

---

13   Probably Richard Mackie (1851–1923); provost of Leith 1899–1908; head of ship broking, steamship, and coal exporting companies; Italian and Swedish Vice-Consul in Edinburgh; Kt 1909; but possibly John Beveridge Mackie (1848–1919); proprietor and editor, *Dunfermline Journal, Dunfermline Express*; author of *The Model Member:* Sir Henry Campbell-Bannerman's Forty Years' Connection with the Stirling Burghs (1914).

14   Only the first letter 'T' of this name is clear. No name of similar length appears in the 1908 or 1909 honours lists.

15   Tree was not knighted in 1908. Next year his wife who had campaigned for a title since 1902 wrote to her friend Asquith begging for an honour. It was granted in June 1909, Tree's additional 'wife' and four natural sons evidently being no impediment. (Maud Beerbohm Tree to Asquith, 20 Apr. 1909, Asquith MSS, vol. 12, ff. 30–1; Madeleine Bingham, *'The Great Lover'*: The Life and Art of Herbert Beerbohm Tree, Hamish Hamilton, 1978, pp. 145, 183–4).

16   Thomas Hardy (1840–1928) declined an honour because '... I am hardly able to realize all its bearings for the moment' and asked that it be postponed for at least a year so that he could have more time to consider it. (Hardy to Asquith, 5 Nov. 1908, Asquith MSS, vol. 11, f. 231). He eventually accepted an O.M. in 1910, after publication of the final part of *The Dynasts*.

17   The Lord Lieutenancy was vacant because of the death that day of the 11th Baron Herries. Asquith probably suggested the Hon. Francis Johnstone (1851–1929); eldest son of Lord Derwent; already Deputy Lord Lieutenant and County Councillor for the North Riding, where the family estates lay; 2nd Baron Derwent 1916. His nephew the 4th Lord Derwent, confirmed that he was a Conservative, though his non-involvement in national affairs resulted in *Dod* never identifying his political sympathies. (Lord Derwent to CH, 12 June 1975).

Oct. 12 Autumn Session. Saw Asquith for 10 minutes in his room after Cabinet, merely discussed with him business of the House.

Oct. 13 I told him behind the Speaker's Chair that whilst the House would accept an increase in Time limit period from 14 to 21 years, it would be unpopular on our side, probably 25 might oppose it – but *if* the [Licensing] Bill was to be saved, the door should be left open for an increase of 14 years to 21, or the Lords would throw it out.

Oct. 14 I told Asquith of Lord Lochee's great disappointment in not having been included in the new shuffle, due to Tweedmouth's retirement, & Fitzmaurice's inclusion in the cabinet.

We discussed who should be undersecretary for Foreign Affairs – he said with a smile: I hear Elibank would like it, I said yes if it was offered, but he is quite happy he says, working with me where he is. He (Master of Elibank) had asked me to name C. Lyell, Sir Edward Grey's Parliamentary Sec. as an aspirant. Asquith said well Trevelyan has prior claims and as he would be a persona grata to Grey I think I will offer it him but I will see Grey this afternoon.

Campbell-Bannerman had told JAP in December 1905 that he did not like Trevelyan but that he would try to find something for him for the sake of his father, whom C.B. thought had been badly treated. (JAP's contemporary notes of events in December 1905, Gainford MSS, 37). Trevelyan was passed over in 1905 and again in April 1908. Trevelyan's father, Sir George Otto Trevelyan, had written to Asquith on 15 April 1908 protesting at the omission of his son from a new ministry in which the sons of other Liberal veterans had been included. Trevelyan was offered the Parliamentary Secretaryship at the Board of Education, not the Foreign Office. He wrote to his father on October 19:

> I never thought that I should be made Grey's under-secretary, it would not have been an impossible position because I have profound confidence in his general policy and studious labours for peace ... Grey would necessarily have felt that he could not have had my full approval in some of his dealings with Russia. consequently, he would probably have been inclined to leave as little as possible to me. (G.O. Trevelyan MSS, 61)

McKinnon Wood moved from Education to under-study Grey. The Times (20 Oct. 1908) said that McKinnon Wood's appointment had caused surprise and commented that he was not 'known to have taken any marked interest in foreign affairs'. McKinnon Wood was, however, a former leader of the Progressives on the London County Council and, at 53, was one of those 'older men' who, as Charles Lyell explained to his mother, 'were very sore at the last redistribution of jobs'. Lyell, 20 years younger than Wood, thought it 'marvellous ... my name was actually considered'. Edward Grey told him that Trevelyan had been 'half

promised' a job and there was 'much sickness' when he was left out at Easter.
(Lyell to Lady Lyell, 14 Oct. 1908, to Sir L. Lyell, 20 Oct. 1908, Lyell MSS).

Oct. 15   Asquith worried a bit over the unemployed problem but told me to look
in at 11.40 on Friday.

In a covering minute on a 'Report on unemployment in the United Kingdom in
September 1908' (Cab. 37/95/123), circulated on October 10, Churchill
commented: 'There can be no doubt that we have already entered upon a period
of exceptional distress and industrial dislocation; and these conditions may be
sensibly aggravated as the winter advances.' (Churchill, Winston S. Churchill,
vol. II, Companion Part 2, p. 842). The honeymooning Churchill had confided to
Masterman on September 20 that he thought the statement from his Labour
correspondents would 'make the Cabinet sit up'. Fearing that 'the LGB can
present a tremendous answer: that all in human power has been done: that no
unemployed are unprovided for' Churchill sought guidance on 'how things really
are behind the grinning mask of fiscal assurance'. (Masterman MSS, A 3/18/1).
On October 14 the Cabinet appointed a new committee on unemployment. This
took responsibility from John Burns who had chaired a previous committee
which had deferred policy decisions until the Poor Law commission reported.
Asquith shared the view of several of his colleagues that Burns was 'entirely in
the hands of the officials'. (Lord Carrington to Sir Thomas Elliott, 14 Oct. 1908,
Elliott MSS).

Oct. 16   He then said, we must defer making any arrangement, but I will
announce the business for next week, & I gave him my draft, which he approved.
    In the afternoon on the licensing bill he indicated a concession on the time
limit might be made on the Report stage.

Oct. 19   Hung about 10 Downing St. to 2.15, when Asquith saw me.   The
cabinet met at 12.40.   Asquith had received my letter at 12.30 – written that
morning, which was as follows:

> In regard to the unemployed question I think the Party would welcome a bill to
> enable ld. rate to be used as a temporary expedient.   The Labour party in the
> country is composed of a variety of elements, & if we now estrange them we shall
> secure no support to enable the govmt to carry half hearted proposals.   If however
> the govmt secure the confidence of the best leaders of the various groups, we shall
> be able to resist both Tory reaction & socialism & drive a wedge between the
> practical & impractical Labour politicians.   An awkward situation will be created if
> we are pressed to give a day, and no bill is introduced.

Asquith said I read your letter to the cabinet which has been somewhat stormy. Ll. George, Winston, Sydney Buxton alone advocate the ld. rate – & Morley would resign at once if we pressed it.

I think we have a strong case without it, but you ought to know the position. There will be another meeting tomorrow & I will make a statement on Wednesday. I said it is no use arguing, but the ld. rate, & local responsibility being shared with the govmt does not mean the right of men to have work provided by the State.

I then left him. He was absolutely cool, & in his statement as to making a reply on Wednesday he was quite conciliatory to the L.R.C. group, & said he recognised that, even if as he assumed his proposals were quite satisfactory, some opportunity for comment might have to be found.

JAP's letter is not mentioned in Asquith's letter to the King on October 20. (RA 29/56). The Tory whips were better briefed. John Burns, talking 'as usual with great freedom' to Lord Balcarres, revealed that the right to raise a penny rate had been 'the bone of contention in the cabinet – and he tells me that the opposition to his views emanated from Lloyd George and Churchill.' (Balcarres' diary, 21 Oct. 1908, Vincent, ed., The Crawford Diaries, *p. 115). Burns fought successfully against the penny rate, arguing that legislation would be needed to empower local authorities to pay wages from rate revenue and that the rate was sure to increase. The government took a cautious approach (Brown,* John Burns, *pp. 142–3). Asquith described for the King the measures the government was to take: increased loans to local authorities, secured on the rates, for improving streets, water works, and sewerage; extra loans (or grants in special cases such as in London) 'where distress prevails'; relaxation of Local Government Board eligibility criteria for applicants and kinds of work allowed; the ship-building programme to be accelerated.*

The extent of Morley's isolation from the rest of the ministry on social questions is illustrated by his preparation for a Cabinet discussion on sweated industries earlier in the year by reading the 1834 Poor Law Report and the works of Dr Chalmers. (Sir Arthur Hirtzel's diary, 19 Dec. 1908, Hirtzel MSS, British Library, Oriental and India Office Collections, Home Misc. 864/1; cf John H. Morgan, John Viscount Morley: An Appreciation and Some Reminiscences, *John Murray, 1924, pp. 81–2).*

Oct. 20 Went in after a cabinet to see Asquith 1.30. I told him Henderson had promised assistance to us in securing licensing bill, on such days as we might desire it, as the Labour MPs were gratified at the promise for a day to debate the govmt proposals. Asquith said he thought there would not be much grumbling at the scheme; but Friday would do the day I suggest as an early day & one which would show earnestness & sincerity by reason of it being an early day.[18] Asquith said I don't think opinion will boil up, but it is better to take it soon – Yes.

Winston Churchill apologised for putting me in the hat the night before when we were run down to 9 on a vote to closure an instruction to the Electric Supply Bill.[19] He & also Loulou told me what the cabinet decided but asked me not to tell their colleagues I knew.

It is more obvious to me than ever the Chief Whip should be in the cabinet, if he is to look after the time of the House & keep Ministers with departments in touch with private members' views.

Oct. 21 Called on Asquith 1.20. He was as usual walking up & down his upstairs room. We he Montagu (his Parl. Secy) & I had a word about H.G. Fordham of Cambridge being given a Knighthood & Asquith agreed it would have to be given after Montagu's expression of regret in June to him.

I then talked over the procedure on unemployed & we agreed to offer a day for the discussion; but would ascertain feeling of House as to which day.

I told him I thought motion would be put up by opposition if opposed by a friend of favourables but not set up supply [sic]. He agreed. We had a word about Electric Power Bills.

I also suggested Soares or Lyell to represent Charity Commissioners & P.M. seemed to think Soares more justified this simple recognition.

He then said he had had a talk with Whittaker before going to bed & sent him home the night before in better humour. I told him his Loulou did not forgive, & it was well for him to have seen Whittaker & I told Asquith how Loulou had turned on Bennett who had criticised the govmt Local Veto proposals that afternoon. Loulou knows he has a language of his own. He thanked Bennett for his kind service. Bennett expressed surprise. Yes said Loulou I need not again trouble to speak again for you in Oxfordshire.

P.M. was amused. He said well the Lady Carlislites, & those anaemic eunuchs were bound to quarrel with the disinterested trust management lot Sherwell Bennett & Whittaker.

Sir Thomas Whittaker, the leading temperance advocate, had criticised Harcourt's efforts in explaining an amendment to the Licensing Bill the previous

---

[18] An early day motion is one for which no specific day has been agreed; the MP proposing it is asking for it to be considered as soon as possible. It is a device used by MPs to express their opinions and to invite support for them, or by an MP hoping that time will be granted by the government.

[19] The instruction was to confer purchasing powers on the LCC. Churchill had moved the motion 'that the question be now put' which had been approved by only nine votes. When the question was put, immediately after Churchill's motion, the government majority was 131.

evening. Harcourt's electoral support mattered to Ernest Bennett because his estates extended into Bennett's Woodstock constituency. Disinterested trust management of liquor sales, as promoted by Whittaker, Sherwell and Bennett, and the Temperance Legislation League meant the retailing of liquor by private philanthropic companies. Lady Carlisle and her 'anaemic eunuchs' – her son Geoffrey Howard, her son-in-law Charles Roberts, and her devoted factotum, and president of the United Kingdom Alliance, Leif Jones – were more interested in promoting abstinence than in elaborate re-organisation of liquor distribution. Further rifts among the temperance forces were revealed early in 1909 when Sherwell voted against a Scottish local option bill. Leif Jones reported to Lady Carlisle on 1 March 1909: 'I had a long talk with Whittaker ... He says Sherwell is really opposed to local option: that he does not approach the question from the same standpoint as Whittaker & I do (!)' (Lady Carlisle MSS, J 23/100). Whittaker was at heart a prohibitionist.

Oct. 22 Had no word with the P.M. except at questions. Licensing conferred cabinet committee.[20]

Oct. 23 Before House met suggested to Prime Minister that I had squared Wedgwood about voting against us on unemployed. Found Hemmerde intending to do same, told him in my opinion govmt would deal with the land question in a bold way in the next session, & he said that would make him hesitate. Asquith told me he & Balfour behind the chair had agreed not to divide but to talk on compensation clauses all the afternoon.

I went over at his request honours list, with the P.M.'s list, & Nash & I prepared a list for preliminary submission to the King. (I off to Sandwich).[21]

Oct. 26 Unemployed Called at 1.40 at No. 10. Explained position in regard to Opposition asking for two days debate.

Balfour anxious to get popularity of urging importance of unemployment:

'He has NO wish to get a fiscalities debate raised' said Asquith, 'as it is all sham. I told him so yesterday.'

We had some talk about honours. He said he was not yet ready to appoint Dr Carlaw Martin a Knight,[22] Dalziel. 1 was too little for Scotland. He proposed to

---

[20] Asquith's Cabinet letters of 20 and 28 October 1908 make no mention of the Licensing Bill, or of a Cabinet committee discussing it.

[21] Before leaving for Sandwich JAP attended a reception given by Lady Denman 'to meet the Prime Minister'. (*The Times*, 24 Oct. 1908).

[22] Martin was knighted the following year, his local member, Winston Churchill, having advised the Prime Minister on 5 May 1909 that Martin 'has been brought to my notice by the Master of Elibank & I will only say that a Kthood conferred upon him wd be from every point of view justified, & wd be vy widely welcomed in Scotland.' (Churchill, *Winston S. Churchill*, vol. II, Companion Part 2, p. 890).

make Sir J. Low of Dundee a baronet. I said I had met him, but he was not now an active Liberal.

He then said Sir Edward Clarke has of course himself to blame but the Tory party have twice treated him abominably & he proposed making him a PC & I said it was a generous act, but it might harden his free trade views, & indirectly help us. Asquith said well I think it would be a nice thing to do.

Sir Edward Clarke (1841–1931), having been Solicitor-General 1886–92, was offered the post again in 1895 on condition that he take no private briefs while in office. Clarke declined, fell out with his constituents over the South African war, and was out of Parliament 1900–6. Returned for the City of London, he immediately encountered the vehement hostility of tariff reformers and retired in June 1906 on medical advice. 'Twice', he said, 'he had been a scapegoat for his convictions.' (The Times, 9 June 1906). Clarke's support for the Liberals over free trade was considered by the Tory Chief Whip his 'fourth act of disloyalty'. (Sykes, Tariff Reform in British Politics, p. 149). In an address at the Inner Temple Hall on 10 July 1908 Asquith had expressed his admiration for Clarke's 'Courage which, though always undaunted, never blusters; persuasiveness which seems rather to win rather than capture assent; eloquence which never sacrifices light to heat …' (H.H. Asquith, Occasional Addresses 1893–1916, Macmillan, 1918, p. 118). The Pease family held Clarke in high regard. Retained as counsel by the Countess of Portsmouth in her suit against Sir Joseph Pease's administration of her estate, he had resigned the brief when Lady Portsmouth criticised his characterisation of her uncle as insufficiently virulent. (Sir Joseph Pease's diary, 21 Nov. 1900, 20 Nov. 1901, Pease MSS).

He then showed me a secret letter he had had from John Sinclair suggesting his elevation to House of Lords to watch Scotch bills & thought moment opportune. Warned Asquith as to Alec Murray's attitude in Scotland on land bill & he showed jealousy of Elibank's work & influence on land bill. I took letter home. I gave the letter back on the front bench & said there was no ground for jealousy. Elibank had been loyal & had united hostile Liberal elements together & there was no ground for criticism. He certainly enjoyed harmless intrigue, but there was no venom vitriol or even vinegar. His action had not been other than helpful in Scotland & Asquith agreed. After a silly speech from Burns, Asquith pulled party together on government's temporary policy in regard to unemployed – a brilliant 40 mins speech. (see record & report *Times* Oct 27 1908). Got to bed at 2.30. A bothering night – Asquith relying on my judgement in ending debate & divisions were alright.

Burns had antagonised Labour members with an unnecessary attack on the unemployable unemployed, and bored the House with details of road grading schemes in Leeds parks and housing in Merthyr Tydfil. He made a gratuitous aside about the Board of Trade which 'he trusted' were devising improved methods of information gathering which might enable them to establish an efficient system of labour exchanges. Nevertheless The Times *described his speech as a vigorous defence of his department while criticising the Prime Minister for still cherishing 'the notion that trade in manacles is free trade so long as the manacles are forged abroad' and failing 'to understand that there is more in the problem than can be explained by "oscillations of trade" to which all countries will always be subject.' Edwin Montagu echoed JAP's assessment of Asquith's contribution to the unemployment debate:*

Wednesday marked another triumph for you and if we have regard to the extraordinary difficulties of the Parliamentary situation – the funk of our Party – the cross currents of opinion – the way in which you succeeded in silencing the Opposition and in making the Labour Party genuinely satisfied despite their papers protestation marked it, if I may so without the least suspicion of flattery, the best Parliamentary performance I have yet seen. It is perfectly true that in the lobbies I heard growls from Oswald Partington and Co. of 'on the Knee to Socialism,' and it is perfectly true that in accordance with the method the Labour Party is pursuing to justify their existence they tabled amendments, but this need not worry you. The debate however on Monday last was not so successful. I think Balfour's criticism of Alden and Robertson was on the whole justified, and I think Pease must be a little conscious of this …

(Montagu to Asquith, n.d. [? 28 Oct. 1908], copy, Montagu MSS)

Oct. 27 Had ten minutes chat. Asquith quiet, cool, & contented as usual. I told him of Hemmerde's land views & excuse for his speech the night before & read extract from his letter. Asquith admitted the strength of the views wh. he and other land reformers had but did not demur [sic] to it.

In the debate on unemployment Hemmerde had said that unemployment in the building trade was due to the high price of land; he blamed the current land system for under-building, overcrowding, and unemployment. He quoted Asquith, Lloyd George and other members of the government to the effect that these related problems could only be overcome by a tax on land values. He concluded that 'He was merely trying to get the party to carry out that for which they were returned to Parliament'. The Liberal MP for Tottenham Percy Alden had congratulated the government on recognising 'the national importance of the problem of unemployment' moving a motion to this effect from which thirteen Liberals dissented. Balfour had indicated that Alden's diversionary attack on tariff reform revealed the half-heartedness of his praise for the government. Alden, J.M. Robertson, and other advanced radicals shared Hemmerde's views on the land question but also argued for a much more ambitious programme of public works. (H.V. Emy, Liberals Radicals and Social Politics 1892–1914,*

Cambridge University Press, 1973, pp. 176–7; José Harris, Unemployment and Politics: *A Study in English Social Policy 1886–1914, Clarendon Press, Oxford, 1974, pp. 223, 227, 230, 240–1). Alden believed that Asquith was sympathetic but that all action was blocked by Burns (Ponsonby's diary, 14 Oct. 1908, Ponsonby MSS, Shulbrede).*

Lloyd George I suggested had given the show away too much for the next budget, & Asquith admitted he was afraid he had said too much.

*In a speech at the Welsh Liberal Convention in Swansea on October 1, Lloyd George had clearly placed on the political agenda the plight of the sick, the infirm, the unemployed the widows, and the orphans. He had proclaimed rhetorically that a few million pounds might surely be spared to save unemployed workmen from hunger and anxiety. (*The Times, *2 Oct. 1908).*

I told Asquith of Elibank's views as to making Williamson a baronet in place of Low. We get nothing for something if latter was done. He said I shall not make Firth a baronet this time.[23]

---

23   Probably Thomas Freeman Firth (1825–1909); prominent in West Riding commercial life; JP and alderman, West Riding; Lib.; Asquith's uncle by marriage; Bt June 1909.

Chapter 4

A Premier's Confidant

Suffragette militancy increased in 1908. Many demonstrations were held and a Women's Parliament was convened in Caxton Hall. There were spectacular interventions in by-elections, increasing disorderly behaviour, and ominously growing indications of links between the unemployed and suffrage activists. A widely publicised plan to 'rush' the House of Commons led to the arrest of three leaders of the Women's Social and Political Union.

*After protracted court proceedings concluding on 24 October 1908 Emmeline and Christabel Pankhurst and Flora Drummond had gone to prison rather than be bound over to be of good behaviour for twelve months. (Wotner & Sons to Chief Clerk, Metropolitan Police Office, 27 Oct. 1908, MEPO 2/1222 x/L03945). In protest, Miss Muriel Matters and Miss Helen Fox had chained themselves to a grille in the Ladies' Gallery before interrupting the Commons' debate on the Licensing Bill. As they refused to produce the keys to the padlocks both they and sections of the grille had to be removed. 'The obnoxious grille', had previously 'resisted all efforts to either displace it or materially modify it'. (Arnold Wright and Philip Smith, *Parliament Past and Present, *Hutchinson, [1902], p. 93).*

Oct. 28, 1908 Did not see the Prime Minister until 10.15. He was then more nettled than I have previously seen him; except for those momentary ebullitions which must occur occasionally in the House of Commons to all those who take part in debate. It was not due to the fact that Suffragettes had chained themselves to the grille & made an undignified scene, or to the uproar in the Strangers' Gallery which really upset him, but to the action of 13 women who had broken in to his serious address at a religious bazaar in Islington. His religious feelings which are not on his sleeve were really hurt, & I was not surprised he showed some warmth when at the conclusion of business he asked the Speaker what steps could be taken to preserve the dignity of the House.

On the afternoon of October 28, Asquith moved the vote of thanks after a bazaar at the Highbury Athenaeum, Islington, in aid of the funds of the Union (Congregational) Chapel, in which he had worshipped when younger. A dozen members of the Women's Social and Political Union had scattered themselves about the hall. As soon as the Prime Minister rose they began their interruptions: 'The women of this country pay rates and taxes. You are their servant. What about Mrs Pankhurst in Holloway? You are responsible for that,

you tyrant.' (The Times, *29 Oct. 1908). The Speaker closed both the Ladies'*
and Strangers' Galleries until further notice.

Oct. 29 I had a friendly chat over business up to Xmas – and talked over what
we could do in carrying over the Housing or other bills. I said I thought we
could drop this bill without much loss to its prospect another session, & pass all
others necessary to our program.

We discussed Electric Supply Bill procedure for Monday night & I told him
of Lough's intentions, & methods he was employing – friendly only on the face
of them.

As MP for Islington (West), Lough was naturally interested in the London
Electricity Supply Bill. Electricity supplies in London were provided by a large
number of private companies who concentrated on supplying rich, and therefore
profitable, areas rather than all of the city. A bill to empower the LCC to spend
more than £4.5 million to buy up all the companies and local authority interests
and to organise a single supplying authority had been withdrawn when the
Municipal Reform Party gained control of the council in March 1907. The 1908
bill, which was passed, merely proposed that the options of the various local
authorities to buy up the companies in 1931 be transferred to the LCC. Lough
obtained a free vote on the bill. For the history of London's electricity supply,
which was not resolved until 1925, see Gibbon and Bell, History of the London
County Council 1889–1939, *pp. 627–31.*

Oct. 30 At 11.30 I called at No. 10, & told Asquith that Furness wanted to
retire from public life, but was prepared if it would help the Liberal Party to put
2,000,000 into shipping – 50 orders for vessels to stimulate trade – he would do
it. He obviously wanted a pat on the back, & would look to a peerage.
Otherwise he would retire into private life without going to the trouble of fresh
enterprise.

Asquith told me he could not see him today, but I could get Lloyd George to
do so. (I found the latter was away as usual – playing golf at Walton Heath! idle
dog that he is).[1] The reason Asquith gave for his inability to see Furness was 2
conferences.

---

1   October 30 was a Friday. Lloyd George had discussed political strategy and the
    plans for his new house at Criccieth over breakfast with the proprietor of the *News*
    of the World. After breakfast he conferred with the Bishop of St Asaph. He was
    back at Downing St the following day. On Sunday he was scheduled to drive to
    Churchill's mother's house at St Albans to lunch and discuss an Irish Land Finance
    bill in a cabinet committee meeting with Churchill, Birrell, and Crewe (Churchill to
    Crewe, 30 Oct. 1908, Churchill, *Winston S. Churchill*, vol. II, Companion Part 2, p.
    843; George Riddell's diary, 30 Oct., 2 Nov. 1908, Lord Riddell, *More Pages From*
    My Diary 1908–1914, Country Life, 1934, p. 4; J.M. McEwen, ed., *The Riddell*
    Diaries 1903–1923, Athlone Press, 1986, p. 21). On November 17 Hobhouse,

One with the Archbishop – negotiations had gone on satisfactorily for a settlement on the Education Question, until the last 2 days, when the Archbishop as the result of confabulations with other Bishops had started a fresh hare. They insisted on voluntary schools in urban districts being paid for out of rates to put them on a plane with other schools. This Asquith agreed with Runciman was absolutely fatal, & nonconformity would resist this. The Archbishop too was making out the whole tendency of a settlement was due to his action, & the Ch. of England had a right to get credit for it. Asquith said I will tell him it is a preposterous contention the nonconformists commenced the concession last summer (May). I said honour should be divided & Asquith said certainly.[2]

I asked Asquith if Lloyd George was loyal, it had been suggested in more than one corner (J. Burns for one) he was afraid of next year's budget, & he & Winston were intriguing for a dissolution in the spring. A. said I do not believe it we must proceed as if there was no foundation for this. I said I had no reason to believe it, & that the intriguing I noticed in July had not been revived since Parl. met this autumn.

A. then told me about his desire to get Lord George Hamilton's Poor Law Report soon, & had meanwhile asked him to let the govmt have the evidence so as to occupy November in framing policy for next session. Lord George yesterday consulted his committee, & Asquith was going to see him this afternoon as to the course they would adopt.

According to Beatrice Webb, the Prime Minister's request was refused 'on the ground that no man could understand the evidence without the majority report!' However, drafts of both the majority and minority reports, and the evidence, were given to Haldane from mid-November 1908 by Mrs Webb who recorded that she had seen some of the evidence on John Burns's table a year earlier. On May 13, her husband had sent Churchill 'the scheme of Poor Law Reform that I am advocating on the P. L. Commission' and all of the evidence on unemployment. Copies of a memorandum embodying Mrs Webb's 'scheme for breaking up the Poor Law' had been sent or given in confidence to Asquith, Lloyd George, Haldane, McKenna, Buxton, Runciman, Harcourt, Samuel, Burns, and McKinnon Wood as well. The same material was also given to front bench Unionists, selected civil servants, journalists, and local administrators.

always ready to believe the worst about the Chancellor, noted that 'Ll. G. had shirked the first meeting to play golf.' (David, ed., *Inside Asquith's Cabinet*, p. 74). Hobhouse was wrong (Jennie Cornwallis-West to Shane Leslie, 14 Nov. 1908, Anita Leslie, *Jennie*: The Life of Lady Randolph Churchill, Arrow, 1975, p. 285).

2   Asquith's correspondence with the Archbishop was circulated to the Cabinet on 18 November 1908. (Cab. 37/96/156). The politics of education in 1908 are clarified in M.J. Wilkinson, *Educational Controversies in British Politics 1895–1914*, Ph.D. thesis, University of Newcastle upon Tyne, 1977, pp. 575–618.

(Beatrice Webb's diary, 15 May, 29 Oct. and 15 Nov. 1908, Passfield MSS;
Barbara Drake and Margaret I. Cole, eds, Our Partnership by Beatrice Webb,
Longmans, Green, 1948, pp. 417–18; Churchill, Winston S. Churchill, *vol. II,*
Companion Part 2, p. 821; Norman and Jeanne MacKenzie, eds, The Diary of
Beatrice Webb, *Vol. Three, 1905–1924, 'The Power to Alter Things', Virago &*
London School of Economics and Political Science, 1984, pp. 93, 102–3). The
commission reported on 4 February 1909.

I told Asquith I had assurances from those in favour of Suffrage that he had
their full support & sympathy, & in the treatment to which he had been
subjected. He seemed to appreciate what I said, & to value the expression of
sympathy.

On October 30 JAP dined at the National Liberal Club with the three senior
whips, Elibank, Lewis, and Norton, and the chairman of the club's political
committee. JAP wanted to see the club's membership of 6000 grow, and be
mobilised as a much more potent force in registration work, speaking,
*canvassing, and the distribution of literature. (*The Daily News, *31 Oct. 1908).*

JAP's ability to take the fight to the country was inhibited by his commitments
at Westminster. As he told his agent, I.M. Peart, in a letter read to a meeting of
the Thaxted Women's Liberal Association on November 7, he was required to be
at the House between 2.30 p.m. and 11 p.m. Monday to Thursday, and until 6.00
p.m. on Friday. He was in charge of all government business, which occupied
the whole of the House of Commons' time during the autumn session.
Nevertheless he had engagements every Saturday in November and was hoping
to address a few meetings on Friday and Saturday evenings in December. 'I
would like the electors to realise that we have already this session passed 34
Government bills through the House of Commons, and 15 other smaller
measures introduced by private members, and that 41 of these have already
*become Acts of Parliament.' (*Saffron Walden Weekly News, *9 Nov. 1908,*
Gainford MSS, 59).

Tuesday Nov. 3 Looked in to ask the Prime Minister not to commit himself too
far in promising to proceed with the Trawling Bill (Moray Firth)[3] – had a word
with him about the Lord Lieut. of Merionethshire – present man said to be dying.
I afterwards found that Lloyd George had put off a baronetcy to Osmond
Williams on strength of his succeeding to the Lord Lieutenancy. I told Asquith I

---

[3] Asked to say whether the government would proceed with the Trawling in
Prohibited Areas Prevention Bill, Asquith could give no date, but promised it would
be at the earliest opportunity after the Scottish Education Bill had been passed. (*PD*,
IV, cxcv, 999, 3 Nov. 1908). The bill was dropped for lack of time on December 9.

thought he would be disappointed. He told me to promise him it in the summer & I did.

I saw C.E. Shaw he promised me £500 down & substantial contributions for 2 to 3 years, which I intimated should reach £2,000 the figure he indicated to Whiteley as I wanted to earmark sums for Midland Federation for a few years ahead.

Edward Grey & Winston were chaffing each other on the Bench at being lowest in ministerial Division list. Winston said Ah but I make speeches in the country – but they don't count said Edward when you make them to please yourself. He certainly does enjoy their success!

According to the regularly duplicated bulletin on ministerial votes, circulated by the Whips' Office, by the week ending 19 December 1908 Churchill had voted in 155 out of a possible 406 divisions, Grey in 162. Asquith had voted in 250, Lloyd George in 290, and JAP himself in 391. (Gainford MSS, 59, ff. 38-41). In October Churchill had spoken twice in Dundee, twice in London, and once in Manchester. He was tied to the Commons more than usual in October and November with the London Electricity Bill and the Port of London Bill. Nevertheless his voting record was the worst in the Cabinet.

Nov. 4 At Cabinet from 12.0 to 12.20. We discussed business – wrangle between claims of Scotland & London for Education & Port of London Bill respectively.[4] I suggested taking an extra day between two stages of Licensing Bill, & this was agreed to. Churchill & George assertive. Crewe asking for time, & asserting Lords could not pass bills if they were jammed up. We had a little explanation as to position of English Education Bill arrangements, I told them my scheme for work was dependent upon whether compromise was secured.

Nov. 9 Had a chat with the P.M. about Lord Robert Cecil's question asking for time to discuss Old Age Pension regulation – asked for Thursday. He decided to give time & I said after 11.0 on Monday 16th. He also agreed to put down allocation of time for report stage of Licensing Bill at 3.45 on Wednesday instead of taking it 2 hours after 11.0 as previously arranged.

He seemed to have enjoyed trip to Devonport to launch the Collingwood on 7th & said the women left me alone, & made a boast of, for this occasion, as a special compliment to Mrs. Asquith.[5] His speech in city given much favour.

---

[4] Both bills were passed in 1908. The Education (Scotland) Bill increased the powers of local school boards, enabling them to compel children up to the age of seventeen to attend evening continuation classes, to supply food and clothing in certain circumstances, and to carry out medical examinations.

[5] H.M.S. *Collingwood*, the latest battleship of the dreadnought type, was not commissioned until 1910. Mrs Asquith launched her with a bottle of Australian wine, probably Harris Irvine's Great Western champagne, 'in accordance with the

Nov. 10 I told Asquith this, & he said well Edward Grey should be given the credit for it. I said what he told me to say.[6] We talked over procedure if Scotch Education Bill was talked out.

Nov. 11 Short interview merely formal about business of House. P.M. in a hurry – lunching out in Balfour Company.

P.M. said after poor A.J.B. how he hates coming to listen to this Port of London Bill, as a city-representative he is forced to by deputations, but he hates the whole thing & cares about [it] even less!

Nov. 12 P.M. quite angry with John Burns & he the P.M. had to throw John Burns over at 8.15 L.G.B. regulations had not carried out his promise.

Asquith had promised that men would no longer be excluded from work provided by money from the Distress Fund because they were in receipt of poor law relief or their names had been on the distress register for two years. The Local Government Board had issued regulations giving the distress committees full discretion. Arthur Henderson, in moving the adjournment, pointed out the difference between actually removing the exclusion and giving discretion to waive it; he proposed that the Local Government Board issue a new Order complying with the letter and the spirit of Asquith's statement. Asquith agreed.

---

desire expressed by King Edward some time ago that wine produced within the empire should be used on such occasions.' (*The Argus* [Melbourne], 10 Nov. 1908, 11 Feb. 1910).

6   In the Prime Minister's annual speech in the Guildhall at the Lord Mayor's Banquet Asquith had discussed economic conditions and the government's remedial action. He also spoke firmly about Britain's attitude to the annexation of Bosnia-Herzegovina by Austria-Hungary while being careful to say nothing to provoke Germany. He and Grey were perplexed by German actions over the Casablanca incident. The fleet had been readied on November 5 in anticipation of a crisis; and Asquith confided to Balfour that night that the government could only explain German policy on the assumption that she wanted war. (Balfour to Lansdowne, 6 Nov. 1908, copy, Balfour MSS, Whittingehame). A perturbed John Morley told his Permanent Under-Secretary on November 6 that he had gone in to ask Grey what was to be said at the Guildhall about Germany. 'Grey (who was not going to be there) had told Asquith to make some commonplaces about friendly relations w. Germany & Italy. J.M. said that this was not nearly enough.' Morley suggested that Asquith should say that he reciprocated the sentiments expressed by the German Emperor himself in an earlier Guildhall speech. Grey, who had forgotten the Emperor's speech 'thought it a good idea: wd J.M. suggest it to Asquith. No, said J.M., you are the proper man; & Grey said he would.' (Hirtzel's diary, 6 Nov. 1908, Hirtzel MSS, British Library, Oriental and India Office Collections, Home Misc 864/1).

'It was a very awkward episode for the Govt.', Sir Courtenay Ilbert recorded,
'Burns had, as in too many cases, allowed himself to be [?counselled] by the
permanent officials of the LGB who had acted with crass stupidity.' (Ilbert's
diary, 12 Nov. 1908, Ilbert MSS, H.C. Lib. MS 72).

Nov. 14 Asquith very pleased with our having got thro' Port of London by
sitting up late night before. He had to climb down over a definition clause on
Licensing Bill.

Nov. 16 Asquith back from Lord Rothschild's. 'I have had some time to think
over our best course' said Asquith, 'in regard to Education. Runciman was bold
enough to chuck The Archbishop's letter into the fire before his face, & to tell
him he must write another, that his proposals were vague & impossible. He
wrote another, like a lamb but it too is far from satisfactory. The nonconformists
had been very good. They have been brought right up to the fence, & I am not
going to throw them over, by asking them to sacrifice everything. We can't go
further with them, they are definite, & the sacrifice of opening public schools to
sects is an enormous concession, but vague assurances as to teachers of new
schools being free from tests won't do. I think we shall break off negociations
and introduce one clause of McKenna's Bill dealing with single School areas to
which no guillotine motion need apply and get away middle of December.'
    Runciman is however going to give the Archbishop one more chance.
    I asked Asquith what about Licensing Bill. 'Oh they (Peers) will reject it.'
    I asked if we should fight Chelmsford, 'Oh yes if you can' – & I said I would
run Dence against Pretyman.

A.H. Dence had been defeated in Essex (Chelmsford) by Sir F. Carne Rasch
Bt in January 1906. His slogan: 'Don't be rash, Vote for Dence' was countered
by the successful Conservative's 'Don't be dense, Vote for Rasch.' (R.J.
Shoobridge to CH, 20 Jan. 1976). On 1 December 1908, at the by-election
following Rasch's retirement, E.G. Pretyman increased the Conservative share
of the poll by over ten per cent. Chelmsford was a safe Tory seat made even
safer by the presence of immigrant Presbyterian farmers from Ayrshire, and
some prominent Quaker Conservatives. The contest was embittered, leading to a
full day's work for magistrates dealing with summonses.

I told A. we had had an excellent meeting in Birmingham on Sat – creating a
Federation for the Midlands & he seemed pleased.[7]

---

[7] The executive committee of the new Midlands Liberal Federation met for the first
time on 18 March 1909.

Nov. 17 Runciman came in at 12.0 he told me that the Archbishop was in bed with neuritis – that he had given him at 5'oclock last night a draft of the Bill – a risky proceeding. He was going to see the new Archbishop of York[8] & the Bp of Southwark & give a definite reply by 2.0 today. He wanted to press the scheme of work to get the bill through as per the enclosed letter.

15 Great College Street,
Westminster
16 Nov. 1908

Confidential

My dear Jack,
    The Prime Minister & I have been considering the programme of the Education Bill. If we give 2 days to the 2nd. Reading discussion, (or what will be equivalent to the 2nd Reading discussion), of the amended bill, we shall have to follow with one day for a closure resolution, 6 days in committee, 2 for Report, 1 for 3rd Reading, making 12 days in all.
    If we start on the 24th. Nov: and work straight through that week sitting also on Saturday 28th. we would finish the committee stage on Thursday 3rd. Dec. On Monday 7th. & Tuesday 8th., we would take Report Stage, on Wednesday 9th. Third Reading, allowing the Lords to start with it on Thursday 10th. Dec. How would that do?
    Will you ring me up at the Education Office tomorrow forenoon & we can arrange a time to call on Asquith to talk this over?
    I presume you agree that the Non conformists say
1.   We cannot turn back now
2.   We must get through with it before they go back to their constituents
3.   They will spend *whatever time* is necessary to get the Bill before Xmas, rather than have no Bill at all.

Yours very sincerely
Walter Runciman

I told him I wanted the 24th for other business.
    We went in to see Asquith together & for 25 mins chatted over the pros & cons. Asquith just back from Windsor – he said the King will be angry if a settlement is not arrived at, but we all thought the Archbishop was too slimy to give satisfactory replies. If he gave them, we agreed for a cabinet to be called early Wednesday 11.0 before Guildhall luncheon to approve. If unsatisfactory negotiation would be broken off & each party would take its own course.
    The Archbishop pressed for teachers to teach any dogma – & all existing sub teachers if promoted to do same. Asquith says for 40 years, they are to dominate in schools over non-conformists, to give this would be to give way with the same result as Liberals gave way in 1874. I won't do it.

---

8   Cosmo Lang's appointment was announced on November 15 but he was not officially nominated until January 1 and not confirmed until 20 January 1909.

In 1874 the 1869 act appointing Endowed Schools Commissioners was due to expire. These commissioners had replaced the Charity Commissioners as inspectors of such schools. The aim of the act had been to include nonconformists. Lord Sandon proposed not only to abolish the Endowed Schools Commissioners but also to reverse the 1869 decision that the Church of England should not be solely responsible for such schools. The 1869 decision had meant that any foundation whose statutes pre-dated the Toleration Acts, was opened up to nonconformists. Lord Sandon's proposal caused a great political storm and in the end the Conservative government withdrew the latter part of the bill. But in return the Liberals had to accept the end of the Endowed Schools Commissioners.

Runciman & I agreed a new bill for a compromise was best, & we must strike whilst the iron was hot, and we could not postpone a bill to another session.

Asquith growling at Questions at Lloyd George's absences – Winston stuck up for him on my other side & said everyman must not be judged by same rules. At the Bd. of Trade the officials regarded him at first as impossible but came to regard him as having done more for their department at the finish than any other minister. I said Yes but he must do his own work even if it is in his own way & not give it to his colleagues.

Nov. 18   After calling at Privy Co. Office to inform FitzRoy I would affirm before the King on Saturday I called at Education. Had 5 minutes chat with Runciman, & went to No. 10 with him & Sir George Murray. Runciman told the latter he would want £150000 more for the Education Bill to secure settlement but it looked on paper like more. Murray thought a second bill necessary as settlement outside McKenna's bill – I said it was in my judgement possible to graft compromise on to the bill, but probably expedient to start de novo.

Runciman told me the Archbishop had accepted all clauses in draft bill except control & power for head teacher to teach dogma & new schools to be built wholly out of voluntary resources, the latter he asked in interests of R.C. who he thought he could speak for. The words of the letter from Archbp were, but these points I do not regard 'as insuperable'. Asquith had at interview with W.R. the night before dwelt on these & would press them in a letter. W.R. asked leave to think over (as I told him I think slowly) whether the latter could be left to Parliament to decide.

They met at 12.0. I went to Guildhall.

Nov. 19   After a cabinet, I went into Asquith's upstairs room to which he had bolted. He said we will introduce a new Bill & what am I to say about 2nd Reading. I said you can I think present the Bill tomorrow circulate it tomorrow night & read it a second time on Wednesday & Thursday & you had better go at once. I told him that the Housing Bill was our difficulty but it would be through by the end of next week. Masterman thought two days should suffice on Report, but Burns's methods would require 4 or 5.

I lunched with him, & after had a chat with Walter Runciman, A.H.D. Acland over the arrangement made by Southwark & the Archbishop.

The Bishop of Southwark, writing in the name of the Archbishop of Canterbury on November 18, had made an important concession expressly limiting the right of head teachers in transferred voluntary schools to give denominational instruction. Existing head teachers could give denominational instruction so long as they held their current appointments. If they held the head teachership of another voluntary school their right was limited to five years from the passing of the legislation. Negotiations had broken down over this issue in 1906; and a fortnight later the rest of the bishops repudiated this and several other elements of the Bishop of Southwark's proposed compromise arrangements. (Cd 4421, lxxxii, pp. 189 ff). Momentarily, however, it seemed as though a breakthrough had been achieved.

Nov. 20 A fine logical speech by Asquith opened the 3d. Reading on the Licensing Bill.

Just before 5.0 I told him Foot & Mouth had broken out in New York State & Carrington hesitated as to closing the ports of New York State. Asquith admitted at once, & agreed with me there was no case for hesitation & the ports should be scheduled. I told Strachey, & in 1/2 an hour cables were issued & instructions given. Bill carried by 350 – 113 amid much gratification by party.

Nov. 21 I went down to Windsor & kissed hands with the King – & affirmed as a P.C.[9]

Mon. Nov. 23 Called on Asquith at 12.45 with Runciman. We urged Asquith to be firm about Wednesday & Thursday being given this week for new Education Bill and we agreed that we must guillotine it if progress was to be secured.

The P.M. hesitated about rushing it, but opposition & criticism was we point out bound to develop on any compromise if not taken quickly, & the opposition would be unduly magnified.

---

[9] JAP kept for his scrapbook (Gainford MSS, 59, f. 17) not only the letters and the form of his affirmation but also the menu card for the seven course luncheon at Windsor, with the seating plan noted on the back. Herbert Samuel, a Jew, took the oath at the same ceremony. (FitzRoy, *Memoirs*, vol. I, pp. 366–7).

*The second reading of the Elementary Education (England and Wales) (No. 2)
Bill began on Wednesday November 25, as urged by JAP and Runciman. Debate
was curtailed, JAP's attempt to avoid a guillotine motion having been rebuffed
by Alick Hood. (Sandars to Balfour, 20 Nov. 1908, Balfour MSS, Add. MS
49765, f. 188). The bill had three main proposals: that rate-aided schools should
be controlled by the local education authority; that denominational teaching
should be paid for by the denominations; and that there should be no religious
test for teachers in the national system. It also proposed that in single school
areas the single school should be in the national system; compensation should be
paid for the transfers. It was hoped that local authorities would make every
reasonable effort to make time and room available so that the children of parents
who wanted them to receive some denominational teaching could do so.
Nonetheless children in the local authority schools not excused by their parents
were to receive 'simple Bible-teaching.' In his introduction to the second
reading Runciman emphasised that the bill was a victory for no sect and that it
was the result of compromise rather than of logic.*

I urged the P.M. to answer Macdonald's question in regard to his consistency
in stating Govmt naval policy was 10% more than 2 Power Standard, & his
previous view, that as stated in accordance with national interests. He wanted to
postpone it, to talk over wording of reply with McKenna. I pointed out any
postponement would be misconstrued so he agreed to say 'Both opinions were
identical in intention.'

*Asquith was correctly perceived by the radicals as having redefined the
formula ('the two-power standard') by which the necessary superiority in
battleships of the British navy was to be calculated. Murray Macdonald, the
pertinacious Liberal MP for Falkirk, sought clarification of precisely what the
government now intended. The wording of the Prime Minister's statement was
carefully considered.*

*JAP later corrected this entry, striking out the paraphrase 'both opinions
were identical in intention' and substituting Asquith's actual reply. JAP stated
that the words 'under existing conditions' in the reply were 'scratched through at
McKenna's insistence by Asquith' but they were in fact used by the Prime
Minister in the Commons. Macdonald's question was: '... whether, in recently
accepting the definition of the two-Power standard as meaning a preponderance
of 10 per cent over the combined strengths, in capital ships, of the two next
strongest Powers, he intended to extend the definition given by himself earlier in
the year to the effect that the standard we have to maintain is one which would
give us complete command of the sea against any reasonably possible
combination of Powers?' Asquith replied on November 23: 'The two statements
are, in my opinion, under existing conditions identical in meaning and effect.'
(PD, IV, cxcvii, 1768).*

I told him about little odds ends of business.

He pointed out Carrington thought Strachey was no help, he did not assuage hostility to his administration, he asked me who I could suggest. I told him Sir John Poynder might take the post. Strachey was a difficulty & had done well in the country.[10]

Tuesday 24 25 26   All these days I had chats with Asquith – he was obviously much worried over the Lords' action in kicking out the Licensing Bill, (which they agreed to do on the 23 at a party meeting at Lansdowne House)[11] and he was more distracted consequently than his wont, & anxious to meet the feeling of the House in regard to more time for a compromise arrangement. I kept sticking in to him, not to give way, & Runciman quietly took my view but not very strongly.

I feel a compromise, unless pressed through quickly here, will fall into one of the many pitfalls which await it from extremists who will set traps on both sides.

Not everyone was perturbed about losing the Licensing Bill. The leading London banker and Liberal MP Edward Holden had 'told the influential members of my Party that I would not go near the House of Commons while this Bill was before them as I hated the accursed thing'. (Holden to I.W. Bentley, 10 Nov. 1908, Midland Bank Archives, 292/47). On November 24 Ilbert congratulated Lloyd George on being given a free hand by the Lords to impose high licensing duties the following spring. The Chancellor said 'it was proposed to hold a thanksgiving service at the Treasury at 10 am next morning'. (Ilbert's diary, 24 Nov. 1908, Ilbert MSS, H.C. Lib. MS 72). George Riddell recorded that the service was scheduled for 10.30 am. (Riddell's diary, 24 Nov. 1908, McEwen, ed., The Riddell Diaries, p. 22).

Friday [Nov. 27]   Negociations not making progress for compromise – none coming from Opposition leaders – Sydney Buxton & Churchill trying to get Asquith to give away the bill, he declined to throw over the principles of bill, when no satisfactory deal possible.

Monday [Nov. 30]   Lunched with A & Mrs Asquith & F. Thomas's at Liberal League Club with [?J ?M. ?P.][12] but no politics discussed. Mrs Asquith told me how a woman with a tiara &c on spat in her face as she walked up the Guildhall

---

10   Strachey remained at the Board of Agriculture until 1911.
11   The vast majority of the 240 or more Unionist peers who met at Lansdowne House on November 24 (not 23) voted to reject the Licensing Bill.
12   JAP's host at this luncheon – probably J.M. Paulton – is identified by three indistinct initials.

with Asquith on Nov. 9 – that she told the Lord Mayor[13] who ordered the woman & her husband to sit at the door nearest the entrance hall, so that they could be easily removed, if they created a scene, or interrupted A's speech.

Tuesday December 1 Asquith on the Bench asked me if I had anything to say to him. I told him Whitley could not conscientiously support the Education compromise & had written his resignation. I thought he was over-worked & needed a holiday – as the reason was not sufficient to take such a course. Asquith had deputations from London M.P.s & Small Holders & then saw Whitley himself.

Tuesday to Tuesday. Dec. 1–8 Saw the slaughter of the Education Bill. The P.M. much concerned I had pressed the bill forward to save it, but with the clergy meeting on the Thursday the P.M. said he could not go on with the contracting out debate, & we had to hurriedly get the Port of London bill on for Friday, after wasting time on small bills on the Thursday.

Friday's cabinet in Asquith's room H. of C. I was sent for – came in at 11.45 Asquith flushed but deliberate found all ministers in agreement the Bill was not to be proceeded with, & withdrawn on Monday. I said it would lead to talk not proceeding with it at 12.00 & if he liked I could arrange for statement, on a motion for adjournment, he said he preferred to wait until Monday & he merely intimated the bill could be withdrawn.

The Education Bill had foundered amid a morass of argument about the arrangements for transfer and contracting out, and a cluster of eleventh hour demands emanating from the Representative Church Council on December 3. Runciman's heavily amended draft letter to the Archbishop of Canterbury signalling the end of negotiations on December 4 is in the Lewis Harcourt papers (Harcourt MSS 440, ff. 151–5). The government's correspondence with the Archbishop was published on December 5. The President of the Board of Education wrote to Asquith on the 6th:

> Now that my efforts have ended in a complete failure I feel that I am to some extent to blame for having laid the Government open to receive a serious blow to its prestige & power.
> Had we succeeded all would have been well, but I fear I was over bold, & the breakdown is I feel much more than a personal matter. Your administration does suffer because I have not succeeded, & as the strength of the Government is of the first importance I feel that I ought to place myself unreservedly in your hands.

---

13 Sir George Wyatt Truscott (1857–1941); printer; succ. his father (Ld Mayor of London 1879–80) as alderman, Dowgate Ward 1895–1941; Lord Mayor, London 1908–9; Kt 1902; Sheriff, London 1902–3; Bt 1909.

Asquith immediately refused Runciman's resignation: 'For the moment I have only to say that you have had my entire sympathy and approval in every step you have taken, and that there is none of my colleagues who stands at this moment higher in my estimation and regard.' (Runciman MSS).

Monday, Dec. 7 I could not see the great man until questions. He was at G Lambton's wedding.[14] At Questions he was flushed, but even there ready to hear anything I had to say on procedure.[15] He had his speech on the funeral of the Bill carefully written out in pencil. He commenced by reading it, but the best part was his tribute to Runciman's effort for peace – he read his peroration as to better to attempt & fail than to be frightened of failure & not make the attempt.

Tuesday December 8 He was having his picture painted until 1.00.[16] I got a good half hour with him discussing public attitude in regard to dissolution. I told him the party was against it, but wanted something said to show we were not taking the Lords rebuff to the Commons lying down. He said 'This is the biggest rebuff the Lords have ever given the Commons & with least justification, & in the face too of enormous majorities. The man in the street does not regard the Licensing Bill as a popular measure but the bill was gaining adherents & the moral forces were all in its favour. I will of course on Friday say something as to our attitude, & the dinner comes to me as very opportune.'[17]

We talked about Elibank & Sinclair each thinking they both knew Scottish feeling the best, about Sinclair & T. Shaw – the latter's jealousy & the other's desire to get to the H of Lords to look after Scotch interests there. He wanted a lead as to whether he should give a Peerage to Sinclair – as a minister it could be given at any time. I said it was a difficult matter & just one of those that was a real petty one in in itself. The thing would be publicly ridiculed: Yes said

---

14   Hon. George Lambton (1860–1945); 5th son of 2nd Earl of Durham; noted horsetrainer; m. Cicely Margaret Horner, elder sister of the Asquiths' daughter-in-law Katherine.

15   Because the committee stage had begun, the only way to kill the Education Bill without stifling all speakers other than the Prime Minister was to move that the chairman leave the chair. Alfred Emmott's diary (8 December 1908; Emmott MSS, ff. 117–18) explains the complications.

16   Asquith, standing in the robes of the First Lord of the Treasury, was being painted by Solomon J. Solomon, R.A. The portrait was presented to the National Liberal Club in December 1909, after being exhibited at the Royal Academy where a 'Votes for Women' poster was stuck to its protective glass. (*The Times*, 8 June 1909).

17   A dinner was to be given to Asquith by Liberal MPs at the National Liberal Club on Friday, December 11, in recognition of the manner in which he had conducted the Licensing Bill through the Commons.

Asquith, at Court he is regarded as C.B.'s natural son & to be promoted will really cause ridicule.[18] He said well think it over, we need not decide today. He deprecated my saying anything to Elibank.

We discussed what would happen if the Lords threw out the budget. He said Keep it at the back of your mind that we may have a dissolution in July if they do so. I pointed out that McKenna thought, no pay to forces & civil service would bring the Lords to their knees. Well it's possible we may be forced, but we shall have £2,000,000 more in hand owing to the Education Bill not going through.

We discussed the Housing bill, its chances & how the Lords would reject it if sent up, owing to insufficient time. I said we must not have another rebuff. The bill was badly drafted. I undertook to make out a statement for him for cabinet on the morrow.

He sent for me at 5.0 to see Sir C. Schwann & others as to a meeting in Manchester in Jany – he demurred, & did not commit himself, but left it to me to decide later.

December 9, 1908   Saw the P.M. after Cabinet. He told me it was arranged to postpone Housing Bill, & to press it through its 2d. Rdg & Comtee rapidly after our return next session. That my draft for his speech was in order as to business to be passed & dropped. Some 20 bills to be pressed & some 10 to be dropped.

He made a very clear exposition as usual, & we got the rule suspended by about 5 o'clock, Eight hours Bill afterwards Port of London Bill at 11.0.

I sent him brief for discussing Bills at Cabinet & for statement in House moving suspension 11 'clk rule.

Thurs. 10 Dec.   After addressing 320 Liberal agents I told Asquith on the Bench that the agents did not want an election now, but had cheered to the echo the statement that I expected the House of Lords would be our issue before the country. Asquith says it is a little nonconsequential!

*A luncheon at the Hotel Metropole was given for the Liberal agents who were conferring in London. JAP was reported to have told the agents that although no-one knew when the election would come, they should keep their powder dry. He added that the election would be fought on the House of Lords and Free Trade. (*The Times, *12 Dec. 1908). Two days later* The Times *published an angry denial by JAP. The luncheon had been a private occasion, with no reporters present. No report had been authorised and the account in* The Times *was inaccurate. The Cabinet had in fact decided on December 9 against an*

---

18   We have been unable to discover any further evidence about this rumour. Sinclair, who had been born in the same year Campbell-Bannerman married, had been C-B's assistant private secretary in the 1890's and a close friendship had culminated in his appointment as C-B's executor.

immediate dissolution, 'at least not before the Budget is over. Cabinet meeting today unanimously agree in favour of putting the Budget through all its stages in the House. The Prime Minister has approved of my plans as they are now.' (Lloyd George to William George, 9 Dec. 1908, William George, My Brother and I, *p. 222).*

I wonder what he will say himself tomorrow when the Party dine him at the Nat–Lib Club! After much diplomatic I made arrangements with Balfour & Hood about business remaining stages of 8 hours Bill. Asquith said it has taken as much negotiating as the Education Bill. I said yes but more successful I hope.

The Miners' Eight Hours Bill achieved its second reading in the Lords on December 15, thereby missing an even greater success. A number of 'backwoods' peers, stirred by Lord Newton's pro forma *rejection motion, had to be dissuaded by Newton from supporting him so as to avoid giving the Liberals and the trade union movement an election issue. (Lord Newton,* Retrospection, John Murray, *1941, pp. 164–5).*

Friday [11 Dec.] Did not see Asquith all day, until after his big speech to 200 of his followers at the National Liberal Club. His speech gave general satisfaction.

To the surprise of John Ellis, who proposed the toast to the Prime Minister, Asquith's speech was 'fully typewritten'. (Ellis's diary, 11 Dec. 1908, Arthur Tilney Bassett, The Life of the Rt. Hon. John Edward Ellis MP, *Macmillan, 1914, p. 249). The Liberal government had fought the 1906 election on Education and Licence Reform, Asquith averred, and it had obtained a clear mandate for its actions. Despite this and support from widely divergent interests the Licensing bill had been defeated by the Lansdowne House Caucus. Asquith went on to invite the party 'to treat the veto of the House of Lords as the dominating issue in politics ...', alluding to the 'great potency and ... great flexibility' of finance as a 'partial solvent' to Lords' obstruction. (Murray,* The People's Budget, *p. 115). 'In the course of the evening,' the Clerk of the House of Commons recorded, 'I had a private talk with Lloyd George about the arrangements for next year's budget which will be a big & contentious measure & will swallow up everything else. The question is whether it can be got through without some form of closure by compartments a procedure which has never yet been applied to Budget Bills.' (Ilbert's diary, 11 Dec. 1908, Ilbert MSS, H.C. Lib. MS 72).*

Monday Dec. 14 Alluding to his speech he asked how it had been received & said it was difficult to steer through the traffic. He asked me whether the party wanted many measures next session. I said NO but each man wanted his own hobby. Yes I see that by the numerous deputations who come to see me. I talked to him about business & moving the suspension of the 9.30 rule for Private Bills.

At 3.00 I told him the adjournment was going to be moved by MacNeill on the statement on Indian [policy] being made in the H of Lords. We arranged that a statement should be made here also, & avoided the adjournment.

J.G. Swift MacNeill and others had already (December 7 and earlier) objected that the government's statement would be made in the House of Lords which was not 'the proper medium for the introduction of legislation' particularly 'having regard to the present relations between the Houses of Parliament'. MacNeill had asked that the papers be presented to the House of Commons first. The statement had been promised 'on or about' December 14; it was given on December 17 because of Morley's indisposition. On December 14 MacNeill was one of several MPs who protested that the Commons should receive the statement and papers before the House of Lords. The statement concerned the government's proposals for administrative reform in India. These included the enlargement of the provincial legislative councils and the extension of their powers to include the discussion of public matters. It was also proposed to introduce greater elected representation of the different communities; to end the 'official majority' whereby Governors had controlled their legislative councils, except in the Viceroy's Legislative Council; to create Executive Councils to advise Lieutenant-Governors; and to advise the appointment of an Indian when the next vacancy occurred in the Viceroy's Legislative Council. Morley emphasised that these reforms (leading to a greater involvement of Indians) were not in response to recent political violence.

Tuesday Dec. 15   Morley wrote Asquith, an astonishing document, resigning because the latter had promised the H. of C. a statement would be made by Buchanan in the House same day as Morley made his in the Lords, & Morley thought his would be anticipated by half an hour.

However I got Crewe to see Lansdowne & he said he would agree to the Lords meeting on the Thursday at 3.30.

When Asquith told me about the resignation I said he is such a child. NO said Asquith he is [a] regular old woman.[19]

---

[19]   Asquith was later to recall that 'Morley had a rather awkward habit of hasty resignation'. (The Earl of Oxford and Asquith, *Fifty Years of Parliament*, 2 vols, Cassell, 1926, Vol. Two, p. 108). 'You seem to be worried today, Lord Morley,' Lloyd George once remarked. 'You will find that the things that upset you most are the trifles,' Morley replied. 'At the present moment I am worrying as to whether I shall accept a dinner invitation.' (Frances Stevenson's diary, 25 Mar. 1934, A.J.P. Taylor, ed., *Lloyd George*: A Diary by Frances Stevenson, Hutchinson, 1971, p. 263).

However the statement on Indian Policy went off in both Houses without trouble. Lord MacDonnell explained the trouble in India was due to Indian division of Bengal.[20]

Thursday Dec. 17   Asquith told me all about Morley, & we merely discussed the winding up of business, & bills to complete.

Elsie & I dined with him & played bridge for a couple of hours with Lady Crewe, Montagu & himself – sat by Mrs Birrell & Mrs Raymond Asquith.

Monday Dec. 21   Saw Asquith at 12.30 & stayed with him an hour. He walked up & down his room, discussed future alterations in personnel of government, Sinclair's ambition to go to H of Lords & relieve the situation at Scotch Office. Never was a minister more painstaking obstinate & less brilliant was his criticism. He quoted the retiring Scotch Perm. Sec. to same effect Macleod & the latter's opinion of the Lord Advocate as being shifty & sharp.

Haldane was sent for & I talked over with them both, Jack Tennant being made under Sec. Board of Trade, Rogers or Poynder at Board of Agriculture, Strachey a Peer, Kemp a baronet.

Asquith's low opinion of Sinclair was expressed more picturesquely to Charles Hobhouse: the Scottish Secretary had 'the brains of a rabbit and the temper of a pig'. (Hobhouse's diary, 3 Aug. 1909, David, ed., Inside Asquith's Cabinet, *pp. 79-80). Sinclair had tried to get both radical small landholding and valuation legislation through the Lords. Asquith dropped the small holding measure but the popular valuation provisions – the precursor of land taxation – were incorporated in the budget for 1909. Ironically it was the alleged need for the Scottish Secretary to be in the Commons that eventually gave Asquith the reason to ask Lord Pentland, as Sinclair became in 1909, to resign in 1912. (Michael Fry,* Patronage and Principle: A Political History of Modern Scotland, *Aberdeen University Press, Aberdeen, 1987, p. 129).*

Tennant, the Prime Minister's brother-in-law, was appointed Under Secretary at the Board of Trade 10 January 1909, Churchill acquiescing with good grace

---

[20]   MacDonnell actually said that, of the areas in which the Lieutenant-Governors were to get councils, Bengal as it then stood was unfit though 'Bengal proper' was very fitted for such a council. He described the division of Bengal in 1905 as 'the greatest blunder' for which everyone concerned denied responsibility. It had in fact been recommended by local officials on purely administrative grounds: they argued that the population of Bengal was too large for a single governor and that the division would cause no difference to the inhabitants since it merely created two administrative areas, the same laws and administrative system being applied in each. Nonetheless the inhabitants did object, and eventually resorted to violence.

when Asquith's intention was revealed to him after Christmas. (Churchill, Winston S. Churchill, vol. II, Companion Part 2, p. 861–2). Neither Francis Rogers (who was unsympathetic to Liberal land policy and voted against the government on rating reform on 25 February 1909) nor Poynder went to the Board of Agriculture. Strachey continued as the Board's spokesman and was appointed Parliamentary Secretary in December 1909. He got his peerage in 1911, having antagonised his ministerial chief and Board of Agriculture officials so much that Lord Carrington had 'written to the P.M. telling him I must get rid of Strachey'. (Carrington to Sir T. Elliott, 22 Sept. 1910, Elliott MSS). George Kemp, a former Unionist free trader, was knighted in 1909; unhappy with disestablishment, Lloyd George's financial policy, and especially Home Rule, he retired from the Commons in 1912, becoming Baron Rochdale in 1913.

Prorogation – winter plans – he asked me to come up & see him at Archerfield for a Sunday, before the recess was over.

Chapter 5

Budget Management

Archerfield, an estate leased for shooting by Margot Asquith's brother, Frank Tennant, was close to five golf courses. The Asquiths often spent September and Christmas there, inviting friends to join them for a few days. The Prime Minister's pre-Christmas vexation with John Sinclair was not abated by a visit from the Scottish Secretary. 'I trust that Sinclair made it clear to you,' he wrote to the Lord Advocate, Thomas Shaw, 'that I am in no way committed, to any of his proposed changes in the Land Bill.' Asquith had been told that Shaw and Sinclair had reached agreement on the conduct of Scottish business, in the two Houses. 'I am heartily glad if this is so.' (Asquith to Shaw, 9 Jan. 1909, Craigmyle MSS). Sinclair was about to be moved to the Lords. In his letter to Lord Knollys asking for the King's approval for Sinclair's peerage, Asquith explained that there were three Scottish ministers in the Commons and none of any standing in the Lords. He added: 'Between ourselves, I think it is in the interest of the Government & of public business: for Shaw is by a good deal a stronger man than his official chief, while Sinclair (who is painstaking) will at any rate be able to speak with first-hand knowledge in the Upper House.' (Asquith to Knollys, 16 Jan. 1909, RA R29/74).

This carefully contrived separation of two troublesome Scots was upset by the sudden death at Cap Martin on February 1 of Lord Robertson, a Lord of Appeal, and former Scottish Solicitor-General and Lord Advocate. Thomas Shaw, an old friend and confidant of Campbell-Bannerman, had held the same succession of offices as Robertson and was keen to have the vacant Lordship of Appeal. Unfortunately, the Lords of Appeal in ordinary received only life peerages. Shaw, as JAP was to learn, tried in vain to persuade Asquith to give him a hereditary title.

16 January 1909   Asquith wired me about the 9th to come for Sunday the 17th. I travelled through the night of the 15th from King's X to Edinburgh, saw Wood[1] of Scotch Liberal Assoc. at breakfast about the Forfarshire vacancy,[2] and reached Archerfield by 11.00 in a furious gale of wind.

---

1   A.D. Wood (–); joint sec. Scottish Lib. Assoc., 1904–1913, responsible for eastern Scotland; sec. Midlothian Lib. Assoc. in 1897–1903; sec. General Bd of Control for Scotland 1913–c. 1930.

2   Forfarshire was Sinclair's seat, vacated by his elevation to the peerage. The by-election was held on February 27. J. Falconer (Lib.) polled 6,422 votes; R.L. Blackburn KC (Con.) 3,970.

Asquith told me Sinclair had bothered him. Otherwise he had a pleasant time, lovely weather, and been out golfing most days. He, Margot, Herbert and Dolly Gladstone alone there – our conversation was general.

Asquith at dinner interesting on Parnell Trial reminiscences: a stupid man with bright flashes. For instance, when Asquith supported Tim Healy as Irish counsel vice Tim Harrington, Parnell said No Healy won't do he has left too much wool on the fence! As an indication of stupidity, he alluded to his telling Webster in cross examination that he had wilfully deceived the House on one occasion. Asquith said the deception was trivial and not worth any such admission, and he told Parnell in consultation immediately afterward, that although the bowling had been wide, he had hit his own wicket – Parnell as a cricketer appreciated the metaphor, but had not realised what he had said at the time.[3]

We played a good deal of bridge after dinner and I had on Monday 18 a good game of golf with the P.M. giving him a stroke and winning by 2 and one.

Asquith explained his views of his law officers. Robson takes legal points, side issues, is lengthy and disappointing in consultation, he should be offered the judgeship (Barnes about to resign) but he did not expect Robson's acceptance. The Lord Ch. had no intention of tempting the Solicitor General. Rufus Isaacs would be offered a vacancy but he thought Simon had done the better of the two in the chipping in at debates, but neither had been able to give time to parliamentary work.

The opportunity to re-assign the government's front-bench lawyers arose from the impending resignation of Sir Gorell Barnes as President of the Probate, Divorce and Admiralty Division. Barnes had been prevailed upon by the Lord Chancellor to accept a peerage and assist with the legal work of the House of Lords and Privy Council. Lord Gorell, as he became, was thereby denied the chance of becoming a Lord of Appeal (with a salary of £6000 a year) although he undertook the same duties on a pension of £3500. (Lord Gorell, One Man ... Many Parts, *Odhams, 1956, pp. 154–5). As Asquith expected, Robson was not tempted by the inducement of elevation to the Lords. (Rowland Whitehead's diary, 26 Feb. 1909, Whitehead MSS, HLRO Hist. Coll. 211). For want of a suitable Liberal the Presidency went to Sir J.C. Bigham, a Liberal Unionist. Bigham retired a year later, ostensibly on health grounds, and the Solicitor-General, Sir Sam Evans, took his place. Isaacs succeeded Evans in October 1910. Robson, his own health broken after bearing much of the brunt of*

---

3   During the special commission of inquiry into *The Times* allegations about 'Parnellism and Crime' in 1888, Parnell admitted under questioning by the Attorney-General, Sir Richard Webster, representing *The Times*, that he had misled the House in 1881 over the continued existence of Fenian secret societies. Parnell had captained a cricket team in Wicklow in the 1870's. Webster was president, Surrey C.C.

defending the 1909 Budget in the House of Commons, became a Lord of Appeal. Isaacs then became Attorney-General, Simon succeeding him as Solicitor-General.

We discussed Gladstone's qualities, which were not appreciated, and certain scandals. Mrs Henry and the King already trying to spoke the wheel of my 'Lady'.

The sovereign's displeasure with Julia Henry had been conveyed to Vaughan Nash by Lord Knollys on 21 December 1908. 'The King has heard a story that the husband of the lady about whom there has been much gossip in connection with Mr L. George, would be if necessary recommended for a knighthood.' If such an honour had been contemplated, the possibility was extinguished by Knollys' next paragraph. 'He too had heard the same story but had told his informant he did not believe it. It was not I who told it to the King, & I have even forgotten the husband's name.' (Asquith MSS, vol. 1, f. 112). Charles Henry got his baronetcy in 1911.

January 22 Went abroad.

February 11 Saw P.M. who told me of his troubles which he took as coolly as ever. Shaw had given him a bad time insisting upon his elevation to High Position in the Lords, to succeed Robertson. The Cabinet had had differences re Navy.

February 15 P.M. explained differences due not to money or policy, but as to whether the 6 new Dreadnoughts should be in estimates, and then 2 withdrawn if other nations did not proceed with their programmes; or whether we should have 4, and undertake other 2 if nations proceed.

I reported gossip about Ll. George's morals, and men being abroad to defame him, and feared actions were pending, and possibly blackmail being levied, position was making things unpleasant, information was being circulated in various quarters.

JAP may not have been aware of the fanciful rumour, recorded on the same day by the Conservative whip, Lord Balcarres, that Margot Asquith's absence abroad at the beginning of the parliamentary session was a sign of 'her frank annoyance with dear Henry for his marked attentions to Miss Maud Allan.' (Vincent, ed., The Crawford Diaries, *p. 121). The Prime Minister's wife had taken a rest cure in Switzerland supplemented, as Asquith told Dorothy Beresford on March 7, by '10 days of movement – seeing people, ordering dresses, going to plays, & so on – in Paris.' (Kidd MSS). The Chancellor of the Exchequer, meanwhile, had real troubles. In January 1909 the Conservative newspaper* The People *published articles implying that Lloyd George (who was not actually named) was about to be cited as co-respondent in a divorce case and that he had paid £20,000 to keep his name out of the case. Less detailed hints of a similar nature had been published in July 1908 in* The Bystander. *That magazine had been forced to apologise and pay 300 guineas in damages. But the story had been magnified in colonial newspapers before being resurrected in* The People. *Lloyd George had taken legal action against the Johannesburg* Mail *whose report that he was in the divorce court was allegedly based on information from the High Commissioner, Lord Selborne. (Sir J. West Ridgeway to Sir Francis Hopwood, 26 Dec. 1908; Lord Crewe to Hopwood, 30 Dec. 1908, Southborough MSS). But rumours were rife in London in February 1909. 'The most common,' Herbert Lewis told Lloyd George on February 27, 'was that his colleagues in the Cabinet had subscribed to buy silence & settle a case out of court. Why, he said, not one of them has sd a single word to me on the subject.' (Lewis's memo. 27/28 Feb. 1909, Lewis MSS, 1963, 3. 19). On March 12, before Mr Justice Lawrence, Sir Edward Carson on behalf of the proprietors of* The People *admitted and apologised unreservedly for the libel they had published. Lloyd George was given the opportunity by his counsel Rufus Isaacs to deny under oath that there was any foundation for* The People*'s story. Accepting £1000, which his solicitors would pass to a charity, Lloyd George indicated through counsel that if there were any repetition of the libel he would pursue the matter to 'the bitter end and would accept no apology'. Letters in the possession of the Lloyd George family point to two possible but unlikely sources of gossip (John Grigg,* Lloyd George: The People's Champion 1902–1911, *Eyre Methuen 1978, pp. 181–9). Bentley Gilbert (David Lloyd George, p. 376) asserts that the £20,000 hush money was not mentioned by* The People *'nor in the trial'. There was no 'trial', and the sum was specifically quoted from an article 'The Price of Peace' by Isaacs in his statement to the court.*

Eight months later Lucy Masterman wrote of a meeting with 'the redoubtable Mrs Henry, with whom rumour at one time linked George's name in connection with the divorce court.' The inherent improbability of Lloyd George offering the millionaire Charles Henry £20,000 apparently did not occur to Mrs Masterman. But she had another good reason to suppose the rumoured association with Lloyd George was baseless. 'She is a large, fat, hirsute Jewess, and the most assiduous climber I have ever came across' who obviously bored Lloyd George. (Lucy Masterman's diary, 1 Dec. 1909, Masterman MSS, B2/2). It is difficult to recognise Lucy Masterman's Julia Henry as the 'dark, tall and very attractive' woman described by Lloyd George's son Richard as 'Lady J., married to an Australian mine owner'. (Earl Lloyd George, Lloyd George, *Frederick Muller, 1960, p. 107). Apart from Julia Henry, the woman whose name was most frequently linked with Lloyd George at this time was Edna May, the retired musical comedy star. Edna May had married Oscar Lewisohn, Julia Henry's brother, in 1907. Stories linking her with Lloyd George recurred as late as*

January 1914. (Lloyd George to Sir Edward Russell, 27 Jan. 1914, Lloyd George MSS, C/7/6/7). On his first appearance in the House after the libel action was settled 'Lloyd George was loudly cheered when he rose to answer a question.' (Ilbert's diary, 16 Mar. 1909, Ilbert MSS, H.C. Lib. MS 72).

February 24   Had 20 minutes chat with P. Minister in his room re Irish debate urging him to wind up. He went into House at 7.00 not having anything in his mind, he made in 10 minutes at the end an epoch speech, touching the real cure for Irish evils, and everything he said was approved. It may secure the Irish vote at Glasgow – the spirit was approved by Nationalists.

Asquith was speaking in the debate on the address to the King. An amendment by Earl Percy proposed to add that the government was totally ineffectual in Ireland and was taking no steps to restore its authority. Balfour had called for a new Crimes Act but Asquith refused, saying that they had never worked. Asquith went on to point out that Balfour himself had been most reluctant to resort to the Crimes Act in 1900 when conditions in Ireland were worse. He concluded by saying that agrarian and political discontent were inextricably intertwined in Ireland and observance of the law could not be obtained till the people were associated with it. A by-election was due on March 2 for Glasgow (Central) following the death of Sir Andrew Torrance, Liberal MP since 1906. The Liberal candidate was T. Gibson Bowles, a former Unionist free trader; the Conservative Charles Scott Dickson KC, who had been nursing the seat for some years. The Liberals tried to concentrate on fiscal issues (the constituency, held by the Tories 1886–1906, included Glasgow's business district) but the Conservatives successfully raised the Irish problem. The Conservative Chief Whip 'apparently had some fear of Scott Dickson wobbling' over tariff reform but steadied him with a warning letter. (A. Chamberlain to Mary Chamberlain, 16 Feb. 1909, Politics From Inside, p. 142). Bowles tried to win free trade Conservative votes by qualifying his support for Home Rule, favouring it only within a United Kingdom framework. The United Irish League did not give Bowles their support until February 27. There were about 2000 Irish in the district. He lost by 2113 votes; 'the Irish injured me, the Unemployed deserted to the enemy & (biggest & worst defection of all) the determining Elector, the business man who last time voted against Balfour & Protection, this time voted against the Gov. & the Budget ...' (T. Gibson Bowles to L. Harcourt, 6 Mar. 1909, Harcourt MSS, dep. 441, f. 26).

At the meeting with me he told me how the Cabinet differences on the Navy had been settled. McKenna made the suggestion after 2 hours and half's discussion, and all concur and are happy. He thought when he got up that morning, all would be up. I told him I had a better opinion of his guidance – and knew he would pull through the difficult situation.

McKenna's suggestion was presumably the 'sudden curve' which Asquith told his wife on February 25, 'developed itself'. (J.A. Spender and Cyril Asquith, Life of Herbert Henry Asquith, *Lord Oxford and Asquith, 2 vols, Hutchinson, 1932, vol. 1, p. 254). Convinced by Asquith's news, JAP informed reporters at the first annual meeting of the Midlands Liberal Federation on February 28 that ministers were in 'perfect agreement upon their policy with regard to the Navy, and to the expenditure to be incurred upon it in the coming year'. (*The Daily News, *1 March 1909). But the rejoicings over the naval estimates had been premature. In the days following the emergence of the sudden curve Asquith was assailed from several directions as McKenna, the Sea Lords, and their opponents sought to interpret the 'concordat' formulated by the Prime Minister. The King had been advised on February 24 of a four point agreement: '(1) 4 new Dreadnoughts to be in any event laid down in the ensuing financial years (2) an Act of Parliament to be passed this Session providing for a programme of naval construction so calculated as to keep us always ahead of the German programme (3) power to be given in the Act to make forward contracts for the ships of next year – so that the government will be able (if so advised) next autumn, to place orders for 4 additional Dreadnoughts, to be laid down not later than 1st April 1910.' (Asquith MSS, 5, ff. 86–7).*

A week of wrangling followed until revelations about German dreadnought construction and gun production conveyed by an Argentine naval mission to Admiral Fisher on March 2 made the Admiralty case for more certainty about the second four ships irresistible. The Cabinet agreed to make provision for eight dreadnoughts, four of which were to be approved for construction only if the international situation warranted it later in the year. McKenna soon made it clear that he regarded this qualification as merely a formality. Lloyd George and Churchill were chagrined to find themselves outmanoeuvred. (Peter Rowland, Lloyd George, *Barrie & Jenkins, 1975, p. 214; Arthur J. Marder,* From the Dreadnought to Scapa Flow: The Royal Navy in the Fisher Era 1904–1914, Vol. I, The Road to War, 1904–1914, *Oxford University Press, 1961, pp. 162–3; Hedley Paul Wilmott,* The Navy Estimates 1906–1909, *unpublished dissertation, University of Liverpool, 1970, pp. 193–216); their policy objections had been substantial and serious not merely,* pace John Tetsuro Sumida, *'contrived ... to discredit' the First Lord or 'placate back-bench Radicals'. (*In Defence of Naval Supremacy: Finance, Technology and British Naval Policy, 1889-1914, *Unwin Hyman, Boston, 1989, pp. 188, 266). McKenna announced to the House of Commons on 26 July 1909 that the second four dreadnoughts would be laid down by April 1910. Doubt persisted publicly until March 1910 about whether the additional ships were part of the 1909 programme. The Cabinet had by then* *decided to lay down five more ships, bringing the total for 1909–10 to thirteen. (Asquith's Cabinet letter to the King, 17 Feb. 1910, Cab. 41/32/4; A.J. Dorey,* Radical Liberal Criticism of British Foreign Policy 1906–1914, *D.Phil. thesis, University of Oxford, 1964, pp. 162–70).*

Two deputations – [Feb.] 24 and 26 – on reduction of armaments. I pointed out, we had no time to devote to subject of armaments as a whole, that each service could be considered on its merits, and I believed would be approved by the Party and I wrote them letters subsequently authorised and approved by the P.M.

*Provoked by a reference in the King's Speech to the increased cost of armaments, the Reduction of Armaments Committee of backbenchers had hoped to obtain precedence for an amendment to the Address regretting the foreshadowed increased outlay on naval armaments. JAP granted them as an alternative an opportunity to move their motion when the House went into committee of supply on the naval estimates. Criticism of army expenditure was to be confined to debate on a resolution relating to the social conditions of private soldiers. (*The Times, *19, 27 Feb. 1909). The National Liberal Federation executive, captured by radicals, continued to press the case against increased naval expenditure. W.P. Byles proclaimed that the Federation would not allow itself to become a wing of the Whips' room. (A.J. Anthony Morris,* Radicalism Against War, 1906–1914: *The Advocacy of Peace and Retrenchment, Longman, 1972, p. 155).*

March 4 Fine peroration by Haldane introducing Army Estimates, in which he dwelt on national advantages by voluntary army as compared to conscription.

*Haldane, of course, did not please everyone. J. St. Loe Strachey (*A New Way of Life, *Macmillan, 1909, p. 67) saw the estimates debate as illustrating the 'absurdities, injustices, and inconveniences caused by this system of conspiring to cajole, or even sometimes to compel, as contrasted with a fair and democratic system of making all share in the performance of a duty which gives security, and therefore is of benefit, to all …'. Haldane's speech had the merit of conformity with Liberal opinion. Montagu had commented to Asquith on February 12 on Haldane's 'everlasting speeches in some of which he finds conscription a debateable question, compulsory military service almost a possible alternative, and such is the state of political excitement, nobody seems to notice it.' (copy, Montagu MSS, Box 1, AS1/1/14).*

Fri. March 5 The prospect of securing the circulation of Navy Estimates before the debate, owing to the delay occasioned by Cabinet differences, compelled

Asquith to ask my presence at the Cabinet this day. I pointed out that the guiding dates were March 22 for Ways and Means resolution if the royal assent to the consolidated fund bill was secured by March 30 – the usual day.[4] Navy Estimates must, therefore, be through on the previous week, and to circulate the estimates on Sat the 13th and take them on the 15th was open to severe criticism.

The Cabinet after discussion agreed to defer their consideration to the 16th – royal assent to be deferred to the 31st, and to circulate statement by Thursday the 11th, the printing of the estimates to be expedited if possible, so as to be in MPs' hands on Sat morning the 13th. All ministers were present but the Lord Chancellor, Lloyd George & Winston doing the talking, McKenna & Haldane making suggestions.

After consultation with authorities in the House, Whitley, & taking Acland Hood into my confidence, I went over at 4.20 to No. 10 Downing Street, and walked straight up to Asquith & told him that I suggested we should not propose the suspension of the 11.00 rule to the end of the month as a debatable motion, but try and secure our money by daily suspensions as necessity required, & give an extra half day to Army Estimates. He agreed, & I mapped out course of business to March 31 on those lines.

Daylight Saving Bill under discussion this day, viz. to alter clocks an hour twice a year to secure health and light – it was suggested that another bill should be introduced to set the thermometer up 10° in winter and 10° in summer![5]

In introducing the naval estimates on March 16, McKenna defended them in terms designed to subdue the government's radical critics. The Conservatives, however, launched a powerful attack questioning the adequacy of the proposed naval construction programme. In his diary on March 17, W.G.G. Leveson-Gower, a House of Commons clerk, summarised: 'An enormous sensation was caused by the debate on Naval Estimates last night, the net result of which seems to be that the Two Power standard is a thing of the past, that Dreadnoughts only

---

4   Normal financial procedures required the passing, before the end of March, of supplementary estimates and excess votes, a vote on account for the civil service and revenue departments, money votes for the the army and navy, and a consolidated fund act to make good the supply granted. Royal assent was needed before payments could be made; and, as the Bank of Ireland was closed on March 31, it was customary to try to complete all these steps a few days before March 30. (Henry Higgs, *The Financial System of the United Kingdom*, Macmillan, 1914, pp. 26–31).

5   Advocates of daylight saving pointed out that it would give more time for outdoor recreation and facilitate Territorial Army training. MPs representing the interests of agricultural labour were opposed but Labour MPs were divided. The bill was referred to a select committee which reported against any legislation 'in view of the diversity of opinion'.

count & that in 3 years we may not have a preponderance of them.' (Leveson-Gower MSS, HLRO Hist. Coll. 123). 'The P.M.'s revelations about the German ship-building have scattered the "Little Navy" people like sheep.' (Leif Jones to Lady Carlisle, 16 Mar. 1909, Lady Carlisle MSS, J 23/100). Two leading radicals, J.A. Murray Macdonald and J.A. Baker, had been away ill but A.G.C. Harvey did not proceed with a critical amendment he had put down. With J.E. Ellis and Sir John Brunner Bt declining to attend a meeting that might countenance any weakening of radical opposition, the remaining members of the Reduction of Armaments Committee were in disarray. (Dorey, Radical Liberal Criticism of British Foreign Policy 1906–1914, *pp. 145–6). Meanwhile, Balfour mistakenly believed he could help the government by pressing for action on the contingent ships. (Rhodri Williams,* Defending the Empire: The Conservative Party and British Defence Policy 1899–1915, *Yale University Press, New Haven, 1991, pp. 164–9).*

[March] 16 and 17   Speaker out of Chair.

Thursday 18th – Monday 22nd [March]   Navy Votes.

March 23   Navy Scare.

Harold Cox came to me & asked me if a compromise was possible to avoid vote of censure which Balfour had tabled on Friday the 19th, asking for eight Dreadnoughts in place of 4 certain & 4 contingent ones to be ordered if required.

He said he came with authority from several of front opposition bench, but not Balfour, & that several rank & file Tories thought that Balfour's tactics were bad.

On the Monday (22) Asquith had told me he thought Balfour had been forced into it by Lee and Pretyman against his saner inclination.

At 10 Downing Street, 1.30 p.m. on this Tuesday, Margot Asquith told me Lady Londonderry had told her that Balfour had done it on his own initiative without consultation with his colleagues. She admitted bad tactics but thought Asquith & Grey ought to have held out in the Cabinet for 8.

I felt inclined to say, I love you Margot, but your judgement is not your strong point, but I merely said we are in a much stronger position with the power which need not be exercised if not needed.

After a Cabinet at the House 6.00 p.m. Asquith told me he was not prepared to budge, that the Tories knew that they were not justified in refusing to accept the Government's pledge to undertake the construction if the necessity arose, & he was not surprised at the overtures.

I told him I would not queer his pitch but I hoped that he would agree with me that if by negotiations I could avoid the Tories making the Navy a party issue it would be best for the country. Yes, he said, I agree, & he left me to carry on negotiations.

I told Cox that if any question was asked the Government could say the subject matter of the ordering of the 4 contingent vessels could be raised again on the construction vote in July & the Government was prepared to then say what progress had been made, & whether they could make any statement public or not as to what further ships they required.

Cox saw Balfour & on

March 24 informed me that Mr. Balfour would not agree to cancel the vote of censure unless Asquith said he would definitely give way on the 'option', & say he would order them in any case.

I told Cox I saw no way of meeting A.J.B., & I hoped he and others who favoured the strong navy view would show their confidence in the Government & their belief that the promise Asquith had given to give the orders if there was a case to give them could be relied upon.

He said he would listen to the debate.

March 25 Saw Asquith 1.30 – but only on business of House, & on possible adjournment on a/c of some dockyard hands having been discharged.[6]

Hood called on me to tell me Lee would move Balfour's vote of censure and Balfour wind up on Monday. I asked him if the Tories would divide. He said 'I don't want to, but I don't see how we can avoid it.' I told him Asquith could not give way; he thought the charge of not accepting his assurance was raising the party issue, & that the rate of ordinary vessels could not be precipitated or accelerated in any case.

Asquith spent the Sunday March 28 at Stocks in Hertfordshire playing in a Balliol Past v Balliol Present golf tourney. Studying his speech notes as he was driven back on the Monday morning, he was 'as nearly perturbed as his self-control would allow when our car broke down with a heated axle at Berkhamsted', and he was transferred to an express train at Watford. (Sir Stephen Tallents, Man and Boy, Faber & Faber, 1943, pp. 135–6). That same morning Lloyd George in an impromptu conversation on Budget tactics agreed with Ilbert that 'if the Govt is weak & the Budget unpopular, the Lords would not hesitate to throw out the Finance Bill in the autumn. He doubts however whether the Opposition are really playing for a general election in the autumn.' (Ilbert's diary, 29 Mar. 1909, Ilbert MSS, H.C. Lib. MS 72).

March 29 Vote of Censure

Asquith told me that he had just been over Edward Grey's speech with him and he said our case is so strong that if 'I was in Balfour's position, I could not

---

6   Of 3,143 men who had been employed in the various government dockyards since October 1908 in an attempt to alleviate unemployment, 1,640 were due to be discharged on March 31.

help withdrawing the vote of censure'. I told Asquith I thought the Tories would divide. I spoke to him about a few appointments McCrae, Atherley-Jones etc & their deserving of reward for long services I criticised Lord Pentland's method of appointing McCrae without consulting me.[7]

I told Asquith I thought some reference should be made by him to the Colonial support offered us in Dreadnoughts.

Like Britain, the dominions had been alarmed by the Admiralty's statement in March 1909 that German dreadnoughts would match the British by 1913. Until then, dominion contributions to the Royal Navy had consisted of direct subsidies: under the 1902 Naval Agreement, Australia paid £200,000 p.a. The Cabinet of March 24 had before it an offer from New Zealand of the gift of one and, if necessary, two dreadnoughts. (Asquith's Cabinet letter to the King, 24 Mar. 1909, Cab. 41/32/8). The gift was accepted and led to the construction of H.M.S. New Zealand. There was strong sentiment in Australia and Canada for similar gifts, but the latter dominions were also able to contemplate the founding of their own navies. Edward Grey tried two alternatives on Harcourt. Were the colonial dreadnoughts to be 'in addition to or in substitution of the ships we ourselves propose or should propose to build?' Either way why not begin them in 1909? If they were to be substitutes for two of the 'hypothetical ships for which no money has yet been voted' it would 'please the Colonies to let them feel that in deference to their zeal all limitations as to when payments for those ships were to begin should be removed, & the ships begun this year.' This ingenious circumvention of the Cabinet's recent compromise was unlikely to appeal to Harcourt, Lloyd George, and others holding out against McKenna's programme. (Grey to Harcourt, n.d. dated by Harcourt 'April '09', Harcourt MSS, dep. 441, ff. 33–4). The 1909 Colonial Conference was invited to consider how best the dominions could help. It called for fleet units to be established by Australia and Canada, to augment the Royal Navy's presence in the Pacific Ocean. The Canadian fleet unit was never built because of doubts of its necessity and a political storm over the form the fleet should take. The Australian fleet unit consisted of the battle cruiser Australia, *ordered 9 August 1909, and the light cruisers* Sydney *and* Melbourne. *(Donald C. Gordon,* The Dominion Partnership in Imperial Defence, 1870–1914, *Johns Hopkins Press, Baltimore, 1965, pp. 187–296; J.A. La Nauze,* Alfred Deakin: A Biography, *2 vols, Melbourne University Press, Melbourne, 1965, vol. II, pp. 515–30, 580-5).*

The vote of censure was debated on Monday March 29 when it was defeated 135–353. Arthur Lee's version of these events is in his A Good Innings: and A

---

[7]   Pentland had appointed Sir George McCrae, MP for Edinburgh (East) as Vice-President and Chairman, Local Government Board for Scotland, thus creating a parliamentary vacancy (Ian Levitt, *Welfare and the Scottish Poor Law 1890–1948*, Ph.D. thesis, University of Edinburgh, 1983, p. 89). Atherley-Jones apparently was not rewarded.

Great Partnership, *3 vols, privately printed, 1939, vol. I (1868–1914), pp. 378–86. His sources, who included the managing director of Vickers, told him that the German naval building programme was much further advanced than the English government admitted or had even calculated. He regarded the speech he made moving the vote of censure as 'probably the most important speech that I ever delivered in parliament' (ibid, p. 382). Grey's reply had been outlined to the Cabinet on March 26 as well as reviewed by the Prime Minister on the day of delivery. (Asquith's Cabinet letter to the King, 26 Mar. 1909, Cab. 41/32/9).*

Sir Edward Grey's speech was magnificent & cut the ground certainly from under the Tories' feet.

McKenna stayed Sunday with me & told me private & secret the information about German intentions, building fast cruisers to destroy British commerce &c, & that obviously we must not now commit ourselves to Dreadnoughts.

McKenna's remark to JAP about the unwisdom of commitment to dreadnoughts signalled his conversion to a view which Fisher had unsuccessfully been preaching at the Admiralty. As Jon Sumida and Charles Fairbanks Jr have shown, Fisher's preference had long been for a faster armoured cruiser. Fisher believed that the dreadnought type had been superseded by the new battle cruiser – what the Germans called 'Grosser Kreuzer'. The Director of Naval Intelligence had learned that the Moltke *was not the same size as the British* Indefatigable *(18,750 tons) but was 22,616 tons and significantly superior. The Tory demand for more battleships (dreadnoughts) was therefore misconceived. A fundamental re-examination of British naval policy from 1909 onwards seems imperative in the light of Sumida's and Fairbanks' arguments. (Charles H. Fairbanks Jr, 'The Origins of the* Dreadnought *Revolution: A Historiographical Essay', The* International History Review, *xiii, 2, May 1991, pp. 246–72; Fairbanks to CH, 4 Dec. 1991).*

He also told me how much he had been disappointed with Winston in the cabinet – his powers of expression were not associated with constructive ability or helpful criticism. In fact his presence was obviously distasteful to all his colleagues in the cabinet.[8]

After unfolding his Budget proposals to the Cabinet on April 7 Lloyd George retreated with his advisers to the house at 4 Chichester Place, Brighton which Lord Rendel had placed at his disposal. He responded in detail on April 16 to a memorandum of the 13th by Harcourt. (Harcourt MSS). JAP and Elsie spent the weekend April 16 to 18 in Paris, dining at the Ritz with Molly Harcourt before

---

[8]   The last eleven words of this sentence appear to have been added on April 19.

going to the latest theatrical sensation, Guitry's 'Le Scandal'. At dinner Molly Harcourt had tried to draw JAP into commenting on 'Winston's latest production in the shape of his letter to Dundee. I confess it strikes me as rather "hot" & not very loyal to his Chief or his colleagues. I asked Jack Pease last night what he thought of it. He replied with a quiet smile – I have yet to know if it had the sanction & approval of the P.M. before giving an opinion!' (M. Harcourt to L. Harcourt, 17 April 1909, Harcourt MSS, uncat.).

April 19 Had a chat with the P.M. about ministers. Lloyd George's methods of finance astonishing, & it was not unreasonable [sic] that he should shut himself up at Brighton, with I suppose his 'entourage' for a week. 'I wrote to him' said Asquith 'on Thursday to ask him if he could say whether he would be ready Monday or Thursday. I have not even yet heard from him'. 'It is a pity', said he that he does not like Hobhouse, he has only Robson to help him. I said Loulou had been working hard at finance. Yes but he does not agree with all we are doing, & has asked me to excuse him defending the budget. His criticisms are points of substance & he knows a good deal about it, & I can't well get McKenna or Runciman. Runciman won't help much but Haldane will on some points. I said well he must accept Hobhouse who was quite a decent fellow to work with, & if Treasury don't like him, other departments feel he gives them attention. He knows what goes on in cabinet said I better than most others & I thought L.G. was his informant. NO said Asquith, There it is thro' a medium at the Treasury. I undertook to communicate with L.G. as to date of budget introduction.

Hobhouse, whose principal informant was probably Sir George Murray, believed that he was regarded by the Treasury as 'the best Financial Secretary they have had for more than a generation'. In his diary on 12 April 1909 he had described the senior Treasury officials as 'in a state of revolt and insubordination which is quite indescribable – my own position vis-a-vis with the Chancellor of the Exchequer is extremely uncomfortable. He will neither give nor receive advice, and regards Murray and myself as mere marplots'. (David, ed., Inside Asquith's Cabinet, p. 77).

April 20 Budget
By arrangement I met Lloyd George in his room to discuss date of Budget, & procedure to enable it to be got through the House. Sir George Murray pressed Thursday, he obviously thought the L.G. ('the goat' as he is nicknamed at the Treasury whose boulder & boulder progression and long hair fit the name) would not be ready.

I advocated no guillotine until after 24 money resolutions had been discussed ad nauseam, when the House, Country, Lords, might swallow it. George wants it ab initio.

I had a subsequent chat with Asquith & then asked Ll. George to join us – he explained how 2 errors had occurred creating deficit of £500,000, had only been noticed that day – one item of £350,000 had been put in, before item had been decided upon, & reappeared afterwards again, when cabinet decided upon it. Chalmers was to sit up, & try how to arrange a graduated tax on ?House property to meet it.[9] Asquith & Loulou dined with me quietly at night & agreed that it had often been tried & they did not envy the Chancellor's job in coping with the difficulties his predecessors had failed to overcome.

They talked at dinner about Joe C's attitude & Jessie Collings on Home Rule when, his Father, said Loulou, & I were at Highbury[10] when the Hawarden balloon went up (H.J. Gladstone Leeds) & as we came into the Hall, Joe said that damned old man has done us again. Joe had been scheming himself not on Council lines & all Sir Wm's arguments had been replied to by Joe & Jessie which Joe & Jessie subsequently used themselves. At Highbury all Joe & Jessie said, these are mere 'administrative difficulties'.[11]

Asquith & Loulou also spoke of Dilke's failing strength his intriguing abilities failing to find a field in the present House. Joe's loyalty to Dilke for putting him in the cabinet first. Asquith thought that Joe should have forced his friend into the witness box to clear himself. Loulou said he was too close a friend to venture to give advice, & he knew Dilke did not know how much counsel in cross examination knew against him.

All would have been changed from lawyers' point of view if Dilke had faced the music – & he would have been high up in public life. C.B. always mistrusted Dilke as a colleague owing to his reputation in 1884 ministry.

Dilke's official career was shattered by his failure to enter the witness box and refute charges of adultery in a divorce suit in 1886. When sent for by

---

9   JAP wrote 'Chambers' but obviously meant Sir Robert Chalmers, Chairman, Board of Inland Revenue. No graduated tax on house property was included in the Budget. An earlier proposal by Lloyd George to tax 'the ground rents of land built upon' was rejected by the Cabinet because it involved interfering with existing contracts. (Asquith's Cabinet letter to the King, 19 Mar. 1909, Cab. 41/32/7).

10   Joseph Chamberlain's Birmingham home.

11   On 13 December 1885 Thomas Wemyss Reid, Liberal editor of the *Leeds Mercury* had urged H.J. Gladstone to give the press guidance on his father's position on Irish Home Rule. Reid argued that Joseph Chamberlain and Sir Charles Dilke wanted to leave the Conservatives in office to deal with Ireland in order to undermine W.E. Gladstone's position as Liberal leader. Chamberlain and Dilke argued that the Conservatives would be split by the Irish problem. Herbert Gladstone revealed his father's conversion to support for Irish Home Rule on December 15 and the news – the Hawarden kite (or balloon) – was published (without authorisation) on December 17 and 18. (See D.A. Hamer, *Liberal Politics in the Age of Gladstone and Rosebery*: A Study in Leadership and Policy, Clarendon Press, Oxford, 1972, pp. 113–16).

Gladstone in 1880 Dilke had refused to join the government unless either he or Chamberlain, the leaders of the radical wing of the Liberal party, were in the Cabinet. Chamberlain got the Board of Trade and Dilke was given only an under-secretaryship, partly perhaps because of Queen Victoria's objection to his earlier republican views. As President of the Local Government Board in 1884, Dilke's preparation of the franchise bill and the consequent redistribution of seats entailed lengthy negotiations with Lord Salisbury which aroused Liberal suspicions. While Campbell-Bannerman was responsible for Irish policy as Chief Secretary, Dilke and Chamberlain were communicating privately with the Nationalists. Dilke voted against the government and Campbell-Bannerman as Secretary of State for War in the 1895 cordite vote which led to the Liberals' resignation (Roy Jenkins, Sir Charles Dilke: A Victorian Tragedy, *Collins, 1958, p. 400n). CB regarded Dilke 'as an intriguer who cultivated the press for his own purposes, as a man who enjoyed showing off his own knowledge for reasons of vanity, and as a man who had no influence or following.' (John Wilson,* CB: A Life of Sir Henry Campbell-Bannerman, *Constable, 1973, p. 462).*

April 22 I told Asquith of my negotiations with Abel Smith & Barnard, & he deplored the E. Herts Liberals making it difficult for Free Trade Unionists to work with us & secure our support.

On 21 January 1909 Lord Robert Cecil had written to Asquith on behalf of the Unionist Free Trade Club to ask whether the remaining Unionist free trader MPs would be allowed a straight fight against attacking tariff reformers. Asquith had replied on January 27 that in nine cases out of ten the central organisation would 'practically have no voice, and the matter would be determined entirely by local conditions and influences'. Asquith's own 'disposition (but I speak only for myself) would be to discourage Liberal opposition to a Unionist Free Trader in constituencies which are what I may call naturally or normally Unionist in general politics'. (Cecil of Chelwood MSS, CHE 93/307–13).

The East Hertfordshire Conservative & Liberal Unionist Association was split over free trade. Abel Smith, their MP, was a leading Unionist free trader. At first the executive committee withdrew support but after the annual election the new committee restored their support. In May 1909 E.B. Barnard (Lib. MP Kidderminster), having fallen out with his constituents over licensing, agreed to contest the division as a Liberal free trader. Consequently there were three candidates: a free trade Unionist, a free trade Liberal, and a tariff reform Unionist (R. Mortimer). JAP was anxious not to split the free trade vote. At his adoption meeting Barnard said that strong pressure had been put on him to withdraw because Abel Smith was a freetrader. Barnard alleged that Abel Smith's position was unclear and he maintained his candidature. In October

1909 following negotiations between Lord Selborne and Austen Chamberlain, both Abel Smith and Mortimer agreed to withdraw to enable Sir John Rolleston to be chosen unanimously as Unionist candidate. Rolleston, a tariff reformer, defeated Barnard by 1,692 votes in the January 1910 general election. (Sykes, Tariff Reform in British Politics, *pp. 179–80, 360; Blewett,* The Peers, The Parties and the People, *pp. 212–13, 217–18).*

April 27   The P.M. sent for me and told me that Riddell wanted a Knighthood and asked me about him. I told him all I knew. He thought he might help a hospital, and use his paper in our favour.[12]

We talked about Welsh Disestablishment Bill, and the intention to proceed with the second reading, and the P.M. said it was his intention to take it a stage on as soon as he could find time. We talked over Poynder & Freeman Thomas being given peerages.

May 11   I explained John Ellis's views of Lloyd George's unthoughtout budget proposals.[13]

Lloyd George had introduced the Budget on April 29 having presented the final version to his Cabinet colleagues on the previous afternoon. Preparations continued late into the evening with the Attorney-General's aid being enlisted to go through points of law on the Budget resolutions 'which the Ch of Ex. does not feel equal to coping with alone'. (Sir A. Thring to Sir W. Robson, 28 April 1909, Robson MSS). In his initial statement and subsequent answers to questions he seemed to have an imperfect grasp of many of its detailed provisions. The veteran Quaker MP Ellis maintained his criticism of the Budget throughout the session: officials had not devoted sufficient time to its preparation; they had been preoccupied by the Licensing Bill – with the result that 1,013 words had to be

---

12   How Asquith became aware of Riddell's aspirations is unclear. Lloyd George may well have told him. JAP certainly advised that Riddell's *News of the World* had become 'a valuable party asset'. Asquith, affecting to barely recall who Riddell was, told J.A. Spender on 10 November 1909 that Riddell had been 'strongly recommend to me on the ground (amongst others) that his paper … had become definitely Liberal'. (Spender MSS, Add. MS 46388, f. 92). McEwen (*The Riddell Diaries*, p. 13), alleges that Riddell's published diary version of his knighthood is 'fiction'. Riddell had recorded for 25 June 1909 that he had been 'recommended by Asquith and Pease' and 'LG surprised'. The manuscript diary 'contains nothing for this day' and McEwen finds it 'hard to see why Lloyd George should have been surprised – clearly no one else was responsible.' Presumably what was surprising was the ease with which an honour had been obtained for a divorced proprietor of a popular Sunday newspaper.

13   With JAP's father Ellis had led the movement opposing the cultivation of opium poppies in India in the 1890's and as Under Secretary for India in 1906 he was instrumental in stimulating government action.

dropped and 7,373 words added and a great deal of parliamentary time wasted.
(PD, Commons xii, 1859–64, 3 Nov. 1909). Lloyd George reminded Ellis of 'one
of those locomotive engines which took up water as they went along'. (A.
MacCallum Scott's diary, 21 May 1915, MacCallum Scott MSS).

On 10 May 1909 Ellis wrote to his old colleague James Bryce that the House
of Commons seemed demoralised and compared Asquith's parliamentary
leadership unfavourably with that of Campbell-Bannerman. (Bryce MSS, UB
22). Nor was Asquith's manifest and growing reliance on JAP's counsel
welcomed in all quarters. Edwin Montagu, the Prime Minister's pps, dispiritedly
reported to Walter Runciman on 12 May 1909 that he had nothing to do and he
never saw Asquith. 'Pease gains in influence and reputation for infallibility
every day.' (Runciman MSS).

May 13 P.M. at 1.30 walked up & down his room, & explained to me his views
on Sinclair's (Pentland's) methods of appointments & asked if he should do a job
for Arthur Murray, or sanction The Master of Polwarth or Agnew,[14] 2 Tories, to
vacant position. [illegible] inspection of Civil ? [sic]

I said appoint a Liberal, these Tory appointments do us immense harm. The
Tories never give us any. He said they once did in appointing J.B. Balfour to
judicial position.[15]

We discussed situation on budget and a few minor matters.

He then referred to Fitzmaurice's illness and desire to retire, it looked like
paralysis & he had declined to accept resignation pending his rest cure. If he
went Sinclair might step into his shoes.

May 14 Religious Disabilities Removal Bill

Made an arrangement with the Prime Minister that I might arrange with
Redmond, that if he withdrew the Bill, the Govmt would appoint a Committee to
inquire into the subject of the form of oath, if any, for sovereign coronation
Declaration.

If Committee reported a satisfactory solution Govmt would undertake to
introduce legislation thereon this Parliament. If not satisfactory, the Government
could not undertake to find a satisfactory formula, but, it would negociate with a
view to doing so, & in the hope that legislation could be introduced thereon, on
its own responsibility.

Redmond saw Healy, & he said that he would sooner die on the floor of the
House than betray the interest of the Catholic Faith by any such arrangement, and

---

14   Probably Sir Andrew Noel Agnew, Bt (1850–1928); barrister and Wigtownshire
     magnate; Liberal Unionist MP Edinburgh South 1900–06; 9th Bt 1892.

15   John Blair Balfour (1837–1905), a Liberal MP and former Lord Advocate, was
     appointed Presiding Judge, Court of Session in Scotland, by the Salisbury
     government in 1899; Baron Kinross 1902.

as a Division would be forced by Healy and Lord Edmund Talbot, the scheme fell through with the result that 2d reading was secured by 13! & the bill was referred to comtee. of whole House, and virtually killed by majority of 3.

The Roman Catholic Disabilities Removal Bill, introduced by William Redmond, had two main aims: to repeal the remnants of the penal laws and to amend or remove the statutory declaration made by the sovereign on his accession. Several MPs opposed the bill on the grounds that the Roman Catholic Church was a political, as well as religious, body. Asquith regarded the bill as 'highly inopportune', despite the fact that some of its provisions coincided with a bill introduced by Gladstone and supported by Campbell-Bannerman and Asquith himself twenty years earlier. Lloyd George and Haldane voted for the second reading; no member of the Cabinet voted against. But, as Harcourt reported that evening to the King, referral to a committee of the whole House was 'tantamount to a Parliamentary sentence of death'. (Royal Archives, R 39/12). Asquith told the King that the proposed reform of the sovereign's oath would make the oath 'an inadequate affirmation of the Sovereign's loyalty to the protestant religion.' (Asquith's Cabinet letter to the King, 12 May 1909, Cab. 41/32/15).

May 18 Churchill came in to see Asquith to complain of his treatment, in not being given half a day to introduce his Labour Exchanges Bill. He was disappointed to an amazing extent. He saw the Speaker who told him he could only give him 20 mins. under 10 mins. rule, which Asquith had publicly arranged was all that he should get. He came then to see me. I pointed out all other ministers equally thought their geese were swans.

In fact Churchill was able to speak at some length about the provision of his bill on the eve of its first reading, May 19, in a debate on the Minority report of the Royal Commission on the Poor Law. The Labour Exchanges Bill, which had been drawn up by William Beveridge, aimed to organise the labour market more efficiently by establishing or taking over existing labour exchanges which would collect and publish information about employment. (Gordon Phillips and Noel Whiteside, Casual Labour: The Unemployment Question in the Port Transport Industry 1880–1970, *Clarendon Press, Oxford, 1985, pp. 76–87; Carolyn W. White, 'The Labour Exchange Bill: Churchill as Social Reformer', Studies in History and Politics, vol. 1, Fall 1980, pp. 11-27). Initially it was opposed by the trade unions who feared that the exchanges would direct potential strike breakers to vacant jobs. This fear was removed by the exchanges displaying information about the existence of disputes and also displaying notices of current rates of pay. The bill was passed in September 1909; Churchill opened the first exchange on 1 February 1910. On 22 August 1909 Churchill wrote to JAP asking him if he could recommend any Labour MPs for the posts of Divisional*

Superintendents, particular MPs whose seats might be usefully vacated. (Gainford MSS, 87).

I told Asquith how delighted I was that such an arrangement had been come to in regard to the Budget Resolutions and that it would reduce force of the Opposition as well as secure a Whit holiday. He then said what a selfish creature Winston is. Yes I said I have however come to tell you what an admirable solution we have got as alternative to several all night sittings and Lloyd George pressing guillotine on Budget Resolutions. This I told Asquith, I must resist & I had told L. George so & it was pleasant to think we should find all going now so much more smoothly.

Parliamentary tactics over the Budget were to be a cause of Cabinet contention throughout the summer. Lloyd George had canvassed with the Clerk of the House of Commons as early as December 1908 the possible need for closure by compartments. With precious hours running out he continually pressed for the guillotine to be applied to Finance Bill discussions. Morley and Harcourt led the opposition to this approach, their reservations about the substance of the Budget implicit in their arguments about tactics. (Harcourt to Lord Welby, 3 May 1909, copy, Harcourt MSS, dep. 441, f. 40; Hobhouse's diary, 17 June 1909, David, ed., Inside Asquith's Cabinet, p. 78).

May 25   Went through list of proposed honours with the Prime Minister & Nash and agreed upon names.

P.M. had to leave to meet Queen on her return to London in the middle.[16] Before discussing names he asked me my opinion of Sir William Collins who he thought might help us through the Budget, as Chairman of Committee. He was under the impression Buchanan could not undertake official work again and he would offer the position to Emmott, whose slow but painstaking chairmanship was not satisfactory to even himself, & he had asked for an administrative post. I said I thought the suggestion admirable.

The previous weekend JAP had been at Sandwich where he had talked to Emmott who urged the government to announce the means by which the report stage of the Budget was to be reached by Whitsuntide. Until this was known, the House would be confused. Emmott expressed no dissatisfaction with his own work, though he admitted, after he had received Asquith's offer of the Under Secretaryship of State for India, that he preferred administrative work to his present position and that Asquith knew this. Buchanan had been ill since mid-

---

16   Queen Alexandra was returning from a Mediterranean cruise and was met by the King, the Prince and Princess of Wales, the Greek and Danish ambassadors, and Sir Edward Henry, as well as Asquith.

April and his predecessor at the India Office, Hobhouse, had acted for him in the Commons. Emmott refused to move after learning from Runciman that Lloyd George wanted to oust him as chairman of committees in order to put a more pliant man in his place (Emmott's diary, 23 May and 16 June 1909, Emmott MSS, vol. I, ff. 166–8, 170–6).

I saw Sir Walter Gilbey who called & told him how pleased I was to know his name would be included among next peers list but doubted any now being made.

Sir Walter Gilbey Bt was one of JAP's biggest campaign contributors in Saffron Walden. He and his sister's husband Charles Gold, MP for Saffron Walden 1895–1900, were especially praised by JAP for their help in the 1906 election. (JAP to H. Gladstone, 27 Jan. 1906, Gladstone MSS, Add. MS 46022, f. 150). Gold was knighted in 1906. When Gilbey's business partner, his wife's brother Sir James Blyth Bt, was ennobled in 1907, the Gilbey family and firm were 'much upset'. Blyth was ten years younger than Gilbey, and allegedly had 'never done anything either for Agriculture or for the Liberal Party in Essex or the adjoining counties'. (Alfred Gilbey to Lord Carrington, 26 July 1907, Campbell-Bannerman MSS, Add. MS 52519 ff. 69–70). Gilbey was still on the list of prospective peers when Asquith was preparing to flood the Lords in 1911; he died a baronet.

June 8   I had a long talk with the P.M. He asked me to stay for Cabinet next day instead of going to Pease & Partners shareholders meeting. We discussed possibility of Buchanan's resignation, it being offered to Emmott and possible delegation of portion of budget to Committee upstairs.

Lloyd George, Robson, Thring, and 'sundry Treasury officials' had conferred on Monday June 7 about the procedure to be followed on the Finance Bill. Ilbert, who joined them, recorded the Chancellor's understanding that Balfour hoped to drive him to adoption of the guillotine. A month earlier Ilbert had discussed the matter with Lloyd George and told him that 'Balfour wd probably be pleased … It wd. enable him to get away earlier, & would supply him with a useful grievance & a useful precedent.' With both the Cabinet and the party opposed to the guillotine, Lloyd George was now considering the possibility of sending part of the bill to a standing committee. Ilbert doubted whether such an innovation would commend itself to the House but agreed in the end to try to devise a plan with Thring. The proposal was to give a day in committee of the whole House for a preliminary discussion of each of the land duties, 'the discussion to be of a second reading order, & the question proposed to be general approval of the tax.' Then Part I of the bill would go to a standing committee while the licence duties would proceed in the committee of the whole

House. 'I have great doubts about the feasibility or acceptability of this scheme',
Ilbert admitted. 'But the Govt. are evidently in a tight place, & something must
be tried.' The Speaker was known to be adverse to this plan but Pease
nevertheless brought it to the Cabinet on June 9. (Ilbert's diary, 11 May, 7 June
1909, Ilbert MSS, H.C. Lib. MS 73).

June 9 attended Cabinet submitted my proposals in regard to delegation of
machinery proposals to an upstairs committee, under a resolution empowering
Minister to move such a reference.
 Cabinet did not consent.
 Ll. George submitted his proposals. Morley demurred.

June 10 Authorised by Asquith & Ll. George to approach Hood. Saw Hood &
Balfour's sec. re some method to expedite work without physical disaster to
M.P.s. – arranged to proceed in ordinary way until Budget Bill had been in
comtee.

June 12 Had a quiet chat with Asquith on situation budget & c.

On April 21 Asquith had introduced the first reading of the Established
Church (Wales) Bill which aimed at the dissolution of the Anglican Church in
Wales by 1 January 1911. As its veto by the House of Lords was certain, the bill
was a mere gesture to the Welsh MPs. On June 10, after a meeting with angry
Welsh members, Asquith had announced that it would be dropped.

June 14 Ll. George, Asquith & I discussed how to deal with Welsh Revolt over
disestablishment. Agreed to give priority in 1910.

The Liberal member for Mid-Derbyshire, Sir Alfred Jacoby, died on June 23.
Jacoby had held the seat since 1885, but in 1906 the Liberals had promised the
next nomination for the seat to the miners who formed a decisive 50% of the
electorate. Foreseeing potential difficulties, JAP wrote to Noel Buxton on June
22:

	June 22 1909.
Private	12 Downing Street.
	S.W.

My Dear Noel,
 No doubt you are aware that, in Mid. Derbyshire there may be an early vacancy,
as I hear that Sir Alfred Jacoby is extremely ill.
 In all probability, an arrangement will be made by the miners to run a
Progressive Labour candidate who will be acceptable to the Liberal Party in the
Division. *If*, however, their lot falls upon a Socialist to whom serious objection is
taken by a large number of the miners and by the Liberal Party, would you be

prepared to allow your name to be suggested? In the event of a Socialist being run, you would, I think, have a very good chance, but, of course, a good deal depends on the man.

Yours faithfully,
Joseph A. Pease.
(Noel-Buxton MSS [Duke University])

No Derbyshire Miners' Federation candidate was available in 1909. But J.G. Hancock of the Nottinghamshire Miners' Association, which had 4000 members in the constituency, was nominated. After signing the Labour party constitution, Hancock was adopted as the official Labour candidate. He then assured the local Liberal association that, although he was forced to be a Labour candidate, his views were those of a progressive Liberal. He was adopted as the official Liberal candidate, campaigned with the support of the Liberal organisation, and won with a reduced majority. (Gregory, The Miners and British Politics, *pp. 145–50.)*

*As Chief Whip, JAP signed a notice on June 21 to all Liberal MPs inviting those 'members who desire that special efforts should be made in the constituencies in support of the Finance Bill' to attend a meeting in Westminster Hall on June 23. (Norman MSS). Addressing the meeting, JAP explained a plan to conduct 'a large campaign throughout the Country' in support of the Budget. Churchill was to chair a proposed executive committee and the former journalist Sir Henry Norman had 'at the request of the Prime Minister, kindly consented to direct and carry out, so far as he may be authorised by the Executive Committee, the Campaign in the Country.' Two whips (Elibank and Whitley) were on the original committee. JAP was coopted shortly afterwards. But, if he had hoped thereby to influence the strategy of the Budget League, he was soon to be disillusioned. The organisation was to be the creature of Lloyd George and Churchill, with Norman as their instrument. Norman as honorary secretary was supported by R.C. Lehmann as honorary treasurer. Churchill had promised at the inaugural meeting that the treasurer would be Alfred Mond 'whose special aptitudes for the accumulation of funds were unimpeachable'. But Mond preferred to give rather than collect. (Speech notes by JAP and Churchill, 23 June 1909, Churchill MSS, C2/42, C9/33). Lehmann was only a collector not, as Koss implies (*The Rise and Fall of the Political Press, *Vol. Two, p. 123), a giver. JAP advanced him £1000 in December 1909 for personal election expenses. Alick Murray later cancelled the debt but Lehmann resigned from Parliament at the end of 1910 'unable to face the enormous expense of another contested election'. (Lehmann's diary, 29 June, 12 Dec. 1910, Lehmann MSS). In the League's first few weeks JAP advanced £1000, foreshadowing a maximum of £5000, and wrote to all Cabinet ministers in response to an appeal from Norman who had encountered 'an almost universal refusal to speak'. For his pains, JAP was reminded by Harcourt on June 30 that the Cabinet had not been consulted* *'as to the policy of the formation of the Budget League or of its subsequent operations.' (Norman to JAP, copy, JAP to Norman, two letters, 29 June 1909, Norman MSS; JAP to Harcourt, 29 June 1909, Harcourt to JAP, 30 June 1909, copy, Harcourt MSS). Harcourt, and a handful of back-benchers who made dissenting noises at the June 23 meeting, still hoped for concessions on land taxation and valuation; they had already received an assurance from Haldane, who chaired the meeting and was president of the new body, that the League would not operate in particular constituencies without the consent of the local MP. (Murray, The People's Budget, pp. 182–3).*

June 23 & 24 Discussed vacancies created by Buchanan & Fitzmaurice's resignations. Agreed to appoint Master Elibank & raise Samuel to Duchy Lancaster.

Both Buchanan and Fitzmaurice were resigning because of ill-health. Elibank and Samuel were appointed on June 29 but deciding on their replacements was a more protracted process. A major fear was the possibility of losing seats when newly promoted men faced by-elections. Geoffrey Howard was ruled out on this basis. And Norman Lamont's narrow majority kept him on a back-bench, albeit as Churchill's pps, although he was the first choice to succeed Elibank as Scottish Whip. (L. Jones to Lady Carlisle, 30 June 1909, Lady Carlisle MSS, J 23/100).

June 29 Asquith saw me & we talked over vacancies possible Under Secretaries.

Masterman, Mond, Charles Roberts, Trevelyan, Montagu. I suggested Lyell, Lewis for secretaries; Partington, Erskine, Lamont for Whips.

Twice in the afternoon I had further talks with him.[17]

Lady Wimborne badgered me for Ivor Guest to be given an administrative post. Lord Swaythling for his son Montagu had badgered Asquith. Asquith expressed his admiration for Jewish ability, & way Samuel had got on, & their pertinacity.

July 1 Saw Asquith 1.20. I told him I thought Agar Robartes might be made the Comptroller of the Household, & the abler whips secured by Gulland for

---

17   The Prime Minister's attention may have been diverted by prolonged skirmishing outside the Commons by 3000 police and a large band of militant suffragettes. (Andrew Rosen, *Rise Up, Women!* The Militant Campaign of the Women's Social and Political Union 1903-1914, Routledge and Kegan Paul, 1974, p. 119). Inside the House, there was restiveness in Liberal ranks about the management of the Finance Bill, especially the infrequent presence of Asquith as Leader of the House (Ilbert's diary, 29 June 1909, Ilbert MSS, H.C. Lib. 73; L. Jones to Lady Carlisle, 5, 6, 7 July 1909, Lady Carlisle MSS, J 23/100).

Scotland, & Partington instead of Lewis. That Masterman's promotion would be unpopular. His supporters were few, & his inclusion was a matter of adverse comment before & would be further criticised. A. replied that there was no comparison between the ability of such a man & Hutton & Soares.

July 1 afternoon I saw Robartes & Gulland the latter pleased, the former hesitated as Lord Rosebery was his leader. I told him the brains which had kept Lord R. stable & the figure he was in Liberal party were in Asquith's, Grey's & Haldane's heads.[18]

July 2 – was at Southport with Prime Minister. Saw agents & stayed at Greaves Hall.[19]

July 3 Asquith asked me as we [were] leaving the station about vacancies. I told him Partington was going to see me that evening & report condition of party in his Division & Soares had asked to be included.

July 4 Had interview with Lloyd George at Ballencrieff[20] & Partington agreed that contest should go forward.

A by-election was necessary because of the proposed appointment of Oswald Partington as Junior Lord of the Treasury. The major incident of the campaign was Partington's challenge to fight a reporter of the Sheffield Daily Telegraph. *The presses of that paper had been used to print the* High Peak Elector, *a campaign newspaper published by Partington's opponent, A. Profumo, which Partington claimed had slighted his wife. Partington was returned on July 23 but with a majority reduced from 788 to 347.*

July 5 P.M. saw Partington & me at 1.0 & agreed.

---

18   Agar Robartes decided to refuse the offer of the Comptrollership on the grounds that he could not vote for the $1/2$d tax on undeveloped land or the tax on ungotten minerals. (Agar-Robartes to JAP, 3 July 1909, Gainford MSS, 87).

19   JAP and Asquith were attending the annual meeting of the National Liberal Federation held on July 1 and 2. Greaves Hall, at Banks, Lancashire, was the seat of Sir Tom T. Leyland Scarisbrick, Bt (1874–1933), Lib. MP Dorset (Southern) 1906–10; Mayor of Southport, 1902–3; his baronetcy had been announced a week earlier. Scarisbrick had built the imposing mock-Tudor house in 1902 to entertain delegates to the annual meeting of the British Association. (John Liddle, 'Estate management and land reform politics: the Hesketh and Scarisbrick families and the making of Southport, 1842 to 1914' in David Cannadine, ed., *Patricians, power and politics in nineteenth-century towns*, Leicester University Press/St. Martin's Press, New York, 1982, p. 161).

20   Ballencrieff, Haddington, was the home of Lord Elibank.

In afternoon P.M. told me of his trouble about Scotch Judgeship, Dewar wanting it. Ure opposed to it being given & vacancy Edinburgh created Sinclair (Pentland) concurred.[21] Decided to wait until next vacancy & Dewar to be then considered. He said he was glad appointments seemed over, he would see Trevelyan tomorrow, & Chichester for Comptrollership.

July 6 Asquith sent for me 5.0 p.m. Found him quite annoyed Trevelyan had refused under sec. L.G. Board – declining to serve under John Burns. Asquith had pointed out the interest in work wh. next session would bring, as compared with the cypher position at Bd of Education. He said however Trevelyan has only looked at it from a selfish point of view, & not how he can help me, & he won't get another chance of promotion.

Although Trevelyan would have accepted the post if offered it in 1905 he was now not alone in his fears about working with Burns. Masterman, on his appointment to the same position in 1908, had also made conditions. Masterman agreed with Labour and Radical critics that the Local Government Board under Burns had done no more for the unemployed than it had done under the Tories. He felt that the Board needed reorganisation under a new head appointed from outside. In his letter accepting the office he noted his understanding that Asquith would enquire into the possibility of achieving these changes and would also seek to persuade Burns to allot 'some definite department of the work' to the Under Secretary. Masterman's friends were agreed that in its unreformed state, the position was 'impossible', a view shared by the previous Under Secretaries Runciman and Macnamara (Masterman to Asquith, 13 April 1908, Lucy Masterman, C.F.G. Masterman: A Biography, Nicholson and Watson, 1939, p. 105). Trevelyan's friends thought that Burns had rejected Trevelyan as Runciman's replacement in 1907 because of his involvement with the land reform group in the Commons. (Crompton Llewelyn Davies to Trevelyan, 7 Feb. 1907; J.C. Wedgwood to Trevelyan, 8 Nov. 1907, Trevelyan MSS, 18; A.J.A. Morris, C.P. Trevelyan 1870–1958, Portrait of a Radical, Blackstaff Press, Belfast, 1977, p. 72).

I saw Grey about Chichester being offered Comptrollership – & he sent for him. Chichester asked for 24 hours to consider offer, he had certain objections to Death Duties in budget.

---

21 There had been by-elections in three of the four Edinburgh divisions (including Dewar's) only two months earlier. In the East Edinburgh by-election the Liberal majority was only a ninth of their 1906 result. This was generally ascribed to the loss of the Roman Catholic vote because of the failure to settle the education question.

July 7   Summoned to cabinet, we discussed questions connected with business of House: Irish land bill, S.A. constitution, supply: & agreed on general scheme for August for our work.

I was authorised to try & get Hood to agree to a discussion on appointing a Cmtee to consider closure resolutions.

Monday, July 12   Asquith told me Lord Liverpool had accepted position of Comptroller.

Thus Liverpool assumed Elibank's royal household duties. Fitzmaurice was replaced as Chancellor of the Duchy of Lancaster by Samuel. Samuel was replaced as Under Secretary at the Home Office by Masterman. Masterman was replaced as Parliamentary Secretary at the Local Government Board by Herbert Lewis. Lewis and Elibank were replaced as junior whips by Partington and Gulland. Buchanan was replaced as Under Secretary at the India Office by Elibank. Hobhouse, who saw Lloyd George's hand behind the promotion of Masterman and Lewis, had noted on July 1 that Asquith had been drinking hard over the past few weeks and had lost 'all pluck where Ll.G. is concerned' (David, ed., Inside Asquith's Cabinet, p. 79).

Wednesday, July 14   He handed me the enclosed mem. written by the King.

Mem
  As Lord Liverpool has now succeeded Master of Elibank as Comptroller of the Household and being a Peer cannot make any communication with H. of Commons & myself – please inform the Prime Minister that I consider it most important that this communication should not cease – & I should wish Mr Fuller Vice Chamberlain who now sends me the telegraphic accounts of the debates in House of Commons should take the duties which Master of Elibank carried out so admirably – so that I should not lose 'touch' with House of Commons.
E.R.
July 14, 1909

Asquith said he found the D. of Connaught that afternoon in a very unbending frame of mind. He declined to go back to Malta. It meant probably Kitchener going & there being no chance of sending the Duke of C. to Canada when Grey left. It was his death warrant, & the King would be very angry at Connaught chucking Malta!

The King's brother, the Duke of Connaught, had grudgingly taken up the newly created Mediterranean command in 1907. On 4 June 1909 he wrote to the Army Council stating that the command was impracticable and a sinecure. Resisting persuasion from Haldane and Asquith, he submitted his resignation on July 22. The Duke had wanted to serve until October but the King made the resignation effective immediately. Kitchener at first declined the post but was prevailed upon by the King to accept on the understanding that it would not prejudice his eligibility for any more agreeable future vacancy. Kitchener aspired to the Indian viceroyalty and had no intention of actually going to Malta. Denied the Indian appointment in June 1910 he withdrew his acceptance of the Mediterranean command. The King's anger with his brother quickly turned to remorse and the Duke did succeed Earl Grey as Governor-General of Canada in 1911. (James Lees-Milne, The Enigmatic Edwardian: The Life of Reginald, 2nd Viscount Esher, *Sidgwick & Jackson, 1986, pp. 165–6, 196–7; Philip Magnus,* Kitchener: Portrait of an Imperialist, *Arrow, 1961, pp. 232–43; Registrar, Royal Archives to CH, 17 Jan. 1989).*

July 16 – attended Cabinet from 11.45 to 1.0. After Ll. George had suggested alterations in procedure which he thought would help, I gave it as my opinion small alterations would occupy a lot of time – 1 or 2 simple large ones we should concentrate upon. 2 were agreed to: powers to be given to Vice Chair and power to accept closure on amendments reserving larger ones.

I then let fly, told the cabinet they were asking the House to do more than was physically possible, prudent or wise in interest of party or for the chances of the Bill, & asked for load to be lightened by 1/2d tax postponed.[22] Ll. George made the usual cabinet threat of resigning if lightening insisted on. Press, country would resist it, & he must ask for whole bill, but would make concessions. Grey & he agreed middle of August arrangements might become possible with Opposition. Ll. G. said he had compromises & concessions in hand to recommend to his colleagues.

The committee stage of the Finance Bill had begun on June 21. Clause 2 was still being considered when JAP was authorised by Cabinet on July 7 to negotiate with the Conservative Chief Whip over closure resolutions. While Lloyd George continued to press for an answer to Tory filibustering, JAP believed a more fundamental change of tactics was essential if Liberal backbenchers were not to be worn out by all night sittings. One solution was to roster batches of Liberal members for a week or two of rest, an arrangement impossible for the exiguous Conservative forces. (G. Lane-Fox's diary, 5 June 1909, Bingley MSS; Frank Dilnot, The Old Order Changeth: The Passing of Power from the House of Lords, *Smith, Elder, 1911, p. 77).*

Writing to J.A. Spender on July 16, Lloyd George conceded that 'real progress' made on the previous Wednesday night 'justified our postponing any consideration of the question of fixing a time limit at this stage.' But if, as was being hinted in parts of the press, the government were to 'lighten' the Finance

---

[22]   JAP pasted into the diary the sheet of notes from which he addressed the Cabinet. They are too cryptic and incoherent to transcribe.

Bill by dropping the land clauses, Lloyd George would 'have to go – I could not possibly assent to such a course.' (Spender MSS, Add. MS 46388, f. 201). After the Cabinet on the 16th Lloyd George and JAP continued their discussions over lunch with the Clerk of the House of Commons who was asked to draft 'some minor amendment of standing orders.' Ilbert's proposed amendment to standing order 26 giving the Chair power to select amendments was considered by Emmott, JAP, and Lloyd George late on July 19. Emmott, obviously out of sympathy with the Chancellor, wanted the government not the Chair to take responsibility for choosing amendments. (Ilbert's diary, 16, 19 July 1909, Ilbert MSS, H.C. Lib. MS 73).

July 19   Saw Asquith at 1.30 as he was starting to go down the Thames to see the Fleet. He was still fuming with indignation, the result of Churchill's speech on Saturday in Edinburgh, he told me that he had written him a curt letter merely to say he had no authority for the statement he had made in regard to a dissolution contained in the peroration & that the matter had not even had cabinet consideration. Crewe had written him in the same sense, & Asquith said the young whipper snapper takes upon himself to say things which in their very character are impossible to consider until the occasion arise.

Churchill's speech responded to one made by Lansdowne on July 16. In his reply to Asquith's letter, Churchill was unrepentant. He claimed that to say a dissolution was inevitable if the Lords insisted on their amendments to the Budget was merely a truism; that in no way could his speech be construed as the announcement of a Cabinet decision. Churchill's letter is printed in Churchill, Winston S. Churchill, vol. II, Companion Part 2, pp. 898–9. As a result, Asquith formally rebuked Churchill in Cabinet: it was inconsistent with Cabinet responsibility to make unauthorised statements on high policy. (Asquith's Cabinet letter to the King, 21 July 1909, Cab. 41/32/26).

July 26   Saw Asquith – & talked over business for next 2 or 3 weeks – decided to postpone budget – unless for 1 day next week to get Consolidated Fund Bill thro' 2d Rdg &c.

With growing fears that the Budget would be rejected by the Lords, the Cabinet's more enterprising political strategists were concocting ever more exotic schemes. JAP remained set on a conventional course of passing a Consolidated Fund Bill to sanction expenditure on administration pending the passing of the Finance Bill and the second Appropriation Bill at the end of the session. The Appropriation Act set out each grant voted by the Commons during the session and provided that the grants be expended on the services for which they were appropriated. It could not be introduced until the financial business of the year was completed in the Committee of Ways and Means. The Finance Act, *granting the duties and taxes required, usually completed the process. On July 29, the Clerk of the House of Commons recorded with dismay that 'Lloyd George has a fantastic notion, probably suggested to him by Winston Churchill, that, for the purpose of putting a stronger screw on the Lords, the passing of the Appropriation Bill ought to be postponed [until] after that of the Finance Bill.' A limited amount of Supply would be ensured by passing a Consolidated Fund Bill. Although the Chancellor had Treasury endorsement of the constitutionality of this ploy Ilbert advised the Prime Minister that 'the Treasury argument was partly unsound, partly too technical to carry weight in the House or the Country, and that the Govt would be forced into a premature discussion of a question which might, and probably would, never arise.' (Ilbert's diary, 29 July 1909, Ilbert MSS, H.C. Lib. MS 73).*

Aug. 12 – called into cabinet to state what dates I proposed to give to budget the following week & to explain how I proposed we could secure clause 14 this week. I said by threat of Saturday sitting & to take it on Friday after 3d Reading of Appropriation Bill. I was entrusted to do this – & got arrangement through later with Hood.

12 Aug 09   10 Downing Street,
                                                          Whitehall, S.W.

Dear Jack
    I do not propose to return to the House after dinner to-night, as I am rather done up with the heat & have to prepare for Bletchley tomorrow.
                                                          Ever yours,
                                                          H.H.A.
                                                          (Gainford MSS, 38, f. 73)

The Cabinet had decided on August 4 that suffragettes held in Holloway Gaol were to continue to be treated as 'ordinary prisoners.' 'If they were made "first-class" misdemeanants, the prisons would soon be full of them, and they could to all intents & purposes carry on their operations in comfort from behind the prison walls.' (Asquith's Cabinet letter to the King, 4 Aug. 1909, Cab. 41/32/30). In anticipation of suffragette protest, elaborate precautions were taken to prevent the Prime Minister's speech to the Bletchley meeting being disrupted. Tickets were sold on condition 'that the holder agrees not to disturb the meeting' thereby giving the organisers a contractual right to eject hecklers. Tickets had to be ordered in advance and signed; they were non-transferable and supplied only the day before the meeting. (Rosen, Rise Up, Women, p. 122).

Chapter 6

Election Planning

26 Aug. 1909 Came back after 6 days absence in Scotland (The Glen) Headlam
& The Grove.[1] Asquith asked me to come into his room after questions. He
showed me a letter from Whitley resigning his position, owing to his wife in
hysteria & illness having stolen groceries at Littlehampton.[2] We sent a
sympathetic telegram declining to entertain his proposal.

We then discussed Sydney Buxton's proposition that Granard should be
offered assistant P.M. General & turned that down as the work related to H. of C.
matters finance & labour. I suggested Henry Norman as one whose services on
the Budget League might be recognised, & the man kept quiet.

We also talked over possibilities of Strachey going to Bd. Agric. – new under
Sec. – and how to get over difficulty of a Treasurer & New Whip.[3]

At 6.40 Asquith sent for me again & discussed the possibilities of a General
Election in January & whether anyone could go round the constituencies &
report. I explained I was seeing all the Federation agents on Friday and could get
all information required.

I was at work on candidates and Labour splits were having my attention & I
hoped I might use influences to avoid three cornered fights, but the L.R.C. group
had no recognised authority over the various socialist sections & trade unions –
& Liberals resented arrangements under which they had the only alternatives of
voting for Socialists or Tories – Asquith talked freely & seemed glad to have
some one to talk over confidential matters with & unburden his soul.

---

1 JAP's fellow guest at Glen August 20–2 was Alfred Lyttelton (Glen Visitors' Book,
  Glenconner MSS). The Peases had Gurney relatives who lived at The Grove, a
  house in Norwich.

2 Marguerita Virginia Whitley (d. 1925); daughter of one of Garibaldi's officers; m.
  Whitley in 1892. On August 30 she was charged with stealing a quantity of potted
  meats. Her Harley Street physician testified that she suffered from 'mental
  depression and capricious appetite … hysteria of a well recognized type – anorexia
  nervosa'. She had refused to submit to his prescribed rest cure so he had forbidden
  her any social duties and given her a special diet. In spite of an embarrassed
  revelation by the prosecutor that the thefts had been going on for eight days, the
  charge was dismissed.

3 Strachey had written to JAP on July 11 complaining that his long services to the
  party had not been recognised, and that he had not been given first refusal of the
  new Under-Secretaryship at the Board of Agriculture. (Gainford MSS, 87). He was
  appointed 20 December 1909.

He seemed to think the lesser lights among the Peers would be too strong for the older heads & that the Lords would throw over the budget.

JAP also described his evening meeting with Asquith in a letter to his wife, 27 August 1909. (Gainford MSS, 520).

The Prime Minister sent for me again at 6.30 & gave me 40 minutes of his time. He wanted to let off steam & talk to me about the position – I don't think he has anyone else with whom he can talk really freely. He feels there is at least an equal chance of the Lords chucking the Budget, owing to the pressure of the less eminent & the hot heads. That if Lansdowne can't lead them his way, he will lead them their way – or as Winston put it, if he can't stop the horse going at the fence, he will try & ride him over it.

He wanted to know about candidates & what the position was – evidently egged on by Winston. I told him what the position was, & that I was meeting the Federation Secretaries in a few days (next Friday) to talk over their constituencies with them & see what was required to be done in the event of a January election.

I explained to him the difficulty of making arrangement in regard to 3 cornered seats with a heterogeneous mass composed of I.L.P. – social democrats – trade unionists of great varieties – individual socialists financed by Tories – and the L.R.C. and Liberal Labour members in the House – no one group could answer for the others – & there was no organised Labour party to deal with in fact – though it was generally assumed the Parliamentary group led by Henderson had influence. I told the P.M.

I was ascertaining the anticipated result of a 3d. candidate so called Labour in the constituencies where they are going to be run, & if negociations could do good, I would try & avoid split elections by *official* Liberals in the constituencies. Arrangements were generally regarded as if [sic] It was of course all heads the labour group win & tails we lose and a temporary arrangement might only mean that we sacrificed our permanent party machine in certain constituencies; & our middle class Liberals much resented being thrown over to the socialists, or forced to become Tariff Reformers & Tories.

Lord R's threatened speech at Glasgow is a topic upon which I cannot dwell I can hardly believe he an ex Liberal P.M. will box the compass – what a fool he is. I have a nice letter from Neil Primrose saying he will have a chat with me when he next is in London. I want to keep him at Wisbech and get him to toe the line. If Lord R. does come out against the budget Neil will be more then ever 'suspect' – & he would have either to chuck Lord R. or the constituency.

                                                              Your loving Jack

It looks like the Session going on into the middle of October – but we will try & stick to the Scotch engagements - and see what happens!

If the Lords are on the chuck, the Government won't hurry up the budget, & we shall have no all night sittings to pass the bill through & the session may drag.

Sept. 6   Prime Minister sent for me at 7.0 – on his return from Lympne Castle. He was full of three suffragettes' action on Sunday, they waylaid him in the porch & battered him as he came out of Church. In the afternoon they had a rope & tried to attack him to nooze him. In the evening they threw 3 big stones through the window.

Haldane was all for severe imprisonment & heavy fines – Gladstone had made arrangements for more protection.

Margot Asquith's brother, Frank Tennant, had engaged the architect Robert Lorimer to restore and enlarge the derelict Lympne Castle overlooking Romney Marsh. The work was undertaken in two stages 1907–9 and 1911–12. (Gavin Stamp and André Goulancourt, The English House 1860–1914: *The Flowering of English Domestic Architecture, Faber & Faber, 1986, p. 106). The Asquiths frequently used Lympne at weekends and holidays until they began to make similar use of Walmer Castle late in 1914. (Baroness Elliot of Harwood to CH, 10 June 1975). The afternoon attack had been made when Asquith and his partners were about to return to Lympne from Littlestone Golf Club. The Times (8 Sept. 1909) reported that Asquith was saved by Herbert Gladstone, who pushed the women out of the clubhouse. Harry Cust, posing as secretary of the club of which he was not even a member, impressed the assailants by telling them that whatever their dispute with the Prime Minister they could not walk on the grass in defiance of club regulations. (W.S. Blunt's diary, 2 Oct. 1909, in Wilfrid Scawen Blunt,* My Diaries: *Being a Personal Narrative of Events 1888–1914, Martin Secker, 1932 [1st edn 1919/20], p. 689; Sir Ronald Storrs,* Orientations, *Nicholson and Watson, 1945, p. 34). It is not clear what had happened to the Special Branch sergeant and constable who were supposed to protect the Prime Minister. (Supt P. Quinn to Commissioner of Police, 7 July 1909, MEPO 2/1297). When the Asquiths entertained at Lympne two weeks later they and their guests had a large police escort.*

None of Asquith's Cabinet letters to the King refers to these attacks on ministers by suffragettes. Gladstone circulated a note to all ministers on September 11 about arrangements for police protection. Ministers were asked to notify the police of their public meetings and their movements. (Runciman MSS). The Special Branch sought Home Office agreement on September 15 to augmenting the CID with two inspectors, eight sergeants, and six constables. (MEPO 3/1310). Gladstone, a supporter of female suffrage, told his brother on September 21, 'We can deal with them as a body easily enough but there are a lot of them almost if not quite mad.' (Gladstone of Hawarden MSS). There was another scare later in the month when the police were informed that some suffragettes were improving their marksmanship in order to shoot Asquith as he entered Parliament. (Asquith MSS, vol. 22, ff. 244–6). Though aware that the Home Secretary had now brought in the Special Branch to counter 'a dangerous conspiracy' Asquith would not permit Gladstone to bring his anxieties to the Cabinet. (Rosen, Rise Up, Women, *p. 127, quoting Gladstone to Grey, 10 Oct 1909, Gladstone MSS, Add MS 45992).*

Haldane said he had been with King at Marlborough Club, & the King said he had read Ministers' speeches & alluded to the Queen & himself having arranged the reengagement of Randolph & said the King the result of an alliance is a 'Cow boy'.

Speaking at Leicester in September Churchill had poured scorn on the 'miserable minority of titled persons who represent nobody, who are responsible to nobody, and who only scurry up to London to vote in their party interests, their class interests and in their own interests'. A letter to The Times *a few days later from Lord Knollys made the King's displeasure clear. The King's suggestion that he had himself to blame for Churchill's existence probably exaggerated the influence of his intervention on the interrupted engagement of Lord Randolph Churchill and Miss Jennie Jerome. (Randolph S. Churchill,* Winston S. Churchill, *vol. II, Young Statesman 1901–1914, Heinemann, 1967, p. 327). Nevertheless he told the same story to Esher on September 5. (Esher's journal, 8 Sept. 1909, Esher MSS, 2/12).*

Asquith says well my observations don't seem to have been taken as a hint – apropos of his speech last week referring to Lloyd George & Winston as colleagues whose picturesque language contained the minimum of indiscretion.

I told him my figures in anticipation of a General Election in Jany.

a majority of 40, Liberals 331 with Labour 24 = 355

over Irish 83 Unionists 222 = 315.

JAP had been briefed by the Liberal agents on September 3. A January election now seemed certain, as the Master of Elibank warned Ramsay MacDonald, reinforcing advice earlier in the year from Masterman and JAP. (MacDonald to Margaret MacDonald, [Spring 1909] and 2 Sept. 1909, Jane Cox, ed., A Singular Marriage: *A Labour Love Story in Letters and Diaries, Ramsay and Margaret MacDonald, Harrap, 1988, pp. 337, 340–1).*

Meanwhile, alarmed at the prospect of a huge deficit, the Treasury favoured a second Finance Bill, shorn of rejected elements. Ilbert argued for a Taxes Continuation Bill that would not concede the right of the Lords to 'dictate the amendment of a Finance Bill.' His views were circulated by Asquith as those of a 'high constitutional authority'. A compromise Finance (No. 2) Bill, securing the income tax and the tea duty, was prepared by early November. But Lloyd George, advised by John Simon and supported by the head of the Inland Revenue, was determined to proceed on the authority of the Commons' resolution, taking the risk of conflict with the courts. Ilbert, who participated in a discussion with Lloyd George, Churchill, Chalmers, and Murray on November 12 and had a further long talk with Lloyd George on November 13, was 'driven reluctantly to the same conclusion. L.G.', he noted, 'wants me to write a memorandum on the question for the Cabinet, saying it would carry great weight.' Stiffened by the advice of the 'high constitutional authority' Cabinet decided that no new legislation was necessary. But, as he told Hobhouse on November 19, Asquith decided to avoid a collision with the courts by refusing to collect any taxes after the prorogation. Thus the government stopped short of the bold course which Lloyd George and Chalmers had been ready to pursue. (Misled by a self-serving letter by Ilbert, Blewett, The Peers, The Parties and the People, *p. 89, writes of 'Ilbert's policy' without mentioning Lloyd George's primary role. Ilbert had been surprised to learn from an article by* The Times' *parliamentary correspondent that the custom of 'collecting taxes under the resolutions' had been given legal validity in numerous judicial decisions. Cf Ilbert to Harcourt, n.d. [?8 Sept. 1909], Harcourt MSS, dep. 441, ff. 62–3; Ilbert's diary, 12, 13 and 16 Nov. 1909, Ilbert MSS, H.C. Lib. MS 73; Hobhouse's diary, 20 Nov. 1909, David, ed.,* Inside Asquith's Cabinet, *p. 82; Murray,* The People's Budget, *pp. 227–9).*

Sept. 8 P.M. told me what had passed in cabinet in regard to the financing the country if the Lords threw out the budget – a new bill saving tea & income tax appeared essential.

8 Sept 09   10 Downing Street,
10.15 p.m.   Whitehall, S.W.

My dear Jack – As I am feeling rather seedy this evening, I think I shd. like to be excused from returning to the House. Will you please tell the two Samuels?[4] I shall be all right to-morrow.   Yours
                                                 H.H.A.
                                                 (Gainford MSS, 38, f. 76)

Forgetting that the same thing had happened on August 12 JAP told his wife that this was 'the first time since I have known him' that Asquith went home early. Sending Elsie a cutting from The Standard *on September 8 headed 'HOUSE OF LORDS AND DISSOLUTION. Radicals and Rejection of Budget. Crisis Imminent. Possible General Election in November' JAP commented that headlines like this 'excited the Politicians. It looks,' he said, 'as if the Lords might say we won't reject the budget, but hang it up over a general election. It is of course the same as rejection, and the adoption of the only direct way of killing a bill by the usual motion, it be read "this day six months"!' JAP could not bring himself to believe that the Lords would be so foolish as to invite the destruction of their power of veto. He forecast going steadily on until the middle of October. Having got to bed at 2.30 am on September 6 and 4.00 am on September 7, he had 'done a deal on the quiet with Hood' to ensure an earlier night on the 8th and 9th. Asquith had exhausted himself by refusing to help with the liquor licensing clauses of the Finance Bill unless Lloyd George let him take*

---

4   Presumably Herbert Samuel and Sam Evans.

complete charge. As JAP told Elsie on September 9 after dining at Romano's with the Chancellor, Lloyd George 'only looks in & on now'. (Gainford MSS, 520). Lloyd George, who had 'hardly been in attendance during the licensing clauses', remained conspicuously fresh. (Lord Balcarres' diary, 11, 17 Sept. 1909, Vincent, ed., The Crawford Diaries, *p. 133).*

Sept. 9   1.30 Prime Minister sent for me & said he had 2 or 3 matters to talk over.

I reported what occurred the previous night. He was evidently seedy the day before, overtired sitting up to 4.0 on Tuesday then a long cabinet & being in charge of Licensing clauses. He said his head ache was gone.

He asked me to whom he should give Lord Carysfort's Lord Lieutenancy & K.P. In regard to former I did not know who were landowners in Wicklow who were friendly.[5] As for K.P. I thought Kitchener if his identity with Ireland could be established would be a good move on his return from India, better than Arran or Mountgarret, the one was only as a support lukewarm, the other was not known. Annerley's Liberalism was a sham.[6] We then discussed South Africa and who was to follow Selborne – P.M. said Sydney Buxton wanted to follow, if he could not get Board of Trade with £5,000 p.a.[7] Churchill wanted S. Africa – but quite unfitted. He asked me about Pentland & I said not big enough & he certainly had no claims, he had done well by the Party & P.M. agreed.

---

5   The Earl of Carysfort, Liberal Unionist Lord Lieutenant of Co. Wicklow since 1890, died on September 4. The 8th Viscount Powerscourt (1880–1947) was appointed to replace him; a Liberal Unionist he owned some 41,000 acres in the county.

6   'Annerley' was probably Luke White, Baron Annaly (1857–1922); 3rd Baron 1888; Ld of the Bedchamber to the Prince of Wales 1908–10; permanent Ld-in-Waiting 1910–21. Annaly, Master of the Pytchley Hunt, had been a Lib. Unionist. He was listed in *Vacher's Parliamentary Companion* as a Liberal but not by the *Liberal Year Book*. He had seats in Co. Kilkenny, Co. Dublin, and Northampton. Neither Annaly nor Lord Mountgarret got the KP. Lord Arran 'one of the richest men in Scotland ... goes now and then to London but always with a guide book to find his way from Piccadilly to Pall Mall.' (Lord Esher to Lord Knollys, 23 Aug. 1908, Royal Archives, Edw VII w41. 59). Arran's KP was announced on October 19. Kitchener, who received the KP in 1911, was born in Co. Kerry and his parents lived there until his mother's ill-health led to their removal to Switzerland.

7   In April 1908 when Asquith had offered Churchill the Board of Trade he said that he intended to improve the status and salary of the office (from £2000 to £5000) though any change would not take effect till the following year. But when the act was passed it did not apply to the current incumbent. Churchill was particularly unfortunate for this change was part of a general review; only the salary of the President of the Board of Trade was limited by statute.

He then asked me what I thought should be done with the suffragettes in gaol who were starving themselves. I said forcible feeding it is the duty of the state during their sentences to see they are properly fed. The P.M. said Gladstone had in cabinet been vehemently attacked by Haldane Runciman & Churchill for not protecting the P.M. & for dealing too leniently with law breakers. Throwing stones imperilling life was an offence which should commit a prisoner to the assizes, & the Judges would know how to deal with their conduct.

He dismissed me, after walking up & down the room for 20 mins. by the usual 'very well'.

Sept. 20 I had a chat at 1.30 after Tweedmouth's memorial service at No. 12. – also another at the H of C for half an hour.
Lord Rosebery after the Glasgow speech

Asquith told me of his correspondence with Rosebery, & how he had told him he & his colleagues could not follow his lead, & unless he resigned his presidency of the Liberal League they would have to do so. Lord R. in reply only said he had not changed but the Party had. Meanwhile Asquith heard from Perks that Lord R's resignation had been sent in *before* the Glasgow speech. Yet this fact Lord R. ignored.

In a widely advertised speech to a meeting of businessmen in Glasgow on Friday September 10, Rosebery had condemned the Budget, and noted in passing that he had long since ceased to be 'in communion' with the Liberal Party. Asquith had written decisively to him the following day. Rosebery had in fact resigned from the presidency of the Liberal League on September 9. He advised Asquith on September 14 that he would no longer sit on the Liberal benches. (Rosebery MSS, 10001). Though urged by Sir J. West Ridgeway and others not to precipitate the League's dissolution 'just at a moment when its existence as a rallying point for moderate Liberals is more necessary than ever', Rosebery recognised the inevitable. On October 5, however, the League resolved to continue at the discretion of its committee. According to Harry Paulton this was the wish of Asquith, Grey, and Haldane who saw the organisation 'as a possible rallying ground in the future.' The League was extinguished on 31 May 1910. (West Ridgeway to R. Whitehead, 30 Sept. 1909, Whitehead MSS, HLRO Hist. Coll. 211; Emmott's diary, [?10] Oct. 1909, Emmott MSS, vol. I, f. 197; H.C.G. Matthew, The Liberal Imperialists: The ideas and politics of a post-Gladstonian elite, Oxford University Press, 1973, p. 120; A.S. King, Some Aspects of the History of the Liberal Party in Great Britain 1906–14, D. Phil. thesis, University of Oxford, 1962, p. 178). Writing to the editor of the British Weekly Dr W. Robertson Nicoll on September 9, Lloyd George had recognised that: 'Everything depends upon what Rosebery says tomorrow: if he indicates that the Bill ought to be submitted to the judgment of the Country, the Tory leaders will be stampeded by the wild men behind them.' 'You always said that the Lords would reject the Budget', Lloyd George acknowledged, 'it looks to me now as if you were right'. (Robertson Nicoll MSS).

The possibility of an election if the Budget passed was then discussed by us. A. seemed to think the advantages of a January election in any case might get rid of awkward questions for the moment & the anti climax of Welsh Disestablishment. It was too patent too that it would be granted as an electioneering move. He said the pros & cons seemed pretty evenly divided.

The Home Rule question – the people of England – would not upset the Lords if they again chucked the bill out, and women's suffrage & other complications come before the next Parliament. The importance of dealing with Poor Law Reform next session he admitted was great.

The timing of the election was a major tactical decision on which the Chief Whip's advice was influential if not determinative. A January poll would give the Liberals the advantage of a fresh register though unemployment might be more severe. If the Conservatives won, their ministers would have to face re-election and they would have difficulty in passing a Budget before March 31. There were practical as well as tactical considerations. It would not have been possible to accelerate the production of a new register because a bill ordering it could not be passed before November. In any case the printing contracts did not provide for delivery or completion until late December. (Harcourt to Monks, 27 Sept. 1909, Harcourt MSS, uncat.). Morley thought that belief in the benefit of a new register was 'mere superstition'. He doubted that the Lords would throw out the Budget but favoured an immediate dissolution if they did. (Hirtzel's diary, 13 Sept. 1909, Hirtzel MSS, British Library, Oriental and India Office Collections, Home Misc 864/1).

Sept. 29 Had an interview with Asquith at 11.0 before cabinet. I placed before him the pros. & cons. of a general election in Dec. or Jany if the budget was thrown out by the Lords. I told him the Speaker's views on the question of guillotining report of Finance Bill, that the debates would be perfunctory & inadequate, that with a stale House we had better let the Opposition select their own topics for attack, and allow them a fortnight or so to bring the Report Stage to an end. He thought that would suffice.[8]

At the Cabinet I gave the pros & cons for a Jany election, & the Cabinet appeared impressed. I asked for directions as to business the following week,

---

8   The Clerk of the House had put similar views to Lloyd George the previous day, noting that it was for the whips to say if the Liberal rank and file were jaded and needed rest. (Ilbert's diary, 28 Sept. 1909, Ilbert MSS, H.C. Lib. MS 73).

and for guidance as to the date upon which Budget League meetings shd be stopped. The latter was referred to Churchill & myself to talk over.

I saw an intrigue threatening by Lloyd George & Churchill in having an organisation with a little money which they thought they might get under their own control. Norman the Secy however is loyal to me & the Party as a whole, & agrees the Budget League should be wound up when the Budget reaches the Lords. Asquith sent for me later & said that he had offered S. Africa to Herbert Gladstone, it was now worth £17,000 a year with £4,000 allowance for travelling, the finest berth in the Empire next to India. Gladstone was going to consult his wife. The apppointment must be made before the end of the year.

We talked of his successor: he favoured Burns, to get him out of the Board of Trade;[9] but he thought the King would jib. Harcourt deserved it & the King would like him as his Chief Sec. of State.

The Under Sec. to P.O. he thought he would give to Montagu & appoint Mallet his Sec. – the under Sec. Bd. Agric. to Strachey.

Gladstone accepted South Africa and took up his appointment in February 1910. His place at the Home Office was taken by Churchill; Buxton moved to the Board of Trade, Samuel to the Post Office, and Pease replaced Samuel at the Duchy of Lancaster. Harcourt was consoled with the Colonial Office the following November; Burns remained at the Local Government Board. Montagu, Asquith's pps, became Under Secretary at the India Office. Sir Henry Norman was given the Assistant Postmaster-Generalship, a newly established post from which he was forced to resign when he was defeated in the general election. He was replaced by Captain Norton. F.D. Acland, Financial Secretary to the War Office, was also defeated; he was replaced by Charles Mallet. Sir Samuel Evans, the Solicitor-General, was appointed a judge and replaced by Rufus Isaacs.

We talked about several matters – Lords attitude to budget – chances of election, Winston proposal to adjourn the House & create a delay before the Lords got budget, so as an election would fall immediately after their action & on the new register in Jany. Such a proceeding Asquith regarded as impossible as tending to expand period of tension.

Tuesday Oct. 5 Travelled up to Grantham with Asquith 7.55 p.m. train, he on his way to see the King at Balmoral, I on my way to Corrour to deer stalk.[10]

I gave the P.M. dinner. He said you know the King's view don't you. I said no. The King, he replied is most anxious that the Lords pass the Budget but that

---

[9]   Burns was at the Local Government Board, not the Board of Trade.

[10] At Corrour, a deer forest in southeast Inverness-shire, between Crianlarich and Fort William on Rannoch Moor, JAP shot four stags over the next five days.

an appeal is subsequently made to justify the continuation of the Govmt's policy. Haldane has just come back & until I (Asquith) pointed out the absurdity of the proposal, Haldane seemed to think there was something in it. When the Lords had climbed down, & we won a victory, there would be nothing to appeal to the country on. I shall point this out to the King.

House adjourned from 8th to 18th.

On October 15 Asquith reported to JAP on his interview with the King on October 11: 'All that the King could extract from the Tory leaders was that they have not yet made up their minds what the Lords are to do.' (Gainford MSS, 87).

Monday 18th Asquith not at questions. I answered the only one addressed to him, at his request.

He sent for me at 6 oclock to go over to 10 Downing St. He at once proceeded to tell me that The King had acquiesced in his view about not having an election if & after the Lords passed the budget. I mentioned Herbert Gladstone going to S. Africa, the King did not like this idea but I argued it & got my way.[11] He said I have been misrepresented by the Press as asking the King to see Lansdowne & Balfour at Buckingham Palace last Monday, the King suggested it & I told him I saw no harm but only good might come of it. The King asked me to come after they left, & seemed surprised that Balfour and Lansdowne could not tell him that they could say what the Lords would do, & they left him without being able even to promise him they would let him know. It was a ridiculous position! I told the King he might show them Murray's Treasury minute showing the chaos finance would be in if they chucked the budget.[12] Balfour & Lansdowne denounced the Dukes for all they were worth to the King. The King was much annoyed at Ll. George's speech at Newcastle which makes things much more difficult for the Lords.

Lloyd George had made three speeches in Newcastle-on-Tyne on October 9 explaining his Budget and the land taxes. He added that if the peers rejected the Budget they would have only themselves to blame for the revolution which would follow: the questioning of the right of the peers to so much wealth and to so much power. 'Should five hundred men, ordinary men, chosen accidentally from among the unemployed, override the judgment — the deliberate judgement — of millions of people who are engaged in the industry which makes the wealth of

---

11   The King's grudging approval of a 'very bad' appointment was conveyed to Asquith three days later. (Knollys to Nash, 21 Oct. 1909, Asquith MSS, vol. 1, f. 206).

12   Murray's memorandum, 'Effect of the rejection of the Finance Bill by the House of Lords', circulated to the Cabinet, 7 September 1909 (Cab. 37/100/121), was given to the Tory leaders on October 12.

this country?' The King was annoyed because he had attempted to lower the temperature of Lloyd George's language that summer and had urged him not 'to set class against class'.

JAP did not mention that at this time he encountered royal displeasure for a similar offence to those of Churchill and Lloyd George. On November 3 he had addressed a meeting of his constituents at Steeple Bumpstead. The Times (4 Nov. 1909) reported him as saying that although the Commons recognised that the Budget had to go to the Lords and have the King's sanction, the Commons did not recognise the right of either King or Lords to reject these proposals from the representatives of the people. On November 4 Lord Knollys suggested to Harcourt that JAP should write explaining the unnecessary introduction of the King's name. JAP wrote at once.

Nov 4 1909
12 Downing Street,
S.W.

Dear Lord Knollys,

In case the summarised report of my speech in todays Press, may be misunderstood, I am writing to you to say that my reference to His Majesty was not intended and did not I am sure convey to my audience that His Majesty has taken any side or might take any particular view in regard to the Budget.

My remarks had reference only to the method by which the veto powers of the Upper House might be limited, & that if the necessity arose advice might be given by ministers to secure the creation of Peers to enable the mandate of the country to be carried through, if ordinary means failed.

I am yours
very sincerely
Joseph A. Pease
(RA W66/95)

The explanation did not impress the palace. The Finance Bill had passed its third reading in the Commons on November 4 and an appeal to the country was increasingly probable.

Copy

B. Palace
5 Nov. 1909

Dear Mr Pease,

I have submitted your letter to the King & he desires me to thank you for what you say in it.

He directs me at the same time to add that he hopes you will agree with him in thinking it will be safer that members of the Government should abstain from introducing his name into their speeches.

K.

(RA R29/104)

Lord Knollys complained to Asquith's secretary that JAP's explanation was not very satisfactory. (Knollys to Nash, 5 Nov. 1909, Asquith MSS, vol. 1, f. 218). Nash responded:

5 Nov. 1909
10 Downing Street,
Whitehall. S.W.

My dear Lord Knollys,

I have shown your letter to Mr. Asquith who asks me to say that he quite agrees that the King's name ought not to be introduced into political speeches, & he desires me to thank you for giving him the opportunity of seeing the terms in which you have brought this home to Mr. Pease. I feel sure (though I am not authorised to say so) that Mr Asquith will mention the matter to Mr. Pease, & I am supplying him with a report of the speech in question.

If I may say a personal word it is that Mr. Pease is the last man in the world to perpetrate, knowingly, a blunder of this description. He would be *most* anxious not to do so; & in my opinion the mistake must have arisen through clumsiness or lack of thought: Please forgive me for obtruding this remark but I know Mr. Pease well, & have a regard for him....

(RA R30/69)

During interval *Nov. 5 to 23* Speculation tending all in direction of Lords throwing out Budget. I wrote to Asquith on 16th telling him I heard even Halsbury had been trying to influence Peers to accept budget but the country peers were too strong for him & the longer headed men with experience & less foolhardy.[13]

On that evening Lansdowne handed in at Lords, Notice of rejection. My private sec.[14] tells me, gossip says, Milner was obdurate & would have led peers against Lansdowne unless he had given way.

Fuller writes to me on 18th:

'Much talk at Windsor last night about the Lansdowne motion. The Tory Lords that I spoke to about it i.e. Gosford & Howe are not at all happy about it. Knollys told me "they are mad". Argyll was quite pleased & thought they were right. My view is that the Lords are fighting a rear guard action.'

---

[13]   JAP's letter of November 16 does not seem to have survived.

[14]   As Chief Whip, JAP had two private secretaries: R.H. Davies and F.R.L. Renbold. Richard Humphrey Davies (1872–1970) was private secretary to Patronage Secretary 1905–16; to H.J. Gladstone 1899–1905; Clerk, Parliamentary Recruiting Committee 1914–16; secretary, Liberal Central Association 1917–26; secretary, Principal of the University College of North Wales (Bangor) 1927–40. Renbold was private secretary to successive Chief Whips 1908–13; superintendent of Patronage Secretary's messengers 1913–16. No letter from either man survives in JAP's papers for 1908–10. We cannot discover where JAP was. The information probably came from Davies.

As Vice-Chamberlain of the Household, the Liberal junior whip John Fuller was well-placed to garner political gossip in royal circles. As a wealthy polo-playing Wiltshire landowner, brother-in-law of Lord St Aldwyn, he was persona grata with the Tory peers in the Queen's Household (Gosford and Howe) as well as the Governor and Constable of Windsor Castle (the Duke of Argyll). The King's private secretary, his Liberal sympathies undisguised, appears to have spoken without inhibition about the sanity of the Conservatives. He had told the Prime Minister on November 15 that the King had said he 'thought the Peers were mad'. (Margot Asquith's diary, 15 Nov. 1909, The Autobiography of Margot Asquith, vol. II, Thornton Butterworth, 1922, p. 126). A fortnight later, in conversation with the Clerk of the Privy Council, Knollys 'stated very gravely and emphatically that he thought the Lords mad ...' (FitzRoy's diary, 2 Dec. 1909, FitzRoy, Memoirs, vol. 1, p. 389).

Late in November JAP joined Walter Runciman for some shooting at Swynnerton Park in Staffordshire which the Oswald Partingtons had leased. Runciman reported to his wife on November 28: 'He has just been telling me about his plans for a deal with the Labour people, & I am strongly of the view that he is doing the job well & fully realises the folly of weakness.' (Viscountess Runciman MSS). So anxious was JAP to avoid the appearance of weakness that Lloyd George had concluded that 'the men at the Whips' Office have a strong personal feeling against the Labour men, & are very reluctant to make a deal with them.' (Ilbert's diary, 13 Nov. 1909, Ilbert MSS, H.C. Lib. MS 73).

Lloyd George feared that JAP's containment policy was founded on a debateable reading of a rapidly changing political climate. He had told Ilbert that the greatest danger to the Liberals would arise from 'a split between Liberalism & Labour such as destroyed Liberalism in Germany & elsewhere.' With a general election looming JAP wanted to minimise conflict with Labour but was not prepared to yield fresh ground. The threat of a Labour candidature in Bishop Auckland, where his brother-in-law Sir Henry Havelock-Allan Bt had succeeded Harry Paulton as the Liberal candidate, had given him the opportunity to 'promote the cohesion of progressive forces' by expressing his views 'in regard to the attitude I suggest should be adopted by those constituencies that are now represented by either Liberals or Trades Union representatives who see eye to eye on the main issues of the election, the Budget and the relations of the two Chambers.' In a letter subsequently published in The Manchester Guardian *(Nov. 17) JAP noted that candidates were being put forward by the Social Democratic and other organisations over which the federated trades unions and the Labour Representation Committee had no control. But for JAP the right principle to observe in the face of a common danger was that 'Liberals should, so far as they can, respect the seats which at the last General Election returned L.R.C. candidates, and that the L.R.C. organisation should respect other progressive candidates standing for seats held by other Labour or Liberal candidates in 1906.'*

Expressing a fear that, without some 'tacit understanding' three-cornered contests in seats like Bishop Auckland and Coventry would lead to Conservative victories by minority votes, Pease affirmed that it was 'essential that, if the Liberal Government came back into power, the anomalies of our electoral laws and the possible representation by a candidate returned by a minority vote shall be removed before another General Election.' But the implied promise of electoral reform had a price. 'If the L.R.C. party have come to stay & will rest content with their present numerical strength for the next Parliament, they would surely not be prejudiced in the long run.' Conversely, if the Labour Party persisted in an aggressive attitude they could not expect official Liberalism to remain passive.

As against the 'innumerable instances' which he could give to show that 'so far aggressive action has almost exclusively been confined to Labour organisations' there were only two cases, Jarrow and Gateshead, where he conceded 'it may be suggested that Liberals are the aggressors.' At Jarrow, Pete Curran who had unsuccessfully challenged the veteran Liberal member Sir Mark Palmer in 1906 had won a by-election in July 1907 on Palmer's death. Curran was elected on a minority vote, the Liberals being assailed by an Irish Nationalist and by the first Conservative to appear for a generation. In Gateshead John Johnson, a Miners' Agent, 'stood under Liberal auspices'. While Johnson had 'changed his party' the Liberals 'have not changed their faith, and see no reason why they should now accept an L.R.C. candidate.'

For the past two years Pease had repeatedly praised the effectiveness of men like Burt, Charles Fenwick, John Wilson, Abraham, Randal Cremer, and Richard Bell, joined in the last Parliament by 'Maddison, [H.H.] Vivian, [John] Ward, [George] Nicholls, [W.E.] Harvey, [Fred] Hall, [John] Wadsworth, [Albert] Stanley and many others'. These 'Labour' men, he insisted, had an increasing and far greater influence for example on the Trades Disputes legislation, than 'the outside group led by Mr Keir Hardie and Mr Henderson.' The most that JAP could find to say for the L.R.C. members was that on occasions, especially during all-night sittings on the Budget, their self-sacrifice had enabled some of the government's older supporters to get to bed at a reasonable hour. Summarising what he would like 'organised Labour in the country to realise' Pease offered four propositions:

'1. That if they now press L.R.C. candidates for seats which were won by Liberals, or Labour members who have not signed the constitution, they must expect retaliatory attacks upon their own candidates standing for those seats which they now hold. In my opinion, and I do not say it as a threat, the Labour party are more likely to be losers if an uncompromising attitude is adopted, and attempts made to win seats held by Liberals and Radicals and instead of having 33 members returned their organisation may be left with reduced numbers in the next Parliament.

2. Liberal legislation has not been in the past, nor in the future is it likely to be, much influenced by members who claim no loyalty to the Government, and decline to work on a common platform for common objects.

3. That the Government have shown by their administrative acts and by the laws that have been passed through the House of Commons that they are practical social reformers, and worthy of confidence.

4. That the issues of the next general election are such as all the Liberal, Radical, and Labour members can whole-heartedly unite in supporting –

   (a) Constitutional reform – making the people's voice supreme.

   (b) The maintenance of Free Trade.

   (c) Social reform advanced on the lines indicated by the Government in regard to unemployment, poor-law etc.

   (d) Measures to secure religious and electoral equality.'

Labour spokesmen were predictably unimpressed by JAP's declarations. The Daily Mail *reported on November 20 that 'the advice to "sit still and be good" seems to cause amusement in the Labour ranks.' Labour leaders let it be known that they were far from content with 33 members, all but one of whom was standing for re-election. Twenty-one other candidates were in the field and seventeen more were on the list of prospective candidates awaiting allocation to constituencies. In Wigan, where a three-cornered fight looked likely, the Liberals were 'apparently preparing a pact to support the Labour nominee.' Arthur Henderson, taking the battle to Bishop Auckland, pointed out that three-cornered contests were 'the outcome of democratic power'. He saw no prospect of agreement on the terms indicated by the Liberal Chief Whip; but, in any case, 'the only way out of the difficulty' would be if a special national conference of the Labour party instructed the executive 'to weigh the strict letter of their constitution in order to expedite thereby a victory for the Budget.' (The Times, 22 Nov. 1909).*

JAP's stand was to be vindicated by the containment of Labour in the January election. Havelock-Allan survived the Labour intervention at Bishop Auckland; and Curran was beaten in Jarrow. (A.W. Purdue, 'Jarrow Politics, 1885–1914: The Challenge to Liberal Hegemony', Northern History, Vol. XVIII, 1982, pp. 182–8). In Coventry, there was no Labour candidate but the Liberals still lost the seat they had won in 1906. Wigan, in which the Liberals had little chance, was left to Labour and won by the miners' Henry Twist. Elsewhere, Labour's pickings were meagre. (Blewett, The Peers, The Parties and the People, pp. 234–65; Trevor Lloyd, 'Lib-Labs and "unforgiveable electoral generosity"',

Bulletin of the Institute of Historical Research, *vol. XLVIII, Nov. 1975, pp. 255–9).*

Although the Liberal war chest had been amply replenished by George Whiteley, the government's wealthy supporters could not expect to get through an election without receiving an appeal from the Chief Whip. On November 30 Pease wrote in his own hand to the Prime Minister's brother-in-law Sir Edward Tennant Bt.

Private
My dear Eddie
    I wonder if you can help me at the present time, in my effort to raise a fund to enable the Party to fight the Tories.
    Begging is always an unpleasant occupation & giving is often the same, but if you could send me a few thousand to enable us to fight seats, which might otherwise go unfought, to the detriment of others, I shall be glad, & your generosity will be much appreciated.
    Please do what you can

Yours very sincerely
Joseph A. Pease

Please mark your envelope in reply "Private"
p.s. If I can help you later in any way of course you can rely on my assistance in another direction.

(Glenconner MSS)

Tennant responded with £4,000. He lost his seat at Salisbury in January and was raised to the peerage as Lord Glenconner in 1911.

Dec. 1   Had a chat on general subjects with P.M. see 3/12.

Dec. 2 Thurs   As I was going out to bring Asquith into the House to make his great speech in protest of Lords' rejection of the Budget (on the Tuesday previous) I met Balfour coming into the House, & as he opened the door behind the Speaker's chair, his back was to me, & he said to Wyndham 'I hate this damned dramatic occasion.' Everyone felt Asquith was as much master of the occasion as he was over his words in which he uttered a speech which must become historical. He was in his best form, & his delivery & matter was of the highest order. Poor Balfour blundered about, & was physically unfit for any attempt to counter the master strokes of our great Prime Minister, who rose to the occasion. Perhaps Gladstone's scorn & rhetoric was greater at his best. He however never had this occasion, but I can still picture him withering his opponents on less occasions just as Asquith did on this one.

    We would have had 360 in the lobby in another half hour. The Tories having no reply, did not attempt to better Balfour's failure, & after Henderson & Bottomley spoke, an early Division enabled the session to be wound up.

Another contemporary Liberal diarist, Rowland Whitehead, the Attorney-General's pps, thought the Prime Minister's speech 'the best I have ever heard from him & I have heard many. Then Balfour halting hesitating ineffective ...' (Whitehead's diary, 2 Dec. 1909, Whitehead MSS, HLRO Hist. Coll. 211). The Times (3 Dec. 1909) did not share these opinions of Asquith's performance: 'Mr Asquith's speech is disappointing because it was upon no higher level than that of ordinary political polemic ...'. But the paper did grant that Asquith was grave, and earnest, and made a 'sonorous' denunciation of the peers.

Friday Dec. 3 Before leaving for my constituency I had a talk over an incident on Thursday in which I denounced Lloyd George for buying funds for the Budget League by selling honours. I said it was scandalous, he took it lying down & Churchill who was in the chair, rebuked me & said what I felt should be reserved for another occasion. We agreed to distribute the funds in assisting the spread of budget literature & posters. Asquith admitted George had told him of a man who would do something for Welsh Education, & asked for an honour & as George left the room G. had said perhaps he may also help the Budget League.[15] I told Asquith what my opinion was of my slippery friends & how I raised cash without ever directly associating distinction with Party help, & alluded to Kleinwort who had that morning responded by a cheque for £20,000 for the election on my bare request.

Asquith might have forgotten, though JAP could scarcely have done so, that Alexander Kleinwort had become a baronet eight days earlier. Searle (Corruption in British Politics, p. 148) obscures the point of this episode by vagueness about the timing of Kleinwort's honour. J.C. Horsfall, a Yorkshire textile manufacturer, whose baronetcy was announced at the same time as Kleinwort's, had given Churchill £15,000 for the Budget League 'Campaign Fund' on 25 August 1909. (Churchill, Winston S. Churchill, Vol. II, Companion Part 2, *p. 905).*

When an ostensibly unsolicited cheque for £10,000 in support of free trade was sent to Churchill by a Dundee jute manufacturer J.K. Caird late in December, JAP expressed his delight to Churchill on December 23: 'It is the right way for money to come in: and I can't help repudiating Horsfalling, – to promise honours in exchange for brass, I have always set my face steadily

---

15   One man who certainly did something for Welsh education, and was knighted in 1909, was E. Vincent Evans, journalist, and leading light of the Honourable Society of Cymmrodorion and the National Eisteddfod Association. But Evans's services were personal rather than financial. None of those honoured in November 1909 was later conspicuous in the cause of Welsh education. Sir Edgar Speyer's privy councillorship is suggestively coincidental, but he was a friend of Asquith. Alfred Mond, who was moving to the safe Liberal seat of Swansea and was the Budget League's principal financial supporter, was created a baronet in July 1910.

against, and I could not help flying at Lloyd George for doing it. Caird now deserves all we can do for him, if it was voluntary as I presume it was.' (Churchill MSS, 2/43; Churchill to JAP, 21 Dec. 1909, Gainford MSS, 87). 'Caird, Esq. (Dundee)' was placed with Kleinwort but not Horsfall on the list of names of those 'whom it was proposed to approach with a view to the submission of their names to the King in the event of a creation of Peers becoming necessary.' (Jenkins, Asquith, p. 540). But it was 1913 before Caird, by then 79, got his baronetcy.

JAP's sensitivity about Budget League fund-raising was unsurprising given that he had advanced £2000 to Lehmann and had met £1500 in speakers' expenses. He had written to Norman on September 20: 'I believe the Budget League have more £.s.d. than they will want'; he staked a claim for the 'credit balance when the League's campaign ends with the passage through the House of the Budget.' (Norman MSS). The Executive committee resolved on October 7 that the 'first charge upon any balance remaining at the end of the campaign should be the repayment to the Party funds of money advanced.' But Lloyd George and Churchill were in no hurry to extinguish their organisation and give up the funds it attracted. Sensing this, JAP wrote to Norman on November 3 reiterating that he could see 'no advantage whatever in the League continuing its existence' after the 'passage or the rejection of the Finance Bill.' Offering to submit accounts 'if required', JAP asked for the £3500 to 'be now sent to me'. (Norman MSS). By November 25 Budget League funds had dwindled to £3000. JAP appealed to Churchill who replied making it clear that the League was not about to wind itself up. Given how valuable the League's work had been to the party, 'I should rather deprecate the casting up of balances in any narrow spirit, & I have no doubt that such is far from your intention.' (Churchill, Winston S. Churchill, vol. II, Companion Part 2, pp. 923–4). JAP's pain was eased by a handsome tribute in Norman's final report to the Prime Minister on November 20 to his full and efficient assistance and 'the great practical value of Mr. Pease's scheme for local Federated Areas ...' But the committee had decided to remain in being during the general election. There would be no repayment to the party; the League itself would need additional funds. (Norman MSS).

We discussed possible new whips & I suggested the team for the new Parliament: Norton, Fuller, Partington, Dudley Ward, Soares, Gulland, Maclean (?Lamont). Strachey to go to the Lords (L.G. Bd.) Whitley to Ch. of Committees in place of Caldwell. We spoke of peerages – after election was over.

By the end of the session JAP had voted in 741 out of a possible 858 government divisions. He had cast 518 votes on the Budget Resolutions and Finance Bill. In a tabulation provided by Cecil Norton on December 7, he was recorded as being absent without a pair on 20 occasions. But, as the voting record now cautiously noted after repeated rebukes from members who believed their absences were not a matter for adverse comment, this figure 'might include pairs which have been privately arranged but were not reported, nor entered upon the daily pair sheets in the "No" lobby.' (Gainford MSS, 87).

JAP's conversation with the Prime Minister about the future composition of the whips' team suggests that at this stage neither man had raised the possibility that JAP might move to a different post after the election. As for the colleagues whose post-election fates were discussed, Norton became Assistant Postmaster-General; Fuller continued as Vice-Chamberlain to the Household; Partington continued as a junior whip; Dudley Ward was appointed Treasurer of the Household; Soares was appointed a junior whip 20 February 1910; Gulland continued as a junior whip. Maclean lost his seat and although he won another seat in December he had missed his chance. Lamont also lost his seat but he retired from politics. Strachey remained at the Board of Agriculture until becoming a peer in 1911. Whitley, who had previously been responsible for arranging the business of the House and appointment of committees, became deputy chairman of ways and means. Caldwell, a great favourite of Lloyd George's because of his readiness to accept closure motions, retired from Parliament. (Masterman, C.F.G. Masterman, p. 145). Gulland, the Scottish Whip, explained the changes in a letter to his aunt, Elsie Gulland Osborne, on 27 February 1910; 'the Master of Elibank is Chief and our friendship brings him to lippen a good deal to me. Fuller comes second, I third.' (Gulland Osborne MSS).

The Prime Minister was to launch the Liberal election campaign at the Albert Hall on December 10. JAP sent him some notes and advice:

10th December, 1909

My dear Asquith,

In case you feel inclined to make an appeal in your Speech tonight for unity all over the Country in support of the great Issues which are presented, I send you particulars of the Situation.

There are in Great Britain 567 Seats. The Liberals are proposing to fight 529, and to leave a clear field for Labour in at least 30 others. In nearly all of these 559 seats the prospective Candidates have already been adopted.

The Labour Members, led by Arthur Henderson, have Candidates out for 33 Seats which they already possess. (These Seats are in nearly every case being respected). And about 21 L.R.C. Candidates are attacking Liberal Seats. It is these seats which in a three-cornered battle may be transferred to the Tory Party. There are in addition to these some 15 to 20 Social Democrat Candidates being put up whose opposition to Liberal Candidates will not cause us much anxiety, as the Liberal Party have no sympathy with their aspirations.

An appeal at the present moment may produce a considerable reduction in the number of L.R.C. Candidates attacking Liberal seats, but you should be very careful to say that your realise that there is no possibility under their constitution of any arrangement being arrived at, but that you must appeal to their generosity pending legislation which will prevent, after another Election, the possibility of a representative of a minority vote securing a seat in Parliament.

The other point upon which I think you might perhaps dwell is that you can make it clear that the Liberal Party has no desire to destroy the Second Chamber, but as it is at present constituted its powers should be limited to revision and delay during the existence of a Parliament. There are a good number of influential Liberals who will be influenced in their attitude by a statement on this point and also by any expression which might lead them to think that in the event of hardships being proved as the result of the present Budget, the Liberal Party have not permanently set their seal and hand on every detail in future Budgets.

(Gainford MSS, 87)

Friday Dec. 10 I sent in mem. to Asquith suggesting he might in his Albert Hall speech appeal to Labour to use common sense to avoid 3 cornered contests, & let Tories in, that we Liberals were respecting 30 Labour seats & 13 other seats of Labour (lately Liberal MP) & to run Lab. candidates against Liberals was suicidal. No arrangement was possible but by another election, minority elections might be avoided by a 2d ballot or its equivalent.[16] I suggested alterations in budget, if proved in practice unfair might be inserted subsequently not this year.

Asquith made a general appeal in his speech. The Albert Hall gathering was very enthusiastic 10,000 men ready to be roused. Afterwards the cabinet officers of London Federation & 2 or 3 private Secretaries & I supped at the Ritz with Harcourt & S. Buxton. I sat opposite Asquith – he talked over Watson's scandalous & libellous poem on him published in America & seemed pleased *The Daily Mail* had not yet reprinted it. The American press had revelled in it. He asked me to call on him next morning.

At tea with the Asquiths one day in June 1909 William Watson (1858–1935) had been offended by Violet's insulting remarks about Campbell-Bannerman. Following the publication of his vitriolic poem, 'The Woman with the Serpent's Tongue' the American press quoted him on December 4 as saying that the poem was 'a composite photograph of ... the physical characteristics of Mrs Asquith and the mentality of Violet Asquith. The latter is the voice of the family and rules them all.' (James G. Nelson, Sir William Watson, Twayne, New York, 1966, pp. 148–51). Asquith could hardly have expected Watson's behaviour. He had once declared himself as 'an early & ... consistent reader & admirer' of Watson's poetry. As he told Watson on 8 January 1905 he had urged Watson's claims to the Poet Laureateship on the death of Lord Tennyson. (British Library,

---

16 Neither the two drafts for the speech in Asquith's papers nor the newspaper reports of the speech mention any such appeal. (Asquith MSS, vol. 48, ff. 129–81, and *The Times*, 11 Dec. 1909).

RP 1740 iv). According to Lord Dunsany (Dictionary of National Biography 1931-1940, p. 893) Watson was one of the few poets considered for the laureateship when Robert Bridges was appointed in 1913 – a somewhat improbable example of Asquithian magnanimity. Watson was knighted by Lloyd George in 1917.

Dec. 11, Sat.   called at 11.0 he was just going down to see Archie Gordon (lover of Miss Asquith) who was supposed to be dying result of accident motor, bladder split & pelvis shattered very little hope.[17]   He asked me my views about ministerial alterations. He told me he was writing Lord Knollys, so that he need not fill up Home Office before elections. He proposed appointing Dudley Ward Treasurer of Household, Strachey under Sec. Agric. Norman Under Sec. P. Office at once I agreed.

We said goodbye – I told him I was sanguine – the party was enthused throughout the country on the Lords veto, but it was doubtful whether the determining elector would be one way. My estimate was[18]

Liberals	315			The actual	275		
Labour	40	}	355	returns	40	}	315
				were			
Tories	233	}	315		273	}	355
Irish	82				82		
	——				——		
	670	40 majority	minority 40				

---

[17]   Hon. Archibald Ian Gordon (1884–1909); 3rd son of 7th Earl (later 1st Marquess) of Aberdeen; died on December 16, three weeks after a car accident. On 29 June 1906, Asquith had assured Lady Aberdeen that Violet was 'very much attached to Archie, but there is nothing in the least exclusive in what she feels for him.' (Aberdeen and Temair MSS, 1/5). Gordon's great love was Ettie Desborough. (Jolliffe, *Raymond Asquith*, p. 145, fn. 1; Nicholas Mosley, *Julian Grenfell*: His life and the times of his death 1888–1915, Holt, Rinehart and Winston, New York, 1976, pp. 113–32). But his sister records that on his deathbed his engagement to Violet 'for some time taken for granted, was now confirmed.' *The Times* obituary (Dec. 17) also mentioned the engagement. 'Violet was able to make him supremely happy', Lady Elcho told Arthur Balfour on December 19. However, the King was told that she had refused him. (Marjorie Pentland, *A Bonnie Fechter*: the life of Ishbel Marjoribanks Marchioness of Aberdeen & Temair ... 1857 to 1939, Batsford, 1952, p. 193; Knollys to Nash, 17 Dec. 1909, Asquith MSS, vol. 1, f. 241; Jane Ridley and Clayre Percy, *The Letters of Arthur Balfour and Lady Elcho 1885–1917*, Hamish Hamilton, 1992, p. 260).

[18]   The rest of this entry apparently was written on 27 January 1910.

The Tories expected a majority independent of the Irish, therefore, & were 50 short of their expectations. Our seats were lost in Home Counties (under pressure).

In the final days before the dissolution there was a spirited debate between ministers and JAP on the timing of the first day of polling. JAP preferred Friday January 14, fearing that the Liberal vote would suffer on the next day when football cup-ties would be held. Lloyd George pressed successfully for Saturday, as did Churchill who wrote to JAP on December 21 'Everyone is clear that no Friday pollings should be possible in any circumstances'. (Gainford MSS, 87; Blewett, The Peers, The Parties and the People, pp. 87–8).

The election demonstrated the determination of Labour to advance independently of the Liberals. The Northern Echo (3 Jan. 1910) reported that JAP had told a Middlesborough audience that although the Liberals thought they could recover 20 to 24 Labour seats they were not contesting 47 of the 78 seats in which there were Labour candidates. Of the remaining 31 constituencies JAP considered that there were seven held by Tories that could be won by Liberals if Labour stood aside. The Liberals were attacking only one Labour held seat (Jarrow) where Pete Curran had been beaten by thousands in 1906 and had won the by-election with less than one-third of the votes cast. Labour was fighting 23 Liberal constituencies.

As for his own constituency battle, JAP told Masterman on 14 January 1910, the election was 'being fought by the Tory Party entirely on Tariff Reform and I admit that I make little effect on the village audiences in explaining Land Reform or the Constitutional Point.' Tory handbills charged JAP with voting against the extension of old age pensions to recipients of outdoor poor relief. Primrose League dames promised agricultural labourers that 'their wages under Tariff Reform will rise from 12/- to 20/- per week and that they will have more employment and cheaper food! Now you understand why it is I enjoy an Election!!' (Masterman MSS, A3/5/6). JAP's enjoyment of the campaign was further diminished when he undertook some injudicious exegesis of the Prime Minister's Albert Hall speech. Believing that the government was pledged to introduce and pass a Home Rule bill in the next parliamentary session, Irish nationalist candidates had muted their opposition to the Budget. But JAP caused consternation after early returns were in by telling a questioner that no pledge had been given over Home Rule. 'What was said was that the ban that was placed by the Liberal Party on itself at the last General Election was removed, so that the Liberals are free, if they so desire, to extend self-government to Ireland'. (The Times, 19, 20 Jan. 1910).

What JAP had not foreseen was that the government's freedom to extend self-government to Ireland was about to be replaced by dependence on Irish support to pass the Budget.

Chapter 7

Among Equals

'The counties have let us down badly', Robert Hudson concluded after the general election. 'The landowner & the farmer alike see gain in Tariff Reform, & they have been putting on the screw to their labourers in a way wh. is hardly to be believed.' (Hudson to Sir William Robson, 25 Jan. [1910], Robson MSS). Only seven Liberals survived the electoral rout in the counties of Sussex, Hampshire, Hertfordshire, Surrey, Essex, Kent, Berkshire, and Oxfordshire. Although buoyed by a campaign contribution of £1000 from Sir Christopher Furness, to 'shew my appreciation of your pluck & recovery from the painful position you were placed in some years ago through no fault of your own', JAP could not hold his seat at Saffron Walden. (Furness to JAP, 19 Nov. 1909, Gainford MSS, 87). There were six categories of 'active opponents of Liberalism' in the constituency, JAP told his former constituents in June – Anglicans, landlords, small shopkeepers and traders, farmers seeking tariff protection, brewers, and those under pressure and influence. (Gainford MSS, 59, f. 146). A seventh category of itinerant propagandists should also be noticed. 'The masterly way you got rid of Pease at Saffron Walden,' Lord Northcliffe told Arthur Mee on 21 January 1910, 'shows me that your are a true disciple of Carmelite thoroughness.' (copy, Northcliffe MSS). The fidelity of Liberals disaffected with the direction of the government's financial and social policies had been further undermined by the circulation of extracts from a letter in which Alfred Pease, alienated from his brother's party, had explained to Herbert Samuel on September 16 why 'I can no longer count myself among your political supporters.' (Gainford MSS, 87 and AEP to JAP, 21 Jan. 1910, Gainford MSS, 88). Col. D.J. Proby (Con.) won by 4,283 to 4,011. (Proby was defeated the following December by A.C.T. Beck by 40 votes).

In June JAP's Liberal supporters presented him with a pair of antique French silver fern pots and a silver plate. (Gainford MSS, 56, p. 114). Harcourt, writing to Asquith on the election results on 26 January 1910, asked if JAP had sufficient funds to fight a by-election: 'he seems to me most essential but I heard from a friend of his that if he was beaten he was inclined to return to business & not to the H. of C.' (Asquith MSS, vol. 12, f. 78). In fact, JAP had an offer from Furness and had been instructed on 26 October 1909 by his wife that if the Liberals won the election 'it must be Cabinet with £4,000 a year or a business position which will allow you enough time to get fresh air & exercise – I shan't *allow you to go on in the present strain.' (Gainford MSS, 85).   On January 26 Elsie wrote twice, concluding: 'I want you to tell Asquith quite frankly how much easier life would be for you with a post in Cabinet & its salary of course I think you would do excellent work administratively.' (Gainford MSS, 88).*

On learning of JAP's defeat the Prime Minister wired on January 12: 'This is the worst incident of the election and grieves me more than I can say ...' (Gainford MSS, 59). Alfred Pease, who had voted against Samuel in Cleveland as 'the only practical way of backing the sound men in the Cabinet', lamented that for the first time since 1865 there was no Pease in the House of Commons: 'they prefer Hebrews & Hungarian Jews'. If JAP was permitted some respite, Alfred suggested, 'we will go and kill a few lions together'. (AEP to JAP, 15, 21 Jan. 1910, Gainford MSS, 88).[1] Several offers of seats soon emerged and JAP made discreet enquires about how quickly writs could be issued for a by-election. Jesse Herbert assured him on January 25 'though I have had Hudson & others here pumping with might & main, they learn nothing from me.' (Gainford MSS, 88).

27 Jan. 1910   Saw Asquith about 4 o'clock & had an hour's chat with him. He urged me to find seats for myself Seely & Acland, – but T.W. Russell, Sir Henry Norman & R.K. Causton would have to wait. I suggested Houghton le Spring for me. Rotherham for Acland & Ilkeston for Seely. Asquith said he could give a peerage to Holland & to Furness who deserved it, but Sir Walter Foster (Ilkeston) was too poor. I said I could not stand for Hartlepool nor Seely either without risk of the loss of the seat.

JAP apparently did not discuss with Asquith the Glasgow (Tradeston) seat which A. Cameron Corbett had indicated was at his disposal. But Corbett, who had resigned the Liberal whip in August 1909 and fought the election as an Independent Liberal Free Trader, had too slender a majority. (EP to JAP, 26 Jan. 1910; The Daily Mail, 25 Jan. 1910). Durham (Houghton-le-Spring) had been the seat of the 84 year old Robert Cameron (Lib.) since 1895; West Riding of Yorkshire (Rotherham) was Sir W.H. Holland's seat but had been held by Francis Acland's father 1885–99; Derbyshire (Ilkeston) Sir Walter Foster's; and Hartlepool, the site of the Furness-Withy ship-building firm, was a Furness family preserve. Sir Christopher Furness was raised to the peerage in July 1910 notwithstanding having been unseated on petition for hiring a band of miners to demonstrate during the election campaign. He was succeeded by his nephew, Stephen Wilson Furness (Cornelius O'Leary, The Elimination of Corrupt Practices in British Elections 1868–1911, Clarendon Press, 1962, p. 223).

---

1   Commiserating as one Chief Whip to another Alick Hood wrote on January 26: 'Of course you will pick yourself a safe seat.' (Gainford MSS, 88).

Despite Asquith's reservations about his means, Sir Walter Foster was immediately 'sounded out' by William Allard who had been assisting the Liberal agent in Saffron Walden. Allard wrote to JAP: 'He is agreeable & has stated his condition – a peerage immediately. He would gladly make way for the Chief Whip or for Col. Seely. He sees no difficulty in securing the selection & election of either but regards the Colonel as the more natural choice.' (28 Jan. 1910, Gainford MSS, 88).

Asquith said he might put Elibank into Scotch Office (Sec.). Move Montagu into Govmt Norton to the P.O., & Loulou to the Home Office.

I showed him scheme of work, & said I would continue my work as Chief Whip, as he urged me to do so, from 12 Downing St.

In spite of the difficulties he had experienced with the Budget League, JAP took time to console Henry Norman on his defeat in Wolverhampton East. 'The Prime Minister wants as many of us back again as he can get and, if I may say so without egotism, he asks me to accept the first Seat where I should have a prospect of success ...' Seely was next in line as the Colonial Office needed its representative in the Commons. Then Acland, as Haldane was very 'seedy' and had lost his pps. 'In the event of no opportunity being afforded to us to return within the next fortnight or so, I think the right course would be for us to place our resignations in the hands of the Prime Minister.' (JAP to Norman, 28 Jan. 1910, Norman MSS). JAP left for Biarritz on January 29. On February 1, Allard reported that Robert Cameron, who 'was amiability itself', said his supporters would be vexed if he stood aside and there would be a three cornered contest. (Gainford MSS, 88). The enquiries continued:

20 Queen Anne's Gate,
Westminster.
Feb 2/10

Dear Mr Pease,

This morning I talked with Sir W. Holland. He was sympathetic open & practical: said the idea of retiring in favor of Francis Acland did *not* appeal to him in the least, that he could not regard the early return to Parliament of F.A. as a national need, but that he regarded the election of yourself (& of Col. Seely) as eminently desirable. He will take two or three days to come to a final decision, meanwhile visiting Rotherham, but he is quite favourable & he went so far as to reduce his terms to writing. (He is indignant that £10,000 was exacted from him for his baronetcy.) I am to see him again at the end of this week. He thought that the cropping up of the Acland name was inevitable; but Col. Seely has told me that Mr Whitley is of opinion that there is adverse feeling to *Arthur* Acland in the West Riding on account of the high County Council rate for Education.

Sir W. Holland considers that the concurrence of the miners is obtainable & that there should not be difficulty in that quarter.

I have conferred with Col. Seely this evening, & he thinks that Houghton-le-Spring should be crossed off the list of possibilities – which I also think is the right course. Mid-day I met Arthur Henderson in St. James's Park. Not disclosing my connection with you, I asked why he did not offer a Durham seat for your acceptance. He replied that the Labour Party resented the Lib. 'annexation' of Bp. Auckland & Gateshead & that John Johnson &, after him, Aldn House would be run for any vacancies that might arise in Durham. He asserted that the unrest among the Durham miners will not last long & that anyhow it would not interfere with the miners' vote controlling any bye-election in the County. With fervour he expressed the hope that another genl. election would *not* take place in the near future. Despite his talk, Arthur gave me the idea of a tired man who is compelled by circumstances to talk boldly & confidently – & who by no means is eager for a quarrel. Still, such talk does not make Houghton-le-S. more attractive or more available.[2]

Tynemouth by the bye is of no use. Last Saturday I discussed it with Jas. Watson. Returning to Art. [sic] Acland, Col. Seely's view is that the West of England is the proper part of the country for him. There is Thornbury Divn., & it is conceivable that either Launceston Divn (where the Acland family have property & which Sir Thos. Acland represented 1885–92) or Camborne Divn. might be vacated on terms. I am carefully enquiring in a preliminary way.

Yours very truly
W. Allard.
(Gainford MSS, 88)

Tynemouth had been held for the Liberals by a barrister, H.J. Craig, who was returned again in December 1910. Athelstan Rendall, Liberal MP for Thornbury, held his seat safely until 1922. The MP for Launceston, G.C. Marks, was knighted in 1911 but he did not vacate his seat, holding it until 1924. Francis Acland was eventually placed at Camborne where A.E. Dunn stood aside in December 1910.

I wrote to him [Asquith] to Cannes from Biarritz that Sir C. McLaren wanted also a peerage but I presumed he would only retire for his eldest son or his son in law (Sir Hy. Norman).[3] My wife wrote him a letter to say she thought I ought to

---

2   Robert Cameron remained MP for Houghton-le-Spring until his death in 1913. At the by-election the local Liberal association, most of whose members were miners, campaigned successfully for a commercial traveller, Tom Wing. The Durham Miners' Association candidate, Ald. W. House, was third with only 22 per cent of the vote. (Maureen Callcott, 'Parliamentary Elections in County Durham Between The Wars: The Making Of A Labour Stronghold', *North East Group for the Study of Labour History Bulletin*, 8 Oct. 1974, p. 15).

3   JAP wrote 'Sir W. McLaren' but was confusing Walter Stowe Bright McLaren (1853–1912) with his brother, Sir Charles McLaren. Walter McLaren, a Quaker industrialist, had been Liberal MP for Crewe 1886–95 and won the seat again at a by-election in April 1910. According to Sir Henry Norman's daughter, Lady Burke, Sir Charles McLaren declined to put his seat at the disposal of his son-in-law, even though Norman had been offered the Under-Secretaryship for Foreign Affairs by Sir Edward Grey (conversation with CH, 23 Nov. 1967).

be in the cabinet before Elibank, & she justified the request on ground of my health. Certainly the strain was telling on me & I felt disinclined to do anything – tired out the defeat told more on me than I realised after the gruelling as Chief Whip for 2 years.

Within 2 days came a line offering me a seat in the cabinet as First Commissioner of Works, I accepted it.

Château de Thorenc,
Cannes.
2 Feb 1910

Secret

Dear Jack,

I have thought over our last conversation, and the impression left on my mind is, that (though willing) you would prefer another office to that of Chief Whip.

In any redistribution of places (and I have not yet determined precisely what is to be done) L. Harcourt must cease to hold his present office.

If, therefore, it suits your wishes, I should be very pleased to make you First Cr of Works, with a seat in the Cabinet.

This would vacate your own place, in which I do not know of anyone who could succeed you with equal advantage to the party, or so large a measure of personal confidence & affection on my side.

The choice – in such an event – would seem to be as follows:

    (1) Elibank – who knows the ropes & is a handy fellow
    (2) F. Acland – no seat!
    (3) Mallet

Have you any one else to suggest?

Norton is clamouring for release & recognition, & might (I think) be put into H. Norman's place, at the Post Office.

Please reply by *return of post* to me here: I shall leave on Monday or Tuesday, at latest.

Yrs always
H.H.A.

Asquith had written to JAP from the Château de Thorenc, Lord Rendel's winter retreat, to which he had invited himself by telegram on January 27. 'I could not understand how it was possible for him to absent himself at so critical a moment', Rendel recorded. Asquith's 'flight is much commented on', Charles Hardinge reported to Lord Knollys on January 29. 'It is regarded as a sign of weakness & a desire to avoid discussion'. (RA W55/91). The Prime Minister had overlooked the fact that he had an engagement to dine and sleep at Windsor. Post-election exhaustion and a need for urgent recuperation was the face-saving explanation. Whatever its additional benefits may have been, Asquith also justified his rush abroad as a mission to revive the spirits of his daughter who was still distressed over the death of Archie Gordon. Violet Asquith, her friend Venetia Stanley, and Venetia's mother, Lady Sheffield, were deposited at Rendel's villa at nearby Valescure. The Prime Minister then spent ten days at

Thorenc where the Charles Hobhouses were already installed. Hobhouse found Asquith 'very pleasant, full of chaff and conversation, eats too little but drinks too much'. (Hobhouse's diary, 2 Feb. 1910, David, ed., Inside Asquith's Cabinet, p. 85). In between long drives in the mountains and short evenings 'filled with either music or a game of bridge' Asquith 'had the opportunity of several times visiting his daughter and noting her happy progress towards recovery of health and spirits'. (Rendel's note, [? Feb. 1910], The Personal Papers of Lord Rendel, pp. 175-80, 233).

Secret   Hotel Regina,
                                                   Biarritz
                                                   Feb. 4. 1910

                                                   12 Downing Street,
                                                   S.W.

My dear Asquith,
    I accept with the greatest of gratitude your kind offer of a seat in the cabinet. I would certainly prefer to be there as Chief Commissioner of Works, rather than continue as Chief Whip.
    My view is that Seely would make much the best Chief Whip. He has a keen sense of duty, a knowledge of men, good manners, popular on both sides of the House, would keep his head in a tight place, and has full confidence in himself.
    He may prefer administrative work, but I think would accept the post if you pressed it on him.
    The Master of Elibank is a bit too scheming, & needs a steady hand over him.
    Acland is not very popular, lacks geniality and influence over men, & I doubt if his health would stand. Mallet's appointment would be too great an experiment.[4]
    But I really have nothing serious to urge against any one of them, & whoever you make, I would help all I could. I am glad you think of giving Norton the Sec. to the Post Office. He deserves the position & would help Sydney as much as anyone.
    With heartiest thanks to you Believe me
                                          Yours very gratefully
                                          Joseph A. Pease
                                   (Asquith MSS, vol. 12, ff. 107–10)

When I reached London Friday 11 Feby Asquith asked me to take the Duchy, Buxton to go to Bd. of Trade, Churchill to H. Office *not* Harcourt. I accepted but after thinking over it, on the Sunday 13th wrote to him to say that I would prefer the P.O. as the office of Duchy did not appeal to me.

---

4   Charles Mallet's background at Balliol and the Bar and his Liberal imperialism may have commended him to Asquith. But JAP was probably aware that he was out of sympathy with many leading Liberals ('Haldane, Grey, Spender, Crewe & the usual crew of quidnuncs who fear strong courses') over the Lords. (Mallet to A. Ponsonby, 29 Jan. 1910, Ponsonby MSS).

JAP's bid for the Post Office rather than the largely honorific Duchy of Lancaster was too ambitious and too late. 'I was bound to offer H.S. the Post Office in the first instance,' Asquith wrote on February 14, 'and he has accepted it. So for the time being, at any rate, you must find occupation, & a certain amount of repose, in the Duchy.' (Gainford MSS, 88). Walter Runciman told his wife that Samuel had asked for 24 hours to consider Asquith's offer of the Post Office. Asked why, he replied 'Because I want to decide whether this means you are going to side track me or not.' (Hilda Runciman's diary, June 1910, Viscountess Runciman MSS). As Chief Whip, Asquith chose Alick Murray. 'Beside Elibank,' J.A. Spender later testified, 'I felt myself a mere beginner in the art of smoothing.' (Life, Journalism and Politics, 2 vols, Cassell, 1927, vol. I, p. 235). It seemed to some observers that the principal reason for Pease's promotion was to get him out of the Whips' Office. Lucy Masterman thought Lloyd George 'thoroughly hates' JAP and was determined that he would not be re-appointed as Chief Whip. (Diary 'Reminiscences' n.d., Masterman MSS, B2/2). Herbert Gladstone complained to his brother on February 1 that 'the Whips' Dept should have warned the Cabinet of the extraordinary & unexpected strength of feeling against the Lords in the North.' (Henry Gladstone MSS). 'Pease is blamed for losing two safe seats one after another,' Emmott recorded on 20 February 1910. 'Ll. G. is now blaming him for losing the last election. He is not clever & why should he be put in the Cabinet?' (Emmott MSS, vol. I, f. 220). If Emmott's mystification was tinged with resentment as a disappointed aspirant for Cabinet office, Runciman's disdain is less easily discounted. 'I cannot understand what fatuity can have possessed Asquith's mind ...' (Runciman to Hilda Runciman, 15 Feb. 1910, Viscountess Runciman MSS).

On the 15th Asquith said Samuel had accepted the P.O. with hesitation, if he had declined he would have offered it to me.

On 16th Feby I attended cabinet as a Privy Councillor. Again on 17th – I kissed hands on the 19th, having audience by myself, King very gracious, cabinet on 22nd (3.45) 25th @ 11.0, 26th @ 11.0 absent at Rotherham.

With Houghton-le-Spring unavailable, JAP was selected for the West Riding seat of Rotherham. He spent most of the fortnight after returning to England campaigning in his new constituency. Sir William Holland had been returned there unopposed in 1906. A Labour candidature was now possible but the local Labour party was dissuaded by Ramsay MacDonald because the time available for the campaign was so short. When Labour's decision was announced, the Conservatives withdrew and JAP, by now Chancellor of the Duchy, was elected unopposed. His election was declared one hour after nominations closed on March 1; he played golf in the afternoon. Labour's decision not to fight the by-

election was recalled the following September, when Joe Pointer, Labour MP for Attercliffe, said that JAP was only MP for Rotherham with the miners' consent and that he had agreed to withdraw at any later date if the miners put up their own candidate. JAP denied this vigorously. (The Rotherham Express, *c. 24 Sept. 1910, Gainford MSS, 59, ff. 154–5).* *But the truth was that the only right JAP had was to contest a seat he would certainly lose if the miners were united against him. He put the best face on it in a letter to the Yorkshire Miners' MP Fred Hall on 8 November 1910:*

> ... In order to avoid any future misunderstanding, you will not mind my placing on record that whilst I may have in private conversation admitted in February, that if I was not opposed by the Labour Party at the bye-election, they should be in no way prejudiced from running a labour candidate at a future election if they thought fit to do so, but I know you will agree that there was never any arrangement for me not to stand again.
>
> It was obvious to me in February, as it is now, that if the miners in the Division were unanimous in the support of another candidate they could carry whom they liked, but my freedom to stand at the next or any subsequent election in the division was never ever questioned.
>
> (copy, Gainford MSS, 88)

The by-election campaign had seen another embarrassment for JAP, what The Daily Chronicle *described on February 26 as 'an extraordinary indiscretion'. JAP's sin was to explain to the Rotherham electors the government's intention – as he understood it – to give the Commons an opportunity before it dealt with the Budget to discuss and vote on proposals on 'how the House of Lords ought to be constituted, and what powers ought to be conferred upon them'. Then, with the Budget passed, the government would proceed with 'the great work of the Session, the reconstitution of the House of Lords'. Assailed by the* Chronicle *and 'advanced Radical' MPs for obscuring 'the clear issue of the veto', JAP hastened to affirm that the government's 'immediate efforts must be centred on the abolition of the veto' while restating his desire for a 'constructive policy, in which the basis of the hereditary system will give way to a democratic basis' (*The Daily Mail, *1 March 1910).*

On March 3d I took my seat in the House.

Sat. Mar. 5 Privy Council at Buckingham Palace Pricking Sheriffs[5] – I dined with the King at night.

---

5   The Sheriffs of each county were appointed annually by the Crown in Council, the Sheriffs of Cornwall and Lancaster being exceptions appointed by the Duke of Cornwall and the Council of the Duchy respectively. The sovereign 'pricked' the names of the Sheriffs on the Roll with an ancient bodkin. (Leonard Courtney, *The*

March 9th   Cabinet 11.30. A cabinet in which it looked like resignation – no chance of Irish support or agreement on reconstitution of 2d Chamber.

In the weeks before JAP took his seat at the Cabinet table the government was on the brink of disintegration. Asquith's admission on February 21 that he had no guarantees to deal with the Lords shook his radical supporters and Nationalist allies. The Nationalists' stance was 'no veto, no Budget'. Lloyd George's objective was to get the Budget through the Commons before the Lords considered the veto resolutions. To this end he was prepared to negotiate concessions with both Redmond and the O'Brien faction. He made fresh overtures to Redmond on March 8, letting him know he was also talking to O'Brien; and he saw O'Brien on the 9th.

Aware of the possibility that the Nationalists could turn the government out, Grey, Haldane, Crewe, Runciman, Churchill, and McKenna advocated reform of the Lords rather than a simple curbing of the Lords' veto powers – the policy foreshadowed by JAP in Rotherham. Sir Charles Hardinge explained to the King's private secretary that Grey 'will insist on a new and strong Upper House on an elective principle with a nucleus of distinguished statesmen who are to be nominated'. (Hardinge to Knollys, 27 Jan. 1910, RA W55/90). Two days later Grey told Runciman 'I should like to go to the country on Finance for the Commons & a scheme for an elective Second Chamber & let the Tories fight for the hereditary principle against it.' (Runciman MSS). Grey thought 'Balfour's game is to tie "Single Chamber" round our necks', force an election by May, and campaign on preservation of a slightly reformed House of Lords and 'an Immense Navy'. (Runciman to H. Runciman, 9 Feb. 1910, Viscountess Runciman MSS). The Foreign Secretary threatened resignation if an elected second chamber was not in the forefront of the government's programme. Harcourt, Morley, and Loreburn were equally resolute that there should be no change in the composition of the Lords. With no apparent prospect of Cabinet unanimity, the Prime Minister had indicated to the King his willingness to consider a 'Round Table conference' as a way of resolving the Lords' issue. By late January (not 'as early as the end of March' pace Professor Gollin) 'the idea of a conference ... was in the air.' (Alfred M. Gollin, The Observer and J.L. Garvin 1908–1914: A Study in a Great Editorship, Oxford University Press, 1960, p. 183; Koss, The Rise and Fall of the Political Press in Britain, vol. 2, p. 138). Reporting a conversation with King Edward on 14 February 1910, Jack Sandars informed Arthur Balfour that 'the King asked the Prime Minister whether he did not think that deliberation by both Parties in Parliament might not contribute to a satisfactory issue. To this the Prime Minister said "You mean

---

Working Constitution of the United Kingdom and its Outgrowths, J.M. Dent, 1905, p. 237).

*a Round Table conference", and upon this being accepted as the correct
description, the Prime Minister appeared to be by no means disinclined'.
Sandars pressed: 'You are clear, Sir, that he did not reject it.' 'By no means'
was the reply. (Sandars MSS, Ms Eng. Hist. c. 760 ff. 45–6). Asquith seems to
have given no hint to his Cabinet colleagues of this discreet signal to the
Opposition.*

*Talking to ministers after the March 9 Cabinet meeting, Charles Hobhouse
(who had extracted from Asquith a promise of the next vacant Cabinet seat as the
price of staying at the Treasury with Lloyd George) was evidently not sorry to
learn that 'no one seemed to have liked J. Pease's translation.' (Hobhouse's
diary, 10 March 1910, David, ed., Inside Asquith's Cabinet, p. 88). JAP kept
more detailed notes of this, the first, Cabinet meeting he attended as a member:*

[*9 March 1910*][6]

Carrington

Compensation to tenants for small holdings – memorandum to be issued.[7]

Grey

Congo – mark time until Belgians have more time to do away with forced labour
– vote necessary – but shd. not disclose necessity before May election.

Haldane – smouldering feeling at home needs to be allayed. Temporise &
give Belgians time to carry out change of policy.[8]

Crewe

Somaliland – March 20 – retirement to coast – Sir Wm. Manning announcement
not to be anticipated.

H. of C. shd. not be kept in dark.

Retire – Berbara – Bulhar – Zeila – friendly tribes encourage to defend
themselves against raids.

Mullah – dervishes – massacres not expected by advisers – before rains break.

Indian Garrison

Retention – 6th bat. disbanded keep arms & ponies.

Propose to circulate Manning's telegrams to members on Palm Sunday – Dal
hunter's tribe may tho' friendly become the raiders.

---

[6]   This entry about the Cabinet meeting JAP attended on March 9 is a separate note to
be found in Gainford MSS, 38, f. 87.

[7]   A bill, passed in 1910, amended the Small Holdings and Allotments Act 1908,
compensating tenants of county councils evicted from their land so that it could be
used for small holdings.

[8]   Expecting a debate the next day on the Belgian Congo, the Cabinet agreed with
Grey that for the time being they must express confidence in 'the declared intentions
of a friendly Government' to progressively abolish forced labour. (Asquith's
Cabinet letter to the King, 9 March 1910, Cab. 41/32/9).

A year earlier the government had asked for a supplement of £47,000 to the estimates in order to increase the garrison in Somaliland. Muhammad bin Abdulla (the Mad Mullah), who had resumed his raids on coastal towns and his attacks on tribes under British control, had been a problem since 1899. He survived partly because of the difficult terrain and partly because of the lack of co-ordination between Britain, Italy, and Abyssinia. A campaign against him 1900–6 had ended with Britain's tacit recognition that the Mullah held a sphere of influence in Italian Somaliland. Winston Churchill had urged withdrawal to the coastal strip after a visit to Somaliland in 1907; the cost of holding the country was more than double the value of the revenue it could raise. His memorandum was circulated to the Cabinet 24 November 1908 (Cab. 37/89/84). The Conservative MP, W.W. Ashley, argued that the government's policy of containment was futile and that the only way to end these raids was by a campaign to capture or kill the Mullah. He argued that earlier campaigns had failed because the troops had been on foot or on ponies; he urged a 500–600 strong camel corps and 1,500–1,200 infantry. Late in 1909 the government sent Reginald Wingate to report; he confirmed Ashley's views. Churchill appealed to Crewe on 6 March 1910 'to secure that the evacuation of Somaliland hinterland takes place now.' *(Crewe MSS). Crewe told the Cabinet on March 9 that Sir William Manning and his military advisers now thought 'the time has arrived when we can safely withdraw the troops from the interior to Berbera & two other coast towns.' (Asquith's Cabinet letter to the King, 9 March 1910, Cab. 41/32/9). The defensive containment policy continued until 1920 when the Mullah was defeated by air power. (PD, Commons, II, 769–819, 15 March 1909; Sir Ronald Wingate,* Wingate of the Sudan: The Life and Times of General Sir Reginald Wingate. Maker of the Anglo–Egyptian Sudan, *John Murray, 1955, pp. 152–3). JAP's brother Alfred had met the Mullah on his hunting expeditions to Somaliland, when the Mullah had acted as an interpreter. The government claimed to have asked for Sir Alfred's advice, but did not reveal what it was. When Sir William Manning's appointment as Commissioner of Somaliland was announced in January 1910, Alfred told JAP that Manning was 'about the most horrid man I ever met' (15 Feb. 1910, Gainford MSS, 88).*

Crewe

Lord Rosebery's motion Monday.

Not easy to be sure of him or his intentions in moving resolutions.[9] Vague discussion – Gov. attitude – critical – but not show his hand – dwell on

---

[9] Rosebery had chaired a House of Lords Select Committee on reform of the Lords in 1907. In 1910, after secret consultations with Balfour, he proposed that the Lords should reform themselves and become a strong, effective second chamber; possession of a peerage should not give an automatic right to vote in the House. His motion was passed with ministerial support on March 22 but not pursued until

differences bet. 2 Houses, deadlock – encourage them to table.
Backwoodsmen not going to be shunted for County Councillors.
Homicide by slaying over budget – suicide by reforming H. of L.
450 – yrs – Beaufort only voted twice. Dd. if he wd. go.
Cease cackle – get to scheme –
Loreburn
   Budget – Inc. Tax resolution embrace whole – answer H. of C.
   649 Resolutions dealing with the H. of C.
P.M.
Doubt whether Resolutions or Budget can ever reach Lords.

March 11th   cabinet at 4.0 at H of C.

During these cabinets we discussed the King's Speech, retirement to coast line in Somaliland – a comtee had agreed to this course before I joined. I pointed out danger the Friendlies were in. Crewe did not think serious massacres probable, & we had armed them.[10]

The first few cabinets the question of the Irish turning the Govmt out was discussed, & we agreed to submit veto resolutions before Budget Bill, but Budget Bill before we ploughed sands. Ministers very firm in their differences of view, always suggesting chucking – but the King told Asquith no other Govmt. was possible & he would not hear of it. Asquith kept very quiet, & let his colleagues have lots of rope.

Grey Crewe & Haldane very firm as to abolition of hereditary chamber & a reconstitution of a useful second one deprived of financial power.

Morley very much against any suggestion to create peers to overcome the deadlock between the 2 houses. Harcourt was for C.B. plan pure & simple, & agreed with Morley to leave the Lords as they were.[11]

The rest of us used all our strategies to secure a compromise by a veto first without prejudice to reconstitution. So matters were left on Sat. March 12th. At Speaker's Dinner I had a chat with the P.M. (also before cabinet in his own

---

November 21 when the Lords resolved *nem. con* that there should be a chamber composed of hereditary peers chosen from among themselves and by the Crown, peers sitting by virtue of offices and qualifications, and others chosen from outside. Rosebery declined Morley's invitation to table proposals for a complete scheme of Lords reform. (The Marquess of Crewe, *Lord Rosebery*, 2 vols, John Murray, 1931, vol. 1, pp. 626–31).

10   A year earlier W.W. Ashley MP had argued against arming the friendly Somali tribesmen; they were very bad shots and very keen traders who were likely to trade the rifles to the Mahdi's supporters (*PD*, Commons, ii, 769–819, 15 Mar. 1909).

11   Campbell-Bannerman's plan, carried by a Commons' majority of 285 on 24 June 1907, was to limit the Lords' veto so that they would be able only to suspend legislation, not definitively block it. He wanted no change in the composition of the House nor its replacement by some form of senate.

room)[12] about Lloyd George's statement and false reasons given as to why Army vote should be for 6 months; but vote on a/c & navy for 6 weeks.

The six-week period covered by the vote on account for the navy would end on May 13 in the middle of the Whitsun recess. On March 10, Lloyd George was asked why this was the period covered instead of the customary four-five months, or a more convenient period. He suggested disingenuously that the government was reverting to the pre-1896 practice by which votes were generally only for a short period so that Parliament could maintain proper control over the executive. Austen Chamberlain replied that the government did not expect to survive for longer than six weeks and by voting money for such a short period aimed to leave the greatest possible financial chaos behind them; there would be no funds to carry on business or to pay old-age pensions till after a general election. Chamberlain pointed to the different periods of the army and navy votes as proof that there had been some change of government policy. In explaining the government's action to the King on March 11, Churchill averred that it was right in the present uncertain circumstances that no more supply should be sought by the vote on account than was sufficient to carry the government forward over the period 'for which they may reasonably expect to be responsible; nor should they ask for an amount of supply which would be out of all proportion to any taxes which the House of Commons has shown itself disposed to vote.' (Churchill, Winston S. Churchill, vol. II, Companion Part 2, p. 993).

March [?12]   I told Asquith the Tories meant a formidable attack on Monday, & I asked him to come in & take part in the debate.

He told me Tim Healy & O'Brien were now ready to have a round table conference & to support the Govmt on terms, present rate of Whiskey tax to be dropped in the budget for 1910–11 & some pension money given to paupers, balance to help tenants purchase. I told Asquith Healy the night before at 11.40 was hidden in the dark in Birdcage Walk talking to Ld Edmund Talbot (Tory Whip) & possibly we could not trust him![13]

---

12   Writing some days later JAP wrongly dated the Saturday as 'March 13th'. His discussions with Asquith had both been on Friday March 11. The Speaker's dinner was a full dress affair given at the beginning of each session for members of the ministry, the mover and seconder of the address, and parliamentary officers. There was a series of five dinner parties each session, 'the second was given to the Opposition, the third to Privy Councillors, the fourth and fifth were given to those whom the Speaker delighted to honour'. The dinners, an invitation to which was held to be a command, were followed by large receptions for MPs, peers, and their wives and daughters. (Hon. Sir Edward Cadogan, *Before the Deluge:* Memories and Reflections 1880–1914, John Murray, 1961, p. 174).

13   JAP's suspicions of Healy ('the master of two-o'clock in the morning tactics' as W.E.H. Lecky had dubbed him) are understandable. Talbot could have been going

16th March   Absent from cabinet. Asquith told me on the 17th, they had had no explosion – after words of veto resolutions had been arrived at Grey had asked if the preliminary point had been agreed to, as to whether the resolutions would be confined in the restrictions of veto powers, to only a reconstitution bill, & whether they should remain after a representative House had been established.

It was after discussion *asserted* that at the previous meeting, an arrangement had been arrived at, that we should agree on veto resolutions but not commit one another to the future as to whether the reconstituted House of Lords should be restricted, & this was accepted.

21st March   George asked leave to approach Redmond & to say he would like a definite reply as to his attitude towards our Budget that he had played long enough with us. Morley, I and Loreburn advocated going forward with veto, & Budget without further trimming or being influenced in our conduct by Irish. This was agreed to. We settled terms of veto resolutions. Asquith asked me to see Thring & fix them up for production on the Tuesday in press. They were agreed to in terms which Loreburn described as (in Latin) 'a crafty gentleman deals in generalities'. Winston got this translation.[14]

Birrell ejaculated 'Yes mashed potatoes'.

March 23   Cabinet H of C @ 11.30

Buxton explained to cabinet his anxiety in regard to possible coal strike N'land & Durham and S. Wales.[15]   He had not so far interfered leaving to Askwith to meet men & masters. The miners had thrown over their own leaders. I pointed out, that whilst the masters had no desire for a stoppage, yet if the men came out, the masters would strenuously seek to recover the position which had been gradually lost, before they reopened their collieries. George recommended Buxton to confer with Mabon, & Sir T. Lewis, who for each side could give unbiassed advice.

George was then asked to state the result of his conference with Redmond, Dillon, Birrell & the Master of Elibank on Monday. The obvious desire was on

---

to his home in Buckingham Palace Gardens via Birdcage Walk. But Healy, who normally stayed at the National Liberal Club when in London, would have been taking an extremely wide detour.

14   Classical scholars whom we have consulted have been unable to suggest what Loreburn's original Latin may have been.

15   The threatened strike was in response to an offered pay increase of 2½ per cent. Following the Eight Hours Act mining productivity had fallen by 5 per cent and South Wales coal owners suffering increased foreign competition had given notice to terminate the existing wages agreement from March 31. The dispute was settled by conciliation and a strike averted.

the part of the Nationalists to find a way for supporting the Govmt on the budget. The *whiskey* tax could expire with current year 1909–10, & could be revised.

In regard to *valuation*, the clause omitted in bill which appeared in original bill could be again inserted. The omission was only made because the sense was implied without it. Declaratory words would meet the case.

Small *brewer* to be exempt – would have to be made up to £1500 or £2000. It already existed to £500, & it was a question of extending principle all round to meet Irish case. Graduated tax was suggested & it was arranged expert advisors shd. be asked if practicable.

There were only 30 in Ireland, 3000 in Gt. Britain. Ah, but said Birrell 30 means a lot in Ireland – & it meant Guinness absorbing them! – yes said George Guinness's shares have risen.

However the meeting ended without any bargain being struck. Cabinet to be consulted on one hand & Irish party on other.

The Irish had argued that the increase in duty on spirit was not only very unpopular in Ireland, but had also led to a decline in consumption and in revenue. One way round this, which would be particularly effective in Ireland, would be to exempt small brewers, and to raise the level of exemption from property valued at £500 to property valued at £1500–£2000. Asquith's Cabinet letter reported that a proposal on these lines would be drafted for Cabinet approval. The King was advised that 'no agreement or bargain of any kind was made or sought for, on the one side or the other'. (Asquith MSS, vol. 5, ff. 202– 3). On March 21, however, Bonar Law had 'got from Lloyd George ... in the smokeroom a statement that dissolution in May was "inevitable" ... He believes the Irish have been squared.' (A. Chamberlain to M. Chamberlain, 21 Mar. 1910, Chamberlain, Politics from Inside, p. 235). If Bonar Law understood Lloyd George correctly, the Chancellor's optimism was premature as well as indiscreet. More likely, Lloyd George was making mischief. Guinness shares rose steadily from a low of 390.41 on 1 January 1910 to a peak of 460.80 during the summer then fell slightly during the second half of the year. With over 90 per cent of the domestic market Guinness were keen to keep their Irish 'rivals' alive lest the company be labelled 'monopolist' (Oliver MacDonagh to CH, 3 Oct. 1991).

Asquith then asked the opinion of the Cabinet on what guarantees he should seek, or what he should say when pressed. It was agreed that the situation about which he could be pressed was hypothetical. If budget rejected – out we must go but assuming budget passed & H of Lords wouldn't consider veto resolution what then? Grey said the Lords would laugh at our proposal, that they should have no power over finance. It would admit their error in November.

Asquith said there are always 3 courses: resignation, dissolution, seeking guarantees. Samuel suggested a Referendum, but not seriously. Asquith said, he presumed, we would not ask the King to do what we could not advise him to do, that is to say that we ourselves would not do in this position viz. create 500 peers at once by adopting the prerogative.

Our composite majority might justify our seeking guarantees if again returned in a new H of C. after Dissolution. George suggested deferring any decision until position arose – bye elections might prove some guide. It was decided a cabinet minute might later on be sent to the King but we could not now foresee the exact situation, or arrive at any decision. We should meanwhile proceed on assumption, that we might have to refer to country, & the P.M. should not be further committed in any replies, but rely upon statement already made, as to consider the advice & taking further steps if crisis arose. Could not go further until question actually arose.

The question was brought closer on March 29 by John Redmond. If the Lords refused to accept the government's resolutions and there were no 'guarantees', Nationalist support would be contingent on an immediate election.

March 30   Cabinet

Crewe reported the retirement in Somaliland had been effected quietly & without disturbance.

Buxton reported his intervention in coal trade disputes, & predicted owing to masters' generous concessions probable settlement. He asked permission if men & masters agreed to introduce the 'Herbert Samuel relief Bill', modifying the hours for Friday & Sats interval between shifts from 17 hours to 13.[16]

Debate arose as to whether the resolutions should be discussed & completed, or whether after we got into comtee, budget should be proceeded with. Arranged to dispose of resolutions first & then take all stages of budget under guillotine – even if Irish rejected them. Govmt declined to accept Redmond's dictation as to how appeal should be made to suit Nationalist party's pretensions to become the leaders of radical party. If Nationalist supported the appeal on vetos would come as a united party except possibly on the question of reconstruction. Haldane suggested a bill to meet both sections. Prime Minister authorised him to proceed therewith.

I was instructed to go on with guillotine resolution on veto, & submit to cabinet my scheme for introducing elections on one day Bill.

---

[16]   An Hours of Labour (Surfacemen) Bill, presented on April 14, fulfilled a by-election pledge given to the ironstone miners in Samuel's constituency in July 1909. (Bernard Wasserstein, *Herbert Samuel A Political Life*, Clarendon Press, Oxford, 1992, p. 112).

On 30 March 1910 JAP had circulated to the Cabinet a 'Memorandum in regard to an early general election' (Cab. 37/102/12) in which he pointed out that none of the government's promises concerning electoral reform had been carried out. The limitation of the ballot to one day would minimise the disturbance caused by the campaign and would favour Liberal and Labour interests: the majority of plural voters were Conservatives, and they would have less chance to exercise their votes. A private member's bill, introduced by A.J. Sherwell, proposed the abolition of plural voting as well as single-day elections, but was talked out by Sir F. Banbury the next day.

In the Commons on March 31, Churchill ended his speech on the government's veto proposals: 'Since the House of Lords, upon an evil and unpatriotic instigation – as I must judge it – have used their Veto to affront the Prerogative of the Crown and to invade the rights of the Commons, it has now become necessary that the Crown and the Commons, acting together, should restore the balance of the Constitution and restrict forever the Veto of the House of Lords.' (PD, Commons, xv, 1583, 31 Mar. 1910). Asquith wrote to Churchill at midnight on March 31: 'You made a most admirable speech: one of your best. The only thing I regret is the last sentence – associating "the Crown" & the people: which I hope may be ignored.' At this time Churchill was reporting to the King the proceedings of the House of Commons. Of this speech, Churchill wrote: 'He [Churchill] trusts Your Majesty will not attach any importance to the crude and strained interpretations which the Opposition's newspapers have placed upon his concluding remarks. They meant and were intended to mean, in themselves and in their context, that the existing Constitutional difficulty will not be relieved by any mere continuance of the breach and warfare between the Lords and Commons, but will require – at a time, in a manner, and under circumstances which cannot now be foreseen – the intervention of the Crown.' (Churchill, Winston S. Churchill, vol. II, Companion Part 2, pp. 1000–2). Alick Murray had broached the idea of royal mediation with the Prince of Wales on March 29. To his horror, he discovered that Churchill , having been told of the conversation, had 'communicated with the King taking my ideas as his own and giving great offence in consequence.' (Murray's memo., 14 April 1910, Arthur C. Murray, Master and Brother: Murrays of Elibank, John Murray, 1945, pp. 46–7).

April 4 Cabinet began at once, usual expressions of differences. Morley & Churchill explained each would have to resign, if there was any question of respectively urging, or not urging the King to create Peers.[17] Morley then reflected upon Churchill's indiscretion on Thursday's debate, when he referred to Commons & King, jointly fighting the peers. Churchill said I thought out what I

---

17 Morley bet Harcourt a halfpenny that the word 'legislative' did not occur in the passage about guarantees in Asquith's Albert Hall speech the previous December. Morley lost. (Harcourt's note, 4 April 1910, Harcourt MSS, dep. 441, f. 145).

was going to say & I am prepared to pay the penalty or forfeit. Asquith came to his rescue at once & said there was no question of either the one or the other.

Asquith is said to have written the King explaining Churchill's indiscretion, & he wrote an appreciative letter to Churchill, but castigating him. We gradually got into smooth water, & after discussing replies to questions to be submitted in the House that day of a non committal character, we talked of the situation, & I told the cabinet my view as to our being manoeuvered by the Tories, away from a conflict on the proposals re veto. We had a preliminary chat over Preamble to the Budget Bill. Asquith asked me to help him on the 7th with guillotining veto Resolutions.

April 6 Discussion on word Elective or Popular in Preamble to Veto Bill – agreed to terms of Preamble Sinclair (= Pentland) dissenting on any reference to subject. Grey pointed out how he had met his colleagues & appealed for reciprocity (to secure unity). Morley said the King wanted each P.M. to nominate 50 Peers in turn!

We discussed for 40 minutes whether any limitation clause should be placed on power (in Bill) to repeal by any veto provision the Septennial Act or quinquennial act after passage of Bill, to prevent one Chamber passing such a bill 3 sessions running. Asquith & each colleague reasoned against this, but W.S.C. stood firm, & was not convinced.

The contentious preamble finally included the words: '...Whereas it is intended to substitute for the House of Lords as it at present exists a Second Chamber constituted on a popular instead of hereditary basis, but such substitution cannot be immediately brought into operation' (PP, 1910, [130], iv, pp. 283–8). 'The great point about the Veto Resolutions,' Emmott concluded on April 23, 'is whether they do really mean Single Chamber Govt.' Churchill had told him during the debates on the amendments to the second resolution that he 'was not averse to limiting the Bills which cd be passed over the heads of the Lords. That is excluding from them bills for dealing further with composition or functions of the Lords or for extending the duration of Parliament.' (Emmott MSS, vol. I, f. 234).

JAP summarised the cluster of arguments presented by Churchill:

Tories always had had the power, bill could not include everything. Speaker wd slap us in the face by ruling it outside resolutions. The Tories could always repeal our bill, & that clause cd always be repealed too & ineffective. Public opinion wd find expression to prevent one party by such means perpetuating itself & c & c. We discussed fair wages terms & how Barnes's question to be put tomorrow could be answered.[18]

April 11. 12. 13. cabinets.

Monday met at 12.45 rose at 2.0
Tuesday " 11.30 " 2.0
Wednesday " 11.30 " 1.40

At these cabinets the questions discussed at great length were: whether the Govmt should amend the budget except in declaratory amendments so as to clear up meaning & intentions of previous budgets, & necessary date alterations, and whether any decision should be arrived at as to our own intentions when the Lords rejected our proposals for the removal of their power over finance & permanent veto of bills. The subordinate questions were time of House & arrangement of business also how to answer question on papers – & attitude on Labour Resolution on Wednesday in regard to legislation to repeal Osborne decision which prevents the use of trade union funds being used for political candidatures & objects & c.

W.V. Osborne, a Liberal, was secretary of the Walthamstow branch of the Amalgamated Society of Railway Servants. He had sought an injunction to stop the collection of a political levy by his union on the ground that candidates sponsored by his and many other unions had to accept the Labour party constitution, and to vote according to the Labour whip. His lawyers widened the challenge to encompass all trade union parliamentary representation. The courts, and the Lords in December 1909, ruled that, as the Trade Union Acts of 1871 and 1876 had not included parliamentary representation in their definition of a union's objects, such activity was outside the unions' legal powers. By implication, many other activities not expressly authorised by the legislation were also threatened. This posed a problem which was to vex the Cabinet for many months. (Michael Klarman, 'Osborne: a judgment gone too far?', English Historical Review, vol. ciii, no. 406, Jan. 1988, pp. 21–39; W.B. Gwyn, Democracy and the Cost of Politics in Britain, The Athlone Press, 1962, pp. 178–204; H.A. Clegg, Alan Fox, and A.F. Thompson, A History of British Trade Unions Since 1889, vol. 1, 1889–1910, Clarendon Press, 1964, pp. 413–19; K.D. Ewing, Trade Unions, The Labour Party and the Law: A Study of the Trade Union Act 1913, Edinburgh University Press, Edinburgh, 1982, pp. 17 37). On

---

[18] It was alleged that the War Office was paying some of its employees less than it would oblige contractors to pay under the fair wages clause of its contract. George Barnes asked if the matter would be put to the Fair Wages Advisory Committee and if the fair wages policy applied to the Admiralty and other government departments. Asquith replied that the War Office was seeking the committee's advice, and that his colleagues were consulting to see how far the clause could be applied to other departments. (*PD*, Commons, xvi, 591–2, 7 Apr. 1910).

April 13 J.W. Turner moved 'That ... the right to send representatives to Parliament and to municipal administrative bodies, and to make financial provision for their election and maintenance, enjoyed by Trades Unions for over forty years, and taken from them by the decision in the case of Osborne v. Amalgamated Society of Railway Servants, should be restored.' (PD, Commons, xvi, 1321, 13 Apr. 1910.) After a long debate, no vote was taken.

Morley at the final meeting took a strong line about our not indicating at present, any intention to advise the King to exercise his prerogative. Lloyd George, said he was prepared to subordinate his own views, & allow whiskey duty to be reduced to secure Irish support for his budget, if we made our position clear in regard to conditional guarantees being secured. If there was no question of the Irish vote he obviously would prefer to adhere to his high tax as he thought, all stocks of whiskey were exhausted, & a continuation of the tax would secure revenue. A good case however could be made out to show from a revenue point of view the tax had been a failure. Grey took the view, that he thought we had all agreed no alteration should be made of substance in the 1909 budget, & we all agreed to this course. I advocated a strong line & read letter from H. Storey, sec. to Yorkshire Lib. Fed. dated Ap 10 on the necessity to obtain conditional guarantees from the King, or resign.

Dear Mr Illingworth,

I am a good deal worried. There are persistent rumours that when the Peers refuse to adopt the Veto Resolutions the Prime Minister will not advise the King to force the Resolutions upon them by a creation of new Peers. It is said that the Prime Minister will be prevented from giving this advice by the fear of losing Sir Edward Grey and Mr Haldane from the Cabinet.

This may be all rubbish, but the rumour is so strong that it is already doing us harm. If, however, it should turn out to be true in fact, it will be disastrous. During the last ten days I have been in many parts of the County; and, what is more, I have addressed a good many meetings, some of them large meetings in the open air. I can assure you that the deadness of the audiences is something that I have never seen before. Judging from the whole experience and from the various questions put in the meetings, I think that what exists is a dull, nervous dread that the Government are not going to take what is regarded as the strong course – viz. the course of giving the advice to the King referred to above. For this same reason, I find it difficult in some places to get meetings at all. The people say that they have done their part, they have given the Government a majority, and now they are not inclined to do anything else until it is seen whether the Government are going to use that majority for the purpose for which it was given.

I can, of course, understand that the Government might hold such views as would lead them to refuse to give this advice to the King, whatever might be the consequences. It is, however, only common sense that the consequences should be known beforehand. If the advice is given, and everybody knows that it has been given, it does not matter what else happens: in that case the Party will fight solid. But if the advice is not given, I do not think there is any doubt at all that the Party will break in two.

Please do not trouble to reply. I am only anxious that whatever I can see here should be known to you also.

Yours very truly,   Harold Storey

It was I said no good to wait, as Morley urged, & then see whether the Lords were impressionable. The party, & that was the majority of the country, looked for a strong line, & would be broken up, if the cabinet showed the white feather, instead of a cheering mass behind us we had a sullen crowd waiting, & watching our every word. To appeal to the country on veto resolutions, would be regarded as the same issue as the last election, & without guarantees we should be regarded as failures. Birrell, Churchill & Carrington all spoke in same sense.

Lloyd George & then the P.M. suggested words to carry out our views, & we agreed if the King could not exercise prerogative of Crown, we could not ask him to do so now but if we had a majority, we should & without this knowledge he would acquiesce *we* could not advise a dissolution; or carry on his government.

Asquith summarised the Cabinet's three days of deliberations in a seven page report to the King on April 13: A 'discreditable transaction' with the Irish had been rejected. If the Lords were to reject or lay aside the resolutions on the relations of the two Houses and there proved to be no other way to accomplish the will of the elected majority, the Cabinet would either resign or advise a dissolution. In no case would they 'feel able to advise a dissolution, except under such conditions as would secure that in the new Parliament the judgment of the people as expressed in the election, would be carried into law.' Asquith concluded with a carefully constructed warning: 'The Cabinet were all of opinion that, as far as possible, the name of the Crown should be keep out of the arena of party controversy.' (RA X11/28).

Fortified by the Cabinet's decision, JAP told a meeting of the Uxbridge Liberal Association on April 13 that, anxious as loyal Liberals were to avoid bringing the King's name into matters connected with party politics, the time was coming 'when they must be more specific in regard to the way in which they would have to advise the King as to the steps which it would be necessary to take in the unfortunate event of the House of Lords again resisting the will of the people'. (The Daily News, 14 April 1910). Late in the evening of April 14 Asquith presented 'The Parliament Bill, 1910' to the House and made a statement with the required specificity. If the Lords rejected the government's resolutions, he would, he said, advise the Crown either that his government must resign or Parliament would be dissolved His government would not seek a dissolution unless a new Liberal government would be granted the conditions to enable it to put 'the judgment of the people' into law – a promise that sufficient peers could be created to enable its measures to pass the Lords.

On April 16 JAP used a tea and soirée at the Rotherham drill hall to issue a guarded rebuttal of Tory press allegations that the government had made an improper bargain with the Irish Nationalists to secure the passing of the Budget: 'if there has been any interchange of opinions between them and certain

Ministers there has not been any arrangement of any kind which I personally or the Cabinet is aware of.' (The Rotherham Express, 23 April 1910). *The Irish had been out-manoeuvred and the Budget, introduced by Lloyd George on April 19, was safe.*

April 20 A very cheery happy cabinet. The prospect of Budget going through, & the fact no concession had been made to the Irish over whiskey was a subject matter of congratulations, & yet their support had been secured.

Lloyd George was congratulated before the whole cabinet on the fact that he had £2,900,000 surplus, after all the chaos to his budget proposals created by the Lords, & Asquith said he would in his letter to the King refer to the position & let him realise what free trade finance could do.

We discussed the giving of money to intermediate education, from stable funds, & not from earmarked whiskey money liable to fluctuations.

We agreed to hand the £2,900,000 surplus – by a clause in budget to ship building.[19]

We discussed merits of issuing Insurance Bill, Invalidity & Pauper Pension Bills, & agreed to the latter as the most important.

We decided to take holiday to May 26th from Thursday 26th April.

We discussed H of Lords procedure re resolution bills & preamble & veto bill being circulated before we rose. Asquith said I told the House that our bill would have a preamble & a lot 'of funny stuff in it'. I was deputed to consider with experts, all elections on one day Bill.

April 27 Runciman explained the decision on the Appeal on the Swansea Schoolmasters salary case, & the views of Hamilton, who had reported, also of Robson, Evans, & Isaacs (the law officers) and it was decided to appeal against Farwell & Cozens Hardy's judgement which assumed the right of the court to decide whether schools were 'efficiently maintained' a different point to that of court below which had only to decide whether under Act of 1902 it was possible to pay salaries to teachers in nonprovided schools on a different basis to Provided schools. As Isaacs thought the Lords must limit the judgement, it was decided to go on. Asquith complained the Govmt had been ill advised, but George & McKenna voiced the opinion of the Welsh local authorities.

---

[19] Asquith wrote to the King that day that the surplus was 'very satisfactory evidence, … of the ill-founded & exaggerated character of the apprehensions, which were so freely & widely expressed, that the scheme of taxation proposed by the Budget would check enterprise, lead to evasion, and fail to provide adequate funds to meet the large additions which have become necessary to the expenditure of the State.' (Cab. 41/32/55). In fact, as the King was told, after subtracting £2.75m suspended 'from the Sinking Fund for the repayment of the National Debt' the surplus was actually just over £200,000. There was no explicit mention in the letter to the King of devoting the surplus to ship-building.

Just before the 1902 Education Act came into force, the teachers at the Oxford Street Church of England School, Swansea, applied for an increase in salary. The school managers thought their request reasonable but decided that it would be wrong on their part to grant it just before the local authority took over responsibility. However the authority refused to alter the salaries, even though they were well below the usual rates. As a result there was much dissatisfaction among the teachers, and many left. The school managers therefore raised private funds to supplement the salaries. In April 1907 the authority raised the salaries of all the teachers in its area except those at this school. The managers appealed to the Board of Education to intervene; the result was an enquiry by J.A. Hamilton KC. Hamilton reported in October 1908 that the authority was in default of its duties because the school was only kept efficient by private contributions to the teachers' salaries. However the ministry rejected his finding, stalled publication of the report, and said that it would not intervene in the dispute. The managers, encouraged by the Conservative leadership's espousal of their cause, then appealed to the Divisional Court to issue writs against the ministry for dereliction of duty. The writs were granted, whereupon the ministry appealed. On 21 April 1910 the Court of Appeal quashed the appeal application, saying that the local education authority must not be allowed to discriminate between the salaries of teachers at provided and non-provided schools. Lord Justice Farwell commented: 'I cannot believe that a public Department such as the Education Office can have been guilty of a course which could only be characterised as flagrant misconduct and I prefer to think that they mistook the law.' (The Times, 22 April 1910). The ministry appealed to the House of Lords but was again rebuffed on 6 April 1911 by which time JAP was President of the Board of Education. (The controversy is chronicled in The Schoolmaster *and is expounded in all its complexity in J.G. Ellis,* The Administration of the 1902 Act in Relation to the Church Schools in Swansea, *M.Ed. thesis, University College of Swansea, 1975).*

Harcourt brought up *Duke of York schools* – & Haldane & Burns supported him in desire to hand these over to the territorials – value £200,000 to £300,000. George urged delay & further consideration.[20]

Parliament Bill was discussed & terms agreed to, to be circulated on Saturday. Lord Chancellor & Crewe dwelt upon the difficulty of their position in the House of Lords. When veto Resolutions came to be considered, & pointed out that

---

[20] The Duke of York's Royal Military School, founded in 1801 and known till 1892 as The Royal Military Asylum, was for army officers' children. The school moved to Dover in 1909, hoping to pay for new buildings by selling its Chelsea site, but the inhabitants of Chelsea campaigned to retain the site as open space. They successfully urged its sale to the Territorial Army as training land.

either we should frame our complete scheme of reconstruction & explain it, or otherwise the issue at an election would be confused with Home Rule, Disestablishment & c.

We then spoke of Referendum – & Churchill naively pointed out that the only consideration which restrained his advocacy was the danger that we should not get the decision we sought. Asquith pointed out the difficulty of securing a decision on an exact question 'Do you approve of the Parliament Bill' as the Opposition would allege the question was– one chamber or two – or fiscal reform.

In February 1909 JAP had spoken at Plymouth of the possibility of appealing directly to the people as a way of passing progressive legislation. This was an expression of 'his own personal and private opinion'. In mid-October 1909 The Times *parliamentary correspondent reported that the government was contemplating a referendum. The story was allegedly based on a leaked memorandum written by JAP for the Cabinet but not circulated. (Ilbert's diary, 26 Oct. 1909, Ilbert MSS, H.C. Lib. MS 73). The memorandum, if it existed, cannot now be found. The Cabinet decided on 27 April 1910 to instruct the Parliamentary draftsman 'to prepare, in outline, for future consideration, a Bill for holding all elections on the same day, and a bill for submitting to popular vote, without the need for a general election, the proposals which the Government have made in regard to the relations between the two Houses of Parliament.' (Asquith's Cabinet letter to the King, 28 April 1910, Cab. 41/32/11). The referendum was extensively canvassed in the constitutional conference in the summer of 1910. After a series of challenges and counter-challenges in the election campaign Balfour pledged on November 29 to submit tariff reform to a referendum and invited the Liberals to do the same with Home Rule. (Vernon Bogdanor,* The People and the Party System: The referendum and electoral reform in British politics, *Cambridge University Press, Cambridge, 1981, pp. 16–24; Mark Stephen Campisano,* The Unionists and the Constitution 1906–1911, *B.Litt thesis, University of Oxford, 1977, pp. 117–21; Patricia Kelvin,* The Development and Use of the Concept of Electoral Mandate in British Politics, 1867–1911, *Ph.D. thesis, University of London, 1977, chapters 9 and 10). When challenged in December 1910 to say why he then was not prepared to submit Home Rule to a referendum JAP was forced to make a lame affirmation of belief in representative government rather than 'a measure such as the Referendum, which will handicap progress'. He had never committed himself to 'the general principle of the Referendum'. (The Times, 8, 9, 12 Dec. 1910).*

Chapter 8

Sovereign Remedies

May 6 1910   Death of the King.   11.45 p.m. Friday 6 May.   On receiving a telegram from Lord Knollys 'most critical' I came up to London, 12.18 a.m. train from D'ton Friday night.   I called on Crewe & FitzRoy (Clerk to Privy Council) at 9.30 & on Harcourt (who had just arrived from Paris.)   I saw Attorney General, & then authorities at both Houses in regard to an 'immediate' meeting, as prescribed by Act of Anne 6. & 7.

We then saw Crewe, Churchill & Edward Grey at the F.O. and decided upon course to take viz. meetings to swear allegiance Monday & Tuesday & the eulogies on Wednesday May 11th & cabinet for 4 o'clock on the 10th.   I attended St. Paul's at 1.0 Memorial service with Grey & Burns.   At 4.0 we attended Privy Council at St. James's & then 120 P.C. took oath of allegiance & I affirmed – rather formidable.

Monday I took my affirmation in House & signed the roll in afternoon, at 9.0 a.m. present at Proclamation at St. James's Palace.

In the midst of his more important activities, JAP found time to go to his tailor to get his clothes 'craped'.   As he explained to his wife on May 7 his affirmation of the oath was formidable because he had to take it alone, after the Protestants and then the Catholics had been sworn in as Privy Councillors en bloc by simply raising their hands or 'kissing the book'.   (Gainford MSS, 520).

Several leading political figures, including the Prime Minister, were out of the country in the first week of May.   Alick Murray had been holidaying with Lloyd George, T.P. O'Connor, Arthur Murray, and Arthur Priestley (the bachelor MP for Grantham) at the Villa Lucertola on Lake Como, lent to them by the banker Hugh E. Hoare.   Learning on May 7 of the King's death Elibank and Lloyd George had returned at once to London.   (Murray, Master and Brother, p. 50).   Asquith, on board the Admiralty yacht Enchantress *en route to Gibraltar, reached London on May 9.   Meanwhile, the absence of both the Speaker and Deputy Speaker made it impossible to comply with 6 Anne c.41 (1708): an Act for the Security of Her Majesty's Person and Government and of the Succession to the Crown of Great Britain in the Protestant Line.   The legislative requirement was that Parliament was not dissolved on the death of the Sovereign; if it was not then sitting, it was to meet immediately.   But no one other than the Speaker and his deputy could take the chair in the Commons.   Accordingly, the House met on May 7, adjourned at once, and did not reconvene until Alfred Emmott returned on May 9. (James William Lowther, Viscount Ullswater, A Speaker's Commentaries, 2 vols, Edward Arnold, 1925, Vol. II, p. 90; Ilbert's diary, 10 May 1910, Ilbert MSS, H.C. Lib. MS 74).*

May 10 Tuesday at 11.0 called on Elibank & discussed dates – we agreed on June 13 to resume work.

At 12.0 proceeded to Marlborough House – & took my affirmation on taking position as his Chancellor of the Duchy – after other Ministers had taken oath & left his presence. I drove with Asquith to Buckingham Palace, told him of the views of the Party in regard to the situation & the importance of going canny in regard to veto proposals & that the Tory party were trying to assert our policy had worried the King into his grave & I reminded him that 8 months before he had told me of the sudden death expected by the Drs.[1]

Cabinet at 4.0

We discussed the Address – condolence & congratulation motions, arranged to meet on June 13. Asquith told us the King took strong objection to Oath on his meeting Parliament for first time & pressed for its alteration as it was offensive to 12 millions of his subjects. We admitted Orange men & Col. Sandys would object to bill but decided to have one drafted. The King told Asquith that when he told Lord Salisbury he could not take such an oath, Lord S. said well you 'then can't be King'.

The King's objection was less to the Coronation Oath than to the Accession Declaration which accompanied it. The Declaration, introduced in 1678 in the panic following the discovery of the Popish Plot, and extended to the sovereign under the Bill of Rights in 1689, had long been a source of friction. Its wording could not be justified or excused.

> I, ..., do solemnly and sincerely in the presence of God profess, testify, and declare that I do believe that in the Sacrament of the Lord's Supper there is not any Transubstantiation of the Elements of Bread and Wine into the Body and Blood of Christ at or after the Consecration thereof by any person whatever. And that the Invocation or Adoration of the Virgin Mary or any other saint, and the Sacrifice of the Mass, as they are now used in the Church of Rome, are superstitious and idolatrous. And I do solemnly in the presence of God profess, testify and declare that I do make this Declaration and every part thereof in the plain and ordinary sense of the Words read unto me as they are commonly understood by English Protestants, without any Evasion, Equivocation, or Mental Reservation whatever, and without any dispensation already granted to me for this purpose by the Pope, or any other authority or person whatsoever, or without any hope of any such dispensation from any person or authority whatsoever, or without thinking that I am or can be acquitted before God or man, or absolved of this Declaration or any part thereof, although the Pope, or any other persons, or power whatsoever, should

---

1 Pease told Hobhouse that Asquith had been warned by Sir Thomas Barlow. (Hobhouse's diary, 15 May 1910, David, ed., *Inside Asquith's Cabinet*, p. 90).

dispense with or cancel the same, or declare that it was null and void from the beginning.

(The Times, 29 June 1910)

Edward VII had sought unsuccessfully to have the 'crude language' objectionable to Roman Catholics expunged. The Salisbury government introduced unsatisfactory compromise legislation which was allowed to lapse after being passed in the House of Lords. Sir Sidney Lee stated that 'King Edward's successor took the oath in its old form.' (Lee, King Edward VII, *vol. II, p. 22–5). But the Accession Declaration was to be significantly modified.*

We discussed pros & cons of postponing veto resolutions & prospects of a possible compromise owing to sentiment being opposed to rushing the new King. No decision taken.

According to Lloyd George, the Cabinet had been close to 'precipitating themselves into a 2nd blunder, they were all agreed & I swung them round. As Samuel said to me "For the second time this year you have succeeded in swinging round the Cabinet when they were on the wrong course".' (Lloyd George to Margaret Lloyd George, 10 May 1910, Kenneth O. Morgan, ed., Lloyd George Family Letters, 1885–1936, *University of Wales Press, Cardiff, and Oxford University Press, 1973, p. 153).*

The King told Asquith today that his Father would be regarded as the Peacemaker between International Powers, & it was his view & his own, an arrangement should be arrived at between contending Parties so that there should be domestic peace on the constitutional differences here at home.

May 12   Cabinet at 11.30. Downing St.

I passed note across to Asquith, that I had on his instructions in Nov. issued instructions to Treasury that all new circulars raising revenue should have cabinet sanction & that I thought this was not observed, & that if there was a general election this year, the character of these might be of importance.

Harcourt was asked to procure a wreath for the cabinet, & the inscription was left to him, also the words to be placed upon the H of C. wreath to be placed against the coffin in Westminster Hall.[2]

Egypt. Grey informed us, that the policy pursued of associating natives in Government had only stimulated agitation to promote our evacuation. The Native Advisers were 3 yrs ago mere dummies, they were now effective, but Gorst was persistently attacked, instead of himself. The National Press was

---

2   We have been unable to find a description of the Cabinet's wreath. Those from Parliament were both of laurel leaves and heart-shaped. Neither the Royal Archives nor Harcourt's papers has any record of the inscriptions.

violent & the position was not improving. If terrorism produced any verdict, other than that of murder, against Wardani (who assassinated Boutros Pasha) it would be a monstrous miscarriage of Justice.[3] Gorst wanted the Govmt to at once transport under martial law 3 leaders, & to make clear we intended to remain in Egypt, & punish by martial law any other cases of assassination by prompt court martial. After an hour's discussion, the latter course was agreed to. The P.M. & Grey to draw up despatch to Gorst. Morley put the question, by transportation without ordinary law, will you deepen the Anti British feeling, or slacken the agitation. He in India had only acted under the law, with a view of asserting the principle that the law must be observed, & had transported under the Act of 1818. He did not know whether the agitation in Egypt was deep or froth & bubble. Grey replied Cromer thought the bubble would be pricked by transportation. The agitation was among the town educated Mohammedans & not likely to spread to the Fellaheens. It was agreed Gorst should be asked the grounds upon which he advocated transportation.

I urged unless definite offences committed we could not take the failure of justice in another case, as our warrant for action; but if terrorism prevailed we should announce our intention of adopting martial law, which under our military occupation we had the right to put into force, whether or not justice was meted out in the trial of Wardani as another assassination might follow, if Wardani was hung. No decision on this point was arrived at.

Lord Ch. thought the Press [illegible] be suppressed. Haldane was told to have a brigade ready to strengthen army of occupation if the circumstances justified it. He warned us of the additional expense, which would mostly fall on Egypt. George recounted conversation held by him with 2 officers returning from Egypt. *Cyprus* – we had an hour's talk on the position there, Churchill had led Cyprians to believe (on his colonial tour) that the grant in aid of £50,000 p.a. would be continued. George had, owing to prosperity in the island reduced it by £10,000 this year. King Harman the Governor had told the people he took their view, & did not support us, a long wrangle occurred between George & Churchill, & eventually the P.M. intervened and whilst condemning the grant, suggested they should send a representative here to consult with Colonial Office & Treasury as to a permanent arrangement – a revolt would thus be stayed in the Island.

Cyprus paid an annual tribute to Turkey of £92,800. The island could not raise sufficient revenue to meet both the tribute and the costs of its own

---

3   Ibrahim Wardani (d. 1910); student; shot Boutros Ghali Pasha 20 February 1910. An extreme nationalist Mohammedan, he claimed that the Copt Boutros was betraying Egypt. He was tried, found guilty, and executed that year. Sheik Shawish El Abdul Aziz, a Moslem nationalist, edited *Al-Liwa*, for which Wardani had worked. He was tried for writing seditious poems, inciting readers to murder. On August 8 he was convicted and imprisoned for three months.

administration so an annual grant was made to cover the difference. In 1907 the grant had been fixed at £50,000 for the next three years. Churchill, on his visit to the island in October 1907, had said that if Cypriot revenue showed an encouraging rise, the grant would not be altered to the disadvantage of the island. The Treasury took the view that the British taxpayer was subsidising the Cypriots but its proposed reduction had resulted in threats of non-cooperation by the island's legislature. The Cabinet sent the problem back to the Treasury and the Colonial Office. JAP's copy of a Colonial Office memorandum on the problem (Mediterranean No. 69) is annotated 'I got this settled J.A.P. by insisting on Ll. George meeting Crewe, Seely & Hobhouse July. J.A.P.' (Gainford MSS, [85]). Sir Charles King-Harman was formally rebuked.

Tuesday May 17[4]   Cabinet at No. 10 at 3.0. In the morning members attended Westminster Hall to receive King's Body – service not very impressive, but well done.

For 50 minutes we discussed the alteration of King's so called coronation oath, & after revueing it, we agreed to Attorney General's form of words, omitting direct reference to Transubstantiation, & left at declaration of protestantism as defined by enactments, Bill of Rights & Act of Settlement. Morley very vehement against any denunciation of any religion. George afraid lest we should bring hornet's nest upon us. It was left that leaders of different thought should appear to be consulted so as to get varying elements with us.

Grey asked leave to transport Sheik Shawish, a journalist from Egypt. We assented if new offence committed undermining our authority, & aimed at Judges who had sentenced Wardani. This lasted 40 minutes. We had a further chat for 40 minutes as to veto being pressed in Lords. Churchill advocated firmness within a month, & such a course might produce compromise. George wanted a further fortnight, but all for compromise & conference. The rest opposed to any policy of rushing the King is suicidal, & would as I said hand over the determining elector in the country to the Tories.[5]

The P.M. said if the King asked if we would confer, he proposed to say yes, if other side would. Their refusal to confer would it was admitted help us – if they agreed, they must give us 17/6 in the £1 as our case for holding office & no longer being forced to plough sands, was overwhelmingly in favour of reform. George urged publicity, Morley Samuel & I quiet conferences such as occurred in 1884 over the franchise.

---

[4]   JAP misdated this entry May 16. Asquith's Cabinet letter to the King (Cab. 41/32/59), describing the same Cabinet, dated the meeting as May 17, the day King Edward's body was brought to Westminster Hall. Both men refer to the meeting taking place on Tuesday.

[5]   This sentence (with 'is' where 'as' is needed) is JAP's own corrected version of two sentences which evidently did not express his meaning: 'The rest opposed to any. The policy of resisting the King is suicidal …'.

May 29, 1910
Headlam Hall,
Gainford

My dear Asquith,

I cordially agree to Crewe's suggestion that Lord R. should be approached, & in the way he recommends. My view is: –

From our own party point of view, we should probably gain by Lord R. proceeding at once with his resolutions, an aggressive act now on his part. – but if there is any chance of a compromise under which Liberals could get their own way in the Lords when they were in power, Lord R should be deterred from proceeding for at least the time Crewe suggests.

Yours ever,
Joseph A. Pease
(Asquith MSS, vol. 23, ff. 110–1)

June 6 1910   Cabinet – 3.0. p.m. 10 Downing St.   Members turned up all looking the better for their outdoor lives.   Lloyd George was heard to murmur something about faces like lobsters.   The question of business was first discussed. It was arranged no statement relating to when the veto should be taken should be made this week.   Lord Crewe said Lord Rosebery was prepared to postpone consideration of his own resolutions so long as the House of Lords had the opportunity to discuss his or their alternative schemes before the veto Resolutions, & he would say so on Wednesday.

Asquith suggested Tuesday week as the day to appoint the civil list Committee & asked us if a seat for King George in Ireland could be included.

Redmond had explained to Elibank he would oppose such a suggestion & raise Castle rule, if this was introduced otherwise the Nationalists would lie low over the civil list.

The Civil List Committee of 21 members, chaired by Lloyd George, was announced 15 June 1910. It reported on July 7, recommending a grant of £470,000, the same as that made to King Edward VII in 1901. (PP, 1910 [211], vi, 315). The Chancellor enhanced the value of the grant by exempting it from income tax. No mention was made of an Irish seat. Returning from a visit to Ireland in 1897, the then Duke of York had sought unsuccessfully to persuade Queen Victoria to establish a royal residence near Dublin. Although there is no record in the Royal Archives, it seems likely that the King had raised the matter personally with the Prime Minister. (Registrar, Royal Archives to CH, 5 Jan. 1993). The Nationalists, as they had in 1901, refused to take part on the committee.

Elibank explained the Irish view, their opposition to any deferring of veto, but not pressing for another General Election before Dec. or Jan.   2 inconsistent views, as Liberal party could obviously not postpone the issue after Lords rejection.

We then discussed whether we should have a conference with Opposition, & we all agreed, except Pentland, that Balfour might be approached by the Prime Minister. Churchill argued at his accustomed length, & with reiteration that the King's name must be associated with the proposed conference. That he wished it, & that to reject it, meant opposing his wishes, that 'The Crown was not made of Gingerbread.' We all were against his view, except Lord Loreburn, who quoted precedents. Harcourt emphatic as to danger of King doing anything except by advice of Ministers.

Asquith & I asserted King's views would be well advertised without any reference by Ministers. We could allude to changed circumstances & altered atmosphere created by the King's death.

The King had told Asquith when he last saw him, he did not know quite how the crisis had arisen – hence Asquith's memorandum (enclosed) which he had circulated.[6] The King also told Asquith a distinguished person approached him to summon a conference, he declined to do it unless advised to do so, & he 'strongly repudiated' taking on himself any initiation.[7] Asquith told the King he must consult his colleagues before tendering advice, & he proposed to see him this evening after the Cabinet.

The attempt made by the late King with Lansdowne & Balfour was not encouraging; but George pointed out circumstances had changed. I said the Tories were anxious we should take the first aggressive step, & to show a disposition to be reasonable, would be tactically wise. We discussed the alteration of the Oath, & Runciman said what he found was the views of certain Free Churchmen – & Asquith said what Cantuar's views were, & I reported Ebor's (Lang) with whom I had travelled to York on the evening of the funeral. They both objected to any reference to the Protestant Faith, as it was no definition. The protestants were those who protested against others! It was agreed to modify Robson's words as drafted by an omission as to Protestant Faith leaving Protestant succession in as defined by enactments.

Earlier in the cabinet. Morley asserted his view strongly, that he wanted to see a weak 2d Chamber, & not a strengthened one like Grey.

Grey admitted he was not tied to one plan but if veto resolutions stood alone without a representative 2d Chamber we should be on wrong lines.

---

6 The memorandum, not enclosed in the diary, presumably was Asquith's Cabinet paper, 'The Constitutional Question: its Origins and Development', 28 May 1910 (Cab. 37/102/20).

7 The King had seen Lord Rosebery on June 4 and also visited Joseph Chamberlain. His diary records his difficulty in understanding what Chamberlain was saying but is silent on what was discussed in the two meetings. (Registrar, Royal Archives to CH, 5 Jan. 1993).

June 8 Cabinet. Asquith read scraps of the proposed draft of Regency bill, indicating character of measures. He dwelt on the clause which appeared in all similar bills, preventing Regent exercising powers to enable certain alterations to be secured by law, & said – the limitation of power of veto might be supported by this precedent.[8]

He referred to his interview with the King on the evening of the 6th. The King said he was pleased at the decision of the cabinet to confer with opposition. He said Balfour was ready to do the same. That he did not want to be regarded as the initiator or umpire but as watching the associations in a friendly spirit. Asquith proposed writing a letter asking Balfour to see him. I suggested the object of the interview should be stated. Asquith replied no not object but the subject.

Asquith said he would refer to the King's attitude. Morley pressed this should be done orally but no reference should be made in letter. Churchill pressed for direct written record, but cabinet came to other decision, recognising everyone would know, & that constitutionally it was right. The King should only act on advice of his Ministers. McKenna & the Lord Chancellor pressed for cabinet decision as to course they would take if conference proved abortive. Runciman pointed out the case for veto, after a conference could never be fully restored. I suggested the period of conference should be regarded as a truce, without prejudice to the future, but we could not publicly assert a threat of our future intentions, Grey, Churchill, Crewe & Lloyd George vehemently supporting this view, which was acquiesced in. It was agreed that the P.M. should at once write A.J.B. asking for the interview, & to leave until the conference met what further steps should be taken. It might quickly decide, & if abortive the margin of difference might be so slight as to alter the course. The Irish were represented by George as most anxious that no decision should be taken in advance. The cabinet lasted only 70 mins.

The Cabinet was substantially united on the idea of a conference under a truce. Relying on third-hand sources, and with a vested interest in exaggerating the influence of his own advocacy, J.L. Garvin told Lord Northcliffe on June 13 that Churchill remained 'dead against' a truce, and Lloyd George was going to make the best of what he believed to be an unwise policy. (Gollin, The Observer and J.L. Garvin, p. 190, is misled by Garvin). The misgivings of Runciman, who thought the chances of success 'infinitesimal', seem to have escaped the notice of both JAP and Garvin. (Runciman to Asquith, 7 June 1910, copy, Runciman MSS). Asquith's letter to Balfour was 'not marked private, indicating that it

---

8   The Regency Bill, which became law on August 3, appointed Queen Mary Regent, should the sovereign die before his heir was of age (eighteen). As Regent, Queen Mary was to swear an oath to maintain the Protestant religion. Should she become a Roman Catholic while she was Regent she would lose all her powers.

reflects a cabinet decision, but the middle class sentiment and wordiness show the composition to be Asquith's own. Balfour's assent to the proposal,' Lord Balcarres observed, 'struck me as wondrous frigid: civil but terse to a point bordering on curtness.' (Balcarres' diary, 10 June 1910, Vincent, ed., The Crawford Diaries, p. 158; the letters are in Asquith MSS, vol. 23, ff. 126–9).

June 10 In response to a telephone message on Thursday from Sir Arthur Bigge, I went to Marlborough House at 10.30 on Friday 10th. Fritz Ponsonby told me they were beginning to get things straightened out a bit at last, but warrants & c had given them a lot of work.

Wallington showed me into the Green Drawing Room, & announced me as The Rt. Hon. Mr. Pease. The King alluded to my absence from London as the reason for his not having seen me before – he asked me to sit by him, in one of the 2 chairs ostentatiously placed in the centre of the room. He at once began to talk about the Duchy of Cornwall, & related how George the III & George IV never got on together, & differed over these Duchy Estates & then proceeded to tell me of incidents where he found Prince Consort had parted with property, which owing to mineral finds had been a bargain to the purchaser in Cornwall, & how the owner on one occasion admitted this. I tried to bring him to the subject of Lancashire Duchy, by telling him my Uncle Lord Ducie[9] had told me about the estates in former years, but that there was this difference, that most of ours were let on repairing leases, which accounted for their reputation, as not so creditable to the Sovereign. He suggested a gradual change in system, so that, the King's name should not be associated with estates, not in a creditable condition. The King then went on to tell me about the revenue from the Duchy of Cornwall, & I stopped him again by showing the Duchy of Lancaster revenue was not much less, & in this way I gradually got him to business.

I told him how much the revenues had increased from NIL in 1837 to £64,000 in 1909, & I hoped we might maintain this – & I looked forward to the gradual development of more mineral Royalties.

I explained to him who the council were. He was astonished at the elderly character of my advisers, & suggested resignations. I pointed out men like Engleheart, Lord Cross, Lord Wolverhampton were harmless, & Sir Dighton Probyn might be left on as a compliment if he desired to serve, but that Sir Wm Carrington the new Privy Purse would be an acquisition.

I asked him his view about what detail I should go into in regard to any evidence I gave to civil list committee. He did not want me to volunteer matter but if pressed be open.

---

[9] JAP's mother-in-law, Lady Alice Havelock-Allan, was the sister of Henry John Moreton, 3rd Earl of Ducie (1827–1921); Lib. MP Stroud 1852–3; succ. father 1853; FRS 1855; Ld Lt, Gloucestershire 1857–1911; PC 1859; member, Prince of Wales's Council 1888–1908.

He said I was to consult George Murray as to Income Tax deductions, but he thought the present amount should be the limit. I said I saw no reason why he should pay any, but he asked what King Edward did, & was ready to do the same.

I explained to him the Exors would take a big slice of the revenue this year. He said as I am executor, it won't make much difference. We discussed sinking fund on mineral Royalties – & he left me to use my discretion but to name proposal, if any substantial alterations. He was very cordial, & I left after 25 mins friendly chat. No other subject was discussed.

June 15   Cabinet. 10 Downing St 11.30.

The P.M. read his & Balfour's letters passed last week. June 9. Asquith wrote, to the following effect, owing to the lamented death of the King & unforeseen change in the political atmosphere, & the alteration of perspective thereby created he wrote to ask whether it might be possible to avoid in the next few months an embittered controversial conflict on the constitutional question. That if he A.J.B. thought a preliminary meeting to privately talk over the suggestion he (the P.M.) would be glad to see him. [sic] Balfour responded & offered to see the P.M. early this week. They met yesterday in the P.M.'s room at the H of C.

Asquith said to A.J.B. of course it was unnecessary for him to explain the position, but His Majesty's position was this; he took no initiative, but cordially sympathised with the effort. Asquith did not recapitulate the points, but it was merely a question as to whether both sides would confer.

The 3 subjects related to

1.   The relations between the 2 Houses in regard to finance.
2.   What could be done to avoid deadlock when one of Houses wilfully disagreed with the other.
3.   What was to be the future composition of the 2d Chamber or House of Lords.

He suggested to A.J.B. – the reference should not be restricted but relate to the above 3 topics. Balfour suggested 8 should be the full number, four from each – they should meet on Friday at 3 p.m. in Asquith's Room.

He said Lansdowne wanted another peer with himself (Crewe suggested Cawdor would be selected) Churchill half suggested Curzon – but Morley said NO.) Austen Chamberlain would be the fourth. Asquith said, Balfour's attitude was cordial in manner, sympathetic in intention & he not only hoped but apparently thought something might come of the conference. Asquith said, he suggested Crewe, the Chancellor of the Exchequer, & although it was an invidious task to suggest names, he had come to the conclusion Birrell would be the right man, his association with the Irish might be an advantage.

Edward Grey suggested as a Celt he would counteract Cawdor's emotional celtic temperament. Asquith said Cawdor was only an intruder in Wales – Birrell repudiated relationship.[10]   Someone suggested they hoped Birrell would be helpful as he would lubricate the conference by his happy impromptus.

Women's suffrage was discussed.   The P.M. said he would receive a deputation from both sides on this 'most repulsive subject'! in a few days, & asked for instructions. Grey took up the women's side & urged that all cabinets were split on the subject, and even though large majority of representatives supported it, no effective opportunity could be given without Govmt help to the majority. The P.M. admitted this, & said with no opportunity for controversial subjects this session, he feared his reply might reproduce violent agitation; but he wanted to say something mollifying enthusiasts of the nonmilitant section – although soothing anticipations might not satisfy even them. Grey asked to be in a position to point out to wait 18 mos. as was not unreasonable. It was agreed, the whole question, if the Govmt remained in power & a majority declared for the principle should be afforded an opportunity by facilities being given next year, but the measure should not be fettered by restricted title from a free decision, so that an undemocratic measure should not be forced on the House, under a limited title.

Crewe, urged the added electorate if added might alter the complexion of anti veto view in the country, & should be hung up until the present constitutional problem settled. Churchill suggested that if militant methods, were adopted, the decision should not be binding on the cabinet. I & the P.M. said this course was not advisable, & wd. be a mistake. Burns, Buxton, & Crewe all urged the illogical character of Shackleton's bill.

David Shackleton's Parliamentary Franchise (Women) Bill, introduced on June 14, was given a second reading on July 12. It proposed in essence that the million women then qualified to vote in local elections should be eligible for the parliamentary electoral roll. It was the minimum acceptable to all suffragists. Despite its 'illogical' character, Burns and Buxton, Birrell, Grey, Haldane, and several junior ministers voted for it. Asquith, JAP, Lloyd George, Churchill, and other members of the Cabinet voted against it – the latter two arguing that it was undemocratic. Churchill, who had at first intended to abstain, 'became convinced that the bill was not only absurd and indefensible in itself, but deeply injurious to the Liberal cause.' Rather than 'purchase an ignoble immunity by silence and abstention' he opted to share the danger of violence to which Asquith and Lloyd George were exposed by their public opposition. (Churchill to Lord Lytton, 19 July 1910, Lytton MSS). 'There is no doubt that Winston Churchill's speech was very powerful', Geoffrey Howard told his mother Lady Carlisle on

---

10   Birrell's supposed Celtic character presumably derived from his Scottish mother and Northumbrian father. The Cawdors had intruded into Pembrokeshire by marriage in the late seventeenth century. They sold 36,000 Welsh acres to pay death duties in 1976. (Philip Beresford, *The Sunday Times Book of the Rich*, Penguin, London, 1990, p. 194).

July 13, 'and had a considerable influence on our people because his case had so much that was true in it'. (copy, Howard MSS, J 30). The bill was consigned to the graveyard Committee of the Whole House. (Leslie Parker Hume, The National Union of Women's Suffrage Societies 1897–1914, *Garland, New York & London, 1982, pp. 74–85).*

We discussed when *Budget* should be taken. Ll George urged July 4, after Brewers returns were in (June 30) and I pointed out Tea duty would be hung up for 4 days. George said he would risk that inconvenience.

Brewers' returns were ordered on 22 February 1910. They gave the number of licences issued to common brewers, licensed victuallers, and retailers of beer on and off the premises, and included details of malt, hops and other cereals consumed, quantities produced, and the amounts collected from the licence and beer duties. The tea duty, with income tax, had to be approved annually. A duty on tea of 5d. per pound had been proposed in the Budget. When a reduction in the duty in favour of Empire-grown tea was proposed, Lloyd George pointed out on July 25 that nine-tenths of tea consumed in Britain was grown in the Empire; such a large loss of revenue was unacceptable. He added that the duty had been 8d. in 1904.

We agreed not to press Appropriation Bill & 2 last votes or so, until we knew result of conference – the weapon was the right Parliamentary over a Tory Govmt if they took office. Asquith said, the weapon of taking 5 weeks supply, & relying on supply as the Power, & not the budget had been fully asserted.

Under the Old Age Pensions Act the pauper disqualification for those lodged in workhouses would lapse automatically at the end of 1910 unless Parliament decided otherwise. Needing four million pounds to cover this consequential expenditure, Lloyd George could be sure only of two million. Uncertain of the tax yield for 1909–10, especially the whiskey tax, he proposed to defer the Budget until July. This would entail collecting tea duty for a few days without statutory or parliamentary authority. The Budget was introduced on June 30 when it was learned that the proceeds of the whiskey tax had been greatly overestimated. Nevertheless the money was found for the pauper pensioners. (Elie Halévy, tr. E.I. Watkin, The Rule of Democracy 1905–1914, *Ernest Benn, 1961, pp. 284–5; Ilbert's diary, 14 and 30 June 1910, Ilbert MSS, H.C. Lib. MS 73).*

We discussed the oath declaration. So many representations had been made in favour of a negative R.C. declaration that he was afraid to proceed. I urged sections would oppose every alteration, & Runciman said he would risk the form already agreed to, & Morley was vehement in condemning any religion.

The discussion seemed as the P.M. said interminable – & although Pentland urged one the view that the central doctrines of the R.C. faith invocation of the virgin & the saints & transubstantiation should be repudiated & the Lord Ch. urged the Ch. of Engld wherein it differed should be accepted – we stuck to the form of positive belief Birrell said if we could not pass it we should remember as martyrs 'The blood of the martyrs was the seed of the Church'. Morley said Gladstone would never have agreed to this alteration, 'Yes, he would' said Asquith, 'but with any amount of reservations'!

We discussed Civil list, & agreed not to give in to Sir D. Probyn's claim to give the Queen £30,000 more for Sandringham upkeep. The King would keep up the estate & shootings. The Queen's House & Gardens & £70,000 was ample.

Grey then told us the position in Crete. Turkey was excited, & desired to satisfy their prestige at the expense of Greece. Crete anxious for annexation by Greece. No oppression existed – autonomy prevailed. Whole Europe agreed to impose, & retain, the present nominal suzerainty of Turkey by force. If necessary to use force to rights of Mussulman representatives & their positions & salaries. If Cretans went to mountains, we should seize 3 ports, call in Mussulmans & land forces & appoint Governor, until reason prevailed.

Crete was an autonomous island under Turkish sovereignty, a position guaranteed by the Treaty of Berlin. The annexation of Crete by Greece would be seen by Turkey as a casus belli *and therefore could not be permitted despite the Cretans' desire. The Cretan Assembly had elected E. Venizelos president of a committee which was to seek annexation. It had also excluded Mohammedan members and officials, and sworn its loyalty to the Greek king. For the moment the Cretans were suppressed by gunboat diplomacy.*

June 23 Cabinet.

D. of Cornwall created Prince of Wales this day as a birthday present.[11] Lord Beauchamp as new President attended his first cabinet.[12]

Asquith commenced by reporting result of conference with AJB. & Co. He ridiculed the Press statements, & read out passage from D. News of 'the Prime donkey' P.W. Wilson – who alluded to 4 meetings & diligence – whereas they had only met on Friday 17th it was 'satisfactory' & a 'friendly tone' existed. It was arranged to circulate some papers, & to resume this afternoon when A.J.B. would circulate a paper producing points for consideration. Asquith reported what passed at the 2 meetings he had with deputations on Monday for & against

---

[11] The Duke of Cornwall was the future King Edward VIII (1894–1972); reigned Jan.– Dec. 1936; abdicated to marry Mrs Wallis Simpson; Duke of Windsor 1937.

[12] Beauchamp replaced Wolverhampton who had resigned on June 20 after four months' absence from official duties.

the suffrage. He alluded to the pro suffrage as consisting of women, & one man the most effeminate one they could find Charles McLaren.[13] Mrs Fawcett made it clear that she would not be satisfied with a barren 2d reading & asked for facilities, for all stages – McLaren asked for 2d reading without prejudice. Brailsford had secured a memorial in favour of the Bill signed by 54 Eng. Libs. 20 Scotch. 7 London 13 Welsh = 94. 26 Tories, 22 Labour Irish 16 total 158. Asquith said not 1/4th.

In course of a long discussion, I urged no facilities now, 2d Reading a dishonest vote, & promise time next session, Grey agree. Lord Chancellor & Ll. George urge no commitment ahead but a 2d. Reading now. Eventually it was decided the P.M. should today state 2d. Reading shd. be given, but no further facilities – opportunities later if H of C. wished. We turned up the P.M.'s words at Albert Hall, he said 'I always turn to this speech with [dread?]' but all he sd was an opportunity wd be given.

Asquith was referring to his election speech, in the Albert Hall on 10 December 1909, to 10,000 men whom The Times *described as 'boiling over with enthusiasm'. Stringent precautions had been taken to keep suffragettes and their male supporters out. But there had been a large meeting of suffragettes in the hall the night before and many hid overnight, in the organ and elsewhere, so there were a few interruptions. On the vote for women, Asquith had simply renewed the pledge he had given in May 1908 to a deputation of Liberal MPs, that the government would introduce a comprehensive reform bill to which women's suffrage amendments could be added. The government would leave the decision to the House of Commons. Asquith may well have suspected that the Speaker would rule, as he did for both the 1910 'Conciliation' Bill and the government's own reform bill in 1913, that the widening amendments proposed by the suffragists were inadmissible.*

Crewe asked for assistance to enable subject matters for next colonial conference to be considered – 2 sections (1.) under P.M. self gov. dominions. (2) Crown colonies & protectorates under him. The question of Colonial P.M.s declining to associate with a Secretary instead of the P.M. would be raised. Buxton, Samuel, Haldane Beauchamp placed on the Committee.

At the 1907 Imperial Conference Alfred Deakin of Australia, supported by Sir Joseph Ward of New Zealand and Dr Jameson of Cape Colony, had asserted that

---

13 Sir Charles McLaren acted as a parliamentary whip for the suffragists. (Linda Walker, 'Party Political Women: A Comparative Study of Liberal Women and the Primrose League, 1890–1914', Jane Rendall, ed., *Equal or Different*: Women's Politics 1800–1914, Basil Blackwell, Oxford, 1987, p. 183). But it was his younger brother Walter, Vice-President of the Men's League for Women's Suffrage, who spoke with Mrs Fawcett for the deputation.

*the attitude of the Colonial Office officials was more suited to the governing of
colonies than to conducting relations with the Dominions. He proposed the
removal of Dominion relations from the Colonial Office; a new Dominions
Office should be established, to be responsible to the Prime Minister. His
proposals were opposed by Canada and not adopted by the conference, but a
separate Dominions division with a permanent secretariat for imperial
conferences was established at the Colonial Office. By 1910 the Colonial
Office's attitude was that there was no longer any demand for the change,
though there was need for more recognition of the growing equality between the
Dominions and Britain. The office also pointed out that, were a new department
to be established, the Prime Minister was far too busy to supervise it. The new
department could be placed under the Lord President, who had no departmental
responsibilities (Sir Charles Lucas, 'Proposed Reorganisation of the Colonial
Office,' 23 July 1910, circulated to the cabinet 26 July 1910, Cab. 37/103/35).
In a Cabinet memorandum of 7 March 1911, Seely (the Under-Sec. at the
Colonial Office) argued that although there was enough work to justify the
establishment of a separate department, it would cost an extra £10,000 in
salaries. Demand for the separation was not sufficient to justify this expenditure
(J. Seely, 'Reorganisation of the Colonial Office,' Mottistone MSS, vol. 10, ff.
120–4; this memorandum is not listed in* Public Record Office Handbooks No. 4,
List of Cabinet Papers 1880–1914, HMSO, 1964). *Harcourt, when he succeeded
Crewe as Colonial Secretary, advised the Cabinet that he and the Prime Minister
would offer to divide the Colonial Office below the level of Secretary of State
(there would be two permanent under secretaries) and to establish a standing
committee which would include Dominion representatives such as the high
commissioners (L.V. Harcourt, 'Suggested Reconstruction of the Colonial
Office,' 22 April 1911, Cab. 37/106/52). Both Deakin and Jameson were out of
office and did not attend the 1911 conference; their demands were not renewed,
and even Harcourt's proposed standing committee was dropped for lack of
unanimous support (*The Times, *9 June 1911). For a fuller account see J.A.
Cross,* Whitehall and the Commonwealth: British Departmental Organisation for
Commonwealth Relations, 1900–1966, Routledge and Kegan Paul, 1967, pp.
17–35.*

Accession declaration discussed for half an hour. The P.M. said in restarting it:
'it will probably lead to our downfall.'

Thring was to be seen by Haldane as to possible modification, of bill enclosed
to avoid non cons. raising disestablishment & the test of the Ch. of Eng. as
qualification for throne.

*The bill as drafted had the sovereign declare that he was 'a faithful member
of the Protestant Reformed Church as by law established in England'. In
deference to their nonconformist supporters, the government pruned the*

reference to the established Church. In spite of objections by the Archbishop of Canterbury the bill introduced by Asquith on 29 June 1910 which became law on August 3 contained this declaration:

> I, ..., do solemnly and sincerely in the presence of God profess, testify, and declare that I am a faithful Protestant, and that I will, according to the true intent of the enactments which secure the Protestant succession to the Throne of my Realm, uphold and maintain the said enactments to the best of my powers according to law. (*PP*, 1910, [286], i, 21; C.L. Berry, 'The Coronation Oath and the Church of England', *Journal of Ecclesiastical History*, vol. XI, no. 1, April 1960, pp. 98–105).

June 29 Cabinet – full attendance
arranged that women's franchise 2d Reading should take place 11th and 12th.

Time table & work for rest of session discussed, we agreed that as Redmond would make a bitter attack on budget next day we should anticipate the position of apparently coming to any decision as the result of his pressure, by announcing at once, that we would postpone to a *winter* session portions of our programme including the Budget Bill – merely winding up supply taking some uncontroversial bills, & the budget resolutions to enable taxes to be collected.

The Prime Minister reported what had passed at the Conference – two meetings had been held in the week. At the first discussions on fundamental & organic laws, & what was confiscatory finance and what wasn't was discussed but not much advance made. The last discussion, was free & open, & means were discussed for providing for a deadlock between the two houses, by means of conferences, joint sittings or by referendum. The 2d alleviation found little favour with the 4 Tories, Crewe pointed out this might be due to their idea of a House of 350 of the present peers, whilst our view was such a scheme became only possible with 150 or so elected members.

A.J.B. was in favour of referendum, Asquith said slightly so, Lloyd George said 'heavily so, but on a *deadlock* only.' There was no fundamental opposition shown or repugnance to the veto, but evidently the Tories were anxious to provide conditions & safeguards, to enable bills to be stopped – but A.J.B. admitted the unfairness of the position Liberal Govmts were in at present, & that it was a ridiculous position. Lloyd George said the 4 Tories wanted to find a path, but he thought whenever they came to the chasm they wanted to go back & find another road, & he doubted whether they would really take the plunge – in either event he thought an autumn session inevitable. Crewe suggested there was another course agreeing on some points, & leaving to H of C. later to thrash out those they failed to agree to.

We discussed Budget & Ll. George laid his facts before the cabinet & figures which showed balance of £861,000 surplus. He proposed to take £451,000 of this for removal of pauper disqualification for one quarter, leaving to future the provision for the 270,000 people who would cost £2,000,000 from the extension of the pension. He had other moneys to provide, so he could not on present taxes which would all remain unaltered, give any relief of taxation – such items as King Edw. Funeral £60,000, Harcourt Palaces £60,000 to make them suitable for new occupants, civil list 30000 Qu. Alexandra, Persian loan £100,000,[14] Unemployed Fund £100,000.[15]

We had to budget for arrears of £30 Millions, 27 had since been collected all Inc Tax. We had lost £3 Millions by rejection of budget last Nov.

Whiskey tax had proved great success reduction of crime 10 millions galls less drunk, less in tots. & few. 1oz cups now replaced 1$^1/_5$ oz cups.

Ll. George was confident his estimates would show the following increases, thus without any additional taxation, make up the additional expenditure of over £9,940,000

Customs	32,095,000	Increase over 1909	1,800,000
excise	34,270,000	"	1,000,000
estate	25,650,000		4,000,000
stamps	9,600,000		1,000,000
Inc Tax	37,550,000		450,000
Land Value	600,000		110,000
Land Tax	2,926,000		
P. Office	23,800,000		1,200,000
Crown lands			
Suez Canal	3,490,000		280,000
miscellaneous	———		———

July 6 The Prime Minister reported progress in regard to Veto Conference.

He alluded to Balfour being away ill (cold), but in his absence they had had most instructive talk with *Butler* from U.S.A. who explained the working of collisions between the 2 chambers in America, & how badly referendum worked, the people being listless to express their votes even when on same paper as

---

14 Following the overthrow of the Shah of Persia in 1909 the new nationalist government had asked Britain and Russia for a loan of £500,000. Because of chronic unrest and antiquated revenue collection procedures Persia was unable to give satisfactory guarantees and no loan was raised. (See below 8 Nov. 1910).

15 The Select Committee on the Civil List recommended a grant of £55,000 to put Buckingham Palace, Windsor Castle, and Marlborough House in order for their new occupants. This was in addition to £47,000 p.a. recommended for upkeep. Harcourt had asked Asquith on May 9 for £150,000 to re-face Buckingham Palace (Asquith MSS, vol. 12, f. 137). Under her husband's civil list, Queen Alexandra was to be given £70,000 p.a. Nonetheless, George V's civil list and pension provisions were only £13,000 more than his father's: savings had been made through some other royal deaths (*PP*, 1910 (211), vi, 315). None of these details was mentioned in Asquith's Cabinet letter.

candidates for whom they did vote 50 to 60% abstaining. The evidence was so illuminating, he would circulate it when prepared & printed – he obviously was a skilled observer.[16]

Morley said, Yes he knows the seamy side, & is not a mere professor – he is a gentleman & scholar, educated in Berlin & a friend of Wilhelm's. Birrell, said on temperance questions, they did vote wet or dry but that was the exception. In America, votes recorded in States for men rather than measures; but legislators were for 1 year only. Haldane – men were as Burke said members not for Bristol but for England 'hear hear!' said Birrell in my ear now sitting for Bristol.

It was proposed to hear *Fielding* from Canada at the next meeting.

Churchill asked any basis of agreement come to. Asquith – not yet.

We next discussed procedure.

Oath Bill – it was decided to go on with it at once & not postpone to autumn – better out of way though useful stick to hold over the Irish. Yes said Birrell I prefer a twig even to nothing. Ll. George – a blackthorn would be better. Crewe – I don't anticipate any difficulty in pushing it through the Lords.

Ll. G. to see Thring – push civil list on & get resolutions ready for tabling.

Supplementary estimates also to be ready.

We talked over Suffrage debate – I urged unanimity in preventing it going upstairs after 2d Reading.

We discussed attitude to Labour M.P.s by P.M. – deputation on Osborne Case. We agreed that although they had no money to carry on electoral work, payment of M.P.s was right policy. Grey agreed control of purse should be in hands of constituents & not in trade organisation. Ll. George said in Wales, only wild men had a chance in labour seats, the best men representatives & not delegates shut out by trade union dictation. Churchill said: let us not be drawn away from the true line.

Cabinet had difficulty in deciding what the 'true line' on the Osborne judgement should be. Labour and union leaders themselves had not reached consensus. (Michael Klarman, 'The Trade Union Political Levy, the Osborne Judgement (1909) and the South Wales Miners' Federation', Welsh History Review, vol. 15, no. 1, 1990, pp. 50–1; Michael J. Klarman, 'Parliamentary Reversal of the Osborne Judgement', The Historical Journal, vol. 32, no. 4, 1989, pp. 895–6). Asquith received a delegation from the Joint Labour Board on July 13. The board (also known as the National Labour Advisory Board) was a representative council of the Trades Union Congress, the General Federation of Trade Unions, and the Labour Representation Committee. It was formed in November 1905 after the Caxton Hall 'concordat' (16 February 1905) in an

---

[16]   The evidence of Nicholas Murray Butler, President of Columbia University, was printed as a Cabinet memorandum on 18 July 1910 (Cab. 37/103/33).

attempt to limit the wastefulness of retaining three separate sets of officials. The delegation urged legislation to resolve the Labour party's financial difficulties, but the Cabinet was unable to settle on a policy before the summer recess. With no lead from ministers, Liberal back-benchers were in disarray. A poll initiated by the editor of The Daily Chronicle *would have revealed their views but was suppressed at Churchill's request. (?Churchill to ?Asquith, undated unsigned copy, Churchill MSS, C2/42).*

July 13   P.M. explained the proposals I had made to him to get through the difficulties, the position we were in, in regard to supply, & so end this period of the session by end of July. Army money was wanted to carry on, a consolidated fund necessary by the 26th vote on a/c necessary if appropriation bill for all supply kept over to Nov. – my scheme was to get report of the one Navy vote this night, proceed to clear off all supply & leave the Declaration, Civil List & Regency Bill to the last 3 or 4 days & if we had to sit longer, so be it. Agreed to. Morley explained despatch he & Grey had drafted to enable troops to be ready to relieve trade post in Thibet, 2000 to go to Gyantse & a small number sent forward without delay to secure safety of post & withdraw them before lives were in danger, but show of strength might enable trade to be resumed when threatened position between Thibetans & Chinese at an end. We anxious not to interfere in internal affairs, but must safeguard the lives of our own people. Such a withdrawal obviously better than any after attack, & under apparent military pressure of other forces, which would lose us prestige. Policy to be indicated to Pekin & object of our troops going forward explained.[17]

We had long explanation from S. Buxton in regard to Copyright Bill, & interest in copyright by author 50 yrs after death. This was approved (though we might be compelled to modify) to enable us to bring our law to same position as other powers as recommended by international conference.[18]

P.M. asked for directions as to the extension from 30 of number of years by L.G.B. for repayment of schools. Burns agreed to extend to 40. Runciman & Carrington urged 50 & latter agreed to, with discretion to reduce to L.G.B.[19]

---

[17]   The Younghusband expedition of 1904 had concluded a trade agreement with Tibet under which a British trade agent was permanently in residence at Gyantse. His life was in danger because of the fighting between the Tibetans and the Chinese.

[18]   Following on Imperial Copyright Conference in May 1910, the Copyright Bill was introduced July 26, withdrawn at the end of the session, and re-introduced in April 1911. Establishing a basis for reciprocal recognition of copyright throughout the Empire (and with other countries adhering to the Berne Convention), it gave authors (and their heirs) of a literary, musical, artistic, or dramatic work the sole right to reproduce that work in their lifetime and for 50 years after their death.

[19]   Local Government Board loans to local education authorities to erect school buildings had been repayable over 30 years; they could now be extended to 50 years.

Runciman urged more money for necessitous school areas & £100,000 agreed to.

P.M. said Sir George Reid had been examined by the *conference* in regard to working of plan in Australia when difficulties recurred between 2 assemblies, & Fielding from Canada, but no help from latter except against Referendum. He thought by next cabinet there would be something to report, as the members must before this part of session came to an end have something more definite, & they must now come to grips; a meeting would be held that evening at 5.0.

When he came to write his memoirs Asquith recalled the contributions of Nicholas Murray Butler and W.S. Fielding but had forgotten Sir George Reid's appearance at the conference. 'We should have been glad, if it had been possible to have had first-hand testimony from witnesses of equal authority as to the experience of the States which form the Commonwealth of Australia ...' In fact, on July 19 Asquith produced 'A Suggested Scheme for Dealing with Deadlocks' based on the Australian constitution. (Earl of Oxford and Asquith, Memories and Reflections 1852–1927, 2 vols, Cassell, 1928, vol. I, pp. 200–1; Cab. 37/103/34; John D. Fair, British Interparty Conferences: A Study of the Procedure of Conciliation in British Politics, 1867–1921, Clarendon Press, Oxford, 1980, p. 89).

July 19 After dining with Harcourt & George at the Ministers' table, we retired for coffee (not forgetting liquors tho' L.G.'s public utterances suggest teetotalism) to the Chancellor of the Exchequer's room.[20] We discussed what was going on at the Conference, & we easily drew L.G. to tell us how Balfour with Lansdowne as his fag (he was his fag at Eton) came in favouring Referendum. Austen & Cawdor were independent but fair – any publicity would endanger success & L.G. deprecated the cabinet knowing in case anything got into the Press. L.G. advocating secrecy of cabinet information was funny! & if we could draw him, obviously Donald of the Chronicle could do so on other occasions.

The conference had not looked at any of Lord Rosebery's suggestions. They had considered referendum & rejected it. They were discussing all schemes suggested in turn & were now on the Ripon plan – joint sessions, with delegation from H. of L. to join Commons. Harcourt's remarks after an hours talk was 'how loose' his views are!

The Ripon plan had been approved by the Cabinet on 23 March 1907 but rejected by the Prime Minister, Campbell-Bannerman, 6 May 1907. C.B.

---

[20] On 1 December 1909 Lucy Masterman had recorded that Lloyd George 'generally teetotals fairly strictly', having observed him recently 'very excited' after one glass of champagne at lunch. (Masterman, *C.F.G. Masterman*, pp. 147–8).

preferred the suspensory veto and took up a 'counter project' devised by his secretaries Nash and Ponsonby. (Ponsonby's diary, 15, 21, 26 May 1907; 1, 9, 16, 27 June 1907; Feb. 1909, Ponsonby MSS, Shulbrede). Why the plan was named after Ripon is a mystery: he was meant to chair the Cabinet committee, which recommended the plan to the Cabinet but he was ill while the committee met (under Loreburn's chairmanship) and contributed little to its discussions. The plan, which seems to have come from Crewe, with a significant amendment by Asquith, was that when the two houses disagreed, a joint vote should be held the following session, the voters comprising all the Commons plus 100 peers. These peers were to include all members of the government in the Lords providing that they did not number more than twenty, plus other peers chosen by the Lords. The main objection Campbell-Bannerman had to the plan was that it necessitated a government majority of at least 70 in order to over-ride the upper house, a point that would have been appreciated by his sometime Liberal colleagues after the January 1910 general election. (See Corinne Comstock Weston, 'The Liberal Leadership and the Lords' Veto, 1907–1910', Historical Journal, vol. XI, 3, 1968, pp. 508–37; Fair, British Interparty Conferences, p. 315, fn. 45).

July 20   Cabinet.

Asquith had asked me to be present instead of going to Darlington for a Pease & Partners meeting.

Buxton referred to N.E.R. strike about which he had no official intimation. Grey (late chairman) said if not ended in 2 days, it would take bigger proportions, aim being to hit R' Way Co – at time of August holidays.

The P.M. said he had just left the King. The King seemed to think a National Memorial to King Edw. which would (in the public eye) compete with that to Qu. Victoria (which cost £220,000) shd be not entertained, but local effort might be encouraged. e.g. The Lord Mayor might open a list for a statue to be erected in the New Broad walk between B'ham Palace & Piccadilly.

The question of a hospital fund, or investigation of diseases of men, animals & plants, was mooted by Crewe, but turned down on the ground no memorial would be popular which took a utilitarian form – & to rope in King Edw.'s name for such a purpose, would find little support – he deserved some direct sacrifice![21]

The P.M. said he could not say anything definite in regard to the conference, finance for the time being had been adjourned. They had had evidence from Murray Butler, Fielding & Reid, & now gravest doubts existed as to the

---

[21]   On May 29, JAP had publicly rejected the idea that King Edward should be 'memorialised' by 'all becoming under an obligation to serve their country', favouring instead 'some great object for the good of mankind, such as a hospital.' (*The Rotherham Express*, 4 June 1910, Gainford MSS, 59, f. 141).

possibility of expediency of the referendum & all 8 members had come to the conclusion it would not afford a way of escape for deadlock.

The discussion was proceeding very fruitfully – a joint session was under discussion. This would not at once change the constitution of H. of Lords & it in Grey's view was less objectionable than the veto unless the latter was accompanied by election principles.

The admissions had gone to great lengths
1. The unfairness of the present position for Liberals when in power.
2. Possibility this could be removed.
3. The necessity for such a conclusion to be reached.

Obviously the Ripon plan presented great difficulties, the crucial question was one of the numbers from the Lords to join with the H. of C.

The Lord Ch. said such a scheme wd. impose fresh responsibility on the Lords. The P.M. said he thought the Tories 'were disposed to agree to the H of C being present in full strength, with delegation from the Lords. He proposed to make some announcement – & any substantial point agreed to before the recess.'

If no 'real hope', it shd. be broken up.

Ll. George dwelt upon necessity of disarming the suspicion held by radicals that the Tories were playing a game. Runciman chimed in – we must not allow the Tories to hobble us in the constituencies.

We discussed the possible alteration of oath declaration again, & how to rebut feeling of many denominations that the protestant declaration was novel. Runciman arranged to circulate paper showing the law as it existed. Birrell says: well it excludes me.

Birrell was an atheist. Nevertheless he joined Asquith and Runciman in introducing the bill to change the Accession oath with its new declaration: 'I am a faithful Protestant.' Lord Balcarres wrote: 'Trouble is brewing about the Declara[tion] Bill. Scotland is apparently up in arms. Noncons. in H. of C. who don't care a fig about the Roman Catholics are furious at the proposal that the Sovereign shall pronounce himself a member of the C/E.' (Lord Balcarres' diary, 20 July 1910, vol. xxi, f. 61, Crawford and Balcarres MSS.) A by-election took place in Liverpool (Kirkdale) on July 20. The Times special correspondent described the campaign on July 18 as 'profoundly affected ... by the nice distinctions of theology.' The winner, Col. G. Kyffin-Taylor (Con.) declared after the poll that the result was 'a declaration that in a Protestant country we should have a Protestant King upon the throne.' (The Times, 21 July 1910).

We then discussed for 50 minutes how to respond to Germany's approach to us in regard to Naval policy. Grey stated in autumn last year, he was approached, but Germany then urged we must be prepared, before entering into negociation to be willing to arrive at a reciprocal understanding not to attack each other in combination with any other power. Grey dwelt upon the difficulty of arranging any formula, & that France & Russia would regard any such agreement with suspicion & all the blessings of the entente with France & Russia would go, & we might be again on the verge of war with 1 or other of these powers.[22] Morley urged from Indian point of view not to do anything to worsen our pleasant happy relations with Russia.

Grey said that the negociations lapsed owing to general election, & then in March when Metternich[23] again approached him, the political situation was too uncertain to justify going on. He Grey would now advocate a similar friendly feeling being created with Germany to that secured by settlement of Morocco question with France. – but no political agreement. If Germany would agree to no expedition or increase of naval law it would reduce her ships to 33 first class battleships by 1920. McKenna said we must then have 60% more – that was the Admiralty margin – & meant our building by that date 52 dreadnoughts. This would be some reduction of our present rate.

We were not allowed by Germany to send our naval attaché into the German yards, on same terms as other powers, & we had a grievance. We pressed him that he did not make out a very good case, as opportunities were given, & excuses could be rebutted if facts were as stated – inconvenience at one moment, would if repeated justify representation of facts. The prevailing opinion of cabinet was not to upset present equilibrium but Grey to put on paper for us proposals which we could place before Germany to bring about cordial relations, a reduction of naval expenditure.

July 29 Last day of summer session. Cabinet met at H of C in the Prime Minister's Room. Full attendance. Buxton asked for leave to deal with a matter connected with some Foreign negociation, & asked not to trouble cabinet with details. The P.M. said we are only too glad to be spared them!

---

[22] Grey had given instructions over a year earlier that the expression 'Triple Entente' was not to be used in dispatches. Convenient as it was, 'if it appeared in a Parliamentary Bluebook it would be assumed to have some official meaning and might provoke inconvenient comment or inquiry'. (Harold Nicolson, *Sir Arthur Nicolson Bart., First Lord Carnock: a study in the old diplomacy*, Constable, 1930, p.308). As late as January 1914 Harcourt denied that there was any such thing as a Triple Entente between Britain, France, and Russia. He insisted that Britain's agreements with the other two powers were separate and limited. (see Cameron Hazlehurst, *Politicians at War: July 1914 to May 1915*, Jonathan Cape, 1971, pp. 112–13).

[23] Count Paul von Wolff-Metternich zur Gracht (1853–1934); German Ambassador, London 1901–12; Constantinople 1915–17.

The Prime Minister read out the terms of the motion agreed to at the Conference, which he was directed to announce.[24] We discussed whether the Irish position could be helped by any consequential question. Redmond, who had not seen the terms had told Birrell he was anxious the Budget should not be passed before the Irish knew where they were in regard to the constitutional question. Obviously they could not support whiskey tax, if they had no quid pro quo to show in answer to Healy & O'Brien's jeers at them having sold Nationalism.

It was arranged that a real effort should be made to conclude negociations either with an agreement, or to break them off if no agreement attainable early in November, & that conference meetings would be held at Crewe Hall early in October. The P.M. stated whilst Government views as to H. of C. having unfettered control over finance had been firmly insisted upon, that no arrangement had been arrived at but the 2d point of Liberals having the right to obtain the passage of their measures through a Tory H. of Lords was accepted by the Opposition, & by means of some joint conference a fair chance should be given.

We discussed whether *Women's suffrage* Bill should be encouraged next session, or this with amended title to Shackleton's Bill & was to open whole question. It was agreed to give no promise at the moment. I pointed out with the constitutional point unsolved & the Irish having the Govmt's life in their power, we could now give no further promise as to facilities next year.[25] We discussed *Payment of Members*. It was thought £220,000 would suffice made applicable to future Parliaments. It was regarded as inexpedient from an electioneering standpoint, though we were all committed to the principle. It was resolved to give privately to the Labour M.P.s an undertaking to take the decision of the House on the proposal in some form, if we remained in power. To amend law owing to Osborne Judgement was rejected as useless to the Labour M.P.s if option was to be given to Trades Unionists to refuse their contributions & no other proposal could be supported. I raised *Cyprus*, & a committee was appointed to consider the grant to be given. I pointed out the great loss to Treasury, by difficulties & unrest if £10,000 not given & some solution not found. Churchill urged his colleagues to be loyal to his pledge to Cypriots. McKenna, Crewe, George, Churchill & P.M. in committee.

---

24   The original handwritten text of the statement read by Asquith to the Commons is reproduced in Murray, *Master and Brother*, p. 53.

25   On July 20 Lloyd George had successfully appealed to a meeting of Liberal MPs supporting woman suffrage not to press the government for facilities for the Conciliation Bill. In reply to a question from Philip Snowden on July 28 he said that no facilities could be granted in the current session. Asquith confirmed the decision in the adjournment debate. (Homer Lawrence Morris, *Parliamentary Franchise Reform in England from 1885 to 1918*, Studies in History, Economics and Public Law, Columbia University, vol. XCVI, no. 2, 1921, pp. 66–7).

We discussed Grey's paper on entente with Germany. We amended same with a view to show Germany our anxiety to place them on a similar footing to France & Russia but in a way not to excite unfriendly feelings in latter 2 countries. Grey promised to circulate amended mem. which he proposed to send to our ambassador to show the German Chancellor & to leave in his possession, & see what became of our 'range finding shot' towards some political understanding, cabinet not prepared to commit nation to definite hand bound terms.[26]

Friday July 29 was the last full day of the summer session. The House met briefly on August 3 and was adjourned to Tuesday November 15.

---

[26] Grey's draft memorandum (Cab. 37/103/36) is dated 26 July 1910. The final version, which adds a sentence about Britain's willingness to discuss a modification 'of the tempo of the rate' of German shipbuilding, is printed in G.P. Gooch and Harold Temperley, *British Documents on the Origins of the War 1898–1914, vol. vi Anglo-German Tension. Armaments and Negotiations, 1907–12*, HMSO, 1930, memorandum enclosed with Grey to Goschen, 29 July 1910, no. 387, pp. 501–2. The final memorandum has the same date as Grey's draft, 26 July 1910.

Chapter 9

Autumn Manoeuvres

Late in September 1910 JAP alerted Asquith to the pressure being exerted by the Yorkshire miners (who constituted more than half the Rotherham electorate) for action on the Osborne judgement. During the last fortnight of October, JAP expected to have to address his constituents. 'I must *state my views or some view on the Osborne Case', he warned on September 29. Asquith had been discussing the subject at Archerfield House with John Simon (who was about to become Solicitor-General) and the Master of Elibank. He had written to Runciman on September 25 agreeing with him that there was 'some danger of our weaker-kneed brethren giving thoughtless pledges ... The word should go round that no promises should be made until the Government have announced their policy.' (Runciman MSS). The word did go round orally from the Whips' Office that backbenchers should not 'entangle themselves' by answering press questions. They should 'wait and see'. (A. Murray to William Jones, 3 Oct. 1910, Jones MSS, 5472). JAP's ideas were set out in a dictated memorandum which he offered to circulate as a Cabinet paper 'with a view of extracting the views of our colleagues'. Asquith responded on October 4 urging JAP to print and circulate his paper and inviting other ministers to 'put down their views in writing' before the Cabinet met at a specially summoned meeting on Thursday October 13. (Gainford MSS, 88). JAP's paper was circulated on October 6.

Memorandum on the Osborne Judgment

(Cab. 37/103/42)

A RESOLUTION was carried at the recent Trades Union Congress, by a vote announced as 1,717,000 to 13,000, in favour of the reversal of the Osborne Judgment. These figures did not fairly represent the views of the members themselves of the various affiliated Trade Unions, but merely represent the total number of members which each delegate represented, and are calculated on the assumption that the views of members coincided with the vote recorded by the delegate who voted for or against the resolution. Each delegate who voted in favour of the resolution gave a vote in accordance with the majority of the views of the group he represented, yet such a vote did not expose the extent of the minority in each group, and it is fair to assume that the aggregate number of Trade Union members who desire their liberty to contribute or not to the maintenance of a Member of Parliament to whom they are politically opposed may be counted by many tens of thousands, if not hundreds of thousands. One Trade Union delegate admitted he and many he represented were personally opposed to the resolution, but as a majority of his members approved, all the members of his own Union were included in the 1,717,000. Such a method of computing votes shows that the figures publicly stated are illusory and misleading.

The two main points decided by the Osborne Judgment were:

Firstly – That Trade Unions must act in accordance with their statutory objects.

Under the law they possess certain powers and privileges enabling the conditions of labour and the pay of wage-earners to be improved or safe-guarded by joint action, which are not extended to other associations. The question appears to me to be: Are the present statutory objects, sufficient? If not, what other objects should be included? If a majority of members desire that there should be compulsory levies from all their members to aid the creation or alteration of laws relating to labour, surely the right course to adopt would be to amend the law so that Trade Unions may possess such additional powers. Such an alteration of the law would not be a reversal of the Osborne Judgment, but an amendment or extension of the law so as to increase the functions of Trade Unions.

What we therefore have really to consider is, whether the powers now demanded should be given to Trade Unions, including ends other than those associated with labour questions.

Are we to admit the demand of Trade Unions, in regard to religion, foreign affairs, treaty rights, Naval and Military services, the character of national recreations, the State control of children, the distribution of wealth, the abolition of private property, the nationalisation of the means of production, &c., that all their members should be compelled to contribute to a fund to elect Members of Parliament who shall on these matters record votes according to the decision of the bare majority of the members of their Unions? Such a proposal is far-reaching and if generally adopted would sap all civil and political liberty among the organised labour classes. I gathered that even at the Trades Union Congress there was a desire expressed that the resolution relating to the religious question in connection with our elementary schools should not be pressed, and does it not stand to reason there must be some limitation as to the objects which shall be promoted by a Trades Union.

Instead of promoting liberty for the Trade Union to extend its field of usefulness, such powers would only promote a system of bondage for the members of such an organisation, and would tend to break up Trade Unionism, and stay the beneficent work of improving labour conditions which Trade Unions have been doing for the last fifty years.

Secondly – That the Trade Unionist cannot be compelled to subscribe to the Parliamentary salary of a Member of whose opinions he disapproves.

I believe that a feeling prevails among many representative Trade Unionists (who have not thoroughly thought out the question) that public recognition should be given to the resolutions passed at their Trades Congress gatherings, and that all their members (like those in Parliament itself) should be governed by a majority, and if a majority decide to nominate a particular candidate for a particular constituency, all members should be compelled to contribute equally to the necessary funds to secure the return and the maintenance of the nominated member. But surely if a contribution from the State purse is found, and each Trade Unionist felt that there exists no further occasion for him to contribute to the election expenses or maintenance of his Trade Union Parliamentary representative, the Trade Unionist is the last man who would have reason to complain? Is it not important that the principle should be maintained in our public life that a Member of Parliament ought to hold himself responsible to the electors in his constituency, rather than to a particular class of individuals, scattered throughout the whole country, who are prepared to pay for his votes and services? If, however, a compulsory Parliamentary levy is exacted, the above principle could not be observed.

To suggest that a definite reversal of the Osborne Judgment is a pledge which is to be asked by Trade Unions of all Parliamentary candidates is to misunderstand the question. The decision given by the Judges in the Osborne Case I submit cannot be amended by a mere Act of Parliament repealing the judgement, and it is necessary for Trade Unionists and electors to come to a clear decision as to the exact alterations in the law they desire. If members of Trade Unions are coerced to support objects to which they take conscientious exception, their only alternative is to resign membership, but to drive a large number of members out of union is not the course which Trade Unionists desire.

It may be asserted that it is impossible to draw a rigid line between the trade policy of a labour organisation, and the general policy of the country, and labour organisations cannot be expected to submit to a rule which prevents them from promoting the interest of their members by general political legislative enactments, as well as by administrative action. It may therefore be advisable to extend the powers of the Trade Unions to some political matters beyond the reach of the Osborne Judgement which have not hitherto been included in the Trade Unions Act; but I suggest we should not compel members of a Trade Union organisation to subscribe to the maintenance of candidates with whom they are not in political sympathy on vital issues altogether outside the sphere of labour, any more than they should be compelled to subscribe to support a particular minister of religion. Such a course is contrary to the principles of liberty, and until a real injustice is created, and after payment of members has been established and tried, we should not at any rate now commit ourselves to support increased statutory powers being given whereby a compulsory levy can be raised for all Parliamentary purposes. The payment of all Members of Parliament, the payment of the Returning Officers at Elections, and the inclusion of additional specific objects in the Trade Union Acts where the members of Trade Unions desire such inclusion, should surely meet the situation.

It is conceivable that certain objects are outside the law, and relate to the work pertaining to Trade Union Congresses or Trades Councils, and that the statutory objects may be enlarged with advantage. By such an extension the *status quo ante* would be at least partially restored, and especially would this be the case if the Labour Party agree to no longer exact a pledge from all their candidates to act together.

JAP's memorandum was followed by an avalanche of submissions from Haldane, Loreburn, Samuel, Buxton (a compendium of relevant trade union rules), Carrington, Robson, and Sidney Webb (circulated by Asquith). All of these reached ministers before October 13. There were two more papers – from Buxton (October 21) and Loreburn (November 3) – before the Cabinet reached a decision. (Cab. 37/103/43–48, 50, 52, 57).

October 13 3.0 p.m. Cabinet summoned as result of my memorandum on Osborne Judgement. The Prime Minister's wishes & views were sought by me in view of campaign in my Division & he sent me this letter.[1] There was a full cabinet.

We disposed of the question of how to deal with Republican Government self set up in Portugal. Grey told us the precedents & we agreed to consult other Powers & suggest following the precedents & intimating that official communications shd. pass with Govmt defacto, but with reserve until Country had in some constitutional manner confirmed the Govmt in its position.

We arranged for a communication to be made seeking the postponement of high duties threatened in January as we were prepared to negotiate for a commercial treaty with Portuguese Nation to meet the grievance relating to our high tariff on their wines as compared with our tariff on wines from other nations. Buxton's memorandum circulated indicated line of alterations possible.

The coup in Portugal had begun on October 4 after a year of ineffectual government. King Manoel took refuge in England. Britain, France, and Spain formally recognised the new government early in November. Buxton had warned the Cabinet in March that 'we are within measurable distance of hostile discrimination by Portugal against our trade' but nothing had happened. Now he circulated a note and memorandum (11 Oct. 1910, Cab. 37/104/49). British trade in Portugal was jeopardised by a treaty just completed between Portugal and Germany, which would give the latter's goods preferential treatment. Moreover the Portuguese threatened to double the duty on British goods unless the British government began negotiations on its duty on Portuguese wine imported into England. Duties on wine imported into England varied according to the strength of the wine. As Portugal's chief exports to England were port and madeira, her wines were the most heavily taxed. Moreover Portugal was virtually the sole importer into England of such wines. Buxton asked for Cabinet permission to begin negotiations on a re-arrangement of the duties. The Portuguese also wanted the terms 'port' and 'madeira' restricted to the genuine products.

We then discussed Osborne Judgement. Loreburn, Samuel, Runciman, Buxton & I taking the view political objects must be conferred as suitable for

---

1 In his letter of October 4 Asquith had enjoined 'we had all better hold our peace in public' until after the October 13 Cabinet meeting. (Gainford MSS, 88).

trade union levies. Burt's position since 1874 shd be restored.[2] Haldane Churchill Birrell Crewe & Asquith McKenna & Burns took the view that to compel a man to subscribe to his political opponent & give him no option except to starve was insupportable – the line of least opposition was to earmark portion for other purposes when differences existed – but such a man would be obviously 'marked'.

Ll. George urged postponement & this was agreed to after 3/4 of an hours discussion. Meantime law officers were to give their views as to the far reaching character or limitation of the decision, & whether funds could go to philanthropic objects, congresses &c &c. It was agreed to defer any Govmt announcement of our introducing a bill for Payment of Members.

A reference to terms for compensating Hong Kong re Opium was raised by Crewe.

In 1908 the Commons had passed a resolution deploring the sale of opium and the Colonial Office ordered the closing of all opium dens in the British Colonies. This had led to a severe drop in government revenue – an estimated loss of $500,000 pa was projected in Hong Kong. Imperial policy was modified: twenty-six divans were closed immediately, the rest being permitted to remain until the end of 1910; the local government received $11,060 compensation. In October 1909 the Hong Kong government estimated its 1910 losses at £19,762 – £23,717. The Imperial Treasury did not reply for six months and then suggested that, as the colony could make up most of its loss from the spirit duty, the Treasury grant should be only £9,000. The Colonial Office pointed out that the spirit duty revenue was still only conjectural and that it had, in any case, been allocated for other items. Crewe wanted the Treasury to pay half the colony's actual losses ('The Opium Question in Hong Kong', 4 Oct. 1910, Cab. 37/103/41). JAP's family had financed the anti-opium lobby from the 1870s; his father was the cause's parliamentary champion in the 1890s. The Anti-Opium Society now approached JAP for help.

Private   Wrea Head,
                                             Scalby,
                                             Yorks   22 Oct 1910
My dear Pease,
    I see you have begun Cabinets, so address this to London.
    The Representative Board of Anti Opium Society desire to see the P.M. & I have consented to introduce a Deputation – You may recollect the *Socy of Friends* tried

---

2   Thomas Burt had advocated payment of MPs since his election in 1874. He himself was paid £350 a year by the Northumberland Miners' Association, in addition to his £150 *p.a.* salary as secretary to the association. In September 1910 Burt had said that labour could only be represented in the Commons through the efforts and contributions of organised bodies of workers.

to do this in July but (for reasons in which I quite concurred) the P.M. thought it premature – Some months have now elapsed & I think the situation has changed.

My object in writing to you is to let you know I have written V. Nash to tell him what is desired – Of course I was aware (to some extent) that the matter is on the carpets (probably even in Cabinet) but it would be unfortunate to have it again put off – I have told V. Nash I am in London Mon. Tue & Wed (31 Oct 1 Nov 2 Nov) & will see him if it is best – *What I want* to avoid *is another refusal.*

You may be interested in knowing that the newborn Lib. Fed. – is doing good work. They made me President for this year & the M. of E comes down on 3 Nov to a private palaver when he will be enlightened I think!

I hope the representatives will do as G. Fox recommended 'speak the truth in love.'

I hope you have had a good recreative term.

Yrs very truly
John E. Ellis

JAP forwarded Ellis's letter to the Prime Minister's office on October 25, with an annotation to Vaughan Nash that he supported the idea that Asquith should see the deputation. 'I have other similar letters pressing me to intervene & press the anti-opium cause on the Govmt & I am with them.' (Asquith MSS, vol. 12, ff. 206–7). However, an unsigned typed 'Memo. as to advisability of receiving a Deputation on the Opium Question from the Colonial point of view', [29?] October 1910 (Asquith MSS, vol. 23, ff. 304–5) urged Asquith to avoid receiving the deputation if possible: accelerating the rate of restriction of opium exports from India would only cause the Chinese to turn to morphine and cocaine; this was to be discussed at the forthcoming conference at the Hague. It was argued that the resulting loss of revenue for Hong Kong and the Malay Peninsula should be spread over a ten year period. A note from the head of the India Office's revenue and statistical department to the Secretary of State's private secretary explained further that, in negotiations with the Chinese, 'H.M.'s G. would not insist on statistical proof that China had reduced its production of opium by 3/10ths but was willing to assume that on the whole the obligation had been fulfilled, and was prepared to extend the arrangement for other [sic] 3 years .... In return our Minister asked that the irregular acts of certain provincial Govts, wh. clearly contravened existing treaty stipulations with regard to foreign opium trade, should be brought to an end. The Chinese Govt. expressed gratitude for these "generous" proposals.' (Sir Thomas Holderness to F.H. Lucas, n.d., Asquith MSS, vol. 12, ff. 212–13). Asquith did not receive the deputation (Religious Society of Friends, Proceedings of Yearly Meeting, 1911, pp. 121, 225).

Nov 3 On receipt of wire from Nash – the P.M's secy – 'P.M. would particularly like to see you tomorrow morning at 1.30' I left Rotherham, & after transacting Duchy business, called on the P.M. The conference had been sitting on the constitutional problem for the 18th & H.H.A. began by saying the position was very critical.

He explained to me that Morley had some weeks ago resigned, but had agreed to defer active resignation until they met. Morley admitted he had intended it for good, but he was easily persuaded to take the Presidency of the Council, Beauchamp did not meet the P.M. in the spirit the P.M. expected, he had not been long in office & might have been more 'generous' in accepting the Office of Works. The P.M. then told me of his difficulty with Seely, having Harcourt put over him in the Commons, & he asked me for my advice as to how to get out of the knot. He had Madras to give away but presumed I did not want it, if I had it might have eased the situation a little, but only so far as Hobhouse & Lloyd George being separated at the Treasury. George had asked for Masterman but the P.M. would not hear of it.

After turning the matter over, I suggested Hobhouse to Madras, & Seely to the Treasury. The P.M. said L.G. did not want Seely. I told the P.M. to put his foot down, that Seely could say 'No' in these times of heavy expenditure far better than Hobhouse could.

The P.M. asked me to see Crewe & Seely. I spent 20 mins with each, & came back & told the P.M. Seely would loyally do his best, if left where he was, but he thought six months would be too long playing 2d fiddle after he had played 1st but he left himself in the P.M.'s hands.

Morley had hinted at resignation in April 1910; on September 12 he invited Asquith unequivocally to appoint a new Secretary of State for India. He renewed his request a month later but was eventually persuaded to stay in the ministry as Lord President of the Council. Churchill had urged keeping Morley, and Crewe had advised Asquith on September 23 to make Morley's retention conditional on his staying at least until the following summer. (Asquith MSS, vol. 12, f. 167). On September 14, Asquith sought Crewe's opinion on moving Crewe himself to the India Office; Buxton or Birrell to the Colonial Office; Samuel to replace Buxton at the Board of Trade; Hobhouse to replace Samuel at the Post Office; Seely to replace Hobhouse as Financial Secretary to Treasury; and either Lord Lucas, Lord Denman, or Lord Willingdon to replace Seely at the Colonial Office. (Crewe MSS, C/40). In mid-October, Asquith's intention was to move Loulou Harcourt from the Office of Works to the Colonial Office and promote Hobhouse to the Office of Works. (Harcourt to Asquith, 16 Oct. 1910, copy, Harcourt MSS, dep. 421, f. 150). Hobhouse learned of this on October 29 when Alick Murray told him of a query from Buckingham Palace about 'what sort of fellow C.E.H. was'. Four days later Hobhouse's hopes were dashed when Morley 'requested to be allowed to stay'. (Hobhouse's diary, 30 Oct. and 4 Nov. 1910, David, ed., Inside Asquith's Cabinet, *pp. 97-8). In the event, the only moves were: Beauchamp to Works; Harcourt, Colonial Office, with Seely, responding to Asquith's request on November 4 for 'an unusual proof of loyalty and good comradeship', remaining as Under Secretary until late March 1911 to dry nurse his new chief. (Mottistone MSS, 1, ff. 292–3; 2, f. 89); Crewe, India Office. See also Stephen E. Koss,* John Morley at the India Office, 1905–1910, *Yale University Press, New Haven, 1969, pp. 66–8 who confuses the issue by supposing that a conversation between Morley and the Clerk of the Privy Council about the Lord President's 'attainment of his eightieth year' referred to the 38 year old Beauchamp rather than Wolverhampton; and Churchill,* Winston S. Churchill, *Vol. II, Companion Part 2, p. 1026). The retiring Governor of Madras, Sir Arthur Lawley, was eventually succeeded by Sir Thomas Gibson-Carmichael Bt. The Master of Elibank had suggested that JAP might accept Madras (Asquith to Crewe, 30 Aug. 1910, Crewe MSS, C/40). But both Elibank and Asquith must have known that Pease could not afford the post. Unbeknown to JAP, Asquith had intended once again to offer him the Office of Works and place Beauchamp at the Duchy. But Almeric FitzRoy, aware that Beauchamp did not want to go to the Duchy, 'went over to see Nash and took on myself to tell him that Beauchamp would have preferred to go to the Office of Works, which would have the advantage of not disturbing Pease.' Nash spoke to the Prime Minister and JAP was undisturbed. (FitzRoy's diary, 2 Nov. 1910, FitzRoy,* Memoirs, *vol. II, p. 419).*

I lunched with the P.M. Sir George Murray & Miss Asquith & Sheila.[3] We talked trivialities a little about Monypenny's book on Beaconsfield & Morley's sarcastic review thereon.[4]

Nov 8 Cabinet 3 p.m. @ No 10. *S. Wales Disturbance Strike* Churchill described the position in *S. Wales* coalfield, the methods adopted against Colliery Proprietors, & the incapacity of local police to maintain peace & order. Infantry were ready at Swindon, & Cavalry at Cardiff, but he hoped 90 horse & 200 men of Metropolitan Police would suffice tonight, & the men's leaders were summoned to meet Askwith at Bd. of Trade tomorrow, which Mabon (Abraham

---

[3] The identity of Sheila is an impenetrable mystery.

[4] 'By some strange and absurd impulse' Morley had agreed to review the first volume of W.F. Monypenny's *The Life of Benjamin Disraeli, Earl of Beaconsfield*, (John Murray, 1910). His signed article appeared in *The Times Literary Supplement*, 27 October 1910, pp. 397–9. Though he ended by describing the book as 'an enterprise … so excellently begun', Morley's tone was predominantly one of faint praise for 'a compact supply of standard and authentic material, honestly provided, so far as an outsider can judge, by an undeniably competent craftsman.' The reviewer confessed: 'I find that my pen has got very rusty, or else I am less easily contented; anyhow it is uphill work.' (Morley to Minto, 27 Sept. 1910, John Viscount Morley, *Recollections*, 2 vols, Macmillan, 1917, vol. II, p. 338).

M.P.) thought would preserve order. Buxton explained the difference between the Rhondda & Pontypridd strikes, but peace in one would solve the hostilities displayed in the other. Use of military were deprecated, especially infantry.

JAP's geography is a little confused. The men at Pontypridd, in the Rhondda valleys, were striking against the Cambrian Collieries Ltd (owned by the Liberal MP D.A. Thomas). The other strike was at Aberdare. The strike in the Rhondda was official and had been building up for some time. Its initial cause was failure to agree to the price to be paid to the miners for digging a particularly difficult seam of coal. A conference of all miners in the coalfield had recommended a strike, with a levy on those still at work to give some strike pay, and a month's notice had been given. That notice ran out on November 1. Clashes had become inevitable when the owners prepared to import blackleg labour. The Aberdare strike was unofficial and broke out suddenly on October 20. Its cause was the sudden stop to the 40-year old perquisite of the miners of taking home waste wood. The management said that in future this could only be done after permission had been obtained and the wood paid for. The two groups of strikers soon united.

JAP's account of the government's response to the Tonypandy riots confirms the official records of Churchill's initial restraint. The Times and opposition MPs criticised his delay in sending in the troops. See R. Page Arnot, South Wales Miners: A History of the South Wales Miners' Federation (1898–1914), *George Allen & Unwin, 1967, pp. 174–231 for a detailed description of the events leading up to and during these days. (There are valuable comments in Jane Morgan,* Conflict and Order: The Police and Labour Disputes in England and Wales, 1900–1939, *Clarendon Press, Oxford, 1987, pp. 44–9, 55, 154–6, 164. The sympathetic paragraphs in Martin Gilbert,* Churchill A Life, *Minerva, 1992, pp. 220–1 should be compared with Paul Addison,* Churchill on the Home Front 1900–1955, *Jonathan Cape, 1992, pp. 142–3 and Alan Watkins, 'The truth about Tonypandy',* The Observer, *10 Dec. 1978, p. 48. An important but neglected contemporary account is in the diary of Maj. Gen. J.S. Ewart, Director of Military Operations, 7–10 Nov. 1910, Ewart MSS.*

Persia Edward Grey described situation, & how George Barclay had exceeded his directions, indicating we might have to protect roads ourselves – such a policy of annexation had not been authorised, & no such step intended, our action limited to preserve the security of the gulf & S. Persian ports for the Imperial Bank of Persia, English in character. We had 2d mortgage after Bank, & could not allow a loan to be advanced by Seligman Bros on strength of this security. Imp. Bank ready to advance at 95 to Seligman's 82$\frac{1}{2}$ – if the amount was properly spent – & we would sanction 10% increase in customs duty. They require £1,200,000 – but all earmarked already except £300,000.

Chaos, brigandage existed & the Persians were like children.

Sir George Barclay, British Minister at Tehran, had been instructed to inform the Persian government that something must be done to open the roads for trade; a force of Persian Cossacks, commanded by officers of the Indian Army, was suggested. Not wishing to insist without any sanctions, Barclay had said that, if there were no improvement, the British government would be compelled to intervene to restore order. Grey had rejected this possibility in the summer of 1910 and informed Barclay that he had exceeded his instructions. (Cab. 37/104/62).

Following the recent installation of a constitutional government, Grey's aim was to rejuvenate Persia under Anglo-Russian official influence. The prospect of Seligman lending £1,200,000 to the Persian government threatened the liens held by the British government and the Imperial Bank of Persia over the revenue from the southern customs. The money (raised from German and other unwelcome sources) would have been lent without strings and would not advance the British objective of improved public order and more efficient administration. Grey strongly discouraged Seligman and supported the Imperial Bank which successfully negotiated a loan in May 1911. (David McLean, Britain and Her Buffer State: *The collapse of the Persian empire, 1890–1914, Royal Historical Society, 1979, pp. 96–101).*

Asquith said the *King* wanted view of cabinet in regard to his visit to India – from 3 wk in Nov. 1912 to Feb. 1913 – to be crowned at Delhi on Jany 1. King very keen to go & spend time here & in Colonies, which his Father spent at Biarritz & Homburg, & Marienbad. Curzon was a strong supporter even to 1, 2 or 3 millions – & the project was well received by Indian authorities especially Sir J. Hewett. Minto appeared to have his doubts & wanted to 'think it over' tendency to dethrone Viceroy. Morley & Crewe thought it would pacify India, but some of the Indian Princes had not recovered from their expenditure 1901–2. I suggested the money should be checked, estimates carefully made, & the P.M. said yes & audited a/cs – & £200,000 should suffice. How much India to find was left over. Morley said:– The King would be in no danger – but that the crowning took place at Westminster & the performance was a 'mere sham' & we had to think of the future. Asquith urged at 45 to be imbued with sense of visiting Empire was alright but the importance of the Constitutional Monarch being in this country & not in India & self governing colonies could not be overlooked. Birrell said he must have a durbar at Dublin & make 'em all screwed in Ireland (*sic*). Ll. George suggested that suspension of sinking fund or increased taxation on borrowing necessary if large sums spent!

Despite Cabinet scepticism this meeting was regarded as giving approval to the idea of a durbar. A committee, chaired by Sir John Hewett, was appointed to organise the event. Among the matters to be arranged was the making of a new crown because none of the English Crown Jewels can be taken out of the country.

There was also the question of royal 'boons'. One suggestion, eventually adopted, was an end to the partition of Bengal. This was opposed by the Viceroy who argued that it would offend Mohammedans (who formed the majority of the population in Bengal). The Viceroy proposed as an alternative a gift of half a million pounds for technical education. See F.A. Eustis and Z.H. Zaidi, 'King, Viceroy and Cabinet: The Modification of the Partition of Bengal, 1911,' History, vol. 49, June 1964, pp. 171–84.

Asquith reported position of Conference. A.J.B. & probably Austen apparently keen to settle, also he thought F.E. Smith & Bonar Law & Curzon. The Liberals had presented an ultimatum as the result of 20 meetings.

1. Is there or is there not to be a distinction between subjects to be submitted to joint conference of 2 houses between organic and constitutional questions & others when deadlocks occurred. It was admitted that disestablishment & Tariffs not subject to organic rule exceptions, and Home Rule might even be accepted, if plan was submitted, & no effort to pass it during course of present Parliament. 'Organic changes' wd include suffrage alterations & any change in law making machinery.

2. If joint committee formed, what was the proportion of Lords to be allowed in to joint conference with People's representatives. Asquith said what the proportion was to be, had not been agreed to, it was x, and Ll.G. had gone as far as it was possible (viz:– with a majority of 96. – average in divisions so far in this session – if Tories had 50 Lords & Libs 9 nominated by the parties in Lords it might mean 55 but if the Peers voted together 33 – not much to carry big bills by! With a majority of 70, such a proportion almost useless).

Asquith preferred not to name what x was.[5] It would be H of C. sitting in pleno & H.L. delegation. The Tories had made no counter suggestion. Finance wd be left to H. of C. to control. Asquith thought the forcing of a Home Rule issue at next election not serious objection, as it wd occur to some extent in any case. That a referendum should be taken on organic changes made such changes next to impossible & was a wily suggestion!

It was agreed to await Balfour's reply to 1 & 2 after he had consulted his old colleagues & we should then be called again together probably on Friday 10th. Lord Loreburn asked for time to consider proposals when submitted & Churchill urged no definite step, before we were consulted. This was assented to.[6]

We then discussed contribution to S.S. Co. for *W. Indies*, this was left to cabinet committee. I suggested £1 from Treasury for £1 of W. Indies up to

---

[5] In the margin adjoining the previous passage in brackets JAP wrote a note from 'a private source': 'our x if published fatal as it was our minimum'.

[6] The Conference proceedings and associated discussions are best followed in Fair, *British Interparty Conferences*, pp. 97–101.

£30,000 – we were saving £20M by contract expiring. This £60,000 would secure service direct.[7]

The question of the taking of land from British Museum for a site for building to be erected thereon to replace present wooden museum belonging to S. Kensington was also referred to cabinet committee.

JAP's original sentence has a number of corrections and deletions and its final form makes little sense. We have, therefore, re-arranged the words to make the meaning clear. The Cabinet had before it a memorandum (26 Oct. 1910, Cab. 37/104/54) by the First Commissioner of Works, Harcourt, in which he described the existing Science Museum as a scandal: one of its buildings was a wooden building which had contained the refreshment rooms of the 1862 exhibition (not the 1851 exhibition as Harcourt wrote). The fire hazard and lack of accommodation had led to the loss of many potential gifts. The two unsuitable buildings in which the museum was housed were about 2,000 ft long and mostly less than 30 ft wide. The Commissioners of the 1851 Fund had agreed to contribute £100,000, and the Treasury a further £160,000, but the project was held up by the trustees of the Natural History Museum who objected to certain boundary changes on the site which they felt robbed them of room for future expansion.

The move to improve the museum had gained momentum on 13 July 1909 when the President of the Board of Education, Runciman, met a deputation led by Sir Henry Roscoe, FRS. The deputation presented a memorial signed by the president, all living past presidents, officers, and 128 fellows of the Royal Society, as well as other leading scientists. Runciman set up a departmental committee, chaired by Sir Hugh Bell, on 26 March 1910. The committee's preliminary report was given to Runciman in July 1910; it presumably prompted the spate of Cabinet memoranda which followed. The committee's final report was published 22 March 1911 and 12 April 1912 and was accepted. The first stage of the rebuilding began in 1914 but it was not completed until 1928. The former refreshment rooms actually remained in use until damage in the second world war rendered them unsafe.

[November 9] Cabinet was summoned at 1.0 to meet at 5.0 at No 10 – absent Harcourt, Runciman & McKenna. The Prime Minister explained he had summoned cabinet in haste, because the conference had held that morning its *final* meeting, and it was admitted the result must be communicated to the world without delay & therefore to the cabinet.

---

7   The Colonial Office recommended a subsidy of £63,000 p.a. for the maintenance of the Royal Mail Steam Packet service to the West Indies. A seven year contract was negotiated but the additional £40,000 p.a. subsidy sought for a direct service to Jamaica was still being discussed at the end of the year. (Cab. 37/104/59).

We had presented our ultimatum – which was the minimum towards the compromise, they (the Liberal 4) were prepared to recommend to their colleagues for acceptance – Balfour had ascertained the opinion of his friends at Lansdowne House – not a happy augury – and they could not see their way to move in the direction indicated. It was therefore useless to go on when they were all unanimously but reluctantly agreed to conclude the meetings & announce without delay the result. The question which they had to determine was:– How far it was desirable & right to indicate the course of the conference, and the causes which had led to the breakdown. As the proceedings from the outset had been conducted in confidence, and frankness had been general due to seal of secrecy, the right course to take was to announce that the conference has come to an end without any agreement & that the parties had agreed that the character of the proceedings precluded any disclosure of what had passed. I deplore the time spent, said the P.M., on futile enterprise – but it has not been fruitless as our opponents realise now the gravity and necessity of doing something constructive in character. A.J.B. proposed to prepare a memorandum which would set out the reasons why from their point of view the conference failed, & would ask the P.M. to present it to the King. Asquith said after carefully considering it, he proposed to take it to show the Tory grounds for breaking off the negociations, but placing also his own views on the memo's record. The unnavigable rock or the rock which they could not circumnavigate, was the possession of machinery which whilst stopping undue rushing of legislation provided a means, when a deadlock occurred, & a machinery which would be applicable to all classes of legislation.

The Tories would not however allow changes which the Liberal party were set on obtaining, but wanted the machinery to apply to alterations of tariffs which would be more far reaching, & which the Tory party wanted.

Balfour had written to Asquith on November 8: 'I am afraid that under existing circumstances there is little use continuing our meetings. I had at one moment greatly hoped for better things.' (copy, Lloyd George MSS, C/6/11/8). Balfour's memorandum, 'The Constitutional Conference' (10 Nov. 1910), with Asquith's marginal annotations was printed as a Cabinet paper (Cab. 37/104/60) and sent to the King on November 14. Balfour divided legislation into ordinary, financial, and constitutional. He claimed that the Conservatives were prepared to abandon the House of Lords' right to reject money bills provided that the House of Commons conceded the Lords' right to discuss bills which had great social or political consequences though technically finance bills. Asquith noted that the Liberals would agree to this although it would be 'most distasteful' to his followers. The two sides had reached little agreement on how to deal with constitutional legislation. The Conservatives wanted any bill which was twice rejected by the Lords to be referred to a plebiscite. The Liberals preferred to hold a general election after the first Lords' rejection. Nor did the two sides agree on the composition of a joint sitting of the two Houses. The Liberals proposed the Commons plus 100 peers; the peers were to include twenty government peers plus 80 elected in proportion to party strengths in the Lords. The Conservatives could not agree to these figures.

Loreburn asked that the proceedings should be recorded, that the information if given would be important. Ll. George urged there would be much peril in any narrative recorded.[8] Asquith said he would like to explain to his colleagues what had generally passed, but the rupture had not come precipitately. Ll. George said outside influences – Halsbury & Londonderry – had prevented A.J.B. & Austen agreeing, & possibly Lansdowne & Cawdor, but they had been all along more difficult.

Asquith said he had informed the King of the result. Crewe urged that the ear of the King should be now secured by the P.M. & that he should not be left to form his own views from the press & his surrounders, as he would have to come to our rescue. Ll. George urged same course, & so did we all. Churchill urged that contingent guarantees should be sought, & the Tories might then realise it would be better to settle than rouse the country against the Lords. It would take a week before we could put, said H.H.A., our cards on the table, but we must adopt the position taken up on April 14. Grey summed it up, we shall dissolve if the King will guarantee us the passage of our bill, if we get a majority, & if opposition don't yield to will of people. Churchill expressed anxiety we should work on line on which we worked in the conference & our opponents should be forced to accept our minimum, & thus avoid letting loose strong feelings by an election.

H.H.A. said the only question is am I to see the King tomorrow. I'm not going to threaten him now that's not the way to approach him. What am I to say? Ll. G.: 'You must do it, you can't reply on a memo, written, he would take up the silliest point, writing thoughts are no use, there is such a difference between talking & reading.' J. Morley's face was a picture! *Crewe* urged the King's frame of mind must be so utilised that he could see our side, & the

---

8   Lord Balcarres, the Conservative whip, had written on June 10:

the danger of the Conference lies in the fact that AJB will probably commit the fatal error of treating George, Churchill & Co. as gentlemen whereas they will descend to any meanness to score a point after negotiations are broken off wh. I look upon as inevitable. So much do I feel this that I am not at all sure that the Chief wd not be well advised in demanding a shorthand note of the proceedings. (Balcarres' diary, 10 June 1910, vol. xxi, ff. 37–8, Crawford and Balcarres MSS).

But, so far as the 1921 House of Lords Select Committee on Lords' Reform could discover, no official records were made. Austen Chamberlain kept detailed notes of the negotiations which were later read and supplemented by Lansdowne.

gravamen of the position. He reads, said Asquith, The Westminster & The Nation & hates The Morning Post & we then all insisted on the P.M. going to Sandringham tomorrow afternoon, if only to show the country we meant business & standing by the position of April 14th as stated to the House.

Winston explained in S. Wales peace rested in Warsaw – no lives lost – but proceedings would be taken against ringleaders caught in lawless acts.

It was arranged Stanton shd. not be seen unless he was deputed by men – not as a self appointed miners leader.[9]

I urged all Election on one day bill, & asked if Budget was to be taken & doubted Irish supporting it without guarantees. George & Birrell said oh yes they would.

Nov 15 Cabinet Buxton reported situation S. Wales – neither side wanted B. of Trade intervention – settlement was moving forward, offer by Masters, if men went back, to consider grievances, supported by Mabon & probably Stanton. Churchill said he cd not keep Metrop. police indefinitely, but bombs, detonators, fuses, pick axe heads, & revolvers were being secreted.

Asquith reported that in pursuance of Cabinet wish he went to Sandringham, had interview of some length, declared interview was asked not with declaration of policy, or to tender advice, but to put H.M. in possession of impressions created by the failure of the conference, & to the 2 points upon which it had broken down. He said he would give A.J.B.'s mem. as to cause of its breakup, & that we should probably recommend an early Dissolution before Xmas. H.H.A. pointed out to H.M. that within 12 months the same issue would be presented to the country twice, & the question of H. of L. must be put into train for final settlement. The H. of L. can't be dissolved, but its powers could be curtailed by invidious selection of summonses to peers, but it was now unconstitutional the alternative could only be by creation as promised by Kg Wm IV in 1832, but the knowledge wd bring about an agreement without its probable exercise. He had yesterday put on paper the 4 alternative courses, at the King's request, & sent it to Lord Knollys. The King was bitterly disappointed at the failure of the conference, but seemed very anxious to do what was right. The 4 courses H.H.A. said were

1. For H.M. to act on prerogative in present H. of C. without dissolution.
2. Immediate dissolution – if endorsed he would [be] willing [to] exercise prerogative, & this intention made public.
3. same as 2 only *not made public*.

---

9   C.B. Stanton, agent of the Aberdare miners, preached confrontation rather than the 'fainthearted, over-cautious, creeping, crawling, cowardly' approach of Mabon. (Peter Stead, 'The Language of Edwardian Politics', David Smith, ed., *A People and a Proletariat*: Essays in the History of Wales 1780–1980, Pluto Press in association with Llafur, The Society for the Study of Welsh History, 1980, p. 163).

4. Immediate election, & an assurance the question would be considered, if
& when the electors endorsed Govmt policy.

*JAP's version of the fourth option was vaguer and softer than the formutation
embodied in Runciman's note made at Downing St the same day: 'Immediate dissoln
with no assurances, but a clear understanding that we ministers are to refuse to take
or retain office unless guarantees are given by the King then.' (Runciman MSS).
While the Prime Minister was outlining the alternative courses open to the King, the
Chief Whip was warning Lord Knollys that Asquith had strained the loyalty of his
party and that any semblance of 'flinching from his duty now the crisis is upon us
again' would encourage 'the Socialist and extreme forces in the country'. Alick
Murray's forebodings about a 'spirit of unrest' pervading 'the working classes'
struck no chord at the palace. 'His Majesty was delighted with the Prime Minister
on Friday,' Bigge reported on November 15, 'and especially with his assurance that
the King would be asked for nothing, no guarantees, no promises during this
Parliament.' (Murray, Master and Brother, p. 61).*

The King asked for the Lords to be given an opportunity to create the crisis
by refusing our Bill – Asquith said such tactics could only be dilatory, & to fog
[sic] the issue off. Morley urged if Lords debated, they might present plausible
alternative proposals. Asquith then explained what had passed at the
Conference, & how the Opposition had no alternative proposals. They discussed
finance, & agreed to Speaker presiding over a tribunal joint character to discuss
what was tacking – & they were within reasonable distance of settlement on
this.[10] They had unanimously rejected the referendum as an instrument for this
purpose after Butler Reid & Fielding evidence. The conference had agreed to
the principle of the joint sitting, & to the delegation of a portion of the Lords.
But no proposals had ever come from any of the 4 Tories no counter proposal
even, although they had been asked for them when they eventually disagreed on
the two points reserved for consultation by A.J.B. with his friends. (Halsbury
Londonderry & Co.)

The 2 points were –
1. applicability of all legislation – to the joint comtee, when deadlock
   occurred Tory party never committed themselves but all organic matters
   they wanted to be dependent on an Election (or referendum possibly)

---

[10] On tacking, the conference had concluded that finance was the business solely of the
House of Commons, provided that, if any provision of a bill which deals with
taxation would also effect important social or political changes through
expropriation or differentiation against any class of owners or property, such a
provision should be treated as ordinary legislation and thus subject to joint sittings
of the two Houses in case of deadlock. It was also agreed that a joint committee of
both Houses, chaired by the Speaker, would decide whether or not any provision
was equitable tacking (Fair, *British Interparty Conferences*, p. 89).

2. The numbers talked of were delegation of 100, Liberal Govmt having power to nominate 20 of that body.[11]

Morley urged desirability of avoiding a debate on the Constit. Question in the Lords. Crewe felt he would be powerless to refuse.

At this stage the King sent into the Cabinet through Lord Knollys a message stating he could not give contingent guarantees and reminded the Prime Minister of his promise not to ask for them during the course of the present Parliament!

We all agreed we could not try & evade the straight issue of resignation, if we had *no understanding*, having regard to the statement of April 14th, & that if Balfour formed a Govmt the King's name would be brought in as a combatant & the Crown suffer in consequence, & it would be known he would not recognise his people's view. We could we thought protect him, & prevent any misrepresentation, though people would draw conclusions, as to assurances &c. Ll. George said Redmond would support us without knowledge or guarantees & if the King declined to have a reference made to his views, or the advice given & taken he thought the confidence was entitled to respect. Grey said if the Irish can give us their confidence blindly surely our own friends can do the same. The cabinet then proceeded to place in writing a memorandum for the King to be given to Knollys, in which we clearly set out our view that course 3 must be adopted and that we wanted an understanding that, in the event of the Lords not giving way, we asked that the constitutional powers of the Sovereign after the election to elect peers should be forthcoming, & no statement would be made to the matter unless & until the occasion arose. Knollys sent the mem. to the King at 3.30 & urged its acceptance & that the King should come up to London.

Almeric FitzRoy recorded on November 16 Morley's agreement that morning 'that the King's position in refusing Mr. Asquith's request [for a dissolution] was a very strong one, and that of the Government, "so far as it was at present developed," very weak.' (FitzRoy, Memoirs, vol. II, p. 422). The memorandum sent to the King is published in Harold Nicolson, King George the Fifth: His Life and Reign, Constable, 1952, p. 136. The government's position was strengthened by the King's belief that Balfour would decline to form an administration if the Liberals resigned. In fact, Knollys had been told by Balfour on April 29 that he would 'be prepared to form a government to prevent the King being put in the position contemplated by the demand for the creation of peers.' But this advice (on which Balfour had second thoughts by October) was withheld from the new King who met Asquith and Crewe at 3.30 pm on Wednesday November 16 to reach an understanding.

---

11   Runciman's pencilled note of 'What happened' according to Asquith at the Cabinet on November 15 records: 'Our 4 stuck to the Ripon plan – 20 Lords nominated by the Govt. of the day, 80 by proportional representation. Thus a 44 Liberal majority would become effective after delays. The Tories would not accept these figures.' (Runciman MSS).

November 16 3.30 Cabinet – Without Crewe & the P.M. We discussed whether H. or Lords should be given opportunity to discuss Parliament Bill – 2 courses open let

1. The Lords drift onto the inevitable shallows if they attempted their own reform through our bill, by amendments, & delay election until next year – or

2. Allow them to go on, but decline to accept an amendment, & to intimate, amendments meant rejection –
   Later course adopted.

E. Grey said to debate our bill was a bare faced pretext – say that again said Carrington.

Asquith then came in: he said they had had a 'considerable battle' twice repeated, but a satisfactory settlement had been secured with a good deal of difficulty. No guarantees or assurances had been given, but an understanding that if the elections results justified it, the King was prepared to exercise his constitutional powers in regard to the prerogative in electing Peers – but the King was very nervous & apprehensive, & afraid of disclosure. Asquith then guaranteed the honour of himself & his colleagues individually & collectively not to publicly or privately give the King away. We then considered Payment of members, Labour parties terms as stated by Henderson to me. We agreed not to make public reference to it this week, but later we arranged scheme of work & date Dissolution. 28–29–30th.

Henderson told me in confidence the demand for the repeal of the Osborne Judgement would die down if only the Govmt would state on Friday that they were prepared to give payment to M.P.s, & the returning officers expenses at elections, so that after this election a bill cd be introduced to find Trade Unions & all other M.P.s in the next House maintenance, but it must also be accompanied by a bill to restore to Trade Unions the same powers to be exercised *voluntarily*, which had been exercised before the Osborne judgement. It was decided not to announce our intentions before next week, as if stated on Friday too much attention would be directed to it, & many people in the country did not like payment of M.P.s, to which we were all individually pledged!

November 17 I prepared with Liddell Guillotine Resolution, & submitted it, & scheme of work to Asquith, who seemed well & not worried. He approved of course suggested. He asked me to show it to Ll. George. I said I had got his instructions, but George would never *read any*thing! & he laughed.

On November 18 the Prime Minister announced the breakdown of negotiations over the House of Lords and an immediate general election. The impending election was as usual preceded by delicate money raising negotiations. JAP, who had left the Whips' Office only 10 months earlier, was once again drawn in:

Private   18 Nov. 10
                                                     Headlam Hall,
                                                    Gainford

My dear Alick,

In reply to your question whether I think you might appeal to Kearley to further help the party having regard to his services and past assistance, I would say that the first time I approached him was when he was still working with Lloyd George at the Board of Trade, & he did not relish remaining on & had no intention (& naturally so) of playing 2d fiddle to Winston. He said the P.M. had offered him a baronetcy, and that George Whiteley had suggested if he liked he thought that generosity might be further acknowledged by a peerage. I think Kearley rather resented the suggestion, but he told me that if he later on took a peerage he would like to voluntarily help the Party by £25,000 or so, but he wasn't going to buy it, I merely thanked him, and there the matter was left.

I afterwards included his name among the Privy Councillors, & I hoped that I might have at the last election received something, I believe he wanted to help me, but he was ill & went abroad, & our interview never came off.

I feel sure that if you now approached him he would like to respond in the direction indicated by him, at the interview I first had with him, & know full well how much a whip needs all he can get for a general election![12]

I am very sincerely

                                                Joseph A. Pease

The Hon. A.O. Murray M.P.

                            (Murray of Elibank MSS, 8802, ff. 146–7)

November 22   *11.30* – Cabinet met & discussed Osborne Judgement. Lord Loreburn, Samuel, Buxton & self going for majority rule – with some conscience safeguard. Grey & Morley anxious for restitution of position but against any compulsion or exemption, anxious for only voluntary contributions without trade union pressure. Churchill, Haldane took an extreme anti Trade Union view supported by Burns.

The Law Officers, Isaacs & Simon explained legal view, the former diffuse (upsetting to Birrell) but Simon very clear – decision arrived wonderfully satisfactory considering different aspects.

On Bench in House, Asquith sought again to defer his answer. I said No – it will look like differences – do it now, & he wrote out his answer on his knee from the rough cabinet notes.

Payment of M.Ps Law altered so that trade unions might after effectively ascertaining decision of members include representation & kindred objects for levies – but no compulsion to contribute. Details of ballot &c left for future – but trade union organisation adoptable.

---

[12]   The letter is quoted, with the unexplained omission from the last paragraph of the words 'needs all he', in Searle, *Corruption in British Politics*, pp. 148–9.

Asquith announced the government's intention to legislate to include among the purposes of trade unions the provision of funds for 'Parliamentary and municipal action and representation and kindred objects.' Union opinion was to be 'effectively ascertained' and there was to be no compulsion. The government had also decided to introduce payment of MPs. (Chris Wrigley, 'Labour and the Trade Unions', in K.D. Brown, ed., The First Labour Party 1906–1914, *Croom Helm, 1985, pp. 139–44).*

We agreed on policy as to suffrage conciliation bill, we realised next session we had no time with 2 budgets – Parliament bill, insurance, payment of M.P.s &c.

Sir Edward Grey had announced on November 12 that there would be insufficient time to secure the passage of a women's suffrage bill before the end of the year. A militant demonstration was planned for November 18 when Parliament was to reconvene. When Asquith stated on November 18 that government business would have precedence until the dissolution on November 28, a deputation of 300 women marched on the House of Commons. In the confrontation that followed, there were 119 arrests. On November 22 Asquith provoked further protest by saying that, if re-elected, the government would give facilities for proceeding with a bill which could be freely amended. Realising that such a bill would have more enemies than friends, the WSPU sent 200 women to Downing Street. The ensuing mêlée resulted in 159 arrests and a severe knee injury to the Irish Secretary, Birrell. Asquith escaped by car but Birrell was set upon by about 20 suffragettes while walking alone across the open space by the Duke of York's column. In struggling to get free he slipped a knee-cap. He was rescued by Lord Crewe's secretary, Lionel Earle, who saw the fracas from a passing car. It was 'a brutal, outrageous and unprovoked assault and it may lame me for life', Birrell told C.P. Scott on 2 February 1911. (Scott's political note, 2 Feb. 1911, Trevor Wilson, ed., The Political Diaries of C.P. Scott 1911–1928, *Collins, 1970, p. 36; Blunt's diary, 28 Jan. 1911, Blunt,* My Diaries, *p. 749; FitzRoy's diary, 24 Nov. 1910, FitzRoy,* Memoirs II, *p. 425).*

November 24   Cabinet – The last of Asquith's during the 1910 Parliament. We were called to discuss the terms of the King's Speech. Birrell in bed, hurt by suffragette crowd 2 days before. McKenna in bed recovering from operation for appendicitis. Asquith pointed out no allusion, following precedent, would be made in Address to Dissolution.

We discussed whether 'shadow' of the late king's death was still on us after six mos. Agreed to insert it into his son's mouth. We combined Foreign Office

& Colonial Office suggestions as to the Newfoundland Fishery arbitration.[13] The rest was easily agreed to, laying stress on removal of pauper disqualification for old age pensions, & increase given to the Navy.

I then asked S. Buxton to say what answer Portugal had given in regard to deferring reciprocal action on our tariff on Port wine, & he said they had agreed to defer the matter for further negociation next year.

Morley & Loreburn then agreed upon the points they would relatively take up. The P.M. complained that he had been unfairly criticised for saying we were now 'at war'. This was of course war of words, since diplomatic negociation had failed. Morley undertook to correct the Archbishop.

In the Lords' debate the previous day on Lord Lansdowne's reform proposals, the Archbishop of York said, with reference to the collapse of the conference between the two parties: 'The Prime Minister has said in vivid language that negotiations have ended, and that war is declared.' The Archbishop went on to appeal for restraint in the use of language on both sides, as the Archbishop of Canterbury had done earlier in the debate. On November 24 Morley expressed surprise at the Archbishop's finding fault with the Prime Minister. The Archbishop (said Morley) had said that the Prime Minister was appealing to force when reason had failed. In fact the Prime Minister had merely been using the language of debate: the war of arguments would now begin. (PD, Lords, 23, 24 Nov. 1910).

The line we should adopt in our speeches on H of L. reconstruction was considered & we agreed to favour reform provided the veto was previously secured, but to resist strengthening the 2d chamber in advance of reform.

We discussed the Lords' Resolutions & all agree to accept any such proposals would be to continue the fight for liberalism with the dice loaded against us, & they would in operation sterilise all advance.

The question of joint session depended upon x, the number of peers (Tory) delegated when we were in Power & [the Lords' proposal would] prevent the

---

13   In his opening paragraph on 6 February 1911 the King said: 'the grievous loss which the Empire has sustained by the death of My beloved Father is uppermost in My thoughts.' Surprisingly, no reference was made to the Newfoundland Fisheries settlement, although nearly a hundred years of diplomatic difficulties had finally been ended. The dispute between Britain (on behalf of Newfoundland) and the United States was submitted to the Hague Tribunal in 1910. The Tribunal's decision, reached on September 7, was largely in Britain's favour, particularly over the definition of the three mile limit's applicability to bays: the U.S.A. had argued that the limit followed the indentations of the bays but the tribunal decided that the limit should be measured from a straight line drawn across the bays (*The Annual Register. A Review of Public Events at Home and Abroad for the Year 1910*, Longmans, Green, 1911, pp. 458–9).

King's exercise of his power to create, & that under their proposals the Budget of last year would still be rejected & to refer big bills to referendum would operate only with Libs in a majority, & would in practice give Lords power to force a Dissolution & in fact that if the H of C. was now impotent at times, it would become more impotent under their proposals.

General Election
November 28 – Dec 16.
1910

Government majority unchanged.

| 1 Lib. less. | 2 Lab. more | 2 Nationalists at expense of Inde Nat. more. |

JAP was in no danger of losing his own seat in December 1910. Sir William Holland, who had been unopposed in Rotherham in 1906, had secured 72.4 percent of the vote (12,225 votes) in January 1910. JAP was given a free run by the Conservatives in March when Holland gave up the seat for him. But Holland's huge majority was, according to JAP, his greatest enemy in the election. Like many Liberals JAP suffered from an old register; there had been 2,000 removals, mostly working men 'whom it was absolutely impossible to bring long distances on a Tuesday'. (The Advertiser, 10 Dec. 1910, Gainford MSS, 59, f. 179).

Although several tradesmen barricaded their shops, and fifty extra policemen were drafted into the town on polling day, the election was 'unusually sober'. (The Advertiser, 17 Dec. 1910, Gainford MSS, 59, f. 180). In the event, of the 20,687 voters still on the register, only 13,896 voted. JAP's majority was 4,874.

Having been scorched as a result of his equivocations over Home Rule in January JAP made sure that there were no doubts about his position. 'Ever since he went to Ireland in 1887, and spent many weeks there under Mr Balfour's coercion, he had been a convinced Home Ruler'. There was one condition: 'the two Parliaments shall not be co-ordinate, and the Imperial Parliament must be supreme ...'. (The Advertiser, 10 Dec. 1910, Gainford MSS, 59, f. 179).

Biographies

Individuals are listed alphabetically by the surname or title by which they were known at the end of the period covered by this volume. Titles may be found in the index under the individual's family name.

Aberdeen, Ishbel Maria Gordon, Countess of (1857–1939); sister of 2nd Lord Tweedmouth; m. in 1877 John Campbell Gordon, **Earl of Aberdeen** (1847–1934). An active Liberal and social reformer. Her husband succ. brother as 7th Earl 1870; Ld Lt, Ireland 1886, 1905–15; PC 1886; Gov. Gen., Canada 1893–8; Marquess of Aberdeen 1916.

Abraham, William (1842–1922); Lib.–Lab. MP Glamorganshire (Rhondda) 1885–1918, Rhondda (West) 1918–20; miner and miners' agent; first pres., South Wales Miners' Federation 1898; PC 1911. Widely known by his eisteddfod name 'Mabon'.

Acland, Arthur Herbert Dyke (1847–1926); Lib. MP West Riding of Yorkshire (Rotherham) 1885–99; succ. brother as 13th Bt 1919; Vice-Pres. of the Council (Minister responsible for Education) 1892–5. Sir William Harcourt wanted Acland as Chief Whip in 1892 but Gladstone insisted on Edward Marjoribanks; father of Francis Acland; declined a peerage 1908.

Acland, Sir (Charles) Thomas Dyke, Bt (1842–1919); barrister and farmer; MP Cornwall (East) 1882–85, Cornwall (North East or Launceston) 1885–92; Parl. Sec., Bd of Trade 1886; 12th Bt 1898.

Acland, Francis Dyke (1874–1939); Fin. Sec., War 1908–10; Lib. M.P. Yorkshire (Richmond) 1906–10, Cornwall (Camborne) 1910–22, Devon (Tiverton) June 1923–1924, Cornwall (Northern) July 1932–39; pps to R.B. Haldane 1906–08; U. Sec. of St., Foreign Affairs 1911–15; Fin. Sec., Treasury Feb–June 1915; Parl. Sec., Bd of Agriculture 1915–16; PC 1915; 14th Bt 1926.

Acland-Hood, Sir Alexander Fuller, Bt (1853–1917); Con. Ch. Whip 1902–11 (Patronage Sec., Treasury 1902–5); Con. MP Somerset (Wellington) 1892–1911; Vice-Chamberlain to Household 1900–2; PC 1904; Baron St Audries 1911.

Agar-Robartes, Hon. Thomas Charles Reginald (1880–1915); Lib. MP Cornwall (Bodmin) 1906 (unseated on petition), Cornwall (St Austell) 1908–15; eldest son of 6th Vt Clifden. Close friend of Rosebery's sons Lord Dalmeny and Neil Primrose, best known for his amendment to the Home Rule Bill 11 June 1912 to exclude Antrim, Armagh,

Down, and Londonderry. Recommended for the VC in 1915 for his part in rescuing a severely wounded sergeant; he died from wounds received in this exploit.

Alexandra, Queen (1844–1925); eldest daughter of Prince and Princess Christian, later King Christian IX of Denmark; m. Edward VII (then Prince of Wales) 1863.

Allard, William (1861–1919); sec., Liberal League 1902–9; trained as Liberal organiser under Francis Schnadhorst in 1880s; sec., Nottingham and Birmingham Lib. assocs; mayor, Kingston-on-Thames 1893; Lib. agent and sec., Home Counties Liberal Federation, his 'desertion to the Lib. Imps … was … on a purely commercial basis of £1,000 per ann. for 5 years certain'. (L. Harcourt to J. Morley, 10 Nov. 1901, copy, Harcourt MSS, dep. 427, f. 175); chief organiser, Liberal HQ 1909–13; sec., Lib. Insurance Committee 1912, Home Rule Council 1913–14.

Allendale, Wentworth Canning Blackett Beaumont, Baron (1860–1923); Capt., Yeomen of Guard 1907–11; Lib. MP Northumberland (Hexham) 1895–1907; Vice-Chamberlain 1905–7; 2nd Baron 1907; Ld-in-Waiting 1911–16; Vt 1911; a frequent sporting companion of JAP; his nephew m. JAP's younger dau., to Prime Minister, 28 Nov. 1910, copy, Harcourt MSS, dep. 462, f. 2).

Alverstone, Richard Everard Webster, Baron (1842–1915); QC 1878; one of the most successful barristers of his time; Con. MP Launceston 1885, Isle of Wight 1885–1900; Attorney-General 1885–Feb. 1886, Aug. 1886–92, 1895–1900; Kt 1885; Bt 1900; Master of the Rolls 1900; PC 1900; Baron Alverstone 1900; Ld Chief Justice 1900–13; Vt 1914.

Argyll, John Douglas Sutherland Campbell, Duke of (1845–1914); Gov. & Constable, Windsor Castle 1892–1914; Marquess of Lorne 1847–1900; Lib. MP Argyllshire 1868–78, Con. MP Manchester (South) 1895–1900; private sec. to father when Sec. of St., India 1868–71; Gov. Gen., Canada 1878–83; m. Princess Louise Caroline Alberta, 4th daughter of Queen Victoria; 9th Duke 1900.

Arran, Arthur Jocelyn Charles Gore, Earl of (1868–1958); 6th Earl 1901; soldier; KP 19 October 1909; PC (Ireland) 1917; Ld Lt, Co. Donegal 1917–20; he had been an hon. sec. of the Liberal League.

Askwith, George Ranken (1861–1942); controller-general, commercial, labour & statistical dept, Bd of Trade 1908–11; barrister 1886; worked with Sir Henry (later Lord) James and specialised as arbitrator in labour disputes; asst sec., railway branch, Bd of Trade 1907–9; chief industrial commissioner 1911–19; KCB 1911; Baron Askwith 1919.

Asquith, Herbert Henry (1852–1928); Prime Minister 1908–16; Lib. MP Fife (East) 1886–1918, Paisley 1920–4; Sec. of St., Home Affairs 1892–5; Chancellor of Exchequer 1905–8; Sec. of St., War 1914; Earl of Oxford and Asquith 1925.

Asquith, (Frances) Katherine Frances (1885–1976); dau. of Sir John Horner and H.H. Asquith's close friend Lady Horner; m. Raymond Asquith 1907.

Asquith, Emma Alice Margaret ('Margot') (1864–1945); m. Asquith as his second wife in 1894; dau. of Sir Charles Tennant, Bt; one of the 'Souls'. She recorded that rumour once said she was to marry A.J. Balfour, to which he replied 'No, that is not so. I rather think of having a career of my own.' *(The Autobiography of Margot Asquith*, Thornton Butterworth 1920–21, vol. II, p. 162).

Asquith, Violet (1887–1969); Asquith's only dau. by his first wife; m. Asquith's private secretary, Sir Maurice Bonham Carter 1915; Baroness Asquith of Yarnbury (a life peerage) 1964.

Atherley-Jones, Llewellyn Archer (1848–1929); Lib. MP Durham (North Western) 1885–1914; barrister 1875; QC 1896; Recorder, Newcastle 1906–29; Judge, Mayor's City of London Court 1913–29; son of Ernest Jones, Chartist leader; published several novels anonymously.

Balfour, Arthur James (1848–1930); Leader of the Opposition 1906–11, 1892–5; nephew of 3rd Marquess of Salisbury, private sec. to his uncle 1878–80; Con. MP Hertford 1874–85, Manchester (East) 1885–1906, City of London 1906–22; Pres., Local Govt Bd 1885–6; Sec., Scotland 1886–7; Ch. Sec., Ireland 1887–91; 1st Ld of Treasury and Leader of H. of C. 1891–2, 1895–1905; Ld Privy Seal 1902–3; Prime Minister 1902–5; 1st Ld, Adm. 1915–16; Sec. of St., Foreign Affairs 1916–19; Ld Pres. of Council 1919–22, 1925–29; Earl of Balfour 1922.

Banbury, Sir Frederick George, Bt (1850–1936); Con. MP City of London 1906–24, Camberwell (Peckham) 1892–1906; Bt 1903; director and chairman, Great Northern Railway; member, Stock Exchange; chairman, Royal Society for the Prevention of Cruelty to Animals; PC 1922; Baron Banbury 1924. 'The uncompromising Champion of the old order … to whom the advent of women to the House was … nothing short of an outrage.' *(The Times*, 14 Aug. 1936).

Barclay, Sir George Head (1862–1921); British Minister at Tehran 1908–12; diplomat; KCMG 1908; KCSI 1913; Minister to Bucharest 1913–21.

Barker, Sir John Edward, Bt (1840–1914); Lib. MP Penryn and Falmouth 1906–10; draper; a leader of the early closing of shops movement; JP Herts; Bt 9 November 1908.

Barnard, Edmund Broughton (1856–1930); Lib. MP Kidderminster 1906–10; suffragist; chairman, Metropolitan Water Board (from 1908) and Lea Conservancy Board; chairman and alderman, Hertfordshire County Council; Dep. Ld Lt, Herts.; Kt 1928. Contested Islington East (Oct. 1917), Hertford (1918) for National Party; supported Churchill's Conservative candidature in Epping 1924.

Barnes, George Nicoll (1859–1940); Lab. MP Glasgow (Blackfriars, later Gorbals) 1906–22; engineer; trade unionist; general sec., Amalgamated Society of Engineers 1896–1908; chairman, Parl. Labour Party 1910; Min. of Pensions Dec. 1916–17; member, War Cabinet 1917–19; Min. without Portfolio 1917–20; resigned from Labour Party when it withdrew from coalition 1918.

Beauchamp, William Lygon, Earl (1872–1938); Ld Pres. of Council June–Nov. 1910 and 1914–15; known as Vt Elmley 1872–91; 7th Earl 1891; Gov., New South Wales 1899–1902; Ld Steward of Household 1907–10; First Commissioner, Works 1910–14; Warden, Cinque Ports 1913–34.

Beaufort, Henry Adelbert Wellington FitzRoy Somerset, Duke of (1847–1924); Marquess of Worcester 1853–99; 9th Duke 1899; Master, Beaufort Hunt 1899–1924; 'for at least two generations a great figure among English foxhunters.' (*The Times*, 28 November 1924). Provoked by the speeches of Lloyd George and Churchill over the 1909 Budget, he expressed a wish to see them 'in the middle of twenty couple of dog hounds', A remark greeted with 'laughter and applause' when quoted in the Lords by Lord Denman (*PD*, Lords, iv, 1207, 29 Nov. 1909). He did not vote in 1910 when Rosebery proposed strengthening the Lords, or in August 1911 when the Parliament Act was passed.

Bennett, Ernest Nathaniel (1868–1947); Lib. MP Oxfordshire (Woodstock) 1906–10; Fellow, Hertford College, Oxford; war correspondent, Crete 1897, the Sudan 1898; pps to Sir E. Strachey 1909; joined Ottoman Army 1911; press censor, Turkish staff, Thrace 1912; British Red Cross Commissioner, Belgium, France, and Serbia 1914–15; special service in Admiralty Intelligence Division; joined Labour Party 1916; Lab. MP Central Cardiff 1929–31; Nat. Lab. MP Cardiff (Central) 1931–45; Kt 1930; member, council of Psychical Research Society, hobbies included investigating haunted houses.

Bigge, Sir Arthur (1849–1931); private sec. to Prince of Wales 1901–10. Asst private sec. to 1880–95, private sec. 1895–1901; private sec. to King George V 1910–31; KCB 1895; PC 1910; Baron Stamfordham 1911.

Bingham, Hon. Cecil Edward (1861–1934); 2nd son of 4th Earl of Lucan; Lt Col. 1st Life Guards 1906–10. He commanded the Cavalry Corps in 1915 and rose to the rank of major-General.

Birrell, Augustine (1850–1933); Ch. Sec., Ireland 1907–16; Lib. MP Fife (Western) 1889–1900, Bristol (North) 1906–18; literary critic; Quain Professor of Law, London University 1896–9; Pres., Bd of Education 1905–7.

Birrell, Eleanor (d. 1915); dau. of Frederick Locker Lampson widow, of Lionel Tennyson, the poet laureate's younger son; m. Birrell as his second wife 1888.

Blyth, James Blyth, Baron (1841–1925); director W. and A. Gilbey, wine merchants and distillers; agriculturalist, viticulturalist and advocate of technical education; philanthropist with special interest in tuberculosis; Bt 1895; Baron 1907; organised Franco–British Exhibition June 1908.

Bodington, Sir Nathan (1848–1911); scholar of Greek; instrumental in the founding of Leeds University; Kt 1908.

Borthwick, Sir Thomas, Bt (1835–1912); JP & County Councillor for Midlothian; chairman, Thomas Borthwick & Sons, colonial merchants; Bt 21 July 1908; created a baron 1912 but died before the patent was made out, his son was created Baron Whitburgh in his place.

Bottomley, Horatio William (1860–1933); Lib. MP Hackney (South) 1906–12, 1918–22; claimed to be the natural son of Charles Bradlaugh; journalist and financial speculator; declared bankrupt several times; founded *John Bull* 1906; found guilty of fraud 1922 and expelled from Parliament.

Bourne, Most Rev Francis Alphonsus, Archbishop of Westminster, (1861–1935); 4th Archbishop, Westminster 1903-35; Bishop, Southwark 1897-1903; Cardinal 1911.

Brailsford, Henry Noel (1873–1958); journalist and leader-writer *Manchester Guardian, Daily News, Nation, Morning Leader, Echo,* and *Tribune*; socialist and pacifist; ardent supporter of women's suffrage (he resigned from *Daily News* 1909 when A.G. Gardiner did not condemn forced feeding of imprisoned suffragettes); sec., Conciliation Committee 1910–12; books include *A League of Nations* (1917); editor, *New Leader* 1922–6; chief leader-writer, *New Statesman* 1930–46.

Bryce, Elizabeth (1843-1939); chairman, 1900; dau. of Thomas Ashton; m. James Bryce 1889.

Bryce, James (1838–1922); Ambassador, USA 1907–13; Fellow, Oriel College, Oxford 1862–89; Regius Professor of Civil Law, Oxford 1870–93; Lib. MP Tower Hamlets 1880–5, Aberdeen (South) 1885–1906; U. Sec. of St., Foreign Affairs Feb-May 1886; founder, *The English Historical Review* 1886; author of *The American Commonwealth* 1888; Chancellor, Duchy of Lancaster 1892-4; Pres., Bd of Trade 1894-5; chairman, royal commission on secondary education 1894-5; Ch. Sec., Ireland 1905-7;

chairman, commission on German war atrocities in Belgium; proponent of a League of Nations; Vt Bryce 1914.

Buchanan, Thomas Ryburn (1846–1911); U. Sec. of St., India 1908–9; barrister; Lib. MP Edinburgh 1881–5, Edinburgh (West) 1885–92 (Lib. Unionist 1886–8), Aberdeenshire (East) 1892–1900, Perthshire (Eastern) 1903–11; Fin. Sec., War 1906–8. 'He has been an intimate of C.-B's, and is of the same type in some ways – only more educated: Balliol, First Class, Fellow of All Souls: unselfish, loyal, plain, assiduous: not exactly popular in the H. of C. – but not otherwise' (Morley to Lord Minto, 15 April 1908, John Viscount Morley, *Recollections*, 2 vols, Macmillan 1917, vol. II, p. 253).

Burns, John Elliot (1858–1943); Pres., Local Govt Bd 1905–14; engineer; member, Social Democratic Federation 1884–9; member for Battersea, LCC 1889–1907; 'independent labour' MP Battersea 1892–5; Lib. MP Battersea 1895–1918; chairman, TUC Parliamentary Committee 1883; Pres., Bd of Trade 1914.

Burt, Thomas (1837–1922); Lib. MP Morpeth 1874–1918; miner; gen. sec., Northumberland Miners' Association 1865–1913; Parl. Sec., Bd of trade 1892–5; PC 1906.

Butler, Nicholas Murray (1862–1947); Pres., Columbia University 1901–45; close friend of James Bryce and Theodore Roosevelt; professor of philosophy and education.

Buxton, Noel Edward Noel (1869–1948); radical; Lib. MP Yorkshire, North Riding (Whitby) 1905–6, Norfolk

(North) 1910–18; joined Lab. 1919; Lab. MP Norfolk (North) 1922–1930 (his wife succeeded him as MP); Min. of Agriculture 1924, 1929–30; Baron Noel-Buxton 1930. Gave up £1000 a year as director of family brewing business to enter Parliament as a Liberal (Lord Wedgwood, *Testament to Democracy*, Hutchinson, [1942], p. 75).

Buxton, Sydney (1853–1934); Postmaster-General 1905–10; Lib. MP Tower Hamlets (Poplar) 1886–1914, Peterborough 1883–5; U. Sec. of St., Colonial Affairs 1892–5; Pres., Bd of Trade 1910–14; Gov. Gen., S. Africa 1914–20; author of *Handbook to Political Questions of the Day* (1880); Vt Buxton 1914, Earl 1920.

Caldwell, James (1839–1925); 'Independent' Lib. MP Lanarkshire (Mid) 1894–1910; Lib. Unionist MP, Glasgow (St Rollox) 1886–92; lawyer; calico printer; Dep. Chairman, Ways & Means and Dep. Speaker 1906–10; PC 1910.

Campbell-Bannerman, Sir Henry (1836–1908); Prime Minister Dec. 1905–Apr. 1908; Lib. MP Stirling Burghs 1868–1908; Fin. Sec., War 1871–4, 1880–2; Sec., Adm. 1882–4; Ch. Sec., Ireland 1884–5; Sec. of St., War 1886, 1892–5; GCB 1895; Lib. Leader in Commons from 1899.

Carlisle, Rosalind Frances Howard, Countess of (1845–1921); dau. of 2nd Baron Stanley m. 9th Earl of Carlisle 1864; social reformer; complete abstainer; president, National British Women's Temperance Association; suffragist; president, Women's Liberal Federation 1891–1901, 1906–14. Reputedly a model for Lady Britomart in G.B. Shaw's *Major Barbara* (1905).

Carrington, Charles Robert Wynn-Carrington, Earl (1843–1928); Pres., Bd of Agriculture and Fisheries 1905–11; Lib. MP Wycombe 1865–8; 3rd Baron Carrington 1868; Gov., New South Wales 1885–90; Ld Chamberlain 1892–5; Earl Carrington 1895; Ld Privy Seal 1911–12; Ld Great Chamberlain 1911–28; Marquess of Lincolnshire 1912; close friend of Edward VII and George V.

Carrington, Lt Col. the Hon. Sir William Henry Peregrine (1845–1914); Keeper of the Privy Purse 1910–14; younger brother of Lord Carrington; commissioned into the Grenadier Guards; Lib. MP Wycombe 1868–83; sec., Ld Great Chamberlain's Office 1870–96; Groom-in-Waiting to Queen Victoria 1880–2; Equerry to Queen Victoria 1881–1901; Extra Equerry to Edward VII 1901–10, George V 1910; Comptroller and Treasurer of Household of George V as Prince of Wales 1901–10; changed name from Carington 1880; GCVO 1911.

Carter, George Wallace (1870–1922); organising sec., Free Trade Union; Jan. 1908–11; private sec. to G. Whiteley as Lib. Chief Whip 1905–8; sec., Home Rule Council 1912–13; sec., National Land and Housing Council 1913–14; sec., Central Land and Housing Council 1914–19; jt hon. sec., Parliamentary Recruiting Committee, Parliamentary War Savings Committee, and National War Aims Committee; CBE 1918.

Carysfort, William Proby, Earl of (1836–1909); a Liberal Unionist; Ld Lt of Co. Wicklow 1890–1909; succ. brother as 5th Earl 1872; KP 1874. As well as owning some 19,000 acres in Ireland and 6000 in England he had a fine library and art collection (including nine Reynolds).

Cassel, Sir Ernest Joseph (1852–1921); one of the wealthiest City financiers; a close friend of King Edward VII nicknamed 'Windsor Cassel'; financial adviser to Churchill family and Haldane, worth over £7,000,000 when he died. GCMG 1905; GCVO 1906; GCB 1909; PC 1902. His only dau. m. W.W. Ashley MP.

Cawdor, Frederick Archibald Vaughan Campbell, Earl of (1847–1911); Vt Emlyn 1860–98; Con. MP Carmarthenshire 1874–85; chairman, Great Western Railway 1895–1905; 3rd Earl 1898; 1st Ld, Adm. Mar.–Dec. 1905; member, Select Committee to consider ways to increase efficiency of Lords 1907; supported Lords' rejection of the 1909 Budget till it had been referred to the country; member, Council of Prince of Wales 1908–10.

Cecil, (Edgar Algernon) Robert (Gascoyne-), Lord (1864–1958); Con. MP Marylebone (East) 1906–10; Ind. Con. MP Hertfordshire (Hitchen) 1911–23; 3rd son of 3rd Marquess of Salisbury; private sec. to father 1886–8; barrister; U. Sec. of St., Foreign Affairs 1915–18; Min. of Blockade 1916–18; Asst Sec. of St., Foreign Affairs 1918–19; PC 1915; Ld Privy Seal, in charge of League of Nations affairs 1923; Chancellor, Duchy of Lancaster, in charge of League affairs 1924–7; dep. leader of British delegation 1929–31; Pres., League of Nations Union 1923–45; organiser of Peace Ballot 1934–5; Nobel Peace Prize 1937; Vt Cecil of Chelwood 1923.

Chalmers, Sir Robert (1858–1938); chairman, Bd of Inland Revenue 1907–

11; asst sec., Treasury, 1903–7; KCB 1908; Permanent Sec., Treasury 1911–13; Gov., Ceylon 1913–16; Joint U. Sec., Treasury 1916 and 1916–19; U. Sec. to Chief Sec., Ireland 1916; PC 1916; Baron Chalmers 1919; Master of Peterhouse, Cambridge 1924–31.

Chamberlain, Joseph (1836–1914); Lib. Unionist MP Birmingham (West) 1885–1914; Chairman, National Education League 1870; Mayor, Birmingham 1873–5; Lib. MP Birmingham 1876–85; Pres., National Liberal Federation 1877; Pres., Bd of Trade 1880–5; Pres., Local Govt Bd 1886; Sec. of St., Colonial Affairs 1895–1903; incapacitated by a stroke 1906.

Chamberlain, (Joseph) Austen (1863–1937); Lib. Unionist MP Worcestershire (Eastern) 1892–1914, Birmingham (West) 1914–37; son of Joseph Chamberlain, half-brother of Neville; Lib. Unionist Junior Whip 1892–5; Civil Ld, Adm. 1895–1900; Fin. Sec., Treasury 1900–2; Postmaster-General 1902–3; Chancellor of Exchequer 1903–5, 1919–21; Sec. of St., India 1915–17; member, War Cabinet Apr.–Dec. 1918; leader, Con. party in Commons 1921–Oct. 1922; Ld Privy Seal 1921–22; took part in Irish negotiations 1921; supported continuation of coalition government Oct. 1922 and was therefore out of office till 1924; Sec. of St., Foreign Affairs 1924–9; Kt 1925; First Ld, Adm. Aug.–Oct. 1931.

Chichester, Jocelyn Brudenell Pelham, Earl of (1871–1926); 6th Earl 1905; Public Works Commissioner; 1918. JAP's sister Lucy was married to a cousin of Chichester's wife.

Churchill, Winston Leonard Spencer- (1874–1965); Pres., Bd of Trade 1908–10; Con. then Lib. MP Oldham 1900–6 (a Unionist Free Trader, he crossed the floor to the Liberals in May 1904); Lib. MP Manchester (North-West) 1906–8, Dundee 1908–22 (Co. Lib. 1918–22); Con. MP Essex (Epping) 1924–45, Woodford 1945–64; U. Sec. of St., Colonial Affairs 1905–8; Sec. of St., Home Affairs 1910–11; 1st Ld, Adm. 1911–15; Chancellor, Duchy of Lancaster 1915; Min. of Munitions 1917–19; Sec. of St., War and Air 1919–21; Sec. of St., Air and Colonial Affairs 1921; Sec. of St., Colonial Affairs 1921–2; Chancellor of Exchequer 1924–9; 1st Ld, Adm. 1939–40; Prime Minister and Min. of Defence 1940–5; Leader of Con. Party 1940–55; Prime Minister 1951–5; (Min. of Defence 1951–2); KG 1953.

Collings, Jesse (1831–1920); Lib. MP Birmingham (Bordesley) 1886–1918, Ipswich 1880–6; ironmonger; a founder of National Education League 1868; Birmingham town councillor 1868–78 (Mayor 1878); advocate of free non-sectarian education and land reform especially through the National Agricultural Labourers' Union; Parl. Sec., Local Govt Bd 1886; followed Chamberlain in Liberal Home Rule split; U. Sec. of St., Home Affairs 1895–1902; PC 1892.

Collins, Sir William Job (1859–1946); Lib. MP St Pancras (West) 1906–10, Derby 1916–18; surgeon & oculist; vice-chairman, LCC 1896–7, chairman 1897–8; Kt 1902; chairman, London Education Committee 1904–6; Vice-Chancellor, University of London, 1907–09; temporary chairman, House of Commons committees 1910; KCVO 1914.

Connaught and Strathearn, Prince Arthur William Patrick Albert, Duke of (1850–1942); 3rd and favourite son of Queen Victoria; soldier; Field Marshal 1902; High Commissioner and C-in-C Mediterranean 1907–9; Gov. Gen., Canada 1911–16; Duke of Connaught and Strathearn 1874.

Cowdray, Weetman Dickinson Pearson, Baron (1856–1927); Lib. MP Colchester 1895–1910; construction contractor; his company discovered oil in Mexico; Bt 1894; Baron Cowdray 1910; Pres., Air Board 1917; PC 1917; Vt 1917; proprietor, *The Westminster Gazette;* chief source of funds for Asquithian Liberals 1918–1927; on his death his estate was worth £4,000,000.

Cox, Harold (1859–1936); Lib. MP Preston 1906–9; journalist; sec., Cobden Club 1899–1904; unreconstructed advocate of 'peace, retrenchment and reform'; denounced Lloyd Georgian finance; Alderman, LCC 1910–12; editor *Edinburgh Review* 1912–29; member, Bryce Commission on German outrages 1915.

Craven, William George Robert Craven, Earl of (1868–1921); 4th Earl 1883; ADC to Viceroy of Ireland 1890–2; Capt., Yeomen of Guard 1911–15; m. in 1893 Cornelia (d. 1961), only dau. of Bradley Martin of New York; drowned. Holidaying in Paris in May 1908 Lady Craven and Mary Harcourt 'witnessed a play which was the most improper & sensuous thing I have ever seen' (Mary Harcourt to Lewis Harcourt, 2 May 1908, Harcourt MSS, uncat.).

Crewe, Margaret, Countess of (1881–1967); dau. of 5th Earl of Rosebery m.

Crewe as his second wife 1899. A leading Liberal hostess.

Crewe, Robert Offley Ashburton Crewe-Milnes, Earl of (1858–1945); Sec. of St., Colonial Affairs 1908–10; Lib. Leader in Lords 1908–16; asst private sec. to Sec. of St., Foreign Affairs 1883–4; 2nd Baron Houghton 1885; Ld-in-Waiting 1886; Ld Lt, Ireland 1892–5; Earl of Crewe 1895; Ld Pres. of Council 1905–8, 1915–18; Ld Privy Seal 1908–11, 1912–15; Sec. of St., India 1910–15; Pres., Bd of Education 1916; Ambassador, Paris 1922–8; Sec. of St., War 1931; Marquess 1911.

Cromer, Evelyn Baring, Earl of (1841–1917); soldier; ADC to Sir Henry Knight Storks 1858–67; private sec. to Lord Northbrook when Viceroy, India 1872–6; first British Commissioner, Egyptian Debt Office 1877–9; British controller 1879; financial member, Viceroy's council 1880–3; KCSI 1883; British agent and consul-general, Egypt 1883–1907; Baron Cromer 1892, Vt 1899; Earl of Cromer 1901; offered Sec. of St., Foreign Affairs December 1905 but refused because of Liberal Party 'socialism' and South African policy; wrote *Modern Egypt* 1907; pres., Dardanelles commission 1916–17 but died before it reported.

Cross, Richard Assheton Cross, Viscount (1823–1914); barrister 1849; partner, Parr's Bank 1862–1914; Con. MP Preston 1857–62, Lancashire (South-West) 1868–85, Lancashire (Newton) 1885–6; Sec. of St., Home Affairs 1874–80, 1885–6; Sec. of St., India 1886–92; Chancellor, Duchy of Lancaster June–July 1895; Ld Privy Seal 1895–1900; GCB 1880; Vt Cross 1886. He drew a political pension of £2,000

p.a. 1892–1914. Despite the declaration that his income without the pension was inadequate to maintain his station in life, he left an estate of £79,299 net.

Curzon of Kedleston, George Nathaniel Curzon, Baron (1859–1925); Irish representative peer 1908–11; suffered from curvature of the spine and forced to wear a steel corset from 1878; traveller and writer; Con. MP Lancashire (Southport) 1886–98; U. Sec. of St., India 1891–2; U. Sec. of St., Foreign Affairs 1895–8; Viceroy, India 1898–1905; Baron Curzon 1898 (an Irish peerage, so that he might return to the Commons); Earl Curzon of Kedleston 1911; pres., Anti-Suffrage League 1912–17; Ld Privy Seal 1915–16; Pres., Air Board 1916; 5th Baron Scarsdale 1916; Ld Pres. of Council and member War Cabinet Dec. 1916–18; organised peace celebrations 1918; Sec. of St., Foreign Affairs 1919–24; Marquess Curzon of Kedleston 1921; Ld Privy Seal 1924–5.

Dalziel, Sir (James) Henry (1868–1935); Lib. MP Kirkcaldy Burghs 1892–1921; journalist; Kt 1908; proprietor, *Reynolds' Weekly Newspaper*; interests in *Pall Mall Gazette* and *Lloyd's News*; PC 1912; helped Lloyd George purchase *The Daily Chronicle* in 1918, and was chairman and political director 1918–21; Bt 1918; Baron Dalziel 1921. Asquith had described him with a tinge of irony as one of those whose 'constant loyalty to the party is a stimulus to those responsible for its leadership' (*Daily Mail,* 9 Nov. 1908).

Davidson, Randall Thomas, Archbishop of Canterbury (1848–1930); ordained 1875; chaplain to Archibald Tait, then Archbishop, Canterbury 1877–82; married Tait's dau.

1878; Dean of Windsor 1883–91; Bishop, Rochester 1891–5, Winchester 1895–1903; Archbishop, Canterbury 1903–28; Baron Davidson of Lambeth 1928.

Dence, Alexander Henry (d. 1949), a director of Brand's, the makers of Essence of Beef, Chicken and Mutton and Essence of Malt Sauce; succ. his father as a director of Hovis Ltd 1919, chairman 1924–49. (*The Hovis Jubilee A brief record of the Company's history between 1898–1948*, privately printed, 1948, pp. 10–11).

Derwent, Harcourt Vanden Bempde-Johnstone, Baron (1829–1916); 3rd Bt 1869; Lib. MP Scarborough 1869–80; Baron Derwent 1881; retired from the Commons to provide a seat for J.G. Dodson, later Lord Monk Bretton, Pres., Local Govt Bd 1880–2, after Dodson's election for Chester was declared void.

Devonport, Hudson Ewbanke Kearley, Baron (1856–1934); Parl. Sec., Bd of Trade 1905–9; Lib. MP Devonport 1892–1910; chairman, Port of London Authority 1909–25 after conducting Port of London bill through the Commons 1908; PC 1909; Food Controller 1916–17; Bt 22 July 1908, Baron Devonport 1910, Vt 1917.

Dewar, Arthur (1860–1917); Lib. MP Edinburgh (South) 1899–1900, 1906–10; Solicitor General, Scotland 1909–10; KC Scotland 1904; Senator, College of Justice, Scotland 1910–17; Baron Dewar (a judicial life peerage) 1910; his father founded the whisky distilling company.

Dickinson, Willoughby Hyett (1859–1943); Lib. MP St Pancras (North) 1906–18; suffragist; joined Labour Party

1930; member, LCC 1889–1907 (dep. chairman 1892–6; chairman 1899–1900); chairman, London Liberal Federation 1896–1918; PC 1914; chairman, League of Nations Society 1915–18; Life President, World Alliance for promoting international friendship through the churches; KBE 1918; Baron Dickinson 1930.

Dilke, Sir Charles Wentworth, Bt (1843–1911); Lib. MP Chelsea 1868–86, Gloucestershire (Forest of Dean) 1892–1911; 2nd Bt 1869; U. Sec. of St., Foreign Affairs 1880–2; Pres., Local Govt Bd 1882–5.

Donald, Robert (1860–1933); editor, *The Daily Chronicle* 1904–18; publicity director, Gordon Hotels 1899–1904; prospective Lib. candidate West Ham (North) 1903–04; GBE 1923. JAP actually wrote 'McDonald' in his diary: Donald was Scottish.

Duckworth, Sir James (1840–1915); Lib. MP Lancashire (Middleton) 1897–1900, Stockport 1906–10; mill-hand at age eight; proprietor, *Cheshire County News* and *Manchester Weekly Chronicle*; director, Boot's the chemist; large scale provision-merchant; an active United Free Methodist; Mayor, Rochdale 1891–3, 1910–11. His knighthood was announced 9 Nov. 1908.

Edward VII, King (1841–1910); reigned 1901–10.

Elgin, Victor Alexander Bruce, Earl of (1849–1917); Sec. of St., Colonial Affairs 1905–8; 9th Earl 1863; Treasurer of Household and 1st Commissioner of Works 1886; Viceroy, India 1894–9.

Elibank, Alexander W.C.O. Murray, Master of (1870–1920); Comptroller of Household and Scottish Lib. Whip 1906–9; Lib. MP Edinburghshire 1900–5, 1910–12, Peebles and Selkirk 1906–10; U. Sec. of St., India 1909–10; Patronage Sec., Treasury 1910–12; PC 1911; Baron Murray of Elibank 1912.

Ellis, John Edward (1841–1910); Lib. MP Nottinghamshire (Rushcliffe) 1885–1910; engineer and colliery manager; U. Sec. of St., India 1905–6; PC 1906.

Emmott, Alfred (1858–1926); Lib. MP Oldham 1899–1911; cotton-spinner; PC 1908; Baron Emmott 1911; U. Sec. of St., Colonial Affairs 1911–14; 1st Commissioner of Works 1914–15; Director, War Trade Department 1915–19; chairman, FO committee to collect information on Russia 1920; an Anglican but Quaker-educated.

Engleheart, Sir (John) Gardner Dillman (1823–1923); member, Council of Duchy of Lancaster 1901–12; barrister 1849; private sec. to Duke of Newcastle 1859–64; Comptroller, Household of Prince and Princess Christian 1866–9; Clerk, Council of Duchy 1872–99; Kt 1892.

Erskine, David Charles (1866–1922); Lib. MP Perthshire (Western) 1906–10; chartered accountant; sec. to Gov. Gen., Canada 1897–8; member and chairman, Bd of Trustees, National Galleries of Scotland 1908–22; pps to Sec. for Scotland 1906–10.

Evans, Sir Samuel Thomas (1859–1918); Solicitor-General 1908–10; Lib. MP Glamorganshire (Mid) 1890–1910; barrister 1891; QC 1901; specialised in workmen's compensation and trade union cases; Recorder, Swansea 1906–8; Kt 1908; Presiding Judge, Probate,

Divorce and Admiralty Division 1910–18; Prize Court 1914–18; GCB 1916.

Farwell, Sir George (1845–1915); Ld Justice of Court of Appeal 1906–13; barrister 1871; QC 1891; additional judge, Chancery Division 1899–1906; Kt 1899; chairman, royal commission on purchase of supplies for the army in S. Africa 1906; the first judge to rule against the Amalgamated Society of Railway Servants in the Taff Vale case. His finding against Sir J.W. Pease in the Portsmouth (q.v.) case ruined the Peases.

Fawcett, Millicent Garrett (1847–1929); president, National Union of Women's Suffrage Societies 1897–1918; dissociated herself from the militant Women's Social and Political Union; m. Henry Fawcett, Professor of Economics at Cambridge and Lib. MP Brighton 1865–74; she and her husband were among the founders of what became Newnham College, Cambridge; joined women's suffrage committee 1867; DBE 1925.

Fielding, William Stevens (1848–1929); Canadian Min. of Finance 1896–1911, 1921–25; journalist for Halifax *Morning Chronicle*; Prime Minister, Nova Scotia 1884–96; represented Canada at League of Nations 1922.

Fisher, John Arbuthnot, Baron (1841–1920); 1st Sea Ld 1904–10, 1914–15; entered navy 1854; Director, Naval Ordnance 1886–91; leading developer of the torpedo; Rear-Admiral 1890; Controller of Navy and a Ld of Adm. 1892–7; KCB 1894; C-in-C North America and West Indies Station 1897–9, Mediterranean 1899–1902; GCB 1902; 2nd Sea Lord 1902–3; recorganised training and education of naval officers; C-in-C Portsmouth 1903–4; Naval ADC to Edward VII 1904–10; reorganised fleet distribution with Germany as most likely enemy; principal supporter of the Dreadnought; OM 1905; GCVO 1909; Baron Fisher 1909 (motto 'Fear God and Dread Nought'); chaired royal commission which recommended change from coal to oil as naval fuel.

Fitzmaurice, Lord Edmond Fitzmaurice, Baron (1846–1935); Lib. MP Wiltshire (Cricklade) 1898–1905, Calne 1868–85, U. Sec. of St., Foreign Affairs 1882–5; Chancellor, Duchy of Lancaster 1908–9; Baron Fitzmaurice 1906.

Fitzmaurice, Maurice (1861–1924); Chief Engineer, LCC 1901–12; Kt 1912; consultant civil engineer 1912–24; his projects included the Forth Bridge, Blackwall Tunnel, Aswan Dam, Vauxhall Bridge, Rotherhithe Tunnel and the addition of 87 miles of piping to London's sewerage system. In 1915 he advised the War Office on drainage in Flanders.

FitzRoy, Sir Almeric William (1851–1935); Clerk, Privy Council 1898–1923; private sec., Duke of Devonshire 1895–8; KCVO 1909; KCB 1911; published *The History of the Privy Council* (J. Murray, 1928).

Fleming, Sir John (1847–1925); timber merchant; Provost, Aberdeen 1898–1902; Kt 26 June 1908.

Fordham, Sir (Herbert) George (1854–1929); brewer; barrister; chairman, Cambridge County Council 1904–19; cartographer and advocate of the study of historical geography in schools and universities; Kt 1908.

Frampton, Sir George James (1860–1928); sculptor and craftsman; his work included 'Peter Pan' in Kensington Gardens, the lions in front of the British Museum, and six statues of Queen Victoria; RA; FSA; Kt 1908.

Frederick, Lt Col. Sir Charles Arthur Andrew (1861–1913); Master of King's Household 1907–13; Dep. Master 1901–7; KCVO 1908; GCVO 1910; KCB 1911.

Fuller, Sir John Michael Fleetwood, Bt (1864–1915); Vice-Chamberlain, Household 1907–11; Lib. MP Wiltshire (Westbury) 1900–11; ADC to Viceroy of India 1894–5; Junior Ld of Treasury 1906–7; Gov., Victoria 1911–14; Bt 1910. 'If Johnny Fuller, with a stake in the country, an officer in the Yeomanry, playing polo, etc, connives at socialism and bolsters up the trade, it is not easy to convince Mr Jones the solicitor, or Mr Smith the builder, or Tom, Dick, and Harry, that we are being beaten in manufacture and threatened with defeat in War.' (George Wyndham to the Hon. Percy Wyndham, 11 Jan. 1910, J.W. MacKail and Guy Wyndham, *Life and Letters of George Wyndham*, 2 vols, Hutchinson, Zurls, n.d. [1924], vol. II, p. 648). Fuller, an alcoholic, was Charles Hobhouse's brother-in-law.

Furness, Christopher Furness, Baron (1852–1912); shipowner, shipbuilder, and industrialist; Lib. MP Hartlepool 1891–5, 1900–10; Kt 1895; Baron Furness 1910.

George V, King (1865–1936); reigned 1910–1936. For the first 26 years of his life his elder brother, Prince Albert Edward, Duke of Clarence, had been heir apparent.

Ghali, Boutros, Pasha (1846–1910); Prime Minister, Egypt 1909–Feb. 1910; a Christian Copt; civil servant; Min. of Finance 1893–1905; Foreign Min. 1905–10; first native-born Prime Minister.

Gilbey, Sir Walter, Bt (1831–1914); founder of W. & A. Gilbey, wine merchants and gin manufacturers; served in parliamentary agent's office after service in Crimean hospital organisation; Bt 1893; keen horse-breeder.

Gladstone, Dorothy Mary Gladstone, Viscountess (1876–1953); dau. of Sir Richard Horner Paget, 1st Bt; m. Herbert Gladstone in 1901.

Gladstone, Herbert John Gladstone, Viscount (1854–1930); Sec. of St., Home Affairs 1905–10; youngest son of W.E. Gladstone; Lib. MP Leeds (West) 1880–1910; Fin. Sec., War 1886; U. Sec. of St., Home Affairs 1892–4; 1st Commissioner of Works 1894–5; Lib. Ch. Whip 1899–1906; Gov. Gen., S. Africa 1910–14; Vt Gladstone 1910. Described by David Lloyd George as '... the best living embodiment of the Liberal doctrine that quality is not hereditary (Laughter, Cheers)' (*The Times*, 16 Oct. 1922).

Godfrey-Faussett, Capt. Bryan Godfrey (1863–1945); equerry to Prince of Wales (King George V from 1910) 1901–36; R.N. (retd 1906); extra equerry to King Edward VIII 1936 and King George VI 1937–1945; KCVO 1919; GCVO 1932. Godfrey-Faussett's wife, Eugénie, the sister of JAP's Liberal parliamentary colleague, Dudley Ward, was an intimate friend of Captain David Beatty, who served as ADC to King Edward VII 1908–10.

Gorell, John Gorell Barnes, Baron (1848–1913); Presiding Judge, Probate, Divorce and Admiralty Division 1905–Feb. 1909 (Judge from 1892); barrister 1876; QC 1888; specialised in commercial and admiralty cases; Kt 1892; PC 1905; Baron Gorell 1909; chairman 1909 Royal Commission on Divorce.

Gorst, Sir (John) Eldon (1861–1911); British consul-general, Egypt 1907–11; eldest son of Sir John Eldon Gorst; barrister 1885; diplomat 1887–1901; adviser, Egyptian Min. of Interior 1894–8; financial adviser 1898–1904; Asst U. Sec. of St., Foreign Affairs 1904–7; KCB 1902; GCMG 1911 'long after he had ceased to be conscious' (Ronald Storrs, *Orientations*, Nicholson & Watson, 1945, p. 77).

Gosford, Archibald Brabazon Sparrow Acheson, Earl of (1841–1922); Vice-Chamberlain to Queen Alexandra 1901–21; 4th Earl 1864; Ld of Bedchamber of Prince of Wales 1886–1901.

Granard, Bernard Arthur William Patrick Hastings Forbes, Earl of (1874–1948); Asst Postmaster-General 1906–9; 8th Earl 1889; ADC to Ld Lt, Ireland 1896–9, to GOC 1st Division, Aldershot 1904–5; Lord-in-Waiting 1905–7; Master of the Horse 1907–15, 1924–36; PC 1907; Senator, Eire 1922–34. Fellow officers in the Scots Guards sent him a telegram late in 1905, purportedly from Campbell-Bannerman, summoning him to accept an under-secretaryship. Meanwhile Lord Tweedmouth had passed on to CB a letter from Lord Carrington on 16 November 1905 describing Granard as 'a very good beast, ... dying to be made a Lord in Waiting, being a "Roman

Candlestick" he might be useful.'
(Campbell-Bannerman MSS, Add. MSS
52518, ff. 12–13). Thus, when the
unsuspecting Granard arrived unbidden,
CB spiked the pranksters by finding him
a place.

**Grey, Albert Henry George Grey,
Earl** (1851–1917); Gov. Gen. and C-in-
C, Canada 1904–11; his term of office
was twice extended: first because of his
own popularity, and then to
accommodate the Duke of Connaught;
grandson of 2nd Earl Grey, the Prime
Minister, and a cousin of Edward Grey;
Lib. MP Northumberland (South) 1880–
5, Northumberland (Tyneside) 1885–6;
succ. uncle 1894; director, British South
Africa Company 1889–1904;
Administrator, Rhodesia 1896–7; Ld Lt,
Northumberland 1899–1904.

Grey, Sir Edward, Bt (1862–1933);
Sec. of St., Foreign Affairs 1905–16;
Lib. MP Northumberland (Berwick-on-
Tweed) 1885–1916; succ. grandfather as
3rd Bt 1882; sent down from Balliol
College for incorrigible idleness 1884;
U. Sec. of St., Foreign Affairs 1892–5;
director and chairman North-Eastern
Railway; Vt Grey of Fallodon 1916.
Grey and JAP were both tutored by
Mandell Creighton.

Guest, Hon. Frederick Edward (1875–
1937); asst private sec. to Winston
Churchill 1907–10; Lib. MP Dorset
(Eastern) 1910–1922, Gloucester
(Stroud) 1923–4, Bristol (North) 1924–
9; Con. MP Plymouth (Drake) 1931–7;
commissioned in 1st Life Guards, served
White Nile, South African War, and
India; ADC to Sir John French 1915,
ASO in East Africa 1916-17; Junior Ld
of Treasury 1911–12; Treasurer of
Household 1912–15; Jt Patronage Sec.,

Treasury and Co. Lib. Ch. Whip 1917–
21; Sec. of St., Air 1921–2.

Guest, Hon. Ivor Churchill (1873–
1939); Lib. Unionist, then Lib. MP
Plymouth 1900–6, Cardiff 1906–10; a
Unionist Free Trader he crossed the
floor in April 1904; Baron Ashby St
Ledgers 1910; PC 1910; Paymaster-
General 1910–12; Ld-in-Waiting 1913–
15; succ. father as 2nd Baron Wimborne
1914; Ld Lt, Ireland 1915–18; Vt
Wimborne 1918; 1st Pres., National Lib.
Party 1931; m. in 1902 Hon. Alice
Katherine Sibell Grosvenor (d. 1948).

Gulland, John William (1864–1920);
Lib. MP Dumfries Burghs 1906–18;
corn merchant; director, Edinburgh
Chamber of Commerce; lecturer on
Commercial Practice, Heriot-Watt
College 1898–9; member, Edinburgh
School Board 1900–6; member,
Edinburgh Town Council 1904–6; Sec.,
Scottish Liberal Committee in House of
Commons 1906–9; Scottish Whip 1909–
15; Joint Parl. Sec., Treasury 1915–16.

Gurdon, Sir William Brampton
(1840–1910); Lib. MP Norfolk (North)
1899–1910; Treasury clerk 1864–1885;
KCMG 1882; PC 1907; Ld Lt, Suffolk
1907–10.

Haldane, Richard Burdon (1856–
1928); Sec. of St., War 1905–12; Lib.
MP Haddingtonshire 1885–1911; Ld
Chancellor 1912–15, 1924; Leader of
Labour peers 1925–8; Vt Haldane 1911.
**Halsbury, Hardinge Stanley Giffard,
Earl of** (1823–1921); barrister 1850;
Solicitor-General 1875–80; Con. MP
Launceston 1877–85; Ld Chancellor
1885–Jan 1886, July 1886–92, 1895–
1905; Baron Halsbury 1885, Earl of
Halsbury 1898.

Hamilton, John Andrew (1859–1934); judge, King's Bench 1909–12; barrister 1883; KC 1901; appeal judge 1912; Ld of Appeal in Ordinary 1913–30; Baron Sumner (life peerage) 1913; took leading part in work of Prize Court 1914–18; Vt 1927; one of only three judges whose judgements were of included in Quiller-Couch's *Oxford Book of English Prose.*

Hamilton, Lord George Francis (1845–1927); chairman, royal commission on the poor law and unemployment 1905–9; Con. MP Middlesex 1868–85, Middlesex (Ealing) 1885–1906; U. Sec. of St., India 1874–8; Vice-Pres. of Council (Minister responsible for Education) 1878–80; 1st Ld, Adm. 1885–6, 1886–92; Sec. of St., India 1895–1903; chairman, royal commission on Mesopotamia 1916–17; leading Freemason.

Harcourt, Lewis (1863–1922); 1st Commissioner of Works 1905–10, 1915–16; private sec. to his father, Sir William Harcourt, at the Home Office and Treasury, and in Opposition 1881–1904; Lib. MP Lancashire (Rossendale) 1904–17; Sec. of St., Colonial Affairs 1910–15; Vt Harcourt 1917; known to his friends as 'Loulou'. Active in party organisations, particularly the Home Counties Liberal Federation, he was a founder of the Free Trade Union. His sudden death in 1922 was attributed to 'misadventure'. He m. 1899 Mary Ethel 'Molly' (d. 1961), dau. of Walter Hayes Burns, the New York banker, and niece of J. Pierpont Morgan.

Harcourt, Sir William George Granville Venables Vernon (1827–1904); barrister 1854; QC 1866; Whewell Professor of International Law at Cambridge 1869–87; Lib. MP Oxford 1868–1880, Derby 1880–95,

Monmouthshire (West) 1895–1904; Solicitor-General 1873; Kt 1873; Sec. of St., Home Affairs 1880–5; Chancellor of Exchequer 1886, 1892–5; aspired to premiership when Gladstone resigned in 1894 but the Queen sent for Lord Rosebery.

Hardie, James Keir (1856–1915); Lab. MP Merthyr Tydfil 1900–15, West Ham (South) 1892–5; miner and journalist; founder, Scottish Labour Party 1888; founder, *Labour Leader* 1889; chairman, Independent Labour Party 1893–1900, 1913–15; helped form Labour Representation Committee 1900; first chairman, Parliamentary Labour Party 1906–7.

Hardy, Sir Herbert Hardy Cozens (1838–1920); Master of the Rolls 1907–1918; barrister 1862; QC 1882; Lib. MP Norfolk (Northern) 1885–99; judge, Chancery Division 1899–1901; Kt 1899; Ld Justice of Appeal 1901–7; Baron Cozens-Hardy 1914.

Harrington, Timothy Charles (1851–1910); Irish Nationalist MP Dublin (Harbour) 1885–1910, Co. Westmeath 1883–5; teacher and journalist; sec., Land League 1882; sec., National League 1882; organiser of the 'Plan of Campaign'; barrister 1887; close friend of Parnell and continued to support him after the divorce case had split the Irish party; Ld Mayor of Dublin 1901–3.

Hatch, Sir Ernest Frederic George, Bt (1859–1927); Lib. Unionist, then Lib. MP Lancashire (Gorton) 1895–1906 (a Unionist Free Trader he crossed the floor to the Liberals in March 1905 and retired in Jan. 1906); m. a dau. of 9th Duke of Leeds; wine merchant; traveller and author; chairman of many departmental committees; Bt 1908; KBE 1920.

Healy, Timothy Michael (1855–1931); Irish Nationalist MP Wexford 1880–3, Co. Monaghan 1883–5, Londonderry (South) 1885–6, Longford (North) 1887–92, Louth (North) 1892–1910, Cork (North East) 1910–18; Gov. Gen., Irish Free State 1922–8. Called to Irish bar 1884, he did not become an Irish QC till 1899. From being one of Parnell's most ardent supporters he became one of his most vigorous attackers when he feared that Parnell's involvement in a divorce scandal would lose the Irish Nationalist cause Gladstone's support.

Hemmerde, Edward George (1871–1948); Lib. MP Denbighshire (Eastern) 1906–10, Norfolk (North-West) 1912–18; Lab. MP Cheshire (Crewe) 1922–4; barrister; Recorder, Liverpool 1909–48; won Diamond Sculls, Henley 1900; bailed out of financial woes in 1909 with £10,000 collected from parliamentary colleagues by Horatio Bottomley (Churchill, *Winston S. Churchill*, vol. II, Companion Part 2, p. 917).

Henderson, Arthur (1863–1935); trade unionist; agent to Sir J.W. Pease, JAP's father, 1895–1903 at Durham (Barnard Castle); after Sir Joseph's death he was elected as Independent Lab. MP for the division 1903–18, Lancashire (Widnes) 1919–22, Newcastle (East) 1923, Burnley 1924–31, Derbyshire (Clay Cross) 1933–5; sec., Labour Party 1911–34; chairman, Parliamentary Labour Party (after MacDonald had resigned at outbreak of war) 1914–17; Pres., Bd of Education 1915–16; Paymaster-General 1916; Min. without Portfolio 1916–17; responsible for reorganisation of Labour Party in 1918 and new constitution encouraging constituency organisations; Lab. Ch. Whip 1914, 1921–3; Sec. of St., Home Affairs 1924; Sec. of St., Foreign Affairs 1929–31; refused to accept 1931 financial cuts, becoming Leader of Labour Party in opposition; pres., World Disarmament Conference 1932–5; Nobel Peace Prize 1934; Wesleyan lay preacher.

Henry, Charles Solomon (1860–1919); Lib. MP Shropshire (Wellington) 1906–18; Co. Lib. MP Shropshire (Wrekin) 1918–19; a wealthy Australian Jew; educated in England and Germany; established C.S. Henry & Co., metal merchants 1882; Bt 1911; m. Julia, dau. of American mining magnate, Leonard Lewisohn. The Henrys entertained political colleagues at Carlton Gardens, on their private nine-hole golf course at Brooklands near Wargrave, and at Parkwood, Henley on-Thames, where the parliamentary cricket match was played. Friends of the Rufus Isaacs, and the Ivor Herberts, they had become close to Lloyd George following the death of his daughter Mair late in 1907 and hosted his trip to Germany in August 1908 (see 4 Oct. 1908).

Henry, Sir Edward Richard (1850–1931); Commissioner, Metropolitan Police 1903–1918; Indian civil servant 1873-1900; special duties, South Africa 1900–1; Asst Commissioner, Metropolitan Police 1901–3; KCVO 1906; KCB 1910; GCVO 1911; Bt 1918. His classification of finger prints was published by the Indian government in 1900 and adopted world-wide.

Henry, Julia (d. 1927), eldest dau. of Leonard Lewisohn, the American 'copper king'; m. (Sir) Charles Henry 1892. Lloyd George's elder son found her attractive and recalled a conversation with his father from which he concluded that the relationship was not platonic (Earl Lloyd George, *Lloyd George*, Frederick Muller, 1960, pp. 107-9). Frances Stevenson recorded that Julia Henry was still 'quite mad' on Lloyd George in 1915 and 1919: 'She ... does not seem to have any pride or self-respect where he is concerned.' She would invite people to dinner to meet him, despite his continued refusal to go, and would then 'explain' to her guests that he preferred to dine alone with her (A.J.P. Taylor, ed., *Lloyd George: A Diary by Frances Stevenson*, Hutchinson, 1971, pp. 74, 190). The relationship ended in 1920 in recriminations over Lloyd George's alleged misuse of £20,000 donated by American friends of the Henrys for British war charities. (Lady Henry MSS).

Hewett, Sir John Prescott (1854–1942); Lt Gov., United Provinces 1907–12; Indian Civil Service 1875; member, Gov. Gen's Council, 1907–12; Kt 1907; chairman, Durbar Committee 1910–13; Con. MP Bedfordshire (Luton) 1922–3.

Hobhouse, Charles Edward Henry (1862–1941); Fin. Sec., Treasury 1908–11; Lib. MP Bristol (East) 1900–18, Wiltshire (Devizes) 1892–5; asst private sec. to U. Sec. of St., Colonial Affairs 1892–5; U. Sec. of St., India 1907–8; PC 1909: Chancellor, Duchy of Lancaster 1911–14; Postmaster-General 1914–15; 4th Bt 1916.

House, William (1854–1917); president, Durham Miners' Association 1900–17;

Durham County Councillor and Alderman 1893–1917; vice-pres., Miners' Federation of Great Britain 1914–17; bottom of the poll in a three cornered contest at Bishop Auckland, January 1910. He stood and lost again in December 1910, and was defeated at the Houghton-le-Spring by-election in 1913 at which the majority of miners supported the Liberal candidate.

Howe, Richard George Penn Curzon, Earl (1861–1929); Ld Chamberlain to Queen Alexandra 1903–25; as Vt Curzon, Con. MP Buckinghamshire (Wycombe) 1885–1900; Treasurer of Household 1896–1900; 4th Earl 1900; Ld-in-Waiting to Queen Victoria 1900–1 and to Edward VII 1901–3; his first wife was Lady Georgina Elizabeth, 5th dau. of the 7th Duke of Marlborough.

Hudson, Sir Robert Arundell (1864–1927); sec., National Liberal Federation 1893–1922; hon. sec., . 1895–1927; asst sec., National Liberal Federation 1886–93; Kt 1906; m., as his 2nd wife, widow of Vt Northcliffe.

Hutton, Alfred Eddison (1865–1947); Lib. MP West Riding of Yorkshire (Morley) 1892–1910; a temporary chairman of committees 1907–09; manufacturer; elected unopposed in 1906 but retired in Jan. 1910.

Ilkeston, (Balthazar) Walter Foster, Baron (1840–1913); Lib. MP Derbyshire (Ilkeston) 1887–1910, Chester 1885–6; Professor of Medicine, Birmingham 1864–92; Kt 1886; Chairman, National Liberal Federation 1886–90; Parl. Sec., Local Govt Bd 1892–5; pres., Land Law Reform Association 1890–1908; PC 1906; Baron Ilkeston 1910.

Isaacs, Sir Rufus Daniel (1860–1935); Lib. MP Reading 1904–13; spent his early years in family fruit merchandising business; barrister 1887; QC 1898; specialised in commercial and trade union cases; Solicitor-General Mar.–Oct. 1910; Kt 1910; Attorney-General 1910–13 (first attorney-general in Cabinet 1912–13); PC 1911; Ld Chief Justice 1913–21; Baron Reading 1914; led Anglo-French mission to USA to ask for American credits, September 1915; Vt Reading 1916; High Commissioner to USA and Canada 1917; Earl of Reading 1917; Ambassador to USA 1918–19; Viceroy, India 1921–6; Marquess of Reading 1926; Sec. of St., Foreign Affairs 1931.

Islington, John Poynder Dickson-Poynder, Baron (1866–1936); Con. then Lib. MP Wiltshire (Chippenham) 1892–1910 (a Unionist Free Trader, he crossed the floor to the Liberals in May 1904); succ. uncle as 6th Bt 1884; member, LCC 1898–1904; ADC to Lord Methuen in S. Africa War; Gov. Gen., New Zealand 1910–12; Baron Islington 1910; PC 1911; U. Sec. of St., Colonial Affairs 1914–15; U. Sec. of St., India 1915–18; chairman, National Savings Committee 1920–6.

James, (Mary) Venetia (d. 1948); dau. of George Bentinck; cousin of Lady Ottoline Morrell, both of them grand-daughters of the 3rd Duke of Portland; m. J. Arthur James, joint heir to an American railway and copper fortune 1885. With Arthur's brother Willie and his wife, part of King Edward VII's circle, fond of horse-racing and German spas. They moved into George Bentinck's former house at 3 Grafton St in the summer of 1893 (Christopher Simon Sykes, *Country House Camera,* Weidenfeld and Nicolson, 1980, p. 153;

Sir Sidney Lee, *King Edward VII, A Biography,* 2 vols, Macmillan, 1925/27, vol. II, pp. 65, 392, 694; Sir Frederick Ponsonby, Lord Sysonby, *Recollections of Three Reigns,* Eyre & Spottiswoode, 1951, p. 21). Her enthusiasm and 'meaningless thrift' as a hostess are recalled in Hon. Sir Edward Cadogan, *Before the Deluge* Memories and Reflections 1880–1914, John Murray, 1961, pp. 167–9. Hilaire Belloc regaled his friends with a ballad whose leading line was 'And Mrs James will entertain the King.' (W.S. Blunt's diary, 5 Dec. 1909, in Blunt, *My Diaries,* p. 699). On King Edward's death his mistress Alice Keppel took refuge from creditors with Mrs James in Grafton St (Anita Leslie, *Edwardians in Love,* Arrow Books, 1974 [1st edn Hutchinson 1972] p. 340).

Johnson, John (1850–1910), treasurer, Durham Miners' Association from 1890; though a member of the ILP was adopted by Liberals at Gateshead, winning a by-election in January 1904. He dropped to the bottom of the poll in January 1910 when he joined the Labour Party and the Liberals successfully ran a candidate of their own. He was actually opposed by the miners at the election because of his support for the Miners' Eight Hours Act.

Jones, Rev. Evan (1836–1915); Calvinist Methodist Minister; pastor of Moriah, Caernarvon 1875–1906; first pres., National Council of Free Churches of England and Wales 1909; noted preacher and publicist.

Kemp, Sir George (1866–1945); Lib. Unionist MP Lancashire (Heywood) 1895–1906, Lib. MP Manchester (North-West) 1910–12; flannel manufacturer; fought in both the South African and First World Wars; Kt 1909; Baron Rochdale 1913.

Keppel, Hon. Derek (1863–1944); equerry to Prince of Wales (King George V from 1910) 1893–1936; Master of Household 1910–36; KCVO 1911; equerry to King Edward VIII 1936.

Kilbracken, (John) Arthur Godley, Baron (1847–1932); Permanent U. Sec. of St., India 1883–1909; private sec. to W.E. Gladstone 1872–4, 1880–2; Fellow, Hertford College, Oxford 1874–81; GCB 1908; Baron Kilbracken 1909.

King-Harman, Sir Charles Anthony (1851–1939); High Commissioner, Cyprus 1904–11; auditor-general, Barbados 1883–93; colonial sec., Mauritius 1893–7; administrator, St Lucia 1897–1900; Gov., Sierra Leone 1900–4; KCMG 1900.

Kitchener, Horatio Herbert Kitchener, Viscount (1850–1916); C-in-C, India 1902–9; soldier and administrator; served in Franco-Prussian war 1870; Palestine Exploration Fund 1874–8; surveyed Cyprus 1878–82; in Sudan Expedition 1884–5; Gov. Gen., Eastern Sudan 1886–8; Adjutant-General, Egyptian Army 1888–92; Sirdar, Egyptian Army 1892–9; KCMG 1894; Baron Kitchener 1898; Chief of Staff, South Africa 1899–1900, C-in-C 1900–2; Vt Kitchener 1902; FM 1909; H.M.'s Agent and Consul General, Egypt 1911–14; Sec. of St., War 1914–16; Earl Kitchener of Khartoum 1914; drowned on his way to Russia.

Kleinwort, Sir Alexander Drake, Bt (1858–1935); merchant banker and insurer; Bt 25 Nov. 1909.

Knollys, Francis Knollys, Baron (1837–1924); private sec. to King Edward VII 1870–1910; private sec. to King George V 1910–13; PC 1910; Baron Knollys 1902, Vt Knollys 1911.

Lamont, Norman (1869–1949); Lib. MP Bute 1905–10; pps to Winston Churchill 1909–1910; asst private sec. to Campbell-Bannerman 1906–08; hon. sec., Scottish Liberal Association 1904–8; 2nd Bt 1913; Member, Legislative Council, Trinidad 1915–23.

Lang, (William) Cosmo Gordon (1864–1945); Canon, St Paul's and Suffragan Bishop, Stepney 1901–8; read for the bar under Sir W. Robson; ordained 1891; achieved fame as a preacher, particularly for the Church of England's Men's Society; Archbishop, York 1909–28; PC 1909; Archbishop, Canterbury 1928–42; Baron Lang of Lambeth 1942. .

Lansdowne, Henry Charles Keith Petty-Fitzmaurice, Marquess of (1845–1927); leader of Con. peers 1903–16; 5th Marquess 1866, Junior Ld of Treasury 1869–72; U. Sec. of St., War 1872–4; U. Sec. of St., India 1880; Gov. Gen., Canada 1883–8; Viceroy, India 1888–94; Sec. of St., War 1895–1900; Sec. of St., Foreign Affairs 1900–5; Min. without portfolio 1915–16. Lansdowne was a Lib. till 1880.

Law, Andrew Bonar (1858–23); Con. MP Camberwell (Dulwich) 1906–10, Glasgow (Blackfriars) 1900–6, Lancashire (Bootle) 1911–18, Glasgow (Central) 1918–23; iron merchant; Parl. Sec., Bd of Trade 1902–5; leader, Con. Party 1911–21, 1922–3; Sec. of St., Colonial Affairs 1915–16; Chancellor of Exchequer 1916–19; member, War Cabinet 1916–19; Ld Privy Seal 1919–21; Prime Minister 1922–3.

Lawrence, Hon. Charles Napier (1855–1927); merchant; director (chairman 1921–4) London and North-Western Railway 1884–1927; Baron Lawrence of Kingsgate 1923; m. in 1881 Catherine Sumner (d. 1934), an American, niece of former U.S. Ambassador in London, James Gerard.

Layland-Barratt, Sir Francis, Bt (1860–1933); Lib. MP Devon (Torquay) 1900–10, Cornwall (St Austell) 1915–18; High Sheriff, Cornwall 1897; Bt 23 July 1908.

Lee, Arthur Hamilton (1868–1947); Con. MP Hampshire (Fareham) 1900–18; soldier 1888–93; professor of military history, strategy and tactics, Royal Military College, Kingston, Canada 1893–8; *Daily Chronicle* special correspondent in Klondyke Gold Rush 1896; military attaché in Washington 1898–1900; Civil Ld, Adm. 1903–5; opposition spokesman on naval affairs 1906–14; special service with Expeditionary Force 1914–15; Parl. Military Sec. to Min. of Munitions 1915–16; personal Military Sec. to Lloyd George at War Office 1916; KCB 1916; Director-General, Food Production 1917–18; Baron Lee of Fareham 1918; Pres., Bd of Agriculture & Fisheries 1919–21; First Ld, Adm. 1921–2; delegate, Washington Disarmament Conference 1921–2; Vt 1922. In 1921 gave Chequers plus an endowment for its upkeep, for the use of successive prime ministers; founded Courtauld Institute of Art 1932.

Lehmann, Rudolf Chambers (1856–1929); Lib. MP Leicestershire (Harborough) 1906–10; chairman, Liberal Publication Dept 1906; barrister; editor *The Daily News* 1901; on staff of *Punch* 1890–1919; oarsman and rowing coach; father of Beatrix, Rosamund, and John Lehmann. He was considered a possible successor to JAP as Chief Whip (L. Harcourt to Asquith, 26 Jan. 1910, Asquith MSS, vol. 12, f. 78).

Lever, Beatrice Levy (d. 1917) m. 1896 **Arthur Levy Lever** (1860–1924), Lib. MP Harwich 1906–10, Hackney (Central) 1922–3; Bt 1911.

Lewis, (John) Herbert (1858–1933); Junior Ld of Treasury 1905–9; Lib. MP Flint Boroughs 1892–1918, University of Wales 1918–22; friend of Lloyd George; Parl. Sec., Local Govt Bd 1909–15; PC 1912; Parl. Sec., Bd of Education 1915–22; GBE 1922.

Lewis, Sir William Thomas, Bt (1837–1914); engineer; chief agent to Marquesses of Bute, retired 1909; served on several coal-mining royal commissions; formed Monmouthshire & South Wales Coal-Owners' Association 1871; urged acceptance of sliding scale 1875; pres., Mining Association 1881; Kt 1885; Bt 1896; Baron Merthyr 1911. (John Davies, 'Aristocratic town-makers and the coal metropolis: the marquesses of Bute and the growth of Cardiff, 1776 to 1947', in David Cannadine, ed., *Patricians, power and politics in nineteenth-century towns*, Leicester University Press/St Martin's Press, New York, 1982).

Liddell, Adolphus ('Doll') George Charles (1846–1920); barrister; private sec., Ld Chancellor 1909–15; asst sec., Ld Chancellor's Office 1888–1919; CB 1908. His memoirs, *Notes From the Life of an Ordinary Mortal* (John Murray) were published in 1911. He unsuccessfully wooed Laura Tennant and Edith 'D.D.' Balfour both of whom married Alfred Lyttelton (Anita Leslie, *Edwardians in Love*, pp. 243–5).

Liverpool, Arthur William de Brito Savile Foljambe, Earl of (1870–1941); soldier; State Steward and Chamberlain, Ld Lt of Ireland 1906–8; 2nd Earl 1907; Comptroller of Household 1909–12; Governor (Gov. Gen. from 1917) and C-in-C, New Zealand 1912–20; PC 1917.

Lloyd George, David (1863–1945); Chancellor of Exchequer 1908–15; Lib. MP Caernarvon Boroughs 1890–1945 (Co. Lib. 1918–22; Nat. Lib. 1922–3); Pres., Bd of Trade 1905–8; Min. of Munitions 1915–16; Sec. of St., War 1916; Prime Minister 1916–22; Earl Lloyd-George of Dwyfor 1945.

Lochee, Edmond Robertson, Baron (1845–1911); Lib. MP Dundee 1885–1908; Civil Ld, Adm. 1892–5, Parl. Sec., Adm. 1905–8; PC 1906, Baron Lochee 1908.

Londonderry, Lady Theresa Susey Helen Stewart, Marchioness of (d. 1919); eldest dau. of the 19th Earl of Shrewsbury; m. the 6th Marquess in 1875.

Londonderry, Charles Stewart Vane-Tempest-Stewart, Marquess of (1852–1915); known as Vt Castlereagh 1872–84; Con. MP Down 1878–84; 6th Marquess 1884; Ld Lt, Ireland 1886–9; Postmaster-General 1900–2; Pres., Bd of Education 1902–5; Ld Pres., Council 1903–5.

Loreburn, Robert Threshie Reid, Baron (1846–1923); Ld Chancellor 1905–12; Lib. MP Hereford 1880–5, Dumfries Burghs 1886–1905; Solicitor-General 1894; Attorney-General 1894–5; Kt 1894; Baron Loreburn 1906, Earl

1911. A keen racquets player, he also played cricket for Oxford for three seasons; a noted wicket-keeper; pres., MCC 1907.

Lough, Thomas (1850–1922); Parl. Sec., Bd of Education 1905–8; Lib. MP Islington (West) 1892–1918; PC 1908; with Campbell–Bannerman's blessing continued as head of Lough Bros, wholesale tea merchants, after appointment as junior minister. Ramsay MacDonald got his first glimpses of political life as Lough's private secretary 1888–91.

Low, Sir James, Bt (1849–1923); maker of confectioneries, jams, and chocolates; Ld Provost, Dundee 1893–6; Kt 1895; Bt 1908.

Lowther, James William (1855–1949); Speaker of Commons 1905–21; Con. MP Rutland 1883–5, Cumberland (Penrith) 1886–1921; U. Sec. of St., Foreign Affairs 1891–2; Chairman, Ways and Means Committee and Dep. Speaker 1895–1905; PC 1898; Vt Ullswater 1921.

Lyell, Hon. Charles Henry (1875–1918); Lib. MP Dorset (Eastern) 1904–10, Edinburgh (South) 1910–16; pps to Grey 1906–11, Asquith 1911–16; severely wounded as artillery officer; asst military attaché, Washington 1918; eldest son of 1st Baron Lyell.

McCrae, Sir George (1860–1928); Lib. MP Edinburgh (East) 1899–1909, Stirling & Falkirk Burghs 1923–4; merchant hosier and mercer; member Edinburgh Corporation; Kt 1908; Vice-Pres. Local Govt Bd, Scotland; Chairman, Scottish Bd of Health 1919–22.

Macdonald, John Archibald Murray (1854–1939); Lib. MP Tower Hamlets 1892–5, Falkirk Burghs 1906–18, Stirling and Falkirk Burghs 1918–22; radical critic of Liberal government's naval expenditure; PC 1916.

MacDonald, James Ramsay (1866–1937); Lab. MP Leicester 1906–18, Glamorganshire (Aberavon) 1922–9, Durham (Seaham) 1929–31; National Lab. MP Durham (Seaham) 1931–5, Scottish Universities 1936–7; sec., Labour Representation Committee 1900–12, treasurer 1912–24; member, LCC 1900–4; chairman, Independent Labour Party 1906–8; chairman, Parliamentary Labour Party 1911–14, 1922–31; Prime Minister and Sec. of St., Foreign Affairs 1924; Prime Minister 1929–35; Ld Pres. of Council 1935–7.

MacDonnell, Anthony Patrick MacDonnell, Baron (1844–1925); entered Indian Civil Service 1865; Chief Commissioner, Central Provinces 1890–3; member, Viceroy's Council 1893–5; KCSI 1893; Lt Gov., N.W. Provinces and Oudh 1895–1901; GCSI 1897; member, Council of India 1902–5; PC 1902; Permanent U. Sec. to Ld Lt, Ireland 1902–8; Baron MacDonnell 1908; chairman, royal commission on civil service 1912–15; member, Irish Convention 1917–18. Richard Holt, his colleague on the civil service royal commission, described him as '... a very decent old boy – but peppery and commonly nicknamed the Bengal tiger ...' (diary, 22 Mar. 1914, Holt MSS). Improbable speculation in 1906 that he might become Chief Secretary for Ireland prompted a denial and the explanation: 'I am too old to learn to tell lies now.' (Sir William Orpen, *Stories of Old Ireland and Myself*, Williams and Norgate, 1924, p. 40).

McKenna, Reginald (1863–1943); 1st Ld Adm. 1908–11; Lib. MP Monmouthshire (Northern) 1895–1918; Fin. Sec., Treasury 1905–7; Pres., Bd of Education 1907–8; Sec. of St., Home Affairs 1911–15; Chancellor of Exchequer 1915–16; chairman, Midland Bank 1919–43.

McLaren, Sir Charles Benjamin Bright, Bt (1850–1934); Lib. MP Leicestershire (Bosworth) 1892-1910, Stafford 1880-6; barrister; nephew of John Bright; through his marriage he obtained interests in steel, shipbuilding, and coal; chairman, John Brown & Co., shipbuilders; his estates included the seaside resort of Prestatyn; a founder of the Eighty Club and National Liberal Club; Bt 1902; PC 1908; Baron Aberconway 1911. McLaren had written to Campbell-Bannerman on 31 May 1902 putting forward his claims for a baronetcy: as well as the 22 elections fought by him, his father, and his brother, and his services to the party, 'I suppose no man built more or finer ships for the Navy than I have ...' (Campbell-Bannerman MSS, Add. MS 52517, ff. 160–1).

Maclean, Donald (1864–1932); Lib. MP Bath 1906–Jan. 1910, Peebles Dec. 1910–22, Cornwall (Northern) 1929–32; Chairman, Ways and Means Committee and Dep. Speaker 1911–18; PC 1916; chairman, Treasury committee on reconstruction of Poor Law and House of Commons Appeal Tribunal; KBE 1917; chairman, Lib. Parliamentary Party 1919–22; Pres., Bd of Education 1931-2.

Macleod, Sir Reginald (1847–1935); Permanent U. Sec., Scotland 1902–9; Queen's and Ld Treasurer's Remembrancer 1889–1900; Registrar-

General, England and Wales 1900–2; 27th Chief of Macleod Clan; KCB 1905.

MacNeill, John Gordon Swift (1849–1926): Irish Nationalist MP Donegal (South) 1887–1918; Professor, Constitutional and Criminal Law, King's Inns, Dublin 1882–8; Professor, Constitutional Law, Irish National University 1909–26.

Maddison, Fred (1856–1937); Lib. MP Burnley 1906–1910; printer; president, TUC 1886; first Labour member of Hull Corporation; Lib. MP Sheffield (Brightside) 1897–1900; contested Darlington 1910.

Mallet, Charles Edward (1862–1947); Lib. MP Plymouth 1906–10; barrister 1889; pps to W. Runciman 1908; Fin. Sec., War Office 1910–11; Sec. for Indian Students at India Office 1912–16; Kt 1917; wrote lives of Lloyd George, Lord Cave, Herbert Gladstone, and Anthony Hope.

Manning, Brig. Gen. Sir William (Henry) (1863–1932); Indian Army 1888–1910; acting Commissioner and C-in-C, British Central Africa 1897–8, 1900–1; Inspector-Gen., King's African Rifles 1901–7; commanded Somaliland Field Force 1902–3; KCMG 1904; acting Gov. and C-in-C, Nyasaland Protectorate 1907–8; Commissioner and C-in-C, Somaliland Protectorate 1910; Gov. and C-in-C, Nyasaland Protectorate 1910–13; Gov., Jamaica 1913–18; Gov., Ceylon 1918–25.

Marchamley, George Whiteley, Baron (1855–1925); Patronage Sec., Treasury 1905–8; Cons. MP Stockport 1893–1900; Lib. MP West Riding of Yorkshire (Pudsey) 1900–8; PC 1907; Baron Marchamley 1908.

Marnham, Francis John (1853–1941); Lib. MP Surrey (Chertsey) 1906–10; member, Stock Exchange; Mayor of Torquay 1926–7.

Martin, Sir Thomas Carlaw (1850?–1920); editor, *Dundee Advertiser* and other Scottish morning journals 1887–1910; chairman, Scottish Agricultural Commissions to Canada 1908, Australia 1910; director, Royal Scottish Museum 1910–16; Kt 1909.

Masterman, Charles Frederick Gurney (1873–1927); U. Sec. of St., Local Govt Bd 1908–9; journalist and author; Lib. MP West Ham (North) 1906–11, Bethnal Green (South-west) 1911–14, Manchester (Rusholme) 1923–4; U. Sec. of St., Home Affairs 1909–12; Fin. Sec., Treasury 1912–14; PC 1912; Chancellor, Duchy of Lancaster 1914–15.

Milner, Alfred Milner, Viscount (1854–1925); barrister 1881; journalist under Morley and W.T. Stead; greatly influenced by S.A. Barnett, a co-founder of Toynbee Hall; private sec. to G.J. Goschen 1883–5 and Dec. 1886–8 when Goschen was Chancellor of Exchequer; active with Goschen in founding the Liberal Unionist Association 1886; director-general of accounts in Egypt 1890; U. Sec., Finance Ministry, Egypt 1890–2; Chairman, Bd of Inland Revenue 1892–7; KCB 1895; High Commissioner, S. Africa 1897–1905; Baron Milner 1901, Vt 1902; an ardent opponent of the 1909 Budget, the Parliament Act and Home Rule; member, War Cabinet 1916–18; Sec. of St., War April–Dec. 1918; Sec. of St., Colonial Affairs 1918–21.

Minto, Gilbert John Elliot, Earl of (1845–1914); Viceroy, India 1905–10; 4th Earl 1891; Gov. Gen., Canada 1898–1904. Francis Grenfell described him as 'a sporting fellow who has ridden three times in the Grand National, and one of the few living who has broken his neck steeplechasing'. (John Buchan, *Francis and Riversdale Grenfell: A Memoir*, Thomas Nelson, 1920, p. 69).

Mond, Sir Alfred Moritz, Bt (1868–1930); Lib. MP Chester 1906–10, Swansea (later Swansea, West) 1910–23, Carmarthen 1924–8; Bt 1910; PC 1913; 1st Commissioner of Works 1916–21; Min. of Health 1921–2; managing director and chairman, Imperial Chemical Industries Ltd and its fore-runners; Zionist; joined Con. Party 1926; Baron Melchett 1928.

Montagu, Hon. Edwin Samuel (1879–1924); pps to Asquith 1906–10; Lib. MP Cambridgeshire (Chesterton) 1906–22; U. Sec. of St., India 1910–14; Fin. Sec., Treasury 1914–Feb. 1915, May 1915–16; Chancellor, Duchy of Lancaster Feb.–May 1915, 1916; Min. of Munitions 1916; Sec. of St., India 1917–22. He described his feeling for Asquith as 'hero-worship', though his marriage in 1915 to the Hon. Venetia Stanley (1887–1948) was one of the greatest emotional blows his hero had to suffer.

Montgomery, Henry Greville (1864–1951); Lib. MP Somerset (Bridgwater) 1906–10; newspaper proprietor; founder, Institute of Clayworkers.

Morley, Arnold (1849–1916); chairman of committee, Free Trade Union: Lib. MP Nottingham 1880–95; Lib. Ch. Whip 1886–92; PC 1892; Postmaster-General 1892–5.

Morley of Blackburn, John Morley, Viscount (1838–1923); Sec. of St., India 1905–10; Vt Morley 2 May 1908 so that he might be spared attendance in the Commons; journalist; editor, *Fortnightly Review* 1867–82; editor, *Pall Mall Gazette* 1880–3; Lib. MP Newcastle-upon-Tyne 1883–95, Montrose Burghs 1896–1908; Ch. Sec., Ireland 1886, 1892–5 (JAP was his pps 1892–5); Ld Privy Seal 1910–14. Author of the *Life of Gladstone* (1903) and many other works.

Mountgarret, Henry Edmund Butler, Viscount (Irish peerage) (1844–1912); High Sheriff, West Riding of Yorkshire 1895; 14th Vt 1900; Baron Mountgarret 1911; Vicary Gibbs (in H.A. Doubleday and Lord Howard de Walden, ed., *G.E.C.'s The Complete Peerage*, St Catherine Press, 1936, vol. IX, p. 328, n.) describes him as a strong Liberal whose even stronger support for the Church of England caused him to oppose the Liberal Education Bill.

Murray, Hon. Arthur Cecil (1879–1962); Lib. MP Kincardineshire 1908–23; 4th son of 1st Vt Elibank; soldier in India; pps Parl. Sec., Bd of Trade 1908–9, to U. Sec. of St., India 1909, and to Sec. of St., Foreign Affairs 1910–14; asst military attaché, Washington 1917–18; director, London & North Eastern Railway 1923–48; author; succ. brother as 12th Baron and 3rd Vt Elibank 1951.

Murray, Sir George Herbert (1849–1936); Permanent Sec., Treasury 1903–11; civil servant 1872–1911; private sec. to W.E. Gladstone 1892–4, Lord Rosebery 1894–5; KCB 1899; GCB 1908; PC 1910; GCVO 1920.

Nash, Vaughan (1861–1932); private sec. to Asquith 1908–12; journalist, *The Daily Chronicle* 1893–9; *The Manchester Guardian* 1900, *The Daily News* 1901; private sec. to Campbell-Bannerman 1905–8; chairman, Development Commission 1912–29; Sec., Min. of Reconstruction 1917–19.

Newnes, Sir George, Bt (1851–1910); owner and founder of *The Westminster Gazette;* Lib. MP Swansea 1900–10, Cambridgeshire (Newmarket) 1885–95; Bt 1895; owner and founder, *Tit Bits* (1881), *Strand Magazine* (1891), *Country Life* (1897), *Ladies' Field* (1898). He fitted out the 1898 South Polar Expedition led by Borchgrevinck.

Norman, Sir Henry (1858–1939); Lib. MP Wolverhampton (South) 1900–10, Blackburn 1910–23; journalist on *Pall Mall Gazette* and *Daily Chronicle* (asst editor 1895); Kt 1906; hon. sec., Budget League 1909; Asst Postmaster-General Jan–Feb. 1910; Bt 1915; PC 1918; traveller, author, and pioneer in wireless telegraphy business.

Northampton, William George Spencer Scott Compton, Marquess of (1851–1913); as Earl Compton, Lib. MP Warwickshire (Stratford-upon-Avon) 1885–6, West Riding of Yorkshire (Barnsley) 1889–97; 5th Marquess 1897; member, LCC 1889–92, alderman 1892–5; Ld Lt, Warwickshire 1912–13; pres. British and Foreign Bible Society and Ragged School Union; philanthropist.

Norton, Cecil William (1850–1930); Junior Ld of Treasury 1905–10; Lib. MP Newington (West) 1892–1916; cavalry officer; Asst Postmaster-General 1910–16; Parl. Sec., Min. of Munitions 1919–21; Baron Rathcreedan 1916.

Nunburnholme, Charles Henry Wellesley Wilson, Baron (1875–1924); soldier and shipowner; Lib. MP Kingston-upon-Hull (West) 1906–7; Sheriff, Hull 1900; his father had been MP for Hull for the preceding 20 years; 2nd Baron 1907; m. a dau. of Lord Carrington; Ld Lt, East Riding of Yorkshire 1908–24.

O'Brien, William (1852–1928); Irish Nationalist MP Mallow 1883–5, Tyrone (South) 1885–6, Cork (North East) 1887–92, Cork (City) 1892–5, 1900–9, 1910–18; journalist; editor, *United Ireland* 1881; from being an extreme advocate of nationalism, he became an advocate of conciliation with Ulster and founded the All for Ireland League which had 7 MPs including Healy.

O'Hagan, Maurice Herbert Townley O'Hagan, Baron (1882–1961); Ld-in-Waiting 1907–10; succ. brother as 3rd Baron 1900; asst private sec. to 1st Ld, Adm. 1906–7; Dep. Speaker and Dep. Chairman of Committees, House of Lords, 1950–8.

Parnell, Charles Stewart (1846–91); Irish Nationalist leader; MP Co. Meath 1875–80, Cork 1880–91.

Partington, Oswald (1872–1935) and the **Hon. Clara Isobel Partington** (1880–1945). Partington, a paper manufacturer, was Lib. MP Derbyshire (High Peak) 1900–10, West Riding of Yorkshire (Shipley) 1915–18; pps to C. Hobhouse 1908; Junior Ld of Treasury 1909–11; 2nd Baron Doverdale 1925. Clara Partington was sister of the Master of Elibank. The marriage was dissolved in 1934.

Paulton, James Mellor ('Harry'), (1857–1923); Lib. MP Durham (Bishop Auckland) 1885–1910; joint hon. sec., Liberal League friend of JAP since Cambridge; war correspondent to *Manchester Examiner* (owned by his father) in Sudan Campaign; private sec. to James Bryce, Hugh Childers, and H.H. Asquith at the Home Office.

Pease, Ethel ('Elsie') (1867–1941); m. JAP in 1886. Her grand-father, Sir Henry Havelock, relieved Lucknow in 1857. Her father, Sir Henry Marshman Havelock-Allan, 1st Bt, received the VC for his conduct at the battle of Cawnpore. Her mother, Lady Alice Moreton , was 2nd dau. of the 2nd Earl of Ducie. EP was such a good horsewoman that her father said he would not permit her to marry anyone who could not out-ride her; JAP did.

Pease, Miriam Blanche (1887–1965); JAP's eldest child; a great friend of Harcourt's daughters; Inspector of Factories 1916–38; Superintending Inspector 1938–42.

Perks, Sir Robert William, Bt (1849–1934); Lib. MP Lincolnshire (Louth) 1892–1910; treasurer, Liberal League 1902–9; solicitor; a partner for 25 years of H.H. Fowler; specialised in railway and parliamentary practice; later a civil engineer; an active Methodist; originator and chairman (1906–8) of parliamentary committee of nonconformists; Bt 1908. Beatrice Webb described him in 1902 'as a repulsive being … A combination of Gradgrind, Pecksniff and Jabez Balfour.' (Norman and Jeanne MacKenzie, eds, *The Diary of Beatrice Webb*, Vol. Two 1892–1905, Virago, 1983, p. 241).

Pirrie, William James Pirrie, Baron (1847–1924); shipbuilder and shipowner; apprenticed to Harland & Wolff 1862, partner 1874, chairman 1895; Ld Mayor, Belfast 1896–7; Baron Pirrie 1906; Comptroller–General of Merchant Shipbuilding 1918; Vt 1921. Just before Pirrie's death he was described by Lord Inverforth as 'probably the richest man in England' (Arthur Pound and Samuel Taylor Moore, eds, *They Told Barron: Conversations and Revelations of … Clarence W. Barron*, Harper Brothers, New York, 1930, p. 167).

Polwarth, Walter George Hepburne Scott, Master of (1864–1944); Dep. Ld Lt, Berwickshire, Haddingtonshire and Selkirkshire; unsuccessfully opposed Haldane in Haddingtonshire elections 1892, 1895; chairman, General Board of Commissioners in Lunacy for Scotland 1897–1909; chairman, Prison Commission for Scotland 1909–29; Ld Lt, E. Lothian 1937–44; 9th Baron Polwarth 1920; Representative Peer for Scotland 1929–44.

Ponsonby, Sir Frederick Edward Grey ('Fritz') (1867–1935); son of Gen. Sir Henry Ponsonby, Queen Victoria's private sec. and brother of Arthur, the Lib. MP; asst private sec. to Queen Victoria 1895–1901; Edward VII 1901–10, George V 1910–14; KCVO 1910; Receiver-General, Duchy of Lancaster; Keeper of Privy Purse 1914–35; Baron Sysonby 1935.

Portsmouth, Newton Wallop, Earl of (1856–1917); U. Sec. of St., War 1905–8; as Vt Lymington, Lib. MP Barnstaple 1880–5, Devon (South Molton) 1885–91 (Lib. Un. 1886–91); 6th Earl 1891. Asquith tutored him in the summer of

1874. He m. JAP's cousin, Beatrice Mary Pease, in 1885. JAP's father, Sir Joseph Whitwell Pease, was one of her guardians. A law suit brought by Beatrice and her husband against her guardians led to a settlement of over £300,000 in shares, cash and costs. (Gainford MSS, 26 and 125; Kirby, *Men of Business and Politics*, Ch. 5). Portsmouth's meanness was notorious. 'Burghclere narrated that when he was dining with P. cigarettes were offered to the guests, but cigars to the host' (Charles Hobhouse's diary, 18 June 1910, Edward David, ed., *Inside Asquith's Cabinet*, From the Diaries of Charles Hobhouse, John Murray, 1977, p. 93). A large landowner in England and Ireland, Portsmouth voted with the 'die-hards' against the Parliament Bill.

Pretious, Ivy Gladys (1880–1958), was appointed secretary of the executive committee of the Free Trade Union in 1903, succeeding Leonard Hobhouse as the FTU secretary in March 1904. Her father had left the family when Ivy was three; her mother's progressive school went bankrupt in 1895. Henceforth Ivy, living at first with Frederic and Ethel Harrison, supported herself and a younger brother. After working with a music publisher, contributing cooking and dressmaking columns to *Our Home*, and teaching in Paris, she spent eighteen months in South Africa with Emily Hobhouse, caring for Boer refugees. Emily's brother, Leonard, took her into the Free Trade Union. She was a friend of Charles Masterman, Hilton Young, Francis Acland, George Trevelyan, Charles Mallet, Tom Kettle, Desmond McCarthy, and John Ward. Secretly engaged to, and jilted by, the Hon. (later Sir) Albert Napier, 9th s. of Lord Napier of Magdala; courted by Reginald McKenna; entranced by a briefly celibate Bertrand Russell; harassed in a cab by Lloyd George; proposed to by Tom Kettle MP; she married in 1909 Charles Tennyson, stepson of Augustine Birrell, junior equity counsel to the Office of Works, later a prominent businessman and writer. 'She is the sort of woman who is apparently very attractive to men & there is always somebody or something on.' (Mary Harcourt to Lewis Harcourt, 27 April 1909, Harcourt MSS uncat.). In March 1909, Miss Pretious (an anti-suffragist) and Margot Asquith were the only women admitted to a large public meeting of the FTU. Although she had organised the women's branch, chaired by Loulou Harcourt's wife, Mary, she remained as the FTU's principal London organiser until she gave up her £900 a year on her marriage. She was awarded the OBE for wartime service supervising the female staff of the Ministry of Munitions. (Hallam Tennyson, 'Sir Charles Bruce Locker Tennyson,' obituary, *Royal Society of Literature Report 1977–78*, 1979, pp. 27–9; Hallam Tennyson, *The Haunted Mind*: An Autobiography, André Deutsch, 1984, pp. 3–9; Charles Tennyson, 'Ivy Gladys Tennyson,' ts, n.d.; Bertrand Russell letters, Ivy Tennyson MSS, courtesy Hallam Tennyson).

Pretyman, Ernest George (1859–1931); Con. MP Suffolk (Woodbridge) 1895–1906, Essex (Chelmsford) 1908–1923; Civil Ld, Adm. 1900–3, 1916–19; Parl. Sec., Adm. 1903–5; Parl. Sec., Bd of Trade 1915–16.

Price, Sir Robert John (1854–1926); Lib. MP Norfolk (Eastern) 1892–1918; surgeon turned barrister; Kt 26 June 1908.

Probyn, Gen. Sir Dighton Macnaghten (1833–1924); Comptroller, Queen Alexandra's Household 1910–24; Extra Equerry to George V 1910–24; soldier; VC in Indian Mutiny; KCSI 1876; Equerry to Edward VII as Prince of Wales 1872–7; Comptroller and Treasurer 1877–91; member, Council for Duchy of Cornwall 1877–1901; Keeper of Privy Purse and Extra Equerry 1901–10; Receiver-General, Duchy of Lancaster 1901–10.

Redmond, John Edward (1856–1918); chairman of Irish MPs 1900–18; Clerk, Commons 1880; a close friend of Parnell even after the split in the Irish nationalists in 1890; Irish Nationalist MP Co. Wexford 1881–5, N. Wexford 1885–90, Waterford 1890–1918.

Redmond, William Hoey Kearney (1861–1917); Irish Nat. MP Wexford 1883–5, Fermanagh (North) 1885–91, Clare (East) 1891–1917; brother of John Redmond; killed on active service.

Rees, Sir John David (1854–1922); Lib. MP Montgomery 1906–10; Con. MP Nottingham (East) 1912–22; Madras civil servant 1875–1900; private sec. to several Governors of Madras; chairman, British Central Africa Co.; director, various Indian railways and tea companies; KCIE 1910; Bt 1919. According to the 4th Lord Glenconner (interview with CH August 1980) he was the lover of Pamela, 2nd Lady Glenconner (later Lady Grey).

Reid, Sir George Houston (1845–1918); first Australian High Commissioner, London 1910–13; barrister 1879; MLA, East Sydney 1880–4, 1885–1901; Min. of Public Instruction 1883–4; Premier, New South Wales 1894–9; MHR, East Sydney 1901–10; Prime Minister, Australia 1904–5; KCMG 1909; Lib. MP St George's Hanover Sq. 1916–18.

Riddell, Sir George Allardice (1865–1934); newspaper proprietor; solicitor 1888–1903; legal adviser and chairman, *News of the World*; Kt 1909; liaison officer between British government and press 1914–18 and British delegates and press at Paris Peace Conference; Bt 1918; Baron Riddell 1920; he gave much time and £100,000 to the Royal Free Hospital; he was also a benefactor of the Eastman Dental Hospital which has a bust of him in its lobby.

Ripon, George Frederick Samuel Robinson, Marquess of (1827–1909); Ld Privy Seal and Leader of Lib. Lords 1905–Oct. 1908; born at 10 Downing St during his father's four month term of office as Prime Minister; as Vt Goderich Lib. MP Hull 1852–3, Huddersfield 1853–7, West Riding of Yorkshire 1857–9; 2nd Earl of Ripon 1859; U. Sec. of St., War 1859–61, 1861–3; U. Sec. of St., India 1861; Sec. of St., War 1863–6; Sec. of St., India 1866; Ld Pres. of Council 1868–73; Marquess of Ripon after his success in settling the *Alabama* dispute with the U.S.A. 1871; Viceroy, India 1880–4; 1st Ld, Adm. 1886; Sec. of St., Colonial Affairs 1892–5. He became a Roman Catholic in 1874 after many years as a zealous Freemason.

Roberts, Charles Henry (1865–1959); Lib. MP Lincoln 1906–18, Derby 1922–3; U. Sec. of St., India 1914–15; Comptroller of Household 1915–16; Chairman, Cumberland County Council 1938–58.

Roberts, Sir John Herbert, Bt (1863–1956); Lib. MP Denbighshire (Western) 1892–1918; chairman, Welsh Liberal Parliamentary Party 1912–18; timber merchant; Bt 25 July 1908; Baron Clwyd 1919.

Robertson, James Patrick Bannerman Robertson, Baron (1845–1909); Ld of Appeal 1899–1909; Con. MP Buteshire 1885–91; Scottish Solicitor–General 1885–6, 1886–8; Ld Advocate 1888–91; Lord Justice-General and Pres. Court of Session 1891–9; chairman, Irish University Commission 1901–4; Life Baron and PC 1909.

Robinson, Sir Joseph Benjamin, Bt (1840–1929); South African gold and diamond mine-owner; active in Kimberley politics: his success in recruiting labourers in South Africa showed that Chinese labour was not indispensable. Bt 1908.

Robson, William Snowden Robson, Baron (1852–1918); Attorney-General 1908–10; barrister 1880; QC 1892; Lib. MP Tower Hamlets (Bow and Bromley) 1885–6, South Shields 1895–1910; Recorder, Newcastle 1895–1905; Solicitor-General 1905–8; Kt 1905; PC 1910; Ld of Appeal in Ordinary 1910–12; Baron Robson (a judicial life peerage) 1910.

Rogers, Francis Edward Newman (1868–1925); Lib. MP Wiltshire (Devizes) 1906–10; pps to C.E. Hobhouse, Fin. Sec., Treasury, 1909–10; Small Holdings Commissioner 1911–25; chairman, E. Wilts Liberal Association.

Rosebery, Archibald Philip Primrose, Earl of (1847–1929); pres., Liberal League 1902–9; succ. grandfather as 5th Earl 1868; U. Sec. of St., Home Affairs 1881–3; Ld Privy Seal 1885; 1st Commissioner of Works 1886; Sec. of St., Foreign Affairs 1886, 1892–4; Chairman LCC 1889–90, 1892; Prime Minister & Ld Pres. of Council 1894–5.

Rotherham, William Henry Holland, Baron (1849–1927); cotton manufacturer; Lib. MP Salford (North) 1892–5, West Riding of Yorkshire (Rotherham) 1899–1910; Kt 1902; pres. Associated Chambers of Commerce 1904–7; temp. Chairman, Ways & Means 1906–10; Bt 1907; Baron Rotherham 1910.

Rothschild, Nathan Mayer Rothschild, Baron (1840–1915); banker and philanthropist; Lib. MP Aylesbury 1865–85; succ. uncle as 2nd Bt 1876; Baron Rothschild 1885; Ld Lt, Buckinghamshire 1889–1915; PC 1902.

Runciman, Walter (1870–1949); Pres., Bd of Education 1908–11; Lib. MP Dewsbury 1902–18, Oldham 1899–1900, Swansea (West) 1924–9, Cornwall (St Ives) 1929–31; National Lib. MP Cornwall (St Ives) 1931–7; Parl. Sec., Local Govt Bd 1905–7; Fin. Sec., Treasury 1907–8; Pres:, Bd of Agriculture 1911–14; Pres., Bd of Trade 1914–16, 1931–37; Ld Pres. of Council 1938–9; 2nd Baron Runciman 1937; Vt 1937.

Russell, Thomas Wallace (1841–1920); Radical Unionist then Lib. MP Tyrone (South) 1886–1910 (crossed floor 1904), Tyrone (North) 1911–18; an anti-Home Ruler; principal promoter of Land Act 1896; Parl. Sec., Local Govt Bd 1895–1900; vice-pres., Dept of Agriculture & Technical Instruction for Ireland 1907–18; Bt 1917.

St Davids, John Wynford Philipps, Baron (1860–1938); Lib. MP Pembrokeshire 1898–1908, Lanarkshire (Mid) 1888–1894; barrister then financier; Ld Lt, Pembrokeshire 1911–32; Baron St Davids 6 July 1908, Vt 1918; PC 1914. His younger brothers, Ivor (later Lord Treowen, who commanded the 38th Welsh division 1915–16) and Owen (shipowner, ennobled as Lord Kylsant), were both elected as Liberal MPs in 1906.

Salisbury, James Edward Hubert Gascoyne-Cecil, Marquess of (1861–1947); ADC to George V 1910–29; Vt Cranborne 1868–1903; Con. MP Lancashire (Darwen) 1885–92, Rochester 1893–1903; U. Sec. of St., Foreign Affairs 1900–3; Ld Privy Seal 1903–5, 1924–9; Pres., Bd of Trade 1905; ADC to Edward VII 1903–10; Ld Pres. of Council and Dep. Leader of Lords 1922–4; Chancellor, Duchy of Lancaster 1922; Leader, Lords 1925–31. An ardent and vigorous churchman, he was also one of the 'Die-Hards' in 1911; throughout the 1930s he continued to agitate for Lords reform.

Samuel, Herbert Louis (1870–1963); U. Sec. of St., Home Affairs 1905–9; Lib. MP North Riding of Yorkshire (Cleveland) 1902–18, Lancashire (Darwen) 1929–35; Chancellor, Duchy of Lancaster 1909–10, May 1915–16; Postmaster-General 1910–14, May 1915–16; Pres., Local Govt Bd 1914–May 1915; Sec. of St., Home Affairs 1916, 1931–2; High Commissioner, Palestine 1920–5; C-in-C, Palestine 1922–5; a prominent Zionist; Leader of Lib. Party in Commons 1931–5, in Lords 1944–55; Vt Samuel 1937.

Sandars, John Satterfield (1853–1934); private sec. to A.J. Balfour 1895–1915; barrister 1877; private sec., Sec. of St., Home Affairs 1885–92; PC 1905.

Sandhurst, William Mansfield, Baron (1855–1921); 2nd Baron 1876; Ld-in-waiting 1880–5; U. Sec. of St., War 1886, 1892–4; Gov., Bombay 1895–9; member, government committee on Government of South Africa 1906; PC 1907; Ld Chamberlain 1912–21; Vt 1917.

Sandys, Col. Thomas Myles (1837–1911); Con. MP Lancashire (Bootle) 1885–1911; an eminent Orangeman, he resigned his seat to provide for the defeated Bonar Law in March 1911.

Sassoon, Lady (1865-1909); Aline Caroline, dau. of Baron Gustave de Rothschild; m. Sir Edward Sassoon 1887; one of the 'Souls'; 'strongly interested in spiritualism. King Edward's yacht *Aline* was named after her. A close friend of Margot Asquith and Lady Horner, she commended her children to their care when she died.

Sassoon, Sir Edward Albert, Bt (1856–1912); Con. MP Hythe 1899–1912; a Unionist Free Trader; 2nd Bt 1896. Flung from his motor car in an accident in Cannes in January 1911, he died the following year and was succeeded as MP by his son, Philip.

Schreiner, William Philip (1857–1919); South African lawyer and politician; member, Cape Colony Parliament 1893–1900; Attorney-General 1893–6; Prime Minister 1898–1900. Senator 1910–14; High Commissioner, Union of South Africa 1914–19; PC 1917. His sister Olive wrote *The Story of An African Farm* (1883).

Schwann, Sir Charles Ernest, Bt (1844–1929); Lib. MP Manchester (North) 1886–1918; Bt 1906; PC 1911; vice-pres., Manchester Lib. Federation; pres., '95' Club; changed name to Swann 1913.

Scott, Sir James William, Bt (1844–1913); head by marriage of the Haslam merchant and textile companies; chairman, Bolton Lib. Assoc for fourteen years to 1907; Bt 1909.

Seely, John Edward Bernard (1868–1947); U. Sec. of St., Colonial Affairs 1908–10; Con. then Lib. MP Isle of Wight 1900–6 (a Unionist Free Trader, he crossed the floor to the Liberals in March 1904), Liverpool (Abercrombie) 1906–10, Derbyshire (Ilkeston) 1910–22; U. Sec. of St., War 1911–12; Sec. of St., War 1912–14; Special Service Officer with Sir John French 1914–15; Commander, 1st Canadian Cavalry Brigade 1915–18; U. Sec. of St. & Dep. Min. of Munitions 1918–19; U. Sec. of St., Air 1919; Baron Mottistone 1933.

Selborne, William Waldegrave Palmer, Earl of (1859–1942); High Commissioner, S. Africa and Gov. and C-in-C, Transvaal and Orange River Colony 1905–10; private sec. to Ld Chancellor, to Sec. of St., War, and to Chancellor of Exchequer 1881–5; Lib. MP Hampshire (Petersfield) 1885–6, Lib. Unionist MP 1886–95, Edinburgh (West) 1892–5; Lib. Unionist Whip 1886–95; 2nd Earl 1895; U. Sec. of St., Colonial Affairs 1895–1900; 1st Ld, Adm. 1900–5; Pres., Bd of Agriculture 1915–16; Warden, Winchester College 1920–5; High Steward, Winchester 1929–42; m. dau. of 3rd Marquis of Salisbury. Edward Grey had been his fag at Winchester.

Shackleton, David James (1863–1938); Lab. MP Lancashire (Clitheroe) 1902–10; cotton operative and trade unionist; member, TUC parliamentary committee 1904–10; pres., TUC 1908–9; chairman Lab. Party 1905; senior labour adviser, Home Office 1910–11; national health insurance commissioner 1911–16; first permanent sec., Min. of Labour 1916–21; KCB 1917; chief labour adviser, Min. of Labour 1921–5.

Shaw, Thomas Shaw, Baron (1850–1937); Ld Advocate 1905–9; Lib. MP Hawick 1892–1909; Scottish Solicitor-General 1894–5; PC 1906; Baron Shaw (judicial life peerage) 1909; Ld of Appeal 1909–29; chairman, various committees including the inquiry into Dublin riots 1914 and state purchase of Scottish liquor trade 1917; Baron Craigmyle 1929; a friend of Andrew Carnegie.

Shaw, Sir (Theodore Frederick) Charles Edward, Bt (1859–1942); Lib. MP Stafford 1892–1910; studied for the bar; merchant and Wolverhampton town councillor; retired from marginal seat Jan. 1910; Bt 1908.

Sherwell, Arthur James (1863–1942); Lib. MP Huddersfield 1906–18; Wesleyan Methodist minister; journalist and author, especially with Joseph Rowntree on liquor trade reform.

Simon, Sir John Allsebrook (1873–1954); Lib. MP Essex (Walthamstow) 1906–18, West Riding of Yorkshire (Spen Valley) 1922–40; barrister 1899; KC 1908; Solicitor-General 1910–13; Kt 1910; PC 1913; Attorney-General 1913–15; Sec. of St., Home Affairs 1915–16, 1935–7; chairman, Statutory Commission to investigate development of Indian government 1927–30; formed Liberal National, later National Liberal Party and supported National Government 1931; Sec. of St., Foreign Affairs 1931–5; Chancellor of Exchequer 1937–40; Ld Chancellor 1940–5; Vt Simon 1940.

Sinclair, John (1860–1925); Sec., Scotland 1905–12; Lib. MP Dunbartonshire 1892–5, Forfar 1897–1909; ADC to Lord Aberdeen in Ireland, 1886 and sec. to him in Canada 1896–7; Baron Pentland 1909; Gov. Gen., Madras 1912–19; m. Lady Marjorie Gordon, only dau. of the Aberdeens 1904. In 1887 he began to study law and economics at Toynbee Hall and in 1889 became a Progressive member of the LCC. He was asst private sec. to Campbell-Bannerman 1892–5, and Campbell-Bannerman's executor.

Smith, Abel Henry (1862–1930); Con. MP Christchurch 1892–1900, Hertfordshire (Hertford) 1900–10; pps to Walter Long Pres., Bd of Agriculture 1895–1900; a prominent member of the Hertfordshire Hunt, he was killed in a hunting accident.

Smith, Frederick Edwin (1872–1930); Con. MP Liverpool (Walton) 1906–18, Liverpool (West Derby) 1918–19; barrister 1899; Solicitor-General June–Nov. 1915; Attorney-General 1915–19; Lord Chancellor 1919–22; Sec. of St., India 1924–28; Kt 1915; Bt 1918; Baron Birkenhead 1919, Vt 1921, Earl of Birkenhead 1922.

Soares, Ernest Joseph (1864–1926); pps to H.J. Gladstone 1906–8; solicitor; Lib. MP Devon (Barnstaple) 1900–11; Charity Commissioner 1908–10; Junior Ld of Treasury 1910–11; Kt 1911; Asst Comptroller, Reduction of National Debt and Life Annuity Office 1911–16. The

Secretary of the Treasury, Sir George Murray, offered the assistant comptrollership of the National Debt Office to Maurice Headlam, a Treasury official. Headlam recorded in his memoirs that the offer was withdrawn and that Geoffrey Howard, another Liberal whip, told him 'that there had been some row in the Whips' office, that Soares had to go, and that this was a convenient way of getting rid of him'. (Maurice Headlam, *Irish Reminiscences*, Robert Hale, 1947, p. 25).

Southwark, Richard Knight Causton, Baron (1843–1929); Lib. MP Southwark (West) 1888–1910, Colchester 1880–5; Lib. Junior Whip 1892–1905 (Junior Ld of Treasury 1893–5); Paymaster-General 1905–10; Baron Southwark 1910.

Spencer, (Charles) Robert, Viscount Althorp (1857–1922); Ld Chamberlain 1905–12; Lib. MP Northamptonshire (North) 1880–5, Northamptonshire (Mid) 1885–95, 1900–5; PC 1892; Vice-Chamberlain, Household 1892–5; Vt Althorp 1905; succ. half brother as 6th Earl Spencer 1910; KG 1913.

Spencer, John Poyntz Spencer, Earl (1835–1910); Ld Lt Northants 1872–1908; as Vt Althorp, Lib. MP Northamptonshire (South) 1857; 5th Earl 1857; Ld Lt, Ireland 1868–74, 1882–5; Ld Pres. of Council 1880–3, 1886; 1st Ld, Adm. 1892–5; Leader of Lib. Lords 1902–5. Suffered a stroke October 1905.

Spender, (John) Alfred (1862–1942); editor, *The Westminster Gazette* 1896–1922; asst editor 1893–6; biographer of Campbell-Bannerman, Asquith, Sir R. Hudson and Lord Cowdray.

Spender, Mary (d. 1947); dau. of W.G. Rawlinson, art-collector and writer on Turner; m. J.A. Spender 1892.

Stanley, Hon. Ferdinand Charles (1871–1935); 5th son of 16th Earl of Derby; soldier; m. 1904 the Hon. Alexandra Frances Anne Fellowes (1880–1955), dau. of 2nd Baron De Ramsey, niece of 8th Duke of Marlborough and of Hon. A.E. Fellowes (Baron Ailwyn 1921); Con. Junior Whip 1900–5.

Stanton, Charles Butt (1873–1946); Miners' Agent, Aberdare; candidate E. Glamorgan 1910; Ind. Lab. MP Merthyr Tydfil 1915–18; Nat. Democratic and Labour MP 1918–22; prominent in British Workers' League 1915–22; joined Lib. party 1928.

Storey, (Edwin) Harold (1869–1956); sec., Yorkshire Liberal Federation 1908–19; Congregational minister 1896–1906; sec., Liberal Publications Dept 1919–36; *The Liberal Magazine* (vol. XLV, no. 52, Feb. 1937, p. 41) called Storey 'the best political pamphleteer of his time'. JAP thought him 'a capable fellow'. (JAP to Asquith, 24 Oct. 1910, Asquith MSS, vol. 23, f. 300).

Strachey, Sir Edward, Bt (1858–1936); Treasurer of Household and Commons spokesman for Bd of Agriculture and Fisheries 1905–9; 4th Bt 1901; elder brother of J. St Loe Strachey, cousin of Lytton Strachey; Lib. MP Somerset (Southern) 1892–1911; Parl. Sec., Bd of Agriculture and Fisheries 1909–11; Baron Strachie 1911; Paymaster-General 1912–15; PC 1912; 'an outstanding example of a progressively-minded, public spirited squire' (*The Times*, 27 July 1936).

Strathcona, Donald Alexander Smith, Baron (1820–1914); Canadian financier, worked his way from clerkship to chief factor, Hudson's Bay Co. 1838–62; Gov., Hudson's Bay Co. 1889; Con. MP, Canadian Parliament 1871–9, 1887–96; KCMG 1886; director, Canadian Pacific Railway Co. 1880–1914; Baron Strathcona 1897; Canadian High Commissioner 1896–1914; raised at his own expense Strathcona's Horse to fight in S. African war 1900. According to E.M. Wrong in *The Dictionary of National Biography 1912–1921*, eds. H.W.C. Davis and J.R.H. Weaver, Oxford University Press, 1927, p. 498, Strathcona 'has been regarded as a great statesman and financier, of the same calibre as Cecil Rhodes, and also as the man chiefly responsible for the increased corruption of Canadian public life in the 'eighties: both estimates are excessive'.

Sturgis, Mark Beresford Russell (1884–1949); asst private sec. to Asquith as Chancellor of Exchequer 1906–8; a private sec. to Prime Minister 1908–10; Special Commissioner of Income Tax 1910; Joint Asst U. Sec. for Ireland 1920–2, and for Irish Services 1922–4; son of Julian Sturgis, novelist; changed surname to Grant-Sturgis 1935; KCB 1923.

Swaythling, Montagu Samuel Montagu, Baron (1832–1911); banker, dealing particularly in foreign exchange; assumed surname of Samuel Montagu in place of Samuel 1894; Lib. MP Tower Hamlets (Whitechapel) 1885–1900; Bt 1894, Baron Swaythling 1907. He was Herbert Samuel's uncle. He debarred his heirs from inheriting his estate should they or their spouses not be professed Jews. Venetia Stanley adopted the Jewish faith in 1915 on her marriage to his son Edwin.

Talbot, Edward Stuart (1844–1934); Bishop of the newly created diocese of Southwark 1905–11; tutor in modern history, Christ Church, Oxford 1866–9; first Warden, Keble College 1869–89; ordained 1870; vicar, Leeds 1889–95; Bishop, Rochester 1895–1905, Winchester 1911–23. Ally of Robert Morant.

Talbot, Lord Edmund Bernard (1855–1947); Con. MP Sussex (Chichester) 1894–1921; 3rd son of 14th Duke of Norfolk; assumed name of Talbot in place of Fitzalan-Howard 1876; resumed latter name 1921; soldier; private sec. to Sec. of St., War 1896–8 and to U. Sec. of St., Foreign Affairs 1898–9; asst sec. to St John Brodrick 1900–5; Junior Ld of Treasury 1905; Unionist Ch. Whip 1913–21; Joint Parl. Sec., Treasury 1915–21; Dep. Earl Marshal of England 1917–29; PC 1918; Ld Lt, Ireland 1921–22; Vt FitzAlan 1921; his family were the leading Roman Catholic laymen in England.

Tennant, (Harold) John (1865–1935); Lib. MP Berwickshire 1892–1918; brother of Margot Asquith; asst private sec. to Asquith as Home Sec. 1892–5; Parl. Sec., Bd of Trade 1909–11; Fin. Sec., War 1911–12; U. Sec of St., War 1912–16; PC 1914; Sec., Scotland 1916.

Tennant, Margaret Mary ('May') (1869–1946); dau. of G.W. Abraham; sec. to Lady Dilke; treasurer, Women's Trade Union League; asst commissioner, royal commission on labour 1891; first woman factory inspector 1893; resigned post on her marriage to H.J. Tennant 1896; member, Central Unemployed Body for London; member, royal commission on divorce 1909–12;

director, women's section, Department of National Service 1917.

Thomas, Sir Alfred (1840–1927); Lib. MP Glamorganshire (East) 1885–1910; construction contractor; Mayor of Cardiff 1881; Kt 1902; chairman, Welsh Parliamentary Party 1897–1910; Baron Pontypridd 1912.

Thomson, Sir Joseph John (1856–1940); Cavendish Professor of Experimental Physics, Cambridge 1894–1919; FRS 1884; pres., Royal Society 1915–20; Nobel Prize for physics 1906; chairman, royal commission on secondary education 1916; Master, Trinity College, Cambridge 1918–40; member, advisory board, Department of Scientific and Industrial Research 1919–27; Kt 1908; OM 1912. Discovered the electron (1897) which he originally called a 'corpuscle'.

Thring, Sir Arthur Theodore (1860–1932); 1st Parliamentary Counsel 1903–17; barrister 1887; Clerk of the Parliaments 1917–30; KCB 9 Nov. 1908.

Tomkinson, James (1841–1910); Lib. MP Cheshire (Crewe) 1900–10; a Quaker; director, Lloyd's Bank; 2nd Church Estates Commissioner 1907; PC Nov. 1909. He died in 1910 after falling off his horse in the Commons' steeplechase. Alfred Pease described him as 'probably the hardest and maddest rider to hounds in England, … an enthusiastic and cheerful Radical, and a militant teetotaller' (*Elections and Recollections*, John Murray, 1932, p. 198).

Tree, Sir Herbert Beerbohm (1853–1917); actor, theatre proprietor and manager; renowned for opulent productions, particularly of Shakespeare; proud of his facial resemblance to Asquith (Percy Burton, as told to Lowell Thomas, *Adventures Among Immortals*, Hutchinson, 1938, p. 181); Kt 1909.

Trevelyan, Charles Philips (1870–1958); Parl. Charity Commissioner 1906–Oct. 1908; Lib. MP West Riding of Yorkshire (Elland) 1899–1918; Lab. MP Newcastle-upon-Tyne (Central) 1922–31; private sec. to Ld Lt, Ireland 1892–5; Parl. Sec., Bd of Education Oct. 1908–14; Pres., Bd of Education 1924, 1929–31; 3rd Bt 1928.

Trevelyan, Sir George Otto, Bt (1838–1928); historian and politician; 2nd Bt 1886; Lib. MP Tynemouth and North Shields 1865–8, Hawick 1868–86, Glasgow (Bridgeton) 1887–97; Civil Ld, Adm. 1868–70; Parl. Sec., Adm. 1881–2; Ch. Sec., Ireland 1882–4; Chancellor, Duchy of Lancaster 1884–5; Sec., Scotland 1885–6, 1892–5. Biographer of his uncle, Lord Macaulay. Father of Charles and G.M. Trevelyan.

Tweedmouth, Edward Marjoribanks, 2nd Baron (1849–1909); 1st Ld, Adm. 1905–8; Lib. MP Berwickshire 1880–94; Comptroller of Household 1886; Patronage Sec., Treasury 1892–4; 2nd Baron 1894; Ld Privy Seal and Chancellor, Duchy of Lancaster 1894–5; Ld Pres. of Council April–Oct. 1908.

Tweedmouth, Dudley Marjoribanks, 3rd Baron (1874–1935); Deputy Asst Adjutant and Quartermaster-General, W. Lancs. Divn Territorial Army 1908–10; Military Sec. to Earl of Selborne 1905–8; 3rd Baron 1909; boxing and dog breeding enthusiast; known as 'Beef' to his fellow officers (Geoffrey H. White

and R.S. Lea, eds, *The Complete Peerage by G.E.C.*, vol. XII, pt 2, St Catherine Press, 1959, p. 87, quoting *The Times*, 26 Apr. 1935). Despatched with his mother to Canada in 1895 after his parents' discovery of his engagement to a Gaiety chorus girl, Maude 'Birdie' Sutherland. A two year engagement was stipulated (Lewis Harcourt's diary, 7, 9, 12, 22, 26 Mar. 1895, Harcourt MSS). Marjoribanks married the Hon. Muriel Brodrick in 1901.

Ure, Alexander (1853–1928); Solicitor-General, Scotland 1905–9; lecturer, constitutional law and history 1878–88; Lib. MP Linlithgowshire 1895–1913; PC 1909; Ld Advocate 1909–13; Ld Justice-General for Scotland and Ld Pres., Court of Session 1913–20; a Lib. imperialist then enthusiastic supporter of Lloyd George's 1909 budget and land value tax proposals; Baron Strathclyde 1914. He once walked from Edinburgh to London and from London to Land's End. For his devastating reply to Balfour's accusation of 'mendacious imagination' see Dilnot, *The Old Order Changeth*, pp. 92–106.

Valentia, Arthur Annesley, Viscount (an Irish peerage) (1843–1927); Con. MP Oxford 1895–1917; Comptroller of Household 1898–1901; prominent in Oxfordshire politics; Baron Annesley 1917.

Walker, Sir Edward Daniel (1840–1919); proprietor, E.D. Walker & Wilson, newsagents and railway bookstall lessees; proprietor, *Northern Echo* 1895–1903; member, Darlington Town Council for 20 years (twice Mayor); Kt 1908.

Wallington, Edward William (1854–1933); groom-in-waiting to George V 1910–32; private sec. to Gov. of Fiji 1883–5, New South Wales 1885–9, Victoria 1889–96, S. Australia 1896–1900, Gov. Gen. Australia 1901–2; Groom of Bedchamber to George V when Prince of Wales 1902–10; private sec. to Queen Mary 1910–19; Treasurer 1919–32; Kt 1916.

Ward, William Dudley (1877–1946); Lib. MP Southampton 1906–22; barrister 1904; pps to L. Harcourt 1908–9; Treasurer of Household 1909–12; Vice-Chamberlain, Household 1917–22; PC 1922. He m. 1913 (she divorced him 1931) Winifred May Birkin, later the Prince of Wales's mistress 1919–34 (Frances Donaldson, *Edward VIII*, Weidenfeld and Nicholson, 1974, pp. 59, 159–60).

Warwick, Francis Richard Charles Guy Greville, Earl of (1853–1924); 5th Earl 1893; as Lord Brooke, Con. MP Somersetshire (East) 1879–85, Colchester 1888–92; a leading Freemason. His wife, Frances Evelyn (1861–1938), the celebrated beauty and mistress of Lord Charles Beresford and the Prince of Wales, was converted to socialism in 1895. Her home at Easton Lodge was a meeting-place for Labour reformers. She stood unsuccessfully for Parliament in 1923 as Labour candidate for Warwick and Leamington.

Wedgwood, Josiah Clement (1872–1943); Lib. MP (Lab. from 1919) Newcastle-under-Lyme 1906–42; naval architect; resident magistrate, Transvaal 1902–4; advocated land valuation taxes; Chancellor, Duchy of Lancaster 1924; PC 1924; the publicity following his divorce in 1919 helped the reform of divorce law; Baron Wedgwood 1942.

White, Sir Luke (1845–1920); Lib. MP East Riding of Yorkshire (Buckrose) 1900–18; solicitor and coroner; Kt 1908.

Whitley, John Henry (1866–1935); Junior Ld of Treasury 1907–10 (unpaid till June 1908); Lib. MP Halifax 1900–28; cotton spinner; PC 1911; chairman of various Commons committees incl. relations of employers and employed 1917–18 which led to consultative machinery including 'Whitley Councils'; Speaker of Commons 1921–8; chairman, BBC 1930–5.

Whittaker, Sir Thomas Palmer (1850–1919); Lib. MP West Riding of Yorkshire (Spen Valley) 1892–1919; hardware merchant then newspaper proprietor/editor; member royal commission on licensing laws 1896–9; chairman and managing director, UK Temperance and General Provident Institution; Kt 1906; PC 1908.

Wilkins, Roland Field (1872–1950); Principal Clerk at Treasury 1908; private sec. to R.W. Hanbury, Austen Chamberlain, and W. Hayes Fisher when they were Fin. Sec., Treasury 1899–1903; Treasury Officer of Accounts 1913–19; Asst Comptroller and Auditor 1920–2; Asst Paymaster-General 1924–35.

Williams, Sir (Arthur) Osmond, Bt (1849–1927); Lib. MP Merionethshire 1900–10; Ld Lt, Merionethshire 1909–27; chairman, Merionethshire County Council 1892–5; Constable, Harlech Castle 1909; Bt 1909 (see 3 Nov. 1908).

Williamson, Sir Archibald, Bt (1860–1931); Lib. MP Elgin and Nairn 1906–18; Co. Lib. M.P. Moray and Nairn 1918–22; merchant with South

American interests; Fin. Sec., War Office and Member, Army Council 1919–21; Bt 1909; PC 1918; Baron Forres 1922. Williamson was one of 249 Liberals listed for ennoblement in 1911 but paid £50,000 for the honour in 1922, surviving allegations of wartime trading with the enemy in Chile. (Riddell's diary, 3 June 1922, McEwen, ed., *The Riddell Diaries*, p. 369).

Willingdon, Freeman Freeman-Thomas, Baron (1866–1941); Lib. MP Hastings 1900–6, Bodmin 1906–10; appointed Junior Ld of Treasury Dec. 1905 but lost his seat; did some secretarial work for Asquith; ADC to Lord Brassey when Gov., Victoria 1897–1900; Baron Willingdon 1910; Ld-in-Waiting 1911–13; Gov., Bombay 1913–19, Madras 1919–24; Vt Willingdon 1924; Gov. Gen., Canada 1926–30; Viceroy, India 1931–6; PC 1931; Earl of Willingdon 1931, Marquess 1936; Constable, Dover Castle and Ld Warden, Cinque Ports 1936–41. He played cricket for Cambridge for four years, captaining them in the last; favourite partner of George V at tennis; the Willingdon Club in Madras and the Willingdon Sports Club in Bombay were open to both Britons and Indians. His wife was Lady Marie Adelaide (d. 1960), dau. of 1st Earl Brassey; they m. in 1892.

Wilson, Philip Whitwell (1875–1956); parliamentary correspondent, *Daily News* 1910–22; Lib. MP St Pancras (South) 1906–10; American correspondent, *Daily News*; writer of many religious books.

Wimborne, Lady Cornelia Henrietta Maria (1847–1927); eldest dau. of the 7th Duke of Marlborough m. 1868 Ivor Bertie Guest (1835–1914), Baron

Wimborne 1880. Four of her five sons were MPs; Winston Churchill was her nephew.

Wolverhampton, Henry Hartley Fowler, Vt (1830–1911); Chancellor, Duchy of Lancaster 1905–08; Lib. MP Wolverhampton (East) 1880–1908; U. Sec. of St., Home Affairs 1884–6; Fin. Sec., Treasury 1886; Pres., Local Govt. Bd 1892–4; Sec. of St., India 1894–5; Ld Pres. of Council Oct. 1908–10; a Vice-Pres. Liberal League, 1902–9; GCSI 1895; Vt Wolverhampton 1908; a leading Wesleyan Methodist.

Wood, Sir Edward (1839–1917); JP for Leicester and Leicestershire; Mayor of Leicester four times; Kt 1906; founded Freeman, Hardy and Willis Ltd, boot and shoe manufacturers.

Wood, Thomas McKinnon (1855–1927); U. Sec. of St., Foreign Affairs 1908–11; member, LCC 1892–1907 (Chairman 1898–9); Lib. MP Glasgow (St Rollox) 1906–18; Parl. Sec., Bd of Education 1908; Fin. Sec., Treasury 1911–2; PC 1911; Sec., Scotland 1912–16; Chancellor, Duchy of Lancaster and Fin. Sec., Treasury 1916.

Wyndham, George (1863–1913); Con. MP Dover 1889–1913; private sec. to A.J. Balfour 1887–92; U. Sec. of St., War 1898–1900; Ch. Sec., Ireland 1900–5; tariff reformer; writer.

Manuscript Sources

The notes and commentaries draw on manuscript sources which have been consulted from 1965 onwards. Some collections of papers which are now in libraries, archives, or record offices were seen when they were still in private hands. The following list indicates the present location of collections so far as it is known to us. But it has not been possible in every case to determine whether papers remain in private possession. For collections thought to be privately held we have given the name of the person in whose care they were according to the last information we have. We have listed only those collections from which documents have been quoted. Many other collections have been examined but have not yielded material of direct relevance. We have sought unsuccessfully for the papers of a number of Pease's colleagues and friends, including George Whiteley, Cecil Norton, Freddie Guest, and Sir Robert Hudson. The diaries of Loulou Harcourt for this period have disappeared.

Aberdeen and Temair MSS (the Marquess of Aberdeen and Temair)
Asquith MSS (Bodleian Library, Oxford)
Balfour MSS (British Library; the Earl of Balfour)
Beaverbrook MSS (House of Lords Record Office; Harriet Irving Library, University of New Brunswick)
Belloc MSS (John J. Burns Library, Boston College)
Bingley MSS (G. Lane Fox)
Blunt MSS (Fitzwilliam Museum, Cambridge)
Bondfield MSS (Vassar College Library)
Bryce MSS (Bodleian Library)
Campbell-Bannerman MSS (British Library)
Carlisle, Lady MSS (Castle Howard)
Cecil of Chelwood MSS (British Library)
Churchill MSS (Churchill Archives Centre, Churchill College, Cambridge)
Craigmyle MSS (Lord Craigmyle)
Crawford and Balcarres MSS (John Rylands Library, Victoria University of Manchester)
Crewe MSS (Cambridge University Library)
Crook MSS (Bodleian Library)
Elliott MSS (Sir Hugh Elliott Bt)

Emmott MSS (Nuffield College, Oxford)
Esher MSS (Churchill Archives Centre, Churchill College, Cambridge)
Ewart MSS (Scottish Record Office)
Gainford MSS (Nuffield College, Oxford)
Gladstone MSS (British Library)
Gladstone of Hawarden MSS (St Deiniol's Library, Hawarden)
Gladstone, W.E. MSS (British Library)
Glenconner MSS (Lord Glenconner)
Gulland Osborne MSS (the late J. Gulland Osborne)
Haldane MSS (National Library of Scotland)
Hamilton MSS (British Library)
Harcourt MSS (Bodleian Library)
Henry, Lady MSS (National Library of Wales)
Howard MSS (Castle Howard)
Hirtzel MSS (Oriental and India Office Collections, British Library)
Holt MSS (Liverpool Record Office)
Ilbert MSS (House of Lords Record Office)
Jones MSS (Library, University College of North Wales, Bangor)
Kidd MSS (the late Dr A. Stokes)
Lehmann MSS (the late John Lehmann)
Leveson-Gower MSS (House of Lords Record Office)
Lewis MSS (National Library of Wales)
Lytton MSS (Lady Hermione Cobbold)
Lloyd George MSS (House of Lords Record Office)
Lyell MSS (Lady Lyell)
Masterman MSS (University of Birmingham Library)
Montagu MSS (Wren Library, Trinity College, Cambridge)
Montagu, Venetia MSS (Wren Library, Trinity College, Cambridge)
Mottistone MSS (Nuffield College, Oxford)
Murray of Elibank MSS (National Library of Scotland)
Nathan MSS (Rhodes House Library)
Noel-Buxton MSS (William R. Perkins Library, Duke University)
Norman MSS (the late Lady Burke)
Northcliffe MSS (British Library)
Passfield MSS (British Library of Political and Economic Science)
Pease MSS (J. Gurney Pease)
Ponsonby MSS (Bodleian Library; Lord Ponsonby)
Ripon MSS (British Library)
Robertson Nicoll MSS (the late Mildred Kirkcaldy)
Robson MSS (P. Audley-Miller)
Rosebery MSS (National Library of Scotland)

Runciman MSS (University Library, Newcastle upon Tyne)
Runciman, Viscountess MSS (University Library, Newcastle upon Tyne)
Samuel MSS (House of Lords Record Office)
Sandars MSS (Bodleian Library)
MacCallum Scott MSS (Glasgow University Library)
Selborne MSS (Bodleian Library)
Shortt MSS (David Ingrams)
Southborough MSS (Bodleian Library)
Spender MSS (British Library)
Tennyson, Ivy MSS (Hallam Tennyson)
Trevelyan MSS (University Library, Newcastle upon Tyne)
Tweedmouth MSS (Ministry of Defence Library, Navy)
Whitehead MSS (House of Lords Record Office)

Index

As all individuals mentioned in the text are identified either in the biographical appendix (page number shown below in bold) or in a footnote or commentary, some of those whose names appear only once are not indexed.

Individuals who were untitled in April 1908 are listed under their family names, with cross-references from titles they received between 1908 and 1910. Those who were titled at the time of their first mention in the text are listed under that title. A very small number of exceptions, such as Lord Alverstone (Richard Webster), are to be found under the better known name by which they are referred to in the text. Those with hyphenated names are listed under the name preceding the hyphen.